The FIGHT That STARTED The MOVIES

NONFICTION

Speed Duel: The Inside Story of the Land Speed Record in the Sixties

I Just Ran: Percy Williams, World's Fastest Human

The Imjin War: Japan's Sixteenth-Century Invasion of Korea and Attempt to Conquer China

America's Man in Korea: The Private Letters of George C. Foulk, 1884-1887

Inside the Hermit Kingdom: The 1884 Korea Travel Diary of George Clayton Foulk

FICTION

Homeowner With a Gun

Bad Elephant Far Stream

The FIGHT That STARTED The MOVIES

THE WORLD HEAVYWEIGHT CHAMPIONSHIP, THE BIRTH OF CINEMA AND THE FIRST FEATURE FILM

SAMUEL HAWLEY

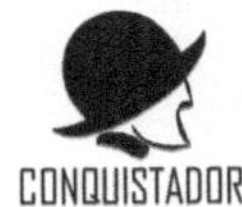

CONQUISTADOR

THE FIGHT THAT STARTED THE MOVIES: THE WORLD
HEAVYWEIGHT CHAMPIONSHIP, THE BIRTH OF
CINEMA AND THE FIRST FEATURE FILM
Published by Conquistador Press, 2016

Library and Archives Canada Cataloguing in Publication

Hawley, Samuel Jay, 1960-

The fight that started the movies : the world heavyweight championship, the birth of cinema and the first feature film / Samuel Hawley.

Includes bibliographical references and index.
Issued in print and electronic formats.
ISBN 978-0-9920786-8-3 (paperback).   ISBN 978-0-9920786-9-0 (html)

1. Corbett-Fitzsimmons fight (Motion picture). 2. Cinematography—History—19th century. 3. Cinematography—Equipment and supplies—History—19th century. 4. Motion pictures—History—19th century. 5. Boxing—United States—History—19th century. 6. Documentary films—History and criticism. 7. Boxing films—History and criticism. 8. Rector, Enoch J., 1863-1957. 9. Corbett, James J., 1866-1933. 10. Fitzsimmons, Robert James, 1863-1917. I. Title.

TR848.H28 2016   777.09   C2016-902813-5
                                                C2016-902814-3

---

www.conquistadorpress.com
info@conquistadorpress.com

Visit the author's website:
www.samuelhawley.com

The author gratefully acknowledges the assistance he received from Enoch Rector's granddaughter, Sara Chermayeff, who sadly passed away on March 16, 2016, and from Sara's daughter Sasha Chermayeff; also from Paul Spehr, former assistant chief of the Motion Picture, Broadcasting, and Recorded Sound Division at the Library of Congress; Leonard DeGraaf at the Thomas Edison National Historic Park; and Dan Streible, cinema studies professor at New York University.

CONTENTS

PROLOGUE

THE SCREENING TOOK PLACE on June 10, 1997 at the National Film Theatre in London, on the south bank of the Thames River overlooking Waterloo Bridge. The audience began filtering in at six o'clock in the evening. They took their seats in the dimly lit auditorium, early birds in the prime central locations, later arrivals fanning out on the sides. There was murmured conversation as the minutes ticked down to the six-thirty show time, heads leaned together, voices kept low.

Tonight's presentation was *The Corbett-Fitzsimmons Fight*. It was scheduled to run for twenty-nine minutes, not much more than a third of its original length. The rest was lost. It had been made without a script, without editing, without sound, without camera movement or artful lighting. Its director, Enoch Rector, had simply filmed a heavyweight title fight in real time, using a huge, human-powered camera called the "Veriscope" that he and his assistants operated from the inside. Rector's film was nevertheless very special, for it had been made before the Wright brothers' first flight, before the Model "A" Ford, even before the Spanish-American War. It had premiered in New York City on May 22, 1897, almost exactly one hundred years before.

It was the world's first feature-length film.

Few in the audience waiting to see *The Corbett-Fitzsimmons Fight* that evening knew much about the story behind its making: about fighters Jim Corbett and Bob Fitzsimmons, whose championship battle at Carson City, Nevada on March 17, 1897 was the subject of the movie; about Enoch Rector, the man who filmed the contest from inside his Veriscope apparatus; about the chain of events that brought them together and the colorful cast of characters involved on the way—inventors like Eadweard Muybridge, Thomas Edison, William K. L. Dickson and Eugene Lauste; visionary hustlers like the playboy brothers Gray and Otway Latham, promoter Dan Stuart and manager William Brady; pugilists like John L. Sullivan, Young Griffo, Peter Maher and the original Jack Dempsey; fight managers and trainers; filmmakers and fakers; businessmen and Wild West legends; lawmakers opposed to prizefighting and determined to shut down the whole thing. It is a tale as rich and complex as the extant footage of Rector's film is deceptively simple, a tapestry of influences in which boxing is deeply interwoven with the birth of the movies.

The fight game was indeed a driving force in the emergence of cinema in the 1890s. Boxing, or more specifically the desire to feed the public's appetite for films of prizefights, provided a major impetus in the evolution of movies from a mere twenty seconds' duration to a full minute, then eight minutes, then feature length; in the invention of projectors to show films on screens to theaters full of people rather than via one-viewer-at-a-time peephole machines; and in the popularization of the idea that a movie was more than just a passing novelty to gape at, but a complete evening of entertainment to rival the theater.

Boxing also gave rise to the concept of the blockbuster motion picture, *The Corbett-Fitzsimmons Fight* being not just the world's first feature-length film but also the cinema's first really big hit. It was shown in theaters across North America and Europe and as far afield as South Africa and Australia, taking in an estimated seven hundred thousand dollars, the equivalent of more than twenty million dollars today. Its success spurred the making of many other fight pictures, notably the hugely successful *Jeffries-Sharkey Contest*, released in 1899 at an unprecedented one hundred twenty-two minutes. Dozens more followed.

And then they disappeared.

The fact was that prizefighting had been illegal all along in most states of the Union. It was this very illegality that helped make fight films such an irresistible money-making proposition, for the laws only barred the holding of live contests, not the exhibition of films.

If a venue could be secured to stage a battle without legal interference, there was a great deal of money to be made from a championship fight—from the selling of tickets to the event itself and, more importantly, from the nationwide exhibition of a film.

It was the 1912 Sims Act banning the interstate transfer of fight films that effectively killed off the business. Denied national distribution, it was no longer financially viable to film prizefights and production thus ceased. The few prints of *The Corbett-Fitzsimmons Fight* still in existence subsequently disintegrated or were thrown out or packed away and forgotten. With the passage of decades, few remembered that it had ever existed.

Its rediscovery a half-century later was thanks in part to handball and in particular to Jim Jacobs, one of the best players in the world in the 1950s and '60s. The sport took Jacobs all over, competing in tournaments and holding clinics. Wherever he appeared he would conclude his presentation by mentioning his second passion, the collecting of fight films, asking his audience for leads. His appeals turned up lost treasures in all sorts of places.

It was after an appearance at the Multnomah Athletic Club in Portland, Oregon that Jacobs was approached by an elderly man who said he had a very old fight film at home in a box. It turned out to be an original reel of *The Corbett-Fitzsimmons Fight*. The fragile nitrate film was two and a half inches wide and had five sprocket holes per frame—the unique format Enoch Rector had had custom made. Another portion of the film turned up in 1982, donated to the Museum of Modern Art in New York by Bob Fitzsimmons' granddaughter. These two finds, restored and transferred onto 35mm stock by the British Film Institute in London, comprised the extant footage screened at the film's centenary in 1997.

By six-thirty most of the four hundred fifty seats in London's National Film Theatre were filled. The lights were dimmed. The curtains parted. The projector began humming in the booth in the back, just audible through the soundproof wall before the piano accompaniment started. A surprisingly large black-and-white image appeared on the screen—no opening titles, just two men in bathrobes entering the ring and pacing about. Amazingly, it was in a widescreen format familiar to modern filmgoers, not the nearly square aspect ratio associated with older movies. It was another of Enoch Rector's innovations, a way to encompass the ring while keeping his cameras in close.

All the people in the moving image were dead now—the fighters, the corner men, the referee, the spectators at ringside, the fans on the bleachers. So were the technicians operating the camera. So were their children. So were most of their grandchildren. One of the figures off to the left was Bat Masterson, former Wild West lawman. He had been hired to oversee security inside the arena. Just out of the shot on the right sat Wyatt Earp, famous for the gunfight at the OK Corral. Others present had fought in the Civil War, had voted for Abraham Lincoln, had known the Union when it had only twenty-five states.

The audience settled back in their seats. Up on the screen, the past continued to flicker.

PART ONE

BEGINNINGS

CHAPTER 1

THE PERSISTENCE OF VISION

THE MOST UNCOMFORTABLE American journey available to the public in 1860 was the Butterfield Overland Mail Company's twice-weekly service between St. Louis and San Francisco. The entire route, twenty-eight hundred miles, was covered nonstop, passengers snatching what sleep they could while the stagecoach jolted along, wolfing down meals and dashing to the outhouse during halts to change horses. The trip took nearly a month. "I now know what hell is like," observed a passenger after enduring the inaugural west-to-east trip. "I've just had twenty-four days of it."

One of the half-dozen intrepid travelers to board the Overland Mail in San Francisco in July of that year was a local bookseller named Eadweard Muybridge, setting out to return to his native England after an absence of eight years. Crammed inside the coach along with bulging mail sacks, his knees pressed against those of the passengers facing, Muybridge had persevered through three weeks of the journey when the coach upset and he received a severe knock on the head. It left him in a coma for nine days. When he awoke he had double vision, impaired hearing and a general debility that would linger for more than a year.

The ensuing lawsuit against the Overland Mail enriched Muybridge to the tune of twenty-five hundred dollars. With this small fortune in his pocket, he set out to master the art of photography upon his delayed arrival in England, specifically the recently invented wet collodion process, superior to the daguerreotype because it produced a negative from which multiple prints could be made.

When he returned to San Francisco in 1866, it was as a professional photographer, a "painter in light." It was a career at which he would excel.

Taking photographs with the wet collodion process was time consuming, difficult and messy. To appreciate Muybridge's mastery of the art form, consider the challenge of capturing a single image in the comfort of a studio in the city, then imagine Muybridge doing so in the wilds of Yosemite Valley, where he did some of his best work. First he had to polish a glass plate to perfect smoothness and carefully clean it to remove any traces of dust. He then carefully "flowed" a mixture of collodion, potassium iodide and ether over the plate and, working inside the stifling little tent that served as his darkroom, immersed the plate in a bath of light-sensitive silver nitrate. After removal from the bath, the plate was placed in a light-tight holder and rushed to the camera—which had already been positioned and focused—speed being essential because the ether on the plate evaporated quickly. Then remove the dark slide from the holder; ease the cap off the lens without jiggling the camera; count off the required number of seconds to achieve the desired exposure; replace the cap and re-insert the slide in the holder; remove the holder from the camera and rush it back to the tent-darkroom; open the holder and remove the glass plate; pour developing solution over the plate, taking care to do so evenly to avoid blotching and ridging; wait for the image to emerge, then pour water over the plate to halt the developing process; place the plate in a bath of fixer to preserve the image; wash the plate in water, then dry it; heat the plate and apply a coat of clear varnish, taking care once again to do so evenly so as not to ruin the outcome; and finally, pack the plate in a box and haul it out of the mountains without dropping it or otherwise smashing it to pieces so that you could use it to make prints to sell to the public. All that... for one photograph.

By the early 1870s Muybridge had built a solid reputation on the West Coast with his scenes of untamed nature and indigenous peoples and his technique of inserting dramatic skies into his pictures. He also did a good deal of architectural work—which is what brought him into contact with railroad tycoon and former California governor Leland Stanford. Stanford owned a number of racehorses and was deeply interested in animal locomotion, in particular the theory, unverifiable with the naked eye, that there was a moment in the stride of a galloping horse when all four of its hooves were off the ground. Stanford subscribed to this theory, called "unsupported transit," a source at the time of much controversy among animal experts. Determined to settle the debate once and for all, he mentioned the problem to Muybridge, who happened to be present in his house taking photographs for Stanford's wife.

"I conversed with him," Stanford later recalled, "about the possibility of taking pictures of a horse moving rapidly. At first he said that it could not be done. Pictures might... be taken on the street, where men and animals were moving slowly, and then touched up to look well. But it was impossible to take a horse while in quick motion; it would make a blur only."

Muybridge himself admitted to having been "amazed at the boldness and originality" of the proposal; as an experienced photographer he understood far better than Stanford the difficulties it posed. The idea was so intriguing, however, that he agreed to explore it, Stanford promising to provide whatever resources were required.

The first step was to come up with a more sensitive emulsion for capturing images taken with the briefest of exposures, mere fractions of a second. "In those days," Muybridge wrote in *Animals in Motion*, "the rapid dry process—by the use of which such an operation is now easily accomplished—had not been discovered. Every photographer was, in a great measure, his own chemist; he prepared his own dipping baths, made his own collodion, coated and developed his own plates, and frequently manufactured the chemicals necessary for his work. All this involved a vast amount of tedious and careful manipulation from which the present generation is, happily, relieved." He also needed a way to achieve the fraction-of-a-second exposure itself. For this he devised a rubber band-tensioned shutter, two slats with a gap in between that snapped down in front of the lens upon the release of a catch.

Muybridge put his new emulsion and shutter to the test in May 1872, attempting to photograph Stanford's racehorse Occident in mid-stride. After a number of failures, a shadow emerged on the glass plate, a vague silhouette that seemed to show all four of the animal's hooves off the ground. The image was of such poor quality, however, that it failed to settle the argument over unsupported transit. A better shutter was needed. And even faster emulsions.

Muybridge, increasingly fascinated by this new field of "instantaneous photography," agreed to keep trying with continued backing from Stanford. Before he could proceed any farther, however, he was arrested for murder.

Eadweard Muybridge was forty-one years old in 1871 when he married shop assistant Flora Downs, a recent divorcee half his age. Four years later, around the time of the birth of their only child, he discovered that she was having an affair with a spendthrift English adventurer named Harry Larkyns, currently employed as drama critic at the *San Francisco Post*. Muybridge confronted the man and warned him off, then sent Flora away to relatives in Portland. These efforts to sever relations between the two lovers failed. They kept in touch by passing letters through the nurse Flora had hired for the baby—letters that in 1874 ended up in Muybridge's hands.

The evidence of his wife's infidelity drove the photographer to despair so extreme that his sweating, quivering appearance alarmed a colleague who ran into him that afternoon. When asked what the matter was, Muybridge replied, "I have something to do."

He boarded a train for the Napa Valley town of Calistoga, where he knew Larkyns had gone to work after leaving his job at the *Post*. He arrived at eight o'clock in the evening and tracked his rival to a house a few miles outside town. There was a blaze of light showing through the windows, loud talk and laughter from a party inside.

"I want to see Major Larkyns," Muybridge announced after knocking at the door. "I will only detain him a moment."

Larkyns, hearing his name, excused himself from the game of cribbage he was playing and peered into the unlit hallway. "Where are you, sir?" he said, puzzled as to who could be calling for him at this late hour. "I cannot see you."

"My name is Muybridge," came the reply. "Here is the answer to the letter you sent my wife."

A shot rang out from the darkness and a bullet struck Larkyns in the chest. "Let me out," he gasped, reeling about and staggering back through the house, Muybridge following, pistol in hand. Before he could fire again, the other men present disarmed him. He instantly grew calm after that, apologizing to the ladies in the room for having caused a disturbance. Larkyns was found dead outside, slumped under a tree.

Muybridge entered a plea of not guilty when indicted for murder. In the trial that followed, his lawyer crafted a defense of justifiable homicide coupled with an insanity plea, witnesses testifying that the crash of the Overland Mail fifteen years before had altered Muybridge, leaving him prone to excitability, impatience and wild emotional swings. The jury accepted the justifiable homicide plea and found Muybridge not guilty. He was released and returned home a changed man. He looked old now, his long beard turned grey, his shaggy hair completely white.

In July 1877 Muybridge resumed his work for Leland Stanford of trying to photograph a horse in motion. Since his earlier efforts, he had come up with new ideas for a more sensitive emulsion and a faster shutter release. By August the newspapers were reporting his success in once again photographing Stanford's horse Occident at a full gallop, this time a clearer picture that seemed to settle the unsupported transit argument once and for all.

But it didn't. Suspicions were raised in some quarters over the authenticity of the image, the position of the horse's legs being so at variance with centuries of painted depictions. The *San Francisco Post*, the newspaper where Harry Larkyns had worked, stood at the forefront of the naysayers, pointing to evidence that the photo had been touched up, questioning the supposedly unnatural position of the driver and scoffing at the overall perspective of the image, which it claimed was suspiciously skewed. "Either that camera did lie," concluded the writer, a friend of Larkyns, "or Stanford has got the most extraordinary horse in the world."

Stanford, openly goaded now by the critics, provided Muybridge with unlimited funds to expand his efforts. He suggested that instead of trying to capture one perfect shot of a trotting horse using a single camera, a dozen cameras should be used in sequence to capture all the animal's motions through one complete stride.

It took Muybridge a year to assemble the necessary equipment, a complicated arrangement of the best English-made cameras and an automatic shutter release mechanism he invented himself. On June 15, 1878, he had everything tested and ready to show to the press. The demonstration, organized to prove that no trickery was involved in the process, was held at Stanford's Palo Alto farm outside San Francisco, where the former governor kept his prize-winning stable of horses.

The day began with Muybridge, shaded under his usual broad-brimmed hat, giving the assembled reporters a tour of the set-up he had erected on the private track. On one side stood a long, white-washed shed, a chest-high opening running its length revealing a line of twelve cameras set twenty-one inches apart. The lens of each camera was pointed at an angled wooden frame erected on the opposite side of the track. This frame was covered with white cotton sheeting to provide maximum contrast against the passing dark figure of a horse and had black lines painted on it—vertical lines, numbered 1 to 21, to measure the horse's forward movement; horizontal lines along the base to measure the height of its hooves. The track between cameras and backdrop was laid with boards, a sprinkling of powdered lime on top to create a reflective surface. Running beneath the boards were twelve tensioned wires, each connected to a battery and one of the cameras. By directing one of the sulky wheels along a gap left in the boards on one side of the track, it would pass over each of the slightly raised wires in turn, pressing them down and thus releasing a catch that in turn released the sliding shutter over the lens of each camera, the slats snapping down with the tension of two rubber bands. The passage in front of the lens of the gap between the slats, Muybridge explained to the reporters, would expose the glass plate inside the camera to light for less than one-thousandth of a second.

Stanford's young trotter Abe Edgington was used for the first test. Upon Muybridge giving the signal, the driver, seated between the two high wheels of the sulky, whipped the horse around the mile-long track and down the stretch toward the cameras at a racing speed of 2:20—a mile in two minutes twenty seconds. Entering the white corridor between camera shed and backdrop, the sulky's left wheel found the gap between the boards to trip the shutters on the twelve cameras, the slats loudly snapping down in such rapid succession that they sounded like a explosive burst. Muybridge and his assistants then removed the exposed plates from the cameras and rushed them into the darkroom built in the shed to be developed. Within twenty minutes they had a series of twelve negatives ready to show, each a distinct and undeniably true image. Together they captured a half-second of real-life movement—and, in images four and eight, all four of Abe Edgington's hooves off the ground.

The second demonstration that followed was even more impressive. The shutter releases on the twelve cameras were rearmed and this time attached to fine threads stretched across the track and brought to just the right tension. The racehorse Sallie Gardner was then ridden down the track at a full gallop, breaking the threads as she passed the cameras to release a rapid-fire fusillade of snaps. The feel of the threads on her chest and the sound of the shutters evidently upset Sallie Gardner, for she made a bound midway through the course and broke her saddle girth. The mishap made the resulting photographs even more compelling, for there, starting in image eight, was the very bound that everyone had seen the horse make, and there in the final shot was the broken end of the saddle girth swinging free.

Eadweard Muybridge's horse-in-motion pictures excited great interest when they appeared in newspapers and magazines worldwide and made his reputation as the "instantaneous photography man." This new-found fame, so much greater than anything he had achieved with his nature photos, spurred him to further efforts. He doubled his photographing set-up to include twenty-four cameras and developed an automatic clockwork shutter release timer that greatly simplified the process by doing away with the myriad of wires and threads. He also started experimenting with the sequential photographing of human subjects, starting in 1879 with three members from the Olympic Club of San Francisco. Muybridge worked with the scantily clad athletes for a day, photographing them—and reportedly himself as well—jumping, tumbling, fencing, wrestling and boxing. It was the start of the human motion studies he would pursue extensively in the coming decade.

Muybridge was also giving lectures to make the most of his fame. They proved popular with the public, audiences laughing out loud when he juxtaposed typical painted depictions of horses, legs splayed out hobby-horse fashion, with an actual photo of Sallie Gardner, her legs in a bunch underneath. The lectures were financially enriching for the photographer but at the same time somewhat frustrating, for Muybridge was not able to show audiences the actual movement he had so painstakingly captured, movement that so clearly existed there in his sequence of photos. He tried to convey a sense of it by using two magic lantern slide projectors side by side to fade one image into the next, but this was much too slow to be effective. He needed to devise a way to project his photos in rapid sequence so that audiences could actually *see* the motion.

It was the magazine *Scientific American* in its October 19, 1878 issue that first put forth a solution, one that was likely already in Muybridge's mind. "We would suggest," the article accompanying engravings of Muybridge's Abe Edgington photos concluded, "that for popular use the photographs should also be mounted on strips for use in the zoetrope."

The Zoetrope, Greek for "wheel of life," invented by William Horner of Bristol in 1834, was a key precursor to real motion pictures. It consisted of a sequence of images affixed around the inside of a drum which had slits cut through the side. By spinning the drum and peering through the passing slits at the images flashing by within, the viewer was presented with a repeating action—a man jumping, a bird flying, a boy dancing a jig. The Zoetrope had not been an entirely original moving image invention but in Muybridge's day it was certainly the best known, having been widely marketed as an optical toy. A more obscure device, the Phenakistoscope, had in fact preceded it by two years. Invented by Belgian Joseph Plateau in 1832, it consisted of a rotating disk with sequential images painted around the edge and a counter-rotating disk on top with slits cut through it to show the images passing by underneath.

With both devices, the Zoetrope and the Phenakistoscope, the rapid passage before the eye of the slits acted like a shutter, intermittently revealing the succession of images as split-second flashes to create the illusion of movement. The illusion works because the retina of the human eye retains an image for a fraction of a second after the image has disappeared, a phenomenon known as the "persistence of vision." If a second image appears before the first image on the retina has faded, and then a third image after the second, and a fourth after the third, the images merge and the brain is tricked into seeing movement.

The device Muybridge invented, christened the Zoopraxiscope, was in essence a Phenakistoscope—the image disk made of glass so as to be transparent—combined with a magic lantern to project the images onto a screen. The technology did not then exist for printing photos directly on glass, so he instead traced them on with paint. By directing light through the disk and on through the lens and by turning a crank to counter-rotate the image disk and shutter disk on top, Muybridge was able to make his horse pictures move on the screen just as the actual animals had done on the track.

"There, Governor," he announced with satisfaction, cranking away at the first private demonstration of his machine in the fall of 1879, "there you have a representation of Hawthorn galloping at a 1:42 gait."

Stanford scrutinized the galloping black silhouette for a few moments, then said, "I think you must be mistaken. That is certainly not the gait of Hawthorn but of Anderson."

He was correct. His horse Anderson had been substituted for Hawthorn without Muybridge's knowledge on the day this particular sequence was taken. The episode was a testament to Stanford's sharp eye for horse movement—and to Muybridge's success at recording it with his multiple cameras and displaying it with his Zoopraxiscope.

In August 1881, Zoopraxiscope and glass image disks stowed in his baggage, Eadweard Muybridge embarked for Europe to give a series of lectures. The tour, arranged by Leland Stanford, was a triumph. For six months Muybridge was feted and stroked in Paris, his presentations attended by leading lights in the sciences and arts and his discoveries praised to the skies. A particularly ardent admirer was Étienne-Jules Marey, a leader in the field of animal locomotion who was developing a hand-held, gun-shaped device for recording sequential images on one piece of film. It was Marey who introduced Muybridge to the gelatin dry plate process, an advance on the cumbersome wet plate process that Muybridge was still using. Muybridge would incorporate it into his work upon his return to the United States, greatly simplifying and improving his instantaneous photography method.

First, however, London awaited. As gratifying as the reception had been in Paris, it was the expatriate Englishman's first London appearance that assured him that he had truly "arrived."

The event was held at the Royal Institution on the evening of March 13, 1882, before an invited audience of highly select guests: the Prince and Princess of Wales, members of the royal family, Alfred Tennyson, Thomas Huxley, the President of the Royal Society, dukes and duchesses and marquises and earls. The luminosity of the assembly made Muybridge visibly nervous and he stumbled through the opening of his presentation before settling down. Soon, however, he had everyone spellbound, presenting a series of horse depictions in art through the ages to point out the mistakes. He then displayed an enlargement of the background of an unidentified but evidently recent painting, ten racing horses with legs splayed out in the accepted notion of grace.

"The attitude is impossible," he observed, comparing the painting to his photos. "If once the animal got into it, he would infallibly break his back in coming down. And all, as you see, are exactly like the first horse and each other. If it be impossible for one horse to assume such an attitude, to find ten horses doing it all at once would be nothing short of a miracle."

The evidence, so contrary to accepted notions and yet so undeniably true, prompted the audience to break into applause. Muybridge then delivered a shock by projecting the full painting from which the debunked background detail had been taken. It was "The Derby Day" by William Frith. Muybridge had just proven that one of England's most celebrated paintings was wrong.

Consternation settled over the hall but did not last long, for Muybridge now began to demonstrate his Zoopraxiscope. As he cranked the sewing machine handle on the projector, the audience watched in wonder as one horse after another galloped in place on the screen, not in crude imitation of life but exactly as a real horse would appear. This was followed by a running deer, a lumbering bull, racing dogs and a trotting pig, then a sampling of Muybridge's human studies, men running and jumping.

Toward the end of the demonstration the Prince of Wales spoke up. "I should like to see your boxing pictures," he said.

"I shall be very happy to show them, your Royal Highness," replied Muybridge. Going through his well-stocked case of glass disks, he extracted the one with the boxers and affixed it to his machine. As he turned the handle, a boxer in green trunks threw a left jab at his opponent in red, one second of real-time movement, repeated again and again.

"I don't know that these pictures teach us anything useful," Muybridge observed as he cranked away to the delight of everyone present, "but they are generally found amusing."

CHAPTER 2

A PUNCH IN THE FACE

BOB FITZSIMMONS FOUND NOTHING AMUSING about his first taste
of boxing. It came when he was eleven years old in the form of a
punch in the face. It shocked him to the core and broke his nose and
dropped him to the ground like a sack of potatoes.

The blow was Bob's reward for trying to fit in. He had been up-
rooted in 1871 at age nine from his native Cornwall in England, his
father James, a police constable and blacksmith, taking wife Jane
and their five youngest children to Timaru, New Zealand to start a
new life. Watching some older boys playing soccer one day, Bob
had kicked the ball back when it came bouncing his way, not noticing the team captain who was running over to fetch it. The well-
meant gesture angered the bigger fellow and prompted the smash in
the face. Returning tearfully home with a bloody shirt and his eyes
turning black, Bob had to endure the further humiliation of being
thrashed by his mother for having gotten into a fight. "Right then
and there," he recalled years later, "I determined to prepare myself
to settle scores with that big coward. From that day on, my sole desire was to become a prizefighter."

Bob could not have found himself in a much more out-of-the-
way place for pursuing such an ambition. The dirt-road colonial
outpost of Timaru had not even existed fifteen years before, prior to
the arrival of the first shipload of settlers from England. Bob nevertheless managed to make a start at figuring out things pugilistic,
watching the occasional amateur bout and practicing with his older
brother Jarrett. Copying the stance of the older men was easy: hands

up, left leg forward, right leg back, feet far enough apart for firm balance, close enough together to allow for brisk movement. Learning to not jerk back or turn away from a punch was much harder. It is an instinctive human reaction—and giving in to it a sure way to lose a fight right at the start. To become a skilled boxer and not just a wild flailer, Bob had to learn to stand face to face with an opponent and "slip" his punches, evading them by ducking or side-stepping or weaving while maintaining the proper stance.

He also had to learn to wrestle, for under the London Prize Ring Rules that had governed boxing for the past century, grabbing hold of your opponent and tussling was very much a part of the game. "No chap had any business in a London ring unless he was a fair nippy wrestler," Bob would recall in 1897. "You had to be up to every trick in the hugging game, and strong into the bargain. Because my legs were always thin, lots of fellows figured they'd never hold up under me in wrestling. That's where I fooled them. My legs never went back on me, and I was always sweet on wrestling from the time I was a kid. Fact is, I learned to wrestle all styles long before I knew anything about sparring. And believe me, that was a big help when I fought with the raw 'uns."

Bob had long since entered the work force by this time, ending his schooling at the age of eleven—he would forever remain a poor speller—to apprentice in Jarrett's blacksmith shop. The freckled, red-haired youth grew up tall and gangly, not at all the sturdy lumber-jack type then considered ideal for the ring. But he won fights just the same, starting with impromptu scraps with local boys, then his first real match in the ring, a London Rules contest against an opponent named Pat Carney.

"You had to look out for yourself more than with the mitts," Bob would remember of that bout, the first of four he fought with bare knuckles, "because there was a hundred little ways of tricking a man with fouls that the referee wouldn't be likely to get on to. And there was them spikes in the shoes! Pat cut me twice after we'd been at it about ten minutes. I had a tear along my left calf, and a gash over my instep. But Pat apologized, said it was sort of accidental, and the referee said nothing. So half a moment later we were locked and wrestling against the ropes, and I spiked Mr. Pat just as accidental as he'd done it to me. He yelled bloody murder, but the referee only grinned and shouted something about 'What's good for the goose is good for the gander,' and Pat shut up. He tried no more monkey business, and neither did I. I put him to sleep fair and square."

It was those long arms of Bob's that did it. They were growing sinewy and strong from shoveling coal into the forge, manhandling horses and working hot iron with a hammer. By his late teens he had a well-muscled torso and back and a superb set of shoulders—and a punch like a turnip swung on the end of a chain.

In June 1882, boxer-turned-showman Jem Mace arrived at the Theatre Royal in Timaru with his touring company of performers, an eclectic mix that included boxers, a wrestler and strongman, a ballad singer and Irish comic and "W.H. Edmunds, lightning sketcher." As an added attraction Mace held an amateur tournament for local boxers under Marquis of Queensberry rules. Bob Fitzsimmons, nineteen years old, six feet tall and one hundred forty pounds, entered the contest and had his first taste of the new style of boxing: padded gloves, three-minute rounds, no wrestling. The gloves were a welcome addition, protecting his hands and allowing for harder hitting, Bob's emerging forte. As for the three minutes of timed action, that increased the tempo of a bout and thus took some getting used to, for no longer could a hurt or tired fighter stall by dropping to a knee in response to a light blow, thereby ending a round. Under the new rules he had to keep fighting until the bell sounded. "The tension's higher with the gloves," Bob would say. "There's more nervous strain."

Bob won all four of his fights in the Jem Mace tournament, all by knock out. He took home a meerschaum pipe as his reward. Three months later, when Mace returned to Timaru for another two-night engagement, Bob faced five more raw opponents in bouts the *Timaru Herald* called "more amusing than interesting as exhibitions of skill, one or two good boxers among them being matched with poor players." Although unnamed, Bob was evidently one of the "good boxers," for he won all five of his fights. For his efforts this time he received a little silver medal worth perhaps a few shillings—and a thorough bruising that had him groaning when he got up for work the next day.

In 1885, when he was twenty-two, Bob left New Zealand for Australia. He needed his own business and the greater income it would provide if he was to get married and start a family, and Timaru was too small to support a second Fitzsimmons smithy. He established a blacksmith shop in Sydney's immigrant Redfern suburb and later relocated to Harris Street down by the docks. In October 1885 he married a Cornwall-born girl named Louisa Johns—her family had emigrated to New Zealand on the same ship as Bob's—and together they had three children. Their first two died before the age of one. Their third child, son Charles, born in 1889, survived.

Shortly before Bob's arrival in Sydney, Larry Foley, the retired heavyweight bare-knuckles champion of Australia, built an athletic hall behind the White Horse Hotel, which he owned. Nicknamed the "Iron Pot," it quickly became Australia's center for boxing, which had fallen into moral disfavor following a much-publicized local death in the prize ring the previous year. It was here that Bob received his first proper instruction, learning the finer points of ring science from Foley and then from "Professor" Peter Jackson, a native of the Caribbean island of St. Croix and the current heavyweight champion of Australia. This included not just the mechanics of punching, but strategy—"generalship," it was called—like dictating the pace of a fight and conserving your strength, maneuvering your opponent into corners, neutralizing his attacks and prompting him to lead with feints.

Bob also got a steady diet of competition, sparring exhibitions and more serious contests for a purse of five or ten pounds. And for the first time he had the experience of facing men who were better than he was. "Mick Dooley had things all his own way with Fitzsimmons in a four rounds contest," the *Sydney Globe* reported on June 4, 1886, "but the latter is fast improving." This was one of the earliest references to Bob fighting in Australia, and one of the last to him being bested. By 1888 he had acquired so much "Foley Polish" that he was easily disposing of opponents and starting to get noticed. The *Sydney Referee* called his March 5th fight against a heavier Bill Slavin "perfect science against a little skill and great strength and reach, and, as usual, science held a strong lead all through. Fitz is ... as thin as a broom handle, but very wiry, and there is no more finished sparrer, after Jackson, ever steps into the square ring. He got all over Slavin, and escaped that cruel left...as easily as falling off a log."

On January 19, 1889, Bob faced Sydney plasterer Jim Hall in the Iron Pot in a scheduled eight-rounder, the gate to go to the winner. Larry Foley posted a placard at the event announcing that it was for the middleweight championship of Australia but it wasn't widely recognized as such. In this era before sanctioning bodies, a championship prizefight came about through a challenge being made and accepted and stakes being posted by each side, winner take all. No such formalities were observed in the Fitzsimmons-Hall fight. Bob in fact was not yet a full-fledged prizefighter. He was no longer a complete amateur, performing as he did for gate receipts and small purses, but he hadn't turned what was then considered fully professional either, putting up the stakes that sanctified a contest. He therefore did not become Australia's new middleweight champion after convincingly defeating Hall in five rounds; through the following year Hall continued to be recognized as holding the title. And when they met again in the Iron Pot in February 1890, this time in a formal title fight for fifty pounds a side, it was Bob who was the challenger and Hall who was the champ.

What happened next would be a source of regret for Bob for the rest of his life. He threw the fight. The betting was heavily in his favor and he was promised half the winnings if he took a dive. "I never suffered so much mental torture before in my life," he later remembered. "What was I to do? I had spent every cent I possessed in training and paying my helpers and, figuratively, I was flat broke. The temptation was too much and I yielded. The incident and the sequel made a black page in my history and how often I have yearned to go back and blot it out."

Bob was in excellent condition at the start of the contest, all bone and muscle and gristle, Hall in visibly poor shape, untoned and soft and panting hard after only two rounds. It appeared Bob was headed for an easy win and the gamblers who had bet on him to an early payoff. And then, in the fourth, he took a right to the jaw—had it been really so hard?—and down he went. It was a spectacular knockout, a Drury Lane special. Bob kicked his legs and rolled onto his back and lay there, flat out, as the referee counted to ten. His seconds dragged him to his corner and propped him on his chair and he slid onto the floor. He was helped through the ropes and led to the dressing room and he was still acting groggy. And then he was handed a fraction of what had been promised and he realized he had made a big mistake.

While there was a sense of incredulity in newspaper reports of the Fitzsimmons-Hall fight, no open suspicions were expressed in print. Following Bob's next fight, however—against an opponent of such rankness that ringside spectators were forced to cover their noses—the *Sydney Referee* made a significant comment. It was one of Bob's unserious efforts, a display of the clowning he sometimes indulged in that in this case went so far that the *Referee* headlined the fight "A Comedy in Nine Acts." "As for Fitzsimmons," the write-up concluded, "he is simply a fool to throw away his reputation as he has been doing lately, and unless he is desirous of being known as champion faker of Australasia he had better fight square and clean, as I know he can if on the job."

With Hall set to depart for America to pursue bigger ambitions, Bob, perhaps to redeem himself, deposited fifty pounds stake money at the *Referee* offices and issued a challenge to fight any middleweight in Australia for the soon-to-be vacant title. No such fight would ever take place. Instead, it was Bob who ended up on the San Francisco-bound steamer and Hall who followed, a year behind. How this came about is unclear. The usual story is that Hall cut his hand in a bar fight and could not make the journey, and that Bob at the last minute was offered his place. Another is that Bob, fearing that his friends would discover he had thrown the Hall fight, took the initiative and decided to leave on his own. Whatever transpired, his departure was hasty, mentioned in the newspapers for the first time on the very day that he left. It was arranged by Tom James, the purser of the steamship *Zealandia* on which Bob would sail. James was a scout of Australian fighters and had already shepherded several prospects across the Pacific. Robert James Fitzsimmons, blacksmith, would be his greatest find.

———— ✳ ————

On the other side of the Pacific Ocean, in San Francisco, James John Corbett, the son of an Irish immigrant livery stable owner, was making his own way into the fight game. As with Fitzsimmons, it had been a bully who gave him his start.

It happened at St. Ignatius Parochial School during recess, in 1878, when Jim was twelve. He had just graduated to the "big yard" where the older boys played, among them "Fatty" Carney, the schoolyard thug. Carney immediately let the new boys know he was in charge by shoving one of Jim's friends. When Jim intervened, Carney glared at him and said, "I'll tend to you after school."

Jim was terrified at the end of the day. He wanted to sneak away but his pride wouldn't let him. Mustering his courage, he went outside and there was Carney, surrounded by a gaggle of schoolboys eager to see a fight. "I had no more idea of sparring than a hog has of Christmas," Corbett recalled fifteen years later. "I had seen one fellow spar, however, and had noticed him looking at his opponent's stomach and hitting for his face. I did the same thing to Fatty and was overjoyed at the result. The longer we fought the more enthusiastic I became. I was not angry; I was simply delighted with the scrap."

The fight ended inconclusively with Carney wrestling Jim to the ground and a passerby breaking it up. It was nevertheless hailed as a victory for Jim, one that earned him a reputation for toughness and left him with a taste for fighting. He began practicing back at the livery stable, "allow[ing] the boys to swing for me to see how nearly I could estimate their reach. Practice enabled me to gauge the blows so closely that I could feel the wind of their gloves on my face." More fights at school followed and soon Jim was expelled. A year at a second school ended with another expulsion and with that his formal education was over. He entered the workforce as a messenger with the Nevada Bank and soon was promoted to assistant teller.

It was at San Francisco's Olympic Club that Jim began seriously to study boxing at the age of eighteen. The manager of the bank where Jim worked had made the suggestion as a more decent way to blow off steam than the fights Jim was now picking in bars down by the harbor. The Olympic had just brought Walter Watson over from England to teach the new "scientific" method and Jim, having had some of the cockiness knocked out of him by the club champion, was determined to learn. He threw himself into it body and soul, early morning runs on a breakfast of raw eggs beaten into sherry, pushing himself until he was exhausted, evening sessions with Watson, learning how to punch, parry, move and evade. By the end of August 1885, after just three months of instruction, Jim was being hailed as "the coming heavyweight of the Club," his reach and strength making up for what he still lacked in skill. By February 1886 he was the Olympic's leading heavyweight boxer, ably challenging Watson—who was admittedly smaller and much older—in amateur bouts.

Everything seemed to be going well for Jim Corbett. He was a well-dressed, well-mannered, well-liked young man with a respectable white-collar bank job and good career prospects. But he wasn't happy. He wanted to marry Ollie Lake, a young lady training to be a school teacher, but she was Protestant and Jim was Catholic and his parents wouldn't agree to a union outside the faith. And so, as Jim's father would see it, he threw away the good life he was building and ran off.

On June 28, 1886, Jim surfaced in Salt Lake City with a manager and a new name, Jim Dillon. He said he was twenty-six years old but in fact was not quite twenty. He had arrived, the *Salt Lake Herald* reported, "with a view of arranging a match with any of our local hitters who may desire to meet him. Mr. Dillon has sparred with nearly all the heavy weights who have visited the coast, and says he is now on his way to New York to arrange a meeting with Mitchell, Burke or Dempsey, or anyone else for that matter. His manager, Harry Eaton, may be found at the Valley House, and he will be pleased to consider any proposition that may be laid before him." A contest was arranged for the very next weekend against beefy local slugger Frank Smith for stakes of one hundred dollars a side. Jim easily won. He next faced Utah champion Duncan McArthur for two-fifty a side. This bout ended in a draw. In the coming weeks Jim appeared in several follow-up "athletic entertainments," serving as master of ceremony and sparring with McArthur and Smith, Ollie helping in the box office selling tickets. She had followed Jim out to Salt Lake City and they had been married by a justice of the peace. "Mr. James Dillon ... has shown himself not only an artist under the

Marquis of Queensberry rules," the *Salt Lake Tribune* concluded, "but a most thorough and well-educated gentleman, who has made a large circle of warm friends in Salt Lake during his stay here." This was the earliest reference in the press to Jim Corbett as a "gentleman." It would not be the last.

And then his father Patrick showed up. He talked Jim into returning home by agreeing to consent to his marriage if Ollie would agree to convert to Catholicism, which she did. The trio arrived back in San Francisco on August 21. Jim and Ollie were remarried in a church the same day.

Jim settled down for a time after that. He found a job as a collector with the Anglo-Nevada Assurance Company and got a place of his own on Fillmore and gave Ollie the quiet life that she wanted, for she considered pugilism "a perfectly horrible business." But it didn't last. In 1887 Jim started working part-time at the Golden Gates Athletic Club as a boxing instructor. In 1888 he quit his job at the Anglo-Nevada to replace the departing Walter Watson at the Olympic Club at a salary of one hundred fifty dollars a month, becoming "Professor Corbett." With his growing reputation as a scientific boxer, he was beginning to feel the pull of the prize ring. The sporting community was clamoring to get him into a fight to the finish, particularly against Joe Choynski (pronounced "Ko-en-ski"), a local rival who was doing everything he could to egg Jim into a set-to. When Jim demurred about fighting for money, he was scoffed at, his foray into professionalism as "Jim Dillon" being well known. "Corbett shows a little backwardness in coming forward and is squeamish about fighting for a stake!" crowed the *Daily Alta California*. "He considers it *infra dig* [beneath him], as it were." This was not entirely true. Jim personally did not have qualms about fighting for money. But the Olympic Club did. And so did his father.

This was why Jim refused to accept the offer of three thousand dollars to fight Choynski at the California Athletic Club, which did not share the Olympic's reticence about prizefights. To appease the Olympic and win his father's grudging acquiescence, Jim agreed to fight Choynski in private and made no mention of the money that would ride on the outcome. As far as Patrick was concerned, it was merely a "boyish affair," two young hotheads going off to settle a feud with their fists. In reality it would be Jim's first professional fight fought under his own name.

Since fistic contests were illegal outside the confines of a club, where they could be labeled "exhibitions," the Corbett-Choynski battle of May 30, 1889 was held in secret, in a barn on a deserted farm north of San Francisco. It was to be a fight to the finish with two-ounce gloves, a quarter the weight of those worn today in most professional bouts, not much more than mittens. The stakes were a thousand dollars a side.

The fight had gone four rounds when the lookout called from the window that a team of horses was approaching. It was the sheriff of Marin County. "Boys, back to your corners," the referee instructed the combatants. And to the handful of panicked spectators: "Gentlemen, stay where you are; there is nothing to be afraid of."

For the next several days San Francisco's sporting element remained in a lather of excitement, alive to every rumor of where the interrupted Corbett-Choynski fight would be held. When word finally got out that it was to be on a barge moored off Benicia, two hundred fifty spectators rushed to the harbor to charter whatever craft they could find for the two-hour trip up through San Pablo Bay.

The principles and their seconds arrived at the barge at six o'clock in the morning, June 5, Corbett with two-ounce gloves as per the agreement, Choynski with nothing. He had forgotten to bring them, he said. It was a ruse to maneuver Jim into fighting with bare knuckles, the Choynski camp having caught wind that he had injured his right thumb in the aborted fight in the barn. Jim, who was indeed injured, insisted on gloves but declined to claim the purse through forfeit. It was finally decided that he would wear his two-ounce gloves and Choynski a pair of regular riding gloves, unpadded, borrowed from a spectator.

The fight began in a light manner, the two men trading quips as they exchanged blows. Corbett: "That was pretty light." Choynski: "That was a good one." Corbett: "Joe, you have got your eye on that bottle." Choynski: "Don't get rattled, Jim." By the seventh round the talking was finished and they were fighting in earnest. By the fourteenth, Choynski's nose and mouth were streaming blood—so much of it that Corbett's gloves were soaked, the pine boards were slippery and several spectators had to turn away to keep down the ham and egg sandwiches they had eaten on the trip out.

Corbett, meanwhile, was hurting—and not just from the steady rain of punishment Choynski was inflicting, the raised seams on his riding gloves leaving a pattern of red welts. Jim had broken his left hand in the fifth and was fighting now with both hands injured, pain shooting up his arm each time he threw a punch. To keep the pain to a manageable level, he tried to connect with his left using only the knuckle closest to his thumb, farthest from the broken bone on the outside of his hand. To do so he had to keep his arm bent and strike at Choynski from the side, rotating his body to deliver a hooking blow. He would later call this a "left hook" and claim to be its inventor. "There it goes again," spectators observed when it landed, driving into Choynski's ribs and right kidney, "touching up" his bloody nose and smashed mouth.

The fight continued for twenty-seven rounds, nearly two hours, until the rising sun was roasting the two men on the uncovered barge and they were staggering with exhaustion, dehydrated, fighting on instinct. Corbett finally ended it with another left, a hugely painful straight left, delivered full force with the last reserves of his strength. It was not a knock-out blow, only a knock down, but it finished Choynski. Woozy from blood loss and utterly spent, he couldn't get up past his knees before the referee counted him out.

Back in San Francisco, Corbett stated that he was through with fighting; that he wouldn't even train anymore. This may have been an emotional response to the suffering he had just endured. In later years he would call this battle with Choynski the toughest of his life. It may, however, have been simply intended to quell his father, who met Jim at the pier with an extremely demonstrative welcome of hugging and kissing. "The old gentleman was excited," the *Daily Alta California* reported, "and it took all of Jim's stern looks to keep him quiet." Was there something about his father that made Jim uneasy; something more than Patrick's strong sense of propriety and disapproval; something slightly "off" that Jim felt he had to appease? In the coming years Patrick Corbett would begin to show signs of mental disturbance that ultimately would lead to a deeply tragic end.

Jim would have felt terrible when he got out of bed the next morning. It was always that way after a hard fight. His face would have been swollen and his head was probably aching. The cuts on the inside of his mouth would have made eating painful. His hands, both injured, would have been swollen and stiff to the point of being almost useless. His battered ribs would have made it hurt to take a deep breath. And yet, just four weeks later, he and Choynski were going at it again, more gently this time in a four-round exhibition. For Jim had no intention of retiring from boxing. He was just getting started. The battle on the barge in fact was something he needed, a baptism by fire that tested his toughness, proving to himself that he could take a "really good licking" and prevail.

If he had had private doubts before, the Choynski fight swept them aside. Jim Corbett had not just the skill but the confidence to take on the best in the world. But would he? With his father's shadow still over him and his wife Ollie disapproving, Jim's future as a prizefighter remained in doubt.

It was a wet, gray afternoon in Sydney, April 16, 1890, when Bob Fitzsimmons locked up his blacksmith shop for the last time and made his way to Admiralty Wharf to board the steamer *Zealandia*. There was a small crowd on hand to see him off, among them his wife Louisa holding their infant son Charles, the hem of her skirt spattered by the mud that lay all around. Bob stowed his bags down in steerage, where he would be traveling, then returned to the deck to wave goodbye.

He was leaving with a letter of introduction from the secretary of the Sydney Athletic Club and a glowing reference printed in the *Sydney Referee*. "He is one of the queerest-looking pieces of pugilistic furniture that ever pulled off a shirt when he is fighting," the *Referee* stated, "and the great 'Frisco club men may smile when they see him perform in the first round or two, but they won't when the feeling is over, and the fight begins in earnest if their money is on the other man. He had not been able to get on many square fights here because all the boys were frightened of the New Zealander. I can earnestly and honestly recommend him to the 'Frisco club as a fine young fellow, as honest as the day, and a more respectable man never broke bread. He is a blacksmith by trade, and his frame is like a long pole bound with whipcord. He is 6ft high and fights 10 st[one] 8 lb. He will go direct to the California Club, and meet his old chum, Peter Jackson, by whom he will be introduced to the committee, and he will be ready to take on any man they like to pit him against—English, American, or Australian."

It was four o'clock, the scheduled hour of departure. The band struck up a fresh tune, the lines were cast off, the *Zealandia* eased away from the wharf and Bob likely shed a few tears. A three-week voyage lay ahead, seven thousand miles via Honolulu across the Pacific. It would be six months before he would see Louisa and young Charley again.

CHAPTER 3

ROOM 5

"I LIKE TO BEGIN at the large end of things," Thomas Edison once told a reporter. "Life is too short to begin at the small end.... We are apt to be impressed by the boulder before us and not reason with the mountain above us that the boulder rolled down from."

For Edison, father of the Phonograph, the electric light, the quadruplex telegraph and a hundred other amazing and useful inventions, the "large end of things" in the late 1880s extended beyond the inventions that continued to flow from his fertile imagination to the very essence of invention itself. He wanted to streamline the creative process, to make it more efficient, and to situate it at the heart of a factory complex purpose-built for turning out his many products.

"I will have the best equipped & largest Laboratory extant," he wrote to a potential financial backer in 1887, "and the facilities incomparably superior to any other for rapid & cheap development of an invention, & working it up into Commercial shape.... [Then] my ambition is to build up a great industrial works in the Orange Valley starting in a small way & gradually working up, the Laboratory supplying the perfected inventions, models, patterns, & fitting up necessary special machinery in the factory for each invention. My plan contemplates the working of only that class of inventions which require but small investments for each and of a highly profitable nature...."

Profitability. For Edison that was key, a way to vet his ideas, for it identified an invention as being of practical value. "Anything that won't sell I don't want to invent," he explained in 1889, "because anything that won't sell hasn't reached the acme of success. Its sale is proof of its utility, and utility is success." He put it even more bluntly to his private secretary Al Tate: "I measure everything I do by the size of a silver dollar. If it don't come up to that standard then I know it's no good." It was an interesting statement coming from a man who personally cared little about money beyond the independence it allowed him to do as he liked.

Edison's vision of a laboratory complex devoted to product research and development in a wide range of fields had become a reality by January 1888, just prior to his forty-first birthday. It was located west of Newark, New Jersey, on a country road a half mile from the Orange train station, surrounded by a white picket fence. There were five structures in total, all of red brick: the main laboratory, two hundred fifty feet long and three stories high, and four smaller one-story buildings for ancillary work.

If you had an appointment to meet Edison himself, you would be led to the main building, glimpsing perhaps through its high arching windows some of the lab employees, Edison's "muckers," bent over their work. Inside the spacious entryway the stockroom might be pointed out by your guide in passing, its thousands of drawers and pigeon holes crammed with every conceivable substance, from angle iron and springs and chemical and mineral samples to feathers and animal skins and spices and grasses. Down the hall was the machine shop; above, two floors containing a second machine shop for more delicate work and a hallway of numbered experiment rooms, all strictly off-limits.

As a visitor, you would be ushered into the library that filled the front of the building, an impressive room designed to communicate the unparalleled achievement that Edison had built up from such humble beginnings as a homeschooled boy selling newspapers and candy. Rich rugs and comfortable armchairs were scattered about; portraits of luminaries hung on the walls; bookcases extended in two tiers most of the way up to the forty-foot ceiling. It was all for show, of course. It did not reflect the man—the self-taught, self-made, ferociously driven genius who cared as little for opulence as he did for clothes and food and personal hygiene. To see anything of the real man here in the library you needed to look into one of the alcoves, at the cot Edison sometimes used for a nap when he had not gotten his full four hours of sleep.

By 1888 it had become somewhat difficult to meet Edison and infringe on his time. His fame was so great and so many people wanted to see him that it was no longer possible to simply drop by his lab for a chat. When Eadweard Muybridge arrived outside the main gate on February 27 of that year, however, there was no question about whether to admit him. He was there by invitation. He was shown right in.

Following his return from his European tour in 1882, demonstrating his Zoopraxiscope and lecturing on motion, Eadweard Muybridge was invited to the University of Pennsylvania to further his studies in what had come to be known as "chronophotography." Over the next several years he captured the gait of nearly every animal in the Philadelphia Zoo, from camel and kangaroo to elephant and tiger, and made a vast number of studies of almost every conceivable type of human movement, his models usually appearing in the nude. Although Muybridge continued to refine his technique and search for faster emulsions, his photographic setup remained fundamentally unchanged from that which he had used to record the gait of Leland Stanford's racehorses. It consisted of a battery of cameras, either twelve or twenty-four, connected to an adjustable mechanism that electrically triggered the shutters in sequence to capture one to two seconds of movement. (Muybridge often used three banks of cameras simultaneously to record an action from different angles.) Since the primary purpose of Muybridge's work was to deconstruct movement in order to analyze its individual "phases," the sequential still images were usually just printed in rows and displayed as-is. For lecture and entertainment purposes, however, it was sometimes useful to reconstruct the short snippet of motion by tracing the photos onto a glass disk and projecting them on a screen via the Zoopraxiscope.

The culmination of Muybridge's work at UPenn was his 1887 masterpiece, *Animal Locomotion*, eleven volumes containing 781 of his motion studies, more than 20,000 individual photographs all together. He also prepared a lecture entitled "Animal Locomotion." His many appearances with it included one before the New England

Society in Orange, New Jersey on February 25, 1888—prompting someone signing himself "A.N. Tinude" to complain to the *Orange Journal* about Muybridge's display of naked flesh before such a "promiscuous assembly," presumably a reference to a mixed audience of men and women.

It is likely that Edison attended this Saturday lecture. Muybridge's visit to his lab occurred the following Monday. In the course of their meeting, Muybridge mentioned that he was working on a new photographic device—just what is uncertain, as it was never built—that could be used to reproduce Secretary of State Thomas Blaine giving a speech, or Edwin Booth performing a soliloquy from *Hamlet*, or Lillian Russell singing a song, "by taking some sixty or seventy instantaneous photographs of each position assumed by the speaker, and then throwing them by means of a magic lantern upon a screen." Muybridge suggested that this prospective invention could be further developed by joining it with Edison's Phonograph, thereby adding sound to the illustration of movement. According to a *New York World* account of the meeting, possibly provided by Muybridge, "This scheme met with the approval of Mr. Edison and he intended to perfect it at his leisure."

While Muybridge's visit certainly helped spark Edison's interest in the challenge of photographically capturing motion, it was not the only factor. Research into chronophotography was heating up in 1888, Muybridge's pioneering work having inspired others to enter the field and develop devices of their own, most notable among them Étienne-Jules Marey in Paris, William Friese-Greene in England, Ottomar Anschütz in Berlin and Frenchman Louis Le Prince, then residing in the UK. Closer to home, Edison may have heard of a paper presented by William Goold Levison to the Brooklyn Academy of Amateur Photographers in June 1888, about an "automatic continuous camera" he had invented. It recorded images in sequence, each on a separate dry plate, as in Muybridge's apparatus, but it did so through a single lens rather than through twelve separate lenses, the plates revolving into position on a wheel. It was "wanting in accuracy of construction," Levison conceded, he having built it himself, but he was confident that "when carefully constructed the camera will operate admirably." With these men and still others now all working in the field, a breakthrough could not be very far off. It was thus an opportune time for Edison to invest a small portion of his inventive power in the problem of photographically capturing motion, for it might lead to another "Edison Wonder" that would astonish the world.

Edison's goal was to do more than merely improve upon the illustration of movement as created by Muybridge's Zoopraxiscope or Anschütz's Tachyscope, increasing the number of sequential photographs taken from one or two dozen to, say, sixty or eighty. He wanted to capture and reproduce extended periods of actual movement by taking *thousands* of photos in rapid succession through a single lens. His initial concept was to adapt the Phonograph to record images rather than sound, in essence replacing a needle inscribing a spiral of sound waves with a lens recording a spiral of tiny photos. To do so required three things. First, the cylinder upon which the images were recorded had to be coated with an emulsion so sensitive that exposures of the barest fraction of a second could be taken. This in itself was a major hurdle, for the evolving science of "instantaneous photography" had not yet advanced to this point. Second, the cylinder had to move intermittently rather than continuously as was the case with sound recording. It had to advance a step, then stop for a photo to be taken, then advance another step, then stop for the next photo, then advance again—on and on, a series of starts and stops occurring some twenty-five times every second, for that was the number of images Edison believed would be needed to trick the human eye into seeing seamless movement. Fortunately, no inventor in the world had more experience with intermittent movement than he, it being central to two of his inventions, the stock ticker and the automatic telegraph.

Finally, a mechanism was needed to flash an image onto the emulsion when the cylinder was stationary, then to block off the light while the cylinder advanced to the next step. This could be accomplished with the 1880s version of a shutter, a rotating disk with slots cut through it like spokes on a wheel. By positioning the disk between the camera lens and the photographic surface and synchronizing its rotation with the cylinder's step-by-step movement, a rapid-fire series of images would be flashed onto the emulsion at exactly the right moment. At least that was the plan.

Preliminary experimental work for the proposed apparatus was done in September 1888, Edison assigning the task to William Kennedy Laurie Dickson, his most experienced man with all things photographic. Dickson had been born in France in 1860, the son of Scottish parents, and educated on the continent and in England prior to moving to the United States in 1879. He wrote to Edison asking for a job that same year, listing his accomplishments and calling himself a "friendless and fatherless boy." His application was rejected. He tried again in 1883, when Edison's various enterprises were booming, and this time was hired. By 1888 Dickson had become a key member of Edison's staff, in charge of testing and photography work and the all-important ore milling department. He was a man of rising substance, recently married to an aging Southern belle twelve years his senior and certainly the most flamboyant and urbane employee at the lab. He was a stylish dresser with a carefully groomed mustache, a debonair and somewhat snobbish dandy with cultured tastes and social ambitions, able to converse in French and German, skilled at playing the violin and a charming performer in musical evenings and *tableau vivant*—in fact, a direct contrast to earthy Edison himself, who was shy in public, unmindful of the social graces and famously careless about his appearance. It is hard to imagine Dickson following Edison's example of bragging about how long he had gone without taking a bath.

Dickson initially expressed doubts about the viability of Edison's Phonograph-camera idea, pointing out that he knew of no emulsion sensitive enough for taking microphotographs at high speeds. "Well, try it," Edison replied; "it will lead to other things." And so Dickson went to work, experimenting with various emulsions, tinkering with microscope lenses, testing materials to use for making cylinder shells. He did so in his spare time, and for no extra pay beyond his twenty-four-dollar salary for a six-day, sixty-hour week, Edison insisting that it not interfere with "the big work at hand." This "big work" was the magnetic separator co-invented by Edison and Dickson that was then the lab's primary focus, a device for enriching the iron content in ore. It promised to revolutionize American industry by utilizing low-grade ore deposits in the eastern

United States near the centers of iron production, thereby doing away with the costly necessity of transporting high-grade ore over long distances. For Edison this was the future, the Next Big Thing into which he was pouring vast amounts of time and money. In comparison, motion photography was little more than an amusing diversion—"a pet hobby," as Edison would later call it.

Encouraged by Dickson's preliminary investigations, Edison filed what was called a "caveat" with the Patent Office, a notification that he was developing a patentable invention. No longer used today, caveats were a sanctioned way in the nineteenth century to establish precedence for an invention, for after being accepted by the Patent Office a rival application could not be accepted for one year. "I am experimenting upon an instrument," Edison's handwritten original of Caveat Number 110, dated October 8, 1888, began, "which does for the Eye what the phonograph does for the Ear, which is the recording and reproduction of things in motion, and in such a form as to be both cheap, practical and convenient." This latter part was important, for it separated Edison's idea from the methods of Muybridge and others, which were generally expensive, labor intensive and inconvenient. His proposed device, Edison went on the explain, would be called a "Kinetograph" (Greek for "motion-writing") when used to record movement and a "Kinetoscope" ("motion-viewing") when used to see the results. (Due to persistent confusion, the two devices would often be referred to at the lab collectively as the "Kineto.") The images would be a mere one-thirty-second of an inch wide, requiring a microscope lens to photograph them and a microscope eyepiece to see them. Assuming a cylinder of similar size to that on the Phonograph and the taking of twenty-five images per second, the device would be capable of recording 42,000 images in total; in other words, twenty-eight minutes of movement. Edison opined that it could be synchronized with a Phonograph to simultaneously reproduce sound and movement, creating an illusion of life so complete that "we may see & hear a whole opera as perfectly as if actually present although the actual performance may have taken place years before."

This opera reference, echoing Muybridge's earlier comment about Edwin Booth and Lillian Russell, was straying into flights of fancy and was removed from the final caveat submission prepared by Edison's lawyers. As for Muybridge himself, he had dropped from the picture. His idea of collaboration did not appeal to Edison at all.

The first version of the cylinder Kinetograph, "Cylinder 1," was constructed in the lab's precision machine shop by Edison's most experienced machinist, John Ott, then passed to William Dickson for testing in the second-floor photographic room, known as "Room 5." Dickson would be initially assisted by Charles Brown, a lower-level Edison mucker paid the hourly rate of twenty-five cents. Their work on Cylinder 1 was largely confined to trying different emulsions and taking single photos, then a handful of photos in succession taken at a very slow speed.

The results were disappointing. The emulsion, made from gelatin or albumen (egg whites), tended to go on lumpy and crack as it dried. The light-sensitive silver halide grains suspended in the goo were also too coarse to allow for any sort of detail in images of microscopic size, and the length of exposure required was too long. The curvature of the cylinder posed yet another problem, for it resulted in images being blurred. A new design, Cylinder 2, was therefore developed and added to Caveat Number 114, a shopping basket filing of dozens of invention ideas lumped together for submission to the Patent Office on March 22, 1889. The most significant change was the switch from a round to a multi-sided cylinder in order to provide a flat surface upon which the photos could be taken. The proposed photo-taking rate was also reduced to "fifteen or twenty times per second." Subsequent test results with Cylinder 2 were scarcely any better. Dickson was getting something, but it wasn't much, only blips and smears of light.

Edison tried again. His next design, Cylinder 3, outlined some time between May and July in Caveat Number 116, would be substantially different. To begin with, the cylinder or "drum" as it was now called was made bigger around and the image size increased to one-eighth of an inch. The rotating disk shutter was also abandoned. Edison instead came up with the idea of using a sparking mechanism to illuminate the subject with flashes of light synchronized to the cylinder's step-by-step movement. Also abandoned was the method of coating the cylinder with liquid emulsion. It would instead be wrapped with an emulsion-coated sheet of a recently developed material called celluloid. The first samples were received at the lab on June 25, 1889 from the John Carbutt Company of Philadelphia, one of the earliest manufacturers of this promising new product, so much lighter and more durable than photographic glass plates. Dickson immediately cut a piece to fit on Cylinder 3 and ran a series of tests.

Lab employee Fred Ott, John's younger brother, served as Dickson's first subject, wrapped in a white sheet and with a white cloth round his head and positioned against a black background for maximum contrast. "[H]e was a comical genius," Charles Brown would later recall, "and we always used to get him because he would cut up monkey shines...." As Fred stood in the ruby red glow of the darkroom light, Cylinder 3 was turned on and began photographing at a rate of eight or ten images per second, its reflector stroboscopically illuminating him as he gyrated and waved his arms. The device was then turned off, the room once again red, the Carbutt sheet was removed from the cylinder and developed, then treated with bichloride of mercury to turn the negative into a positive image. The result was a black sheet covered with nine rows of little white splotches, some two hundred all together. This was affixed to a glass cylinder which was installed on Cylinder 3 in place of the metal cylinder that had been used for photographing. A synchronized light source was placed inside the glass for illumination and a microscope eyepiece installed in place of the lens, thereby turning the device into a Kinetoscope viewer.

What Dickson saw, peering through the eyepiece as the cylinder rotated and the images spiraled past, was a ghostly blob of light, barely identifiable as human much less recognizable as Fred, pulsing and jerking for a period of ten or twelve seconds. It was nowhere near what Edison had envisioned. Doubling the image size to a quarter inch in subsequent tests produced somewhat better results but it was still far short of what was required. To attain acceptable quality with the emulsions at hand would require that images be made even larger and that the cylinder upon which they were recorded in turn be impossibly big.

Dickson would sporadically tinker with the cylinder apparatus for another year, prompted by Edison's lingering desire to link Kinetograph to Phonograph to create moving images with synchronized sound. But it was a developmental dead end. The various versions of the cylinder machine would be eventually shelved and the ghostly record of Fred Ott's gyrations, dubbed *Monkeyshines*, filed away. The way forward lay with the celluloid Dickson had just started using. It opened up a whole new approach to photographically capturing motion, one that employed a long strip of what would soon be called "film."

CHAPTER 4

CHAMPION AND CONTENDER

The Oceanic Steamship Company's steamer *Zealandia* docked in San Francisco on the evening of May 10, 1890, having completed the voyage from Sydney in twenty-four days. She carried a cargo of bananas to restock city markets, a full compliment of passengers filling the cabins, a large bundle of cigars that the ship's quartermaster tried to smuggle onto the wharf through a porthole, and prizefighter Bob Fitzsimmons traveling in steerage.

There were those among the *Zealandia* crew who were not sorry to see Bob disembark the next morning. He had made a habit during the crossing of tripping them and trying to egg them into taking a swing at his balding head. There was no meanness in it. It was just Bob's way, laughing with youthful exuberance as he dodged and parried and danced away from the blows, getting a little exercise to break the monotony of the long trip.

Hauling his bags and armed with a letter of introduction, Bob made his way to the California Athletic Club on New Montgomery Street behind the Palace Hotel. It was a large, three-story stone structure, certainly more stately that Larry Foley's "Iron Pot" back in Sydney, and reputedly the richest athletic club in the world. Inside, he met President Fulda and other luminaries of the institution and was reunited with his old instructor, Peter Jackson, temporarily employed at the CAC as a boxing instructor.

On the following Thursday Bob was tested against another instructor in the CAC's third-floor arena, going three rounds under the sputtering glare of arc lights. Impressed with his performance, the club decided to place him in an already scheduled fight to the finish against middleweight Billy McCarthy, which they were about to cancel on account of McCarthy's opponent falling sick. It was a tremendous stroke of luck for Bob, a case of being in the right place at the right time, for McCarthy was a recognized contender. He had faced world middleweight champion Jack "Nonpareil" Dempsey in February inside the CAC's own ring under these very arc lights, going twenty-eight rounds before finally succumbing. And the purse—one thousand dollars to go to the winner. It was a magnificent payday compared to the paltry sums Bob had been getting in Australia. There must have been a gleam in his eye and a smile on his lips as the offer was put to him and he nodded his head.

The fight took place on May 29, 1890, in front of a crowd restricted to ticket-holding club members. It was one of the rules that had to be observed when holding a prizefight in San Francisco to keep the authorities from interfering. Bob was introduced as the middleweight champion of New Zealand. Stripped down to his fighting outfit, he was observed by the *Daily Alta California* to be "so ungainly in appearance that he would never be picked out of a crowd as a man who had defeated formidable opponents." The electrical timer was started and the bell automatically sounded—the CAC had the latest equipment—and Bob proceeded to beat McCarthy into bloody submission, needing only nine rounds to accomplish what Dempsey had done in twenty-eight. It was an impressive performance, proof that this recent arrival was the coming thing, just like his Antipodean friends had been saying. Bob took the purse, the big fat beautiful purse, sent some of it to his wife for cabin-class passage from Sydney, kept back a little for his modest expenses and put the rest in the bank.

Just a few blocks away, Jim Corbett and his wife Ollie had taken up residence in the first-class Florence Hotel, just round the corner from the Olympic Club where Jim was back working as a boxing instructor. He was now a full-fledged prizefighter with a big reputation, known across the country as a leading contender for John L. Sullivan's heavyweight title.

It had happened like this. Five months after Jim's battle on the barge with Joe Choynski, a new weekly publication appeared in San Francisco called *The Illustrated World*, sixteen pages of pretty pictures, gossipy stories and no-holds-barred reporting that would soon attract libel lawsuits. Jim's face was splashed across the front page of the first issue, dated November 2, 1889. "James J. Corbett—The Coming Champion of the World!" it was headlined. And underneath: "Pin this to your hat!" As a marketing tactic, the publisher sent complimentary copies of this inaugural issue to major cities in the East, placing Jim's name and face before sporting enthusiasts there for the first time.

Among those happening upon a copy was heavyweight contender Jake Kilrain. Earlier that year, Jake had faced Sullivan in an open-air title bout in Mississippi—the last heavyweight championship, it would turn out, under the old bare-knuckles rules. Kilrain had lost that fight but was still thought one of the best, for it had taken Sullivan seventy-five rounds to defeat him. Now, gazing at Corbett's visage on the cover of *The Illustrated World*, Kilrain and his manager decided he would make good fodder for Jake's next fight, a West Coast pretender with an inflated reputation and rich backers to ensure lively betting. A telegram was accordingly sent to San Francisco inviting Jim to face Kilrain for six rounds, twenty-five hundred dollars to go to the winner, a grand to the loser. To avoid the trouble that had dogged the Kilrain-Sullivan contest—both men were subsequently indicted for illegal prizefighting—the bout would be held at New Orleans' Olympic Club, an ostensibly members-only affair under the new Marquis of Queensberry rules. "I was dumbfounded," Jim would later recall, "but also very proud that I was recognized as a boxer of enough merit to cope with a man like the famous Kilrain, and I was also tickled to think that my name was known outside of California!"

Ignoring his father's and his wife's disapproval, Jim was on the first train heading east as soon as the expense money arrived. He was a four-to-one underdog going into the February 17, 1890 fight and, at one-eighty-three, nearly twenty pounds lighter than Kilrain. But it didn't seem to phase him a bit. Jim was in such good spirits when he entered the ring, smiling and nodding and waving, not at all disturbed by the sight of the sullen, heavily mustached Kilrain who was about to destroy him, that he was cheered by the crowd for being such a game mark.

By the second round, however, it was apparent that Kilrain was the mark. Unable to engage in the in-fighting that was an integral part of a London Prize Ring contest, the bigger man grew frustrated as Jim picked him apart from a distance. "Foul!" the spectators roared when Kilrain repeatedly rushed in to clinch and wrestle and employ the moves he was best at. The referee broke them apart and Jim, still smiling, returned to his steady jabbing, bloodying and maddening Kilrain, then wearing him out. At the end of six rounds the crowd was yelling "Corbett! Corbett!" and the referee awarded the obvious decision to Jim. "My Dear," Jim telegraphed Ollie after. "Have won my fight easily. Didn't get a scratch."

His resounding victory over the great Kilrain catapulted Jim to heavyweight contender status. It was a role he took to with ease, as if he had been born to it, expecting it all along, quietly biding his time. When Kilrain, stunned at the outcome, demanded a rematch, Jim coolly brushed him aside, saying that he had a reputation now and intended to make the most of it. When Kilrain went on to make a host of excuses for losing—"squealing," as one paper called it, "like every fairly whipped duffer"—Jim just ignored him. He had his eye on bigger game now. He was after John L. Sullivan's crown.

Sullivan, of course, was in no hurry to put his title on the line. He was too busy using it to make money. With the legal impediments then imposed on prizefighting, restricting it to private clubs where few people could see it, there was great public demand for ring champions to give sparring exhibitions. This was the real pay-off that came from making a name in the fight game and winning a title, the sack of gold waiting at the top of the mountain. For most it meant going on the road with a sparring partner, giving nightly demonstrations on stages across the country, pulling punches so nobody got hurt as the money was raked in. For Sullivan, more popular than any previous fighter, the presentation was more elaborate, a full-blown play written especially for him, a melodrama entitled *Honest Hearts and Willing Hands* that culminated in an exciting mock battle in which he sparred for three rounds. Big John wasn't much of an actor—he tended to bawl out his lines like a tough in a barroom—but that didn't matter. Audiences were happy just to see him in the flesh, to hear his booming voice, to watch him use his terrible fists. And he willingly obliged. He toured the United States and then Australia with his crowd-pleasing potboiler, earning a fortune and burnishing his reputation as the invincible champion without ever having to fight a real fight.

Following his victory over Jake Kilrain, Jim remained for two months in the East, giving sparring exhibitions, winning new fans and making money. As one prominent Eastern sportsman marveled, "The enthusiasm over him among those who have seen him perform amounts almost to a craze." It was the emerging "Gentleman Jim" persona that did it, the combination of pugilistic skill, physical beauty and refined manners; a fighter who, after besting a man with his fists, could slip into evening wear and be charming at a party, sipping champagne.

When Jim finally took the train back to San Francisco, it was to return to his old job at the Olympic Club as boxing instructor with a big raise, his national prominence outweighing the club's scruples about his professionalism. As the summer of 1890 gave way to autumn, Jim was once again "Professor Corbett," working two hours a day at the Olympic for a bank manager's salary while he waited for his shot at the title—a shot that Sullivan was not yet ready to give him. The champ preferred to have the contenders do all the fighting amongst themselves while he continued to enjoy life and tour with his show.

One of the most formidable of these contenders was Peter Jackson, Bob Fitzsimmons' old instructor in Sydney. Jackson had come to America in 1888 to challenge Sullivan for the title but Sullivan refused to fight him because he was black. Jim Corbett had no such reservations. In December 1890 he accepted a lucrative offer from the California Athletic Club to face the Australian for a purse of $10,000. It was his biggest yet but it wouldn't be an easy payday. Unlike Kilrain with his old-fashioned bare-knuckles in-fighting, Jackson was skilled at the Marquis of Queensberry game. He was also significantly bigger than Jim.

It was at this point that Patrick Corbett raised an outcry. On January 1, 1891, after the Corbett-Jackson matchup was made public, a letter to the editor appeared in the *San Francisco Morning Call* in which Patrick publicly castigated his son. "I wish," it read, "in justice to my family, you would state in your paper that such a match cannot or will not take place, as I will not permit him to disgrace his family in this city in that way." When contacted for further comment, Patrick had even more to say the next day, claiming that he would "go before the Grand Jury" and have Jim "indicted and then bound over to keep the peace." He would use every means, legitimate or otherwise, to stop the battle, "for by the Eternal I would rather see him lying out there at Lone Mountain than the tool of a band of sharpers, Kearney-street loungers and sure-thing gamblers. I do not care so much about the matter myself, but it is for Jim's sisters, who are grown-up ladies, and for his five younger brothers that I wish to avoid his becoming a professional pugilist or fighting any contest before a club to a finish for a purse.... Of course I cannot control his actions abroad, but he shall not publicly disgrace us here in San Francisco."

"My father is very foolish and hotheaded in acting as he does in this matter," Jim responded. "I am ranked as one of the leading pugilists of the world, and I am in the business to stay. I agreed to fight Jackson, and I will do so when the time comes." A CAC director chimed in with, "The old man is making a monkey of him.... [T]he big boy deserves better treatment from his family." Others were less sympathetic, suggesting that the whole thing was an advertising ploy to draw attention to the fight.

Nothing came of Patrick's outburst or of the private beseeching that Jim's mother did. The fight would go ahead as planned. Jim resigned again, this time for good, from his position as the Olympic Club and headed East for another tour giving boxing exhibitions. He would return to San Francisco in March.

Bob Fitzsimmons' demolition of Billy McCarthy put him on the fast track for a shot at the middleweight title. Two months later, on July 28, 1890, he was in New Orleans to score an effortless victory over Arthur Upham, knocking out the billed "Middleweight Champion of the South" after "playing" with him, as the *National Police Gazette* put it, for five rounds. The Olympic Club in New Orleans was so impressed with Bob's performance that it offered a purse of $5,000 for a fight to the finish between him and world middleweight champion Jack Dempsey. Clubs in New York and Galveston subsequently entered the bidding and the price rose to $10,000. Finally, toward the end of October, the Olympic raised its offer to $12,000, the biggest purse ever put up by a club, and a deal was made. For blacksmith Bob, who had come to America just six months before, traveling humbly in steerage, the potential payday represented half a lifetime spent hammering at the forge. Perhaps it was to mark this momentous change in his fortunes that Bob shaved off his mustache. He would remain clean-shaven for the rest of his life.

By this time the Fitzsimmons family was reunited. Bob's wife Louisa and infant son Charley arrived by steamer in San Francisco on October 27 and took the train across the country to join him in Bay St. Louis, Mississippi, where he had gone to prepare for the upcoming Dempsey encounter. Louisa would prepare the meals and take care of the cottage that served as Bob's and manager-trainer Jimmy Carroll's training camp. It was a secluded place, ideal for Carroll's purpose of keeping Bob out of the public eye until the fight.

Unlike Dempsey, who was working hard to drop fat as he continued to put on sparring exhibitions, Bob went into training already in good shape. He was not burdened with the bad habits shared by so many prizefighters, the overeating and carousing, the heavy drinking, the staying up late. He therefore did not have to subject himself to the bodily trauma that Dempsey was undergoing. For Bob, pre-fight training was about honing and maintaining his already high level of fitness and watching his diet to make the agreed-upon weight limit, one hundred fifty-four pounds.

None of this was much appreciated by those placing bets on the contest. Bob was the favorite among New Orleans locals who had seen him polish off Upham but throughout the rest of the country betting was squarely on Dempsey. Dempsey was the "Nonpareil," after all, the fighter without equal, the victor in all his many fights except one—which hardly counted, he having been dropped by a pivot blow, ruled illegal. He would also be fighting at his natural weight, whereas Bob, at a shade under six feet, would no doubt be starving and in turn weakening himself to appease the scales.

Dempsey was also by far the more popular fighter, for he was considered American whereas Bob was foreign. John L. Sullivan succinctly expressed the public sentiment on the eve of the match— in the middle of his play *Honest Hearts and Willing Hands*, which was showing in Chicago. During a tender scene, just prior to delivering the line, "Never mind, mother, I'll take care of you," John L. strode to the footlights and bellowed in his inimitable style, "Dempsey will lick this here bloke Fitzsimmons because I'm an American and he's an American, too—see?" He then marched back to the actress playing his mother and said, "What I just said goes, but never mind, mother, I'll take care of you."

The open-air amphitheater at the Olympic Club was expanded in preparation for the match, bleachers built in tiers to give everyone a clear view of the covered ring of packed sand. Despite the hefty admission price of ten dollars, nearly four thousand spectators filed into the place on fight night, January 14, 1891, among them Jim Corbett, who had worked New Orleans into his sparring tour to take in the fight. It was a motley assembly, club members and respectable men of substance rubbing shoulders with ruffians, gamblers and hoods, everyone hunkered in jackets and overcoats against the cool evening air. A large number of police were on hand to maintain order in the event that the crowd got unruly. They circulated in the aisles between the bleachers and were stationed behind the barbed wire fence that encircled the ring, ready to beat back any attempt to rush it. They were also keeping a sharp lookout for women, who by law were not allowed to be present. It was rumored that at least ten disguised females were hiding in the stands, but only one, wearing men's clothing and her hair cut short, was discovered. The unsympathetic audience jeered as she was hauled off in tears.

Fitzsimmons and Dempsey appeared shortly after nine o'clock. "I'll bet $2,000 on Dempsey!" a fan shouted from somewhere in back. This was met with cries of "Go soak your head!" and "Smother yourself!" The two fighters stripped and were weighed at ringside as per the agreement, both coming in at around one-fifty. Bob was four inches taller than Dempsey, his reach clearly greater and the muscular development of his upper body impressive. He appeared nervous, however, whereas Dempsey was calm and relaxed.

They met in the center of the ring to hear the referee go over the rules. Dempsey, perhaps in a bit of gamesmanship, offered Bob a bet of one thousand dollars. "Haven't got the money," Bob tersely replied. They shook hands and Bob added, "May the best man win, Jack."

"He will," said Dempsey.

The gloves, examined by the police to ensure they met city ordinance specifications, were laced on.

The opening bell sounded and Bob came out the aggressor. Dempsey held his own until the third round, then caught a right in the face and went down. He managed to get up and last out the round but Bob had permanently seized the advantage. He continued to pummel Dempsey through the following rounds, breaking his nose and making the blood flow, swelling his face and battering his body and sending him back to his corner groggy for a reviving swig of brandy. By the tenth, even Dempsey's most ardent supporters had to concede that he was outclassed by the gangly Australian. But Dempsey, with magnificent heart, refused to give up, robbing Bob of the five-grand bonus he had been promised if he won inside ten. Rendered almost defenseless, Dempsey absorbed terrible punishment and was repeatedly knocked down, yet he kept getting up. Bob began to hold back, giving the champ the opportunity to concede and spare himself the indignity of a knock out. "Quit, Jack," he urged. "I don't want to hurt you any more."

"You fight," Dempsey gasped back. "I'm not done yet."

And so the contest went on, Dempsey struggling through the eleventh round, then the twelfth, tottering back to his chair for another swig from the bottle. "He's out!" the crowd cried when Bob beat him down again in the thirteenth. But again Dempsey slowly, painfully rose to his feet, sand caking the blood on his face. There were no knock-down rules then. This could have gone on all night, as long as the champion's spirit held out. Bob, the half-smile he had worn through the early going now faded, had no choice but to deliver a deliberate *coup de grâce*. He smashed Dempsey behind the ear as soon as his gloves were up off the sand, knocking him down again, this time for good. The Nonpareil made another valiant effort to rise, then fell back insensible as the referee counted him out. His seconds carried him back to his corner, propped him on his chair and plied him with what was left of the brandy. As the ex-champ revived and realized what had happened, he dropped his face into his gloves and wept.

Bob left the ring looking almost as fresh as he entered, marked only slightly on the cheek from a head butt. He had earned the respect of the crowd not just for his prowess but also for his sportsmanlike conduct. "[E]ven the most chagrined friends of the vanquished," stated the *Johnstown Daily Republic*, "are forced to admit that he is the fairest and most humane fighter that has ever done battle in the ring." Bob had also earned a great deal of money, the $11,000 that was the winner's share of the purse plus another $7,200 in gifts from grateful supporters who had won large sums on the fight. He got dressed and proceeded to the hotel where Louisa was waiting to tell her the good news.

John L. Sullivan was among the many shocked by Dempsey's defeat. "Say, are you giving it to me straight?" was his response upon first hearing the news. Asked to account for the loss, he pointed to the rigors of training. "[I]t is not the actual fighting," he said, "but the training that breaks a man up." John had lost several hundred dollars on the fight but it wasn't the money that upset him. It was the knowledge of how Jack, whom he considered a friend, must be feeling. "I guess it's all up with Dempsey now," John sadly mused before going to bed. "He'll never recover from this licking. The poor fellow's heart must be broken."

Dempsey never did recover. He contracted tuberculosis shortly thereafter and died in 1895, a month short of his thirty-third birthday.

On the morning after the fight, as Bob was strolling about the streets of New Orleans soaking up the adulation, he was approached by the famous sporting promoter "Parson" Davies with a proposition. Davies, who had arranged Jim Corbett's latest tour of the East, wanted to sign Bob up for a similar show, an "athletic combination" that he would headline, sparring a few rounds and perhaps giving a talk. It was the first of several lucrative offers that would be placed before Bob in the days that followed. As the new middleweight champion, the money was just starting to roll in.

But would he remain a middleweight? That's what the papers wanted to know. At six feet tall and with a magnificent reach, Bob had the frame of a heavyweight if not the poundage. And as his demolition of Dempsey had shown, he was clearly better suited for the ultimate class. After complimenting Bob on his "humane" ring conduct, the *Johnstown Daily Republic* went on to state that "he had no business in the arena with Dempsey; he is simply a heavyweight sweated out and trained down to a requisite figure. He is as tall as Sullivan and with a longer reach. Fed up to 180 pounds he would give the Boston boy the hardest time he has yet experienced. He could play with Kilrain like a child." There was in fact already a rumor in circulation that a heavyweight contest was being arranged between Bob and Jim Corbett.

"There is nothing in that," responded Bob's trainer Jimmy Carroll. "Fitzsimmons is a middleweight, and there is no use for him to go after heavyweights. He might make the same mistake as Dempsey and be sorry. It is not good policy for a man to go outside of his class."

"Corbett is too clever, and too big," was all Bob had to say. "Middleweights are good enough for me."

Jim Corbett returned to San Francisco in March 1891 to prepare for his upcoming fight with Peter Jackson. Jake Kilrain, in town to face George Godfrey and still smarting from his loss to Jim, commented in the papers that Jackson would "punch Corbett full of holes and cut him into ribbons." Jim returned the favor by saying that Kilrain would lose to Godfrey, then attended the fight to see his prediction come true. "Why," he was overhead exclaiming as he watched the action, "he [Kilrain] is the slowest man in creation."

The betting was against Jim going into the Jackson fight, an indication that his national reputation was not entirely fistic but had a good deal to do with how he looked and how he behaved. As the *New York Sun* described his ring appearance in that city the previous year, "the general impression was that he was too handsome, too refinedly put together to make a fighter for a man's life.... He is a tall chap, being close on to Peter Jackson's length, and he, too, has a phenomenal reach. He doesn't look so big or heavy as the colored man, but that is because he is far more symmetrically built. His shoulders are broad and his chest deep. His skin is of a delicate white, and this appearance is one of the signs that give Corbett an effeminate appearance. His arms are smooth and not too large.... His body tapers to the waist in delightful lines.... His legs are 'poems'." Could a fighter with the beautiful body of a classical statue, with legs like "poems," take on the likes of Peter Jackson? Many had doubts.

The fight took place on May 21, 1891, at the California Athletic Club in front of a crowd of eight hundred. It would be the longest battle of Jim's entire career, sixty-one rounds lasting until one-thirty in the morning, an almost inconceivable four hours and five minutes. The first thirty rounds were slow—cautious, technical fighting with just a few bright moments of "hot work," neither man wanting to take any risks. "I had my friends to look after," Corbett said after. Jackson used almost identical language: "I tried to protect my friends." They were referring to their supporters who had bet money on them, in some instances more than they could afford.

By the thirtieth round Jim and Peter were even and had nowhere to go but to exhaustion. As the rounds continued to pile up the steam drained from their punches, then their arms played out altogether and hung at their sides as they circled each other and the crowd trickled away. By the sixtieth round, with the two combatants just walking around, the referee was obliged to step in and ask what they intended to do. "I am doing the best I know how," Jim replied. So was Peter. The fight continued for one more round, then, by mutual consent, was declared a draw. "No money!" cried the disgruntled spectators still present. "What did we pay twenty dollars for? Keep them there all night!"

Although officially a draw, the fight was effectively a victory for Jim. He had fought the most formidable heavyweight contender to a standstill, thereby proving that he was not just "scientific" and pretty to look at, but tough, one of the best. He also proved something to himself. Where the Choynski fight had affirmed Jim's ability to take punishment and prevail through pain, facing Jackson was a valuable test of his endurance. To stand for sixty-one rounds against such a tough opponent, he had had to reach down deep for the strength to keep going. He had found that strength. And he had kept going—far beyond his previous limits. Even months later, he would claim to still feel the effects.

Fortunately for Jim, a talked-about rematch against Jackson never came off. Frustrated by the racial prejudice that denied him a shot at the title, the Australian would largely drop out of contention to play the lead in the play *Uncle Tom's Cabin*. As an added attraction between acts, he sparred three rounds with Joe Choynski, who played a slave driver in the show. When they were finished with their nightly exhibition, Peter would put his white Uncle Tom-wig and mustache and eyebrows back on and proceed with the play's emotional finale, forgiving his persecutors for the beating that would lead to his death.

Two months after the Corbett-Jackson fight, John L. Sullivan appeared in San Francisco with his play, the final stop in his American tour before heading to Australia. When he returned, he told reporters, he would at last be free to defend his title, to prove to the world that he was still the best. His play, *Honest Hearts and Willing Hands*, was "a potpourri of rubbish made up of scraps from Boucicault and Joe Murphy," the *Morning Call* reported, but it was enthusiastically received and played to full houses, John's every word and movement being met with laughter and applause. "I laughed till I cried," Ollie Corbett said of the performance she and Jim attended. "Of course, [Sullivan] did not mean to be funny, but he was funny, awfully funny."

On June 24, 1891, the evening before John L.'s departure for Australia, he and members of his theatrical company agreed to appear at a benefit for Jim Corbett, organized to raise money to compensate Jim for the lost payday from the Jackson fight. The evening's entertainment was to culminate with the last act of John's play, with Jim taking the place of John's usual opponent. San Franciscans, wild to see a fistic encounter between native son Jim and the heavyweight champ, lined up outside the Grand Opera House long before the doors opened.

They would be disappointed. The two men, sparring in suits at John's insistence, exchanged only the tamest of blows before shaking hands. The *San Francisco Morning Call* called the whole thing "an immense fake." The *Chronicle* headlined its report "Gentleman John met Gentleman Jim," coining the nickname that would stick with Corbett for the rest of his life.

For Jim, the unserious match was still a revelation, worth a great deal more than the money that was raised. Facing Sullivan in the flesh, he saw that the legend who had popularized the knockout, who had laid so many opponents out cold rather than wearing them down as was the usual outcome of fights in the bare-knuckle era, was not as invincible as most people assumed him to be. Jim saw that John L. was aging, overweight and out of shape, breathing hard after just a few minutes; that he was slow and obvious with his punches; that he often left his chin completely exposed.

"Billy," Jim whispered between rounds to his second, Billy Delaney, "I can whip this fellow!"

"Well, don't say anything about it now," replied Billy. "Keep it to yourself."

CHAPTER 5

SWITCH TO CELLULOID

ON AUGUST 3, 1889, Thomas Edison, traveling incognito, boarded the mail steamer *La Bourgogne* in New York for the seven-day Atlantic crossing to attend the Paris Exposition. He went at the urging of his doctor, the years of overwork and strain from his many projects and business endeavors having undermined his health and left him in need of a rest.

It was at this juncture that William K. L. Dickson, in charge of motion picture work at Edison's lab, made the crucial transition from cylinders to celluloid film. The switch occurred in July. Dickson began by hand-cutting a sheet of Carbutt "Eclipse" celluloid, the company's most light-sensitive product, into narrow pieces that he glued end to end to create strips two or three feet long. These were tested in a new apparatus that advanced the strip horizontally past a lens by means of a gear fitting into notches cut into the top edge of the film, the size of the images being taken increased yet again to half an inch.

The Carbutt celluloid proved an imperfect product. It lacked the sensitivity that Dickson was after, it was too thick to wind onto reels to allow for longer strips to be used and the crude splices tended to catch and tear. By working a series of fourteen-hour days, however, Dickson, assisted now by Fred Ott, managed to capture something to show Edison before he left for Paris.

A more impressive demonstration was prepared for Edison's return in early October. Dickson would insist for the rest of his life that he altered this Kinetograph strip machine to project a moving image on a screen and synchronized it with a Phonograph to add sound. What Edison supposedly saw projected was Dickson raising his hat and saying, "Good morning, Mr. Edison. Glad to see you back. I hope you are satisfied with the kineto-phonograph." This claim has been generally passed off as one of the bigger exaggerations to which Dickson was prone. Edison himself would deny there having been any screen when he was asked about this incident in a later lawsuit against a rival company Dickson helped form. Edison lab employee Eugene Lauste, who had been present in the room installing the screen, would state that Dickson did indeed make an attempt at projection—with no sound—but with dismal results. "[T]he pictures was blur and out of focus," Lauste recalled in 1930, writing in imperfect English; "also the film jump from the sprocket...consequantly [sic.] the show was a failure, and Mr. Edison leave the room with dissatisfaction.... My conclusion is that Mr. D. has told this story to so many people that he think now was a fact."

Whatever Edison saw upon his return from Paris, the strips of celluloid Dickson had begun to experiment with were the way forward. Celluloid held the promise for larger and thus clearer images to be taken and for longer periods of movement to be captured, if only it could be made more light sensitive and thinner for winding onto reels.

Fortunately, such a product was almost at hand. It was being developed in Rochester, New York in the factory of George Eastman. The year before, in July 1888, Eastman had come out with a revolutionary new camera, the Kodak, that allowed for a hundred photographs to be taken before reloading. It worked by means of a long roll of emulsion-coated paper that was advanced by turning a key—a reel-to-reel delivery system much like in Edison's own stock ticker and automatic telegraph. This "stripping paper" was not suitable for Dickson's motion photography work, but the long strips of celluloid Eastman was working to perfect for a new and improved version of the Kodak certainly were. The product was made by "flowing" the liquid material onto a long glass table and letting it dry into a transparent film that could be cut into strips. Dickson saw a sample around July 1889 and acquired a roll for testing in late August, before the product hit the market. It was a thing of beauty, fifty feet long, wonderfully thin and splice-free. The emulsion tended to peel off, resulting in a delay in the product's release, but this problem was soon mostly fixed. Increasing the fineness of the light-sensitive grains to give Dickson the image clarity he wanted would be an ongoing challenge. So would maintaining quality, for the manufacture of photographic emulsion was a dicey proposition in these early years, a bad batch following a dozen good ones for no apparent reason. "I am considering whether we shall start a Praying Department," George Eastman would joke in a letter in early 1892, scratching his head over yet another inexplicable failure.

It was this new Eastman film that Dickson used in his evolving Kinetograph camera starting in late 1889. He was now situated in a separate photo studio he had constructed while Edison was away in Paris, vibration from the elevator and machine shops in the main lab building having hampered work in Room 5. He began with three-quarter-inch-wide strips, punching holes along the top edge to advance them past the lens by means of a toothed gear. The holes were soon moved to the bottom edge to prevent slippage and misalignment, then were placed on both sides, necessitating an increase in film width to a full inch. To punch these holes, a perforating machine powered by a sewing machine foot treadle was built, an adaptation of an earlier Edison invention for perforating paper recording strips for the stock ticker and automatic telegraph.

"Figure 46 is a kinetoscope. The sensitive film is in the form of a long band passing from one reel to another in front of a square slit as in Figure 47; on each side of the band are rows of holes exactly opposite each other...."

So began Edison's description of the latest iteration of his moving picture apparatus, executed on December 9, 1889 as part of Caveat Number 117. The caveat was filed with the Patent Office the following week—and then the project was effectively shelved. Dickson devoted minimal hours in early 1890 to improving the camera, then ceased work altogether. The magnetic ore separator was consuming almost all his attention, his oversight required at the installation of massive ore crushers and separating machines at a mine site at Ogdensburg in upstate New Jersey, where an entire mountain was to be leveled and processed into iron. For Edison, it was becoming the biggest obsession of his life, far more important and *useful* than a moving picture machine, which was for mere entertainment. It was thus not until October 1890, with the Ogdensburg facility up and running, that Dickson was able to devote significant time and energy to pushing the Kineto project ahead.

He was now working on two distinct and separate inventions: a Kinetograph camera for photographing motion and a Kinetoscope viewer for seeing the results. One reason why these two terms were often confused, even by Edison's own staff, was that until this point they had been essentially a single device with interchangeable parts—metal cylinder or glass cylinder, lens or eyepiece, intermittent drive or continuous drive—installed for either photographing or viewing. This approach had ceased to be practical by 1890. The challenges of photographically capturing motion, Dickson had learned, were different from those of presenting the results to the viewer. Two separate machines thus had to be built.

What Dickson came up with by the following spring, lab employee William Heise now working as his main assistant, was a Kinetograph camera that could photograph at a claimed rate of forty frames per second. To maximize exposure time for clearer photos, he was on his way to achieving an intermittent movement whereby the film was in motion for just one-tenth of the time and at rest, an image being taken, for the remaining nine-tenths. This meant that the film had to move *fast* when it was in motion, accelerating to fifty miles per hour and then coming to a dead stop—*forty times every second*. This was extremely jarring and apt to damage the celluloid strip, yet another problem Dickson would have to address. To illuminate the subject, the idea of a stroboscopically flashing light synched with the camera, used for the Cylinder 3 *Monkeyshines* tests, had been abandoned. From now on Dickson would rely on direct sunlight, pulling back the curtains in the new photography building to let it stream in. To obtain an intermittent exposure synched with the film's intermittent movement, a revolving disk shutter was used.

For viewing the results, the idea of projection, which was proving difficult to achieve, gave way to a more readily achievable Kinetoscope peephole device. It moved the film continuously rather than intermittently as in the Kinetograph camera, a revolving disk shutter momentarily "freezing" each image as it raced past the eye of the person peering in. Although it used the same-sized film as in the camera, the drive mechanism had to be altered with slightly smaller sprocket wheels to account for the fact that the celluloid shrank during the developing process, after being chemically treated, washed and dried.

This Kinetoscope viewer was demonstrated for the first time on May 20, 1891, to delegates of the Federation of Women's Clubs attending a convention in Orange. Following a gathering at Edison's house hosted by the inventor's wife Mina, the ladies were bundled into their carriages for the short ride down to the lab and were each treated to a glimpse through the eyepiece of the new invention. Members of the press were invited to the lab for a similar sneak peek a week later, the *Sun* and *Herald* sending reporters down from New York. Their firsthand accounts were picked up and nationally reported.

The device that was shown was not much to look at, just a rough pine box—like "a packing case for shoes or boots," observed the *Sun*—with a light source inside and a silver dollar-sized hole cut in the top. The strip of film it held was of very short duration, not much more than two seconds, the ends glued together so that it ran in a loop. "The machine was started and I looked through the orifice," the man from the *Herald* reported. "What I saw was the form of a man [Dickson] about an inch in size bowing and raising his hat. The motions were natural and continuous and no break could be detected between them. The picture I saw was only a negative, photographed on an endless slip."

The film was run at different speeds to demonstrate how the movement was jerky at a slower rate and smooth and seamless at the maximum speed of forty-six frames per second. This impressive rapidity, nearly triple the sixteen-frames-per-second rate of the coming silent film era and nearly double the twenty-four-frame rate standard today, was necessary to overcome the flicker caused by the continuous—as opposed to intermittent—movement of the film and the general crudity of the equipment.

In speaking about his new invention in the press, Edison returned to his original conception of combining it with the Phonograph to reproduce moving pictures with sound. The rudimentary box the reporters had seen was in fact only the "germ" of a much greater wonder he planned to have ready in time for the Columbian World Exhibition in Chicago in 1893. He spoke of a nickel-in-the-slot "kineto-phonograph" like the coin-operated Phonographs in parlors springing up across the country, evidently imagining it as a peep-hole Kinetoscope viewer with Phonograph eartubes attached. But then he went off on a flight of fancy about people having such machines in their homes whereby moving images would be projected. "My intention," he said, "is to have a happy combination of electricity and photography that a man can sit in his own parlor and see reproduced on a screen the forms of the players in an opera produced on a distant stage, and, as he sees their movements, he will hear the sound of their voices as they talk or sing or laugh." The invention had exciting possibilities in the sporting arena as well, for "it will be possible to apply this system to prize fights and boxing exhibitions. The whole scene with the comments of the spectators, the talk of the seconds, the noise of the blows, and so on will be faithfully transferred."

It was all very thrilling. Just imagine, the *Sun* reporter enthused, being able to watch Madame Patti singing "Home, Sweet Home" just as clearly as if you were seated in the front row at the theater, only the colors missing, and all for only five cents. In the field of sports, you could witness Princeton sprinter Luther Carey set the record for the hundred-yard dash, or observe from ringside "the terrible blows by which Fitzsimmons disposed of Dempsey."

Edison's new invention, as astonishing as it seemed, was not hailed by all. The *Brooklyn Daily Standard* took a dim view of the machine's potential sporting applications. "The worst of it is that prize fights and horse races are to be reproduced," grumbled the paper. "Sporting events recorded with absolute accuracy. The confounding instrument is called the kinetograph...." Writing in the *New York Herald*, English novelist Walter Besant foresaw the invention leading to a very dark future, with theaters closed and people staying at home to watch "photographed puppets for actors and bottled voices for the dialogue."

"How can we expect anything else?" bemoaned Besant's imaginary old man living in the year 1940. "How can we get acting when an actor's sole occupation is to play before an electric camera? Who wants to become an actor any longer? There is no longer the sympathy of the house—the applause. Oh! The art of acting is dead—dead. Edison, the inventor, killed it."

> *Dear Sir: I notice in the N. York Sun of the 28th an account of your new invention the Kinetograph. I think it most wonderful and would like so much to exhibit it in our southern towns. When you have them ready for exhibition would you lease me an outfit?* (Eugene Elliott to Thomas Edison, June 5, 1891)

> *Will you oblige me by answering wheather [sic.] the Kinetograph is ready for the market or how I could get one for exhibition purposes terms etc.* (G. Don Portez to Thomas Edison, June 11, 1891)

> *The writer of this is from Australia & wishes to know if you will sell him the privilege to exhibit the Kinetograph in the Australasian colonies when it is completed.* (John Lyons to Thomas Edison, Sept. 5, 1891)

> *I notice mention in the papers of your invention of the Kinetograph.... [O]n what terms can a responsible person secure the use of one? I want one to travel with as a public exhibition with some of the choicest reproductions of our leading speakers, lecturers and musicians.* (P. W. Singleton to Thomas Edison, Nov. 25, 1891)

The public announcement of Edison's latest invention attracted considerable attention and in turn inquires from entrepreneurs eager to acquire it for various business ideas. Some were understandably confused as to what it could actually do, for Edison, as was his habit, had let his vision of future wonders—projected moving images, synchronized sound, home viewing—overwhelm the reality of the actual device that was being developed. In response to the many purchase and lease requests and agent applications, a similar letter therefore went out from Edison's secretary Al Tate: "Replying to your letter of [DATE], the invention therein referred to is not yet ready for the market."

There were a number of problems that still needed addressing. First, Dickson required better lenses for both the Kinetograph camera and the Kinetoscope viewer. He had particular difficulty acquiring the former, pressing the Gundlach Optical Company of Rochester for months before he got what he wanted. "The lense [sic.] is entirely unfitted for our work," he impatiently wrote in August 1891, sending the first sample back. What he required was a lens with a large aperture to admit the maximum amount of light to allow for high-speed photographing. It needed to encompass a scene thirty feet across at a distance of twenty-five or thirty feet and produce a sharply focused image no more than one and a half inches across. ("I order a lens to give me 1½" circle & you send me one giving me 3" circle," he fired off to Gundlach in September. "You do not fulfill your part.") It also had to have the maximum depth of focus, for unlike in still photography, where an object could be brought into focus by changing the distance between the lens and photographic plate by means of an expandable bellows, with motion picture photography no such adjustment could be made once the camera was in operation. "For what use could I make of a lens that would have to be changed during a taking," Dickson wrote to Gundlach later that year in December. "The subject approaching & receeding [sic.] from lens would make it in focus & then out of focus. Our first machine is ready & have been depending on you to furnish the lenses." Dickson engaged in similar correspondence with Bausch and Lomb for a Kinetoscope lens. He eventually rejected the idea of a binocular eyepiece, which required careful focusing and the exact positioning of the eye, and opted instead for the simplicity and cheapness of a single lens.

Another hurdle was the quality of the film Dickson was receiving from Eastman. The emulsion no longer peeled off the celluloid altogether but there was still a tendency for it to lift up at the edges, a problem known as "frilling." Even worse, the metal sprockets often tore the perforations as the film passed through the camera, the abrupt, wrenching stops and starts of the intermittent movement subjecting the celluloid to more strain than it could bear. Wrapping the sprockets with velvet cushioned the film somewhat but this wasn't enough. What was needed, Dickson implored Eastman, was thicker, more robust film—something that could stand up to the rigors of passage through the camera and to the constant usage it would be subjected to in the Kinetoscope viewer. Eastman fortunately had something in the works he was willing to let him try, a double-coated film that was still being experimented upon. When Dickson placed his first order in November 1891—the high price left him "somewhat stunned"—it was for twenty-seven rolls with the company's most light-sensitive emulsion for use in the camera and a similar quantity of its least sensitive product for making copies of maximum clarity for use in the viewer, all of it with "the skin very tough." It would take several more months of testing and problem-solving and back and forth correspondence, but Eastman eventually came up with a product that met Dickson's demands.

By this time Dickson had finalized the format of the film he was using, making a series of decisions that continue to be felt to this day. For maximum clarity, he increased the width yet again to one and three-eighths of an inch and he changed the shape of the photographed images from a circle to a frame-filling rectangle. These rectangular images were one inch wide by three-quarters of an inch high, the perforations on either side numbering precisely four to a frame, or "phase," to use the Muybridge term that Dickson adopted. The frames were oriented landscape-fashion and situated one on top of the other, the film running through the camera vertically rather than horizontally as had been the case from the 1889 strip machine up to at least mid 1891. This overall format, arrived at by Dickson by early 1892, would become the almost universal movie industry standard in the coming decades, known by the metric equivalent of its width as "35mm film."

By the summer of 1892, William K. L. Dickson had his camera in good working order. He had his lenses and a supply of durable film and an enlarged space in the photography building to work in. He was ready, as he jocularly put it in a letter to Eastman, "to chew up film."

Of the four known films he and assistant William Heise shot between July and October, three were of sporting subjects, Dickson inviting a group of athletes down from neighboring Newark to appear before his camera. They were German-Americans from the Newark Turnverein club under gymnastics instructor George Seikel. The first pair demonstrated the sport of wrestling, the space within which they were to confine their movements delineated by a low railing set against the black backdrop covering the studio's rear wall. The second pair, identically positioned, gave a brief display of fencing. The third pair laced on padded gloves and boxed. Fifty feet of film was presumably used to record each demonstration, this being the length of the rolls ordered from Eastman. With some two feet unusable at either end, necessary leader for threading the film through the camera and winding it onto the reels, a total of perhaps seven hundred sequential images would have been shot of each sport. Assuming a filming speed of forty frames per second, which Dickson claimed, the result would have been motion pictures around seventeen seconds long. The short work was done and the athletes went home. Then, thinking better of it, they demanded payment, which they received, making them the first paid actors in movie history.

The films were not perfect to Dickson's critical eye. He did not like the shadows cast by the sunlight streaming in obliquely though the studio's skylight and south-facing window. But that could be remedied with the new studio he was planning to build. As for the rest—the working of the camera, the clarity and steadiness of the images—it was all really quite good.

Dickson and Heise shot a fourth film, of themselves, during this period of experimentation. They did not engage in mock sparring as Dickson's assistants did several times for earlier tests, or in anything like *Monkeyshines* clowning. This film would be more static and more solemn. It begins with Heise standing alone, the camera moved closer to show his burly form from the knees up, his white shirt and straw boater in sharp contrast against the black backdrop. Dickson then enters the frame from the right, perhaps after turning on the camera, and shakes him by the hand. In the few frames of this short film that still survive, we see these two men congratulating each other, celebrating their achievement of capturing practical, viewable and soon-to-be marketable motion pictures.

By this point the patenting process for the Kinetograph camera and Kinetoscope viewer had been underway for a year. The initial August 1891 filing was rejected because it encompassed both inventions in a single application. Two separate applications were subsequently drawn up and submitted in April 1892. The one for the Kinetoscope sailed through the review process and patent was granted in February 1893. The Kinetograph application, however, met considerable resistance, the Patent Office examiner pointing to competing patents, notably by Louis Le Prince and William Friese-Greene. While the patent for the "Kinetographic Camera" would eventually be granted in August 1897, the ground was already laid for a series of lawsuits that would be fought from the late 1890s until 1910 and beyond, the motion picture patent wars to decide who had priority in the invention of the technology for making movies. The question of "Who was first?" would remain contentious and lead to an anti-Edison backlash and Dickson-slighting by those anxious to highlight the work of others. What is often overlooked in this debate is that Edison and Dickson were doing more than inventing a single piece of motion picture machinery. They were inventing an entire motion picture system. It was a system that included a camera and a viewer and a film format, and the machine that was built at the Edison lab to trim and perforate film prior to use. There was also the equipment that Dickson devised for developing long strips of exposed film by winding it around drums that could be revolved through chemical baths. He initially had a rubberized drum and trough constructed to his specifications, then switched to lacquer when the rubber started to crack. To make copies of films, he built an apparatus that would be instantly recognized by filmmakers today as a contact printer. And then there was the very concept of what to *do* with this system—the camera, the viewer, the perforator, the developing equipment, the printer—how to turn it into a *business* by making short films and presenting them to the public by means of a coin-operated peephole machine.

William K. L. Dickson, under Edison's sporadic direction and assisted by lab employees John and Fred Ott, Charles Brown and

William Heise, did all this. He did it while attending to his numerous other duties, which continued to include addressing the many problems at the Ogdensburg mine. It entailed long hours of work and unremitting pressure throughout 1892 and into the following year. It is thus not surprising, in early February 1893, that he suddenly had to go away for a while.

He had suffered a nervous breakdown.

CHAPTER 6

※

THE HEAVYWEIGHT TITLE

BOB FITZSIMMONS WAS RIDING HIGH after defeating Jack Dempsey to claim the middleweight title. It was his turn now to play coy, choosing who he would fight and how much money he would accept to do it. No more thousand-dollar or even five-thousand-dollar purses for him. From now on it would be ten grand, twenty grand or more. "What I want to point out," stated one disgruntled observer, "is that the Australian, like all other latter-day champions, tramps roughshod over all customs and rules as soon as they become the alleged champions. They all have an idea...that they have a perfect right to dictate any terms to anybody who want to fight them." *Bloody right, mate*, Bob might have replied.

In the meantime, while he waited for an acceptably lucrative challenge, Bob went on the stage. He signed on to appear for eight weeks in a musical comedy entitled *Fashions*, about the ups and downs of a family with upper-class tastes and lower-class means. In the free and easy manner of theatrical productions in that era, the third act was rewritten to include a fight scene featuring Bob and sparring partner Billy Woods going at it for three rounds. They were non-speaking parts, Bob and Billy first appearing as guests at a reception at the Manhattan Athletic Club, then having their set-to in eight-ounce gloves—derided as "pillows"—so as not to run afoul of city ordinances and state laws.

If Bob had any misconceptions that theatrical work would be easy, they were knocked out of him when the play hit Buffalo, New York on March 30, 1891. He was fighting a cold and the cast kept forgetting their lines and the *Buffalo Express* reviewed the whole thing as "rank," suggesting "Slops" as a more suitable title. Even the boxing, which was usually a surefire crowd pleaser, met with a tepid response, Bob looking ill and unable to hold his own against Billy. He was on the mend and his sparring more impressive by the time the play reached Pittsburgh. The rest of the production, however, continued to be panned. "*Fashions* is probably the worst conglomeration that was ever honored with a title," stated the *Pittsburgh Dispatch*. "It is an insult to actors to ask them to appear in it, and torture to the audiences that witness it." Torture or not, the audience went away happy, Bob's rousing ring performance having been thoroughly enjoyed.

Australian middleweight champion Jim Hall, the one man on record as having beaten Bob, had by this time arrived in the United States. Bob was openly saying now that he had thrown the Hall fight in Sydney for the paltry equivalent of seventy-five dollars but many assumed this was just an attempt to paper over a legitimate loss. Of all the challengers on the scene, Hall seemed the most likely to give Fitzsimmons a real fight, the sort of fight sporting men wanted to see. New Orleans' Olympic Club as usual took the lead in putting up a purse to host the bout but it had stiff competition this time, rival clubs wanting to get in on the prizefight bonanza after hearing that the Olympic had cleared as much as $75,000 on the Dempsey-Fitz contest. In the end it was the Minnesota Athletic Club that offered the biggest purse for Hall vs. Fitz. The fight was scheduled for St. Paul on July 22, 1891.

It never took place. The public outcry in St. Paul was too great, prizefighting being denounced as "savagery" and "barbarism." "The gladiators in ancient times massacred one another in imperial Rome," proclaimed Roman Catholic archbishop John Ireland on the eve of the contest. "Are we going back to those days of infamy? Prize fighting is a step on the road to these conditions." Forcefully reminded that state law forbade prizefighting, the local sheriff was instructed to close down the contest. For Bob, it was a huge disappointment. He had not only missed out on a $11,000 payday and wasted three months of training, he had lost the chance to redeem himself for taking a dive in Sydney, which he had come to deeply regret.

Bob's next opportunity to fight for a major purse didn't come until March 2, 1892, when he faced Irish heavyweight champion Peter Maher—back at the reliable Olympic in New Orleans, where a gloved contest could be pulled off without interference. It was a momentous bout in that it marked Bob's formal entry into the heavyweight division. He had insisted after winning the middleweight crown that he had no intention of venturing outside his class, but the sporting world had other ideas. There had been something slightly distasteful about how foreigner Fitzsimmons had destroyed American hero Jack Dempsey with his four-inch height advantage and much greater reach, and the biggest demand wasn't to see him repeat the performance on another smaller opponent. Rather, it was to see him take on heavyweights, six-footers like he was, albeit carrying twenty pounds more. It was thus from the heavyweight ranks that the most lucrative opportunities beckoned. And it was to the heavyweight ranks that Bob went.

Freed from middleweight constraints, Bob trained up rather than down for the Maher fight and stepped through the ropes weighing one-sixty-five, the heaviest of his career. Maher, at one-seventy-eight, was still substantially bigger, with a vicious, dangerous look that warmed the hearts of his supporters, who were proclaiming he would win "without turning a hair."

He almost managed it too. In the very first round, when Bob got careless and rushed in after knocking Maher down, breaking his thumb in the process, Maher countered with a stiff left that in turn dropped Bob, followed by a right as he struggled to rise. Had the bell not sounded—Bob's seconds flouting the rules by helping him back to his corner—it would have ended right there. Chastened, Bob settled down and began to steadily pick his opponent apart. He concentrated especially on Maher's lip which he had split in the first, nursing his injured right hand and mainly using his left. Choking on his own blood, smeared with gore from hair to waistline, Maher grew increasingly frustrated and, like an infuriated bull, started making mad rushes and wild swings. "You're a cur," he roared, impotent and increasingly exhausted. "Why don't you fight?" Bob just laughed and kept shifting and jabbing—and in the seventh unloading a pivot blow, which the rules allowed. He had no intention of playing Maher's toe-to-toe game.

By the end of the twelfth Maher had had enough. He returned to his corner and the towel was thrown in. "You did very well," Bob said, rushing over to shake Maher's hand and kiss him on the forehead. "So did you," Maher huskily replied. A flask was produced and they shared a drink. One swig was enough for Bob. Maher, despondent, kept at it. He was still drinking on the train back to New York when he opened the window and tried to hurl himself out. Bob was among those in the car who rushed over to stop him.

"Peter Maher's dream is over," concluded the *New York World*. "His first showing with a clever man proved him to be a clumsy, lumbering fellow, and some think a trifle shaky in the region of the heart." English heavyweight champion Charley Mitchell put it more sharply, stating that Maher "ought to be ashamed to own himself an Irishman, and Irishmen ought to be ashamed that he is one of them. He is the most cowardly fighter, to my mind, that ever stepped in the ring. Fitzsimmons, on the other hand, is a wonderfully clever fighter, and a surprise."

"Sullivan could lick a room full of such men," growled another observer, dismissing both.

Four days after the Fitz-Maher contest, an earthquake shook the fight world. It came in the form of a letter published in newspapers across the country, stating that John L. Sullivan was at last ready to defend his heavyweight title. "[T]his country has been overrun with a lot of foreign fighters," John L. stated, "and also American aspirants for fistic fame and championship honors, who have endeavored to seek notoriety knowing full well that my hands were tied by contract and honor. I have been compelled to listen to their bluffs without making reply on account of my obligations. But now, my turn has come. . . .

"I hereby challenge any and all of the bluffers who have been trying to make capital at my expense to fight me either the last week in August, this year, or the first week in September this year, at the Olympic Club, New Orleans, for a purse of $25,000 and an outside bet of $10,000, the winner of the fight to take the entire purse. . . .

"I give precedence in this challenge to Frank P. Slavin, of Australia, as he and his backers have done the greatest amount of blowing. My second preference is the bombastic sprinter, Charles Mitchell, of England, whom I would rather whip than any man in the world. My third preference is James Corbett, of California, who has achieved his share of bombast. But in this challenge I include all fighters—first come, first served—who are white. I will not fight a negro. I never have. I never shall."

The whole thing had the look of Sullivan bluffing the bluffers. Why, for example, was he specifying the purse? That was for the club hosting the fight to decide. And why single out "Paddy" Slavin, who was heading off to fight in England? And the demand for an immense side bet of ten thousand dollars—that seemed like a ploy to make the challenge too rich to take up. "[H]e must be crazy or thinks I am," Mitchell responded, suggesting twenty-five hundred instead. This led to a public exchange of insults. "Poor little 210-pound baby!" sneered Sullivan. "It's wonder to me that he is permitted to go out without a nurse." Mitchell spat back that Sullivan was an "old woman" and a "bad impersonation of an actor." And his play was "rotten."

While Sullivan and Mitchell were busy trading insults, Jim Corbett was working behind the scenes to snatch up the challenge. His savvy new manager, William Brady, would be of great assistance in this. The two men had known each other since their youth in San Francisco, when Brady was hustling selling peanuts and Jim a bank clerk. In the succeeding years, as Jim rose to prominence in the ring, Brady had become a successful theatrical producer, reviving old plays and grafting on splashy new effects. Their paths crossed again in the summer of 1891, when Brady, learning through a friend that Jim aspired to be an actor, cabled him an offer to appear in his latest play, *After Dark*. It was a non-speaking part, just some boxing between Jim and sparring partner Jim Daly that Brady slapped onto the production to enhance its appeal. The experience nevertheless fanned Jim's theatrical ambitions into full flame. "I haven't got a line to speak in *After Dark*," he said later that year in November, "but a great many actors have begun that way, haven't they? I'm thinking of having a play especially written for me, so that I can star, have lines to speak, and get a chance to show the public that there are no flies on my elocution…. Yes, I'm going to study hard and after a while come out as a bona fide actor."

When Sullivan's challenge appeared in the papers, Brady quietly put down a deposit of a thousand dollars for the side bet while Jim rounded up backers to cover the rest. There would be no equivocating, no negotiating, no hemming and hawing like Charley Mitchell was doing. Jim accepted all the champion's terms. A matchup was therefore quickly arranged. "He'll be an easy mark," Sullivan commented before going on the stage in Chicago. "Why, [Corbett] can't punch a hole in a pound of butter…. He's a pretty boy now, but his mother won't know him when I'm through with him. I admire his pluck, though." The articles were signed at the offices of the *New York World* on March 15, a representative standing in for John L., Bob Fitzsimmons among the onlookers. By the end of the day the Olympic Club in New Orleans had agreed to host the contest and put up the $25,000 purse, the biggest ever offered up to that time, and the deal was struck. When Mitchell cabled later with a counter-offer to keep the game with Sullivan going, he was sent the reply: "Your wire received too late. Sullivan and Corbett matched…."

The following week, Mitchell showed up drunk at the New York theater where Jim was appearing and tried to pick a fight. Although insulted by the Englishman and egged on by onlookers, Jim refused to be provoked, adding further to his gentlemanly image. "I am perfectly satisfied that the American public will not take any stock in a bullying rough like Mitchell," Jim said the next day, "and if I ever have the good fortune to meet him in the ring I'll teach him a lesson in politeness which he will not soon forget."

After a flattering physical examination by a New York doctor ("I have never seen such a magnificent specimen of muscular development"), John L. Sullivan went into training at Hampton Bays on Long Island. There was a lot of work to be done, more than just "a shampoo and a shave," as one supremely confident supporter put it. John was out of shape and at least forty pounds overweight, for he did not believe in exercising, watching his diet or moderating his heavy drinking when not in training. "Some athletes pride themselves on being in condition always," he said, "but this I do not approve of, for I reason that a man continually in training keeps nature up to its highest tension and without any relaxing he soon becomes mechanical and more like a steel spring than nature's own." His entourage included several experienced trainers, notably William Muldoon, but they were there just to assist. Big John had fixed ideas about the sort of preparation he needed and did not take kindly to being told what to do.

The first step was a laxative treatment. John prepared the dose himself, stewing a tea of zinnia, salts, manna and black licorice on the stove for two hours. For the first two days of training he did little more than drink this mixture and sit around waiting for it to have its effect. Then came the liver pills. Then he was ready to get down to work.

After rising between six and seven o'clock and having a sponge bath, John would take a stroll to work up an appetite for a steak or mutton chop breakfast, then rest until ten. After that came a brisk twelve-mile walk, bundled up in a heavy sweater with a wide belt cinched round his middle "to take the fat off." Upon his return, John's trainers would rub him down and cover him with blankets to prolong his perspiring. Then it was either a cold-water shower or a plunge in the ocean, John's ever-present valet, "Jap," hovering nearby with towels and the ubiquitous sweater. A session of rehearsing for his new play, *The Man From Boston*, scheduled to open following his defeat of Corbett, came next. By then it was lunchtime and John would be hungry, apt to march into the kitchen and bellow, "Want my dinner!" if service was slow. It was another meat-heavy, no-vegetable repast. John generally refused to eat vegetables while in training, with the notable exception of celery, which he consumed by the bunch. He also restricted his intake of liquid, drinking only enough to quench his thirst.

The afternoon consisted of another bracing dip in the ocean, then up to two hours throwing the medicine ball, using very light dumbbells (anything over four pounds could leave a fighter "muscle bound") and skipping rope, which John considered the best exercise for building up his "wind." He did not punch a heavy bag, which he said was only for show. He preferred to hit a ball hung on a rope, making it bounce off the ceiling. He did no sparring either, as he believed he did not need it. When this final session of daily work was complete, he had another rubdown, a meat-heavy supper and was in bed by ten.

Although this may not have been the best way to prepare for a fight, John L. accomplished a good deal in his three months of training. He went off the booze, dropped thirty pounds and regained most of the stamina he had lost in the previous three years of hard living. Most visitors who made the trip out to Long Island to see him came away reassured that he was rounding into prime condition for hammering Corbett into jelly. For some, however, John's weight remained a concern. One discerning observer at one of his rubdowns pronounced his buttocks "fleshy," which was troubling because "that portion of the body tightens up in training as quick, if not quicker, than any other part. If the buttocks have not tightened up it is safe to conclude there is fat elsewhere on the body."

At his training camp at the oceanfront resort town of Asbury Park, New Jersey, Jim Corbett's days were regimented much like John's but with certain variations: handball first thing in the morning, even though Jim's trainers didn't think it did him any good; running as part of his roadwork, whereas John mainly walked; heavier resistance training, including the use of a pulley apparatus; punching the heavy bag; and plenty of sparring. Overall, Jim trained harder than the champ and was more amenable to accepting guidance—although he did have a strong stubborn streak, which elicited from his trainers the frequent comment, "Of course, if you say so it's so." He certainly ate more as well, for he was trying to keep weight on, not lose it. Steaks and roasts ladled with gravy, potatoes, cobbler and cream, mutton chops with the fat still on—visitors to Asbury Park were astonished by what Jim packed away. "Don't you think it will hurt him?" one asked after witnessing a particularly prodigious meal. "Look at him," was trainer Billy Delaney's reply. Jim did indeed look to be in excellent shape, one hundred eighty-five pounds on a six-foot-one frame. By August he was so dominating sparring partner Jim Daly that a bigger man, two-hundred-thirty-pound wrestler John McVey, had to be hired.

An additional facet of Jim's training was mental, building up his confidence to take on the Sullivan legend. He knew how John L.'s imposing reputation and presence could defeat an opponent before a fight ever started—and so did John. "I am only training hard to oblige my friends," the champ reportedly told visitors to his Long Island camp. "I don't have to do it, for Corbett is so scared of me that he will fret himself half to death before the fight takes place." It was bluff, of course, part of the psychological game John L. was so good at. But at the same time, Jim could not have possessed the degree of confidence he claimed—not with the image of what Sullivan's reputation could do etched on his brain. Back in 1884, when Jim was seventeen, he had seen John L. go against local Olympic Club boxer George Robinson in San Francisco's Mechanics' Pavilion. He had seen Robinson, so wary of the fabled punches, drop to the ground more than fifty times in four rounds, sometimes before Sullivan had even taken a swing. He had heard and perhaps contributed to the cries of "Coward!" and "Cur!" Jim was a vastly superior fighter to Robinson but he was still human. Preparing himself mentally to meet Sullivan, particularly with so many pundits proclaiming that he was certain to lose, must have taken a considerable effort of will.

Having the ever-confident William Brady as his manager must have helped. Brady was so sure of Jim's victory that he commissioned a play to be written for him to cash in on the heavyweight crown that was yet to be won. The formulaic melodrama, which incorporated incidents from Jim's own life, was initially titled *Gentleman Jim*, then renamed *Gentleman Jack* when it was pointed out that so obvious a ploy would turn audiences off. Jim and John L. were thus both busy learning lines for plays starring the "Champion of the World" as they trained for their upcoming battle. The rival productions were scheduled to open a month after the contest, on the very same night.

John L. Sullivan arrived in New Orleans weighing slightly over two hundred ten pounds. He looked to be in excellent condition, "stout" in the best sense of the word, and impressed everyone who attended his training sessions. "I never saw such power," observed President Charles Noel of the Olympic Club, overlooking John's graying hair. "He hits like a steam engine," commented another. Bob Fitzsimmons, in town for the fight, was also among the spectators. He had a greater appreciation than most of Corbett's skill as a boxer but, seeing Sullivan now, so indomitable, so massive, it was hard to imagine he could lose to a man weighing only one-eighty-five. That was the majority opinion, even in Corbett's hometown of San Francisco: Jim, for all his ring "science," lacked the weight and power to topple John L.

Jim still had his share of fans, a minority who believed he would win and a wider group who admired his gameness. They mobbed him as he left Asbury Park and again at the station. They crowded round whenever he stepped off his private rail car on the journey south. They formed a gauntlet in New Orleans, shaking his hand and slapping his back and jostling his baggage until his special jug of apple sauce fell out and broke.

The contest took place on September 7, 1892—a Wednesday, when the Olympic Club liked to hold its big fights. It was a sultry evening and a portion of the tarpaulin covering the arena had been pulled back to let in the breeze. Sullivan arrived first, claiming he felt "as fine as a colt in clover." He donned green tights and his usual black leather boots, the kind that had been spiked full of holes in his last title defense three years before, against Jake Kilrain under the now-eclipsed London Prize Ring rules. He had had special high-heeled boots made in New York but hadn't brought them because they hadn't felt right. He would therefore be stepping into the ring two inches shorter than Corbett, but still looking bigger, weighing thirty pounds more.

He wouldn't be wearing his thick belly wraps either. Jim, through manager Brady, had raised a last-minute stink about the "pitch pine plasters" the champ liked to wear under his tights. "Those pitch plasters serve as a sort of armor," said Brady. "After a little while they become a hard mass of pitch and cloth, and it is almost impossible to make any impression through them. The rules call for bare skin. Corbett didn't bargain to fight a man in a coat of mail." When informed that the Olympic Club had disallowed the wrappings, John L. blustered that he "didn't give a blank. He'd let the blank plaster go to blank if there was any kick about it from that young feller."

Jim, the "young feller," arrived fifteen minutes later, at eight-thirty, looking like a dude in a straw boater and making a show of not having a care in the world. He donned an abbreviated pair of trunks that left a good part of his buttocks showing and the green silk belt that Ollie had made. He won the coin toss and thus the winning corner, the one Fitzsimmons had occupied in his victories over Dempsey and Maher. The Sullivan crowd took this as a bad sign.

There were ten thousand men crammed into the arena by fight time, another towering financial success for the Olympic. Hundreds of thousands more were in vicarious attendance across the country, gathered in saloons and pool halls and hotel lobbies and in front of newspaper buildings—anywhere there was a telegraph wire and an operator to decipher the dots and the dashes.

"8:44—Official timekeeper R. M. Frank takes his seat and tests the electric bell ... 8:52—Sullivan enters the ring, closely followed by Corbett. Both greeted with tremendous applause."

In New York City, the throngs exceeded those that had gathered when Benjamin Harrison won the last presidential election. They gathered at newspaper row in clusters of two and three thousand, reading the bulletins as they were posted on blackboards and banners.

"8:55—Prof. John Duffy, the referee, enters the ring ... 8:59—Capt. Barrett and Mr. Spori are weighing the gloves."

Atop the Pulitzer Building on Park Row, two columns of lights had been set up, green for Sullivan, white for Corbett, to indicate who had the advantage in each round. Inside, ensconced in the offices of the *World*, Ollie Corbett followed the news with extreme trepidation.

"9:00—The men go to the middle of the ring to receive instructions ... 9:03—The men are putting on the gloves."

Sullivan was glaring at Jim, giving him the full intimidation treatment, Jim in turn making a point not to notice. He walked about the ring smiling and nodding and waving at people in the audience he didn't know—looking everywhere except at John L.

"9:06—The men shake hands ... 9:07—The referee calls time."

Sullivan went on the attack as soon as the bell sounded, lunging at Jim with monstrous lefts and rights, Jim dodging and dancing and feinting, not throwing anything in return, just feeling him out. It quickly became apparent that the champ, while a ferocious slugger, was not a particularly skilled boxer. He had a habit, for example, of slapping his left thigh before throwing his right, telegraphing his main weapon. Jim noted the weaknesses, the opportunities, but bided his time. As agreed upon with trainer Billy Delaney, he would hold back and not take any chances until Sullivan began to tire and grew careless.

The fight continued in this manner for the first two rounds, Sullivan the aggressor, Jim on the defense, the audience started to hiss at what they saw as the challenger's "running away." Then, in the third, Jim started to turn up the heat. He drew first blood in the fifth with a shot to the nose that split open the bridge and rocked Sullivan badly. Confidence soaring, Jim was tempted to go on the offensive, to move in close for the finish. Delaney, leaving off his fanning between rounds, reined him back in. "You said you were going to take your time," he reminded his fighter. "What are you going to take any chances for?"

In the opposite corner, John's seconds sponged and rubbed and fanned but remained silent. The champ fought his fights the way he conducted his training, on his own terms, wanting no advice, brooking no interference. *Drink*, he would say, and the bottle would he thrust to his lips.

By the tenth round Jim's methodical jabbing had had a shocking effect. Sullivan's face was battered and his wicked smile long gone. His nose was streaming blood and he was spitting out red. His tights were sagging, revealing the rolls of fat on his sides and his stomach, a physique that appeared much older than his thirty-four years. And he was breathing hard, "puffing like a porpoise" as the *New York World* put it, on his way to exhaustion while Corbett still appeared fresh and unmarked.

To Bob Fitzsimmons, seated in a private box with Joe Choynski, the whole thing must have appeared very familiar, for it was a repeat of his own fight with Maher. "Come on!" Sullivan bellowed at one point in frustration, just like Maher, wanting Jim to stand toe to toe and trade punches. But Jim kept dancing and dodging and jabbing, working away at the split nose and the big unwrapped belly, Sullivan's return shots flailing through air.

An upset was coming. Excitement crescendoed not just in the arena but across the country. In Washington D.C., outside the *Post* and *Star* newspaper offices, immense crowds surged and swayed as they followed the action via bulletins projected with a stereopticon onto a wall. "Sixteenth Round—John leads and is met by a straight left on the chin..." At the Orpheum Theater in San Francisco, the audience roared as two boxers reenacted the contest in a ring on stage, cued by cables read out from a telegraph stand set up behind. "Eighteenth Round—Both men cautious. Corbett again put his left on John's nose..." At Battery D in New York City, a visual representation of the fight using puppets was being met with derision. It was so crude, not at all the lifelike show the advertisements had promised, that the audience began to jeer, demanding to hear only the cables. "Twentieth Round—Corbett rushes John to ropes, landing three times on head and stomach..." At a saloon in Cincinnati, Ohio, so many people had crammed in to follow the fight that the floor collapsed and tumbled them all into the cellar.

Delaney cut Jim loose in the twenty-first round, for Sullivan was done in, his legs visibly shaking. Jim answered the bell thinking it might take another ten rounds to break his opponent completely. But then he tagged John on the jaw and saw his eyes roll back and he knew he had him. He moved in and unloaded everything, no longer saving his hands. Overpowered, John dropped. When he struggled halfway up, his gloves just leaving the sand, Jim delivered the *coup de grâce*, knocking him out. The battle had lasted an hour and twenty-one minutes. After ten years and six months, the world had a new heavyweight champ.

Pandemonium erupted in the stands and rippled outward via telegraph wire—to Quarantine in New York City, where the cry that sounded across the harbor led some to think that cholera had flared up anew; to Pittsburgh, where Corbett supporters, hitherto quiet in the pro-Sullivan crowd gathered in front of the *Dispatch* office, finally gave vent to their feelings; to Indianapolis, where the hawkers and shoeshine boys working the throngs knocked off their labors to join the celebrations; to the Hayes Street home of Jim's parents in San Francisco, where Patrick Corbett's initial burst of exaltation was followed by wishes that Jim would at last give up prizefighting, now that he had won the laurels he craved.

Back in the ring, Jim was momentarily feeling something other than elation. "I should have felt proud and dazed," he revealed in his autobiography *The Roar of the Crowd* a quarter century later, "but the only thing I could think of, right after the knockout, was Sullivan lying there on the floor. I was actually disgusted with the crowd, and it left a lasting impression on me. It struck me as sad to see all those thousands who had given him such a wonderful ovation when he entered the ring turning it to me now that he was down and out."

The conflicted feelings did not last long. As Sullivan's seconds dragged him to his chair, Jim raised his arms in victory and started jumping around, hugging his seconds and William Brady. Then he shook hands with John, who had regained his senses and risen unsteadily to his feet. The ex-champ then turned to the spectators and, hanging onto the ropes for support, delivered one of the speeches for which he was famous. "Ladies and gentlemen," he said, "it is the old, old story, the story of a young man against an old one. There are gray hairs in my head and I should have known better." His voice broke. He paused to master himself. "I can only say," he hoarsely continued, "that I am glad that the championship is to remain in America. That is all I've got to say."

Led back in his dressing room, John broke down and wept. "Well, Sullivan is done, Charley," he said to his corner man, Charley Johnson. "Corbett is the cleverest man in the world. But I am awfully sorry you lost, Charley, and I can't get over it." Johnson, who had put up most of the $10,000 side bet, stroked John's hair and tried to offer comfort, saying that it wasn't over, that John could build himself back up and reclaim the title. But John had already started on his first bottle of beer. "I felt like I was standing on a bridge with water all around me," he mused, reflecting on the new experience of being knocked out. "I was falling in the water. I tried to catch myself, but I toppled over and could hear the water all around me." He called for another bottle and broke down again. "I don't suppose that the people will want to come and see my play now," he wept. He would continue to drink on into the night.

In his neighboring dressing room, Jim was being shouted at and jostled by newsmen. "Don't get so excited," he snapped, growing testy. "I know I won, and I know you are glad of it, but don't try to crowd me to death." Congratulatory cables were pouring in. A messenger arrived to say that Jim's wife was on the wire and would he like to exchange a greeting. "Oh, I can't go now," Jim said. "Just give her my love and tell her that I am all right, feeling well and not a bit hurt." He declined a celebratory glass, pointedly drinking only milk, then started to boast about how easy he had found the fight, "simply a walkover and the softest kind of a snap," and how good he felt, so fresh that he could go out and run ten miles. There was just some soreness in his right thumb from delivering the finishing blow.

A knock at the door. It was Bob Fitzsimmons wanting to offer his congratulations. "Don't let him in," Jim barked. "I don't want to see him. The big duffer would not come near me before the fight, and I don't want to see him now."

Bob persisted, peeping over the top of the door. He was committed now to the heavyweight ranks and that meant making his presence known to the champ. *Jim, Jim*, he called out.

Jim just ignored him.

Jim made several stops on his triumphal journey back to New York to appear in sold out performances of the play *After Dark*, William Brady seizing every opportunity to make money off the new heavyweight title. It was a glorious end to Jim's stint as a dialogless theatrical star. Less than a month later, on October 3, 1892, he opened in Elizabeth, New Jersey in his own play, *Gentleman Jack*, about young bank clerk Jack Royden who gets the girl and knocks out the dastardly villain—a thinly disguised Charley Mitchell—in an elaborately staged fight scene that comprised the final act. Catastrophe was averted at the last minute when John Donaldson stepped into the part of "Twitchell" after Jim Daly, Corbett's usual sparring partner, quit in protest of Corbett's refusal to ease up on his punches. The plot was hackneyed but Jim's performance surprisingly good, audiences roaring their approval when he proclaimed, "I will defend the championship of America against the world!" Brady, playing the role of Jack's father, was so delighted with how it came off that he "seemed disposed at several points to dance a coltish hornpipe," according to the *New York World*. Jim of course had his share of detractors—the *New York Sun* critic referred to "his small ability as an actor" and the *New York Press* called his delivery "amateurish"—but the play nevertheless went on to enjoy great success, earning Jim more than he could ever hope to make in the ring.

John L. Sullivan, meanwhile, had embarked on a successful run with his own potboiler, *Captain Harcourt, or The Man From Boston*, which opened in Harlem the same day, October 3. The people, it turned out, still wanted to see him—which was fortunate, for John needed the money. When he made his entrance on opening night following the prompt, "Here comes Captain Harcourt now!" the audience rose to its feet and cheered for three minutes.

As for Bob Fitzsimmons, he was touring with a vaudeville show billed as "Bob Fitzsimmons's Athletic and Specialty Company. A Cyclone of Success!" By all appearances he was doing well for himself, wearing expensive suits and silk cravats and throwing money around as he angled for a shot at Corbett's new title. But all wasn't rosy with Ruby Robert. He was in fact heading for a very big fall. It would wreck his marriage and leave him broke, sleeping in a police station, unable to pay for a room.

CHAPTER 7

PREPARING FOR MARKET

WILLIAM DICKSON WAS AWAY from the Edison lab for ten weeks following his nervous breakdown in February 1893. He had "gone to Florida for his health," the *Orange Chronicle* noted, "being much affected by brain exhaustion." Accompanied by a fellow lab employee and friend, he took the train down to Edison's cottage at Fort Myers for an all-expenses-paid vacation, sharing the house with Edison's father, Samuel, who was wintering there with James Symington, his frugal caregiver. "I feel very sure," Dickson wrote pathetically to Edison's secretary Al Tate while en route, "that I shall very soon begin to improve & return better able to cope with my duties."

His appetite certainly improved very quickly—so much so that Symington, who considered a dollar fifty a sufficient weekly expenditure per person for groceries, wrote to Thomas Edison to complain. "It cost 11 dollars each a week to keep them gentleman with their nigger cook," he stated. "Every Gastronomic Device that could be thought of was brought into registration." For exercise, Dickson did some hunting—he was an excellent shot—and went on photographing expeditions. He also took great interest in Samuel, for this was the father of Edison, the progenitor of the great man, and he seemed even more eccentric than the son. Samuel insisted, for example, on wearing the oldest, most threadbare shirts, the fabric so far gone that the washerwoman expressed doubts they would hold together. Dickson was of course very curious about this and embarrassed Symington by asking why Edison's father dressed in rags. "What could I say," Symington reported to Edison in his letter, not wanting to admit to outsiders that the old man had dementia. "I could only say that he had such a contempt of dudes that his prejudices went to the other extreme and that you knew nothing of it."

Back at the lab, increasingly desperate inquiries were being received regarding progress on the Kinetoscopes that were to be manufactured for the planned exhibit at the Columbian Exposition in Chicago. Al Tate had arranged the sale of the concession to a group of investors, the machine was virtually production-ready, everything was set for the debut of Edison's latest wonder...but no Kinetoscopes were being made. Edison had applied the brakes to the project. He would not agree to give the go-ahead until Dickson returned and pronounced the Kinetoscope ready. As Tate confided in a letter to Dickson, however, the main impediment was that Edison's "attention is so much absorbed by Ore Milling affairs he cannot devote much time to other matters. Unfortunately, the 'other matters' suffer because of this." The Ogdensburg iron ore mine, operating at a large monthly loss, had already been shut down once for redesigning and would soon be shut down again, Edison's personal investment in the venture on its way to totaling two million dollars. Compared to this all-important work, the Kinetoscope was for Edison a minor distraction, a novelty of possibly only short-term market potential that would fade after the public had had its fill. The silent peephole machine may have even been something of a personal let-down, for it fell short of his grander vision of presenting moving pictures with synchronized sound.

When Dickson returned to the lab in April, apparently fully recovered, the Kinetoscope project was thus at a standstill. And on May 1 the Exposition in Chicago opened without the planned one-hundred-fifty-machine display. The coin-in-the-slot Phonograph exhibit attracted a steady stream of people and turned a handsome profit; people lined up to see Eadweard Muybridge illustrate motion with his Zoopraxiscope and twenty-four-image disks; they paid good money for a fleeting glimpse of movement on Ottomar Anschütz's Tachyscope with its similarly limited number of sequential pictures. But the more impressive Kinetoscope, sure to "pay $1000 a day," according to one of Tate's investors, was nowhere to be seen.

With the Columbian Exposition debut a bust, Edison settled on a more modest unveiling for the Kinetoscope at the monthly meeting of the Physics Department at the Brooklyn Institute on May 9, the invention's first public showing outside the lab. A lecture was presented by department president George Hopkins, then the audience lined up for a peek into the one existing production model that Dickson had set up on the stage. What they saw was a blacksmithing scene arranged against the now standard black backdrop, a man and two assistants heating iron in a forge and hammering it on an anvil, then passing around a bottle for a hurried drink.

Al Tate's disappointed investors continued to hope that a reduced number of Kinetoscopes might still be got ready before the close of the Exposition. An initial order of twenty-five machines was given to an Edison lab employee in June to complete on contract but even these failed to materialize as summer gave way to fall. This was partly due to the fact that the employee, rumored to have a drinking problem, was unable to fulfill the contract and eventually had to be fired. A more important reason for the delay, however, was that Edison was letting the project slide—first through neglect, iron ore consuming his attention, but also due to reluctance to launch a new business at a time when the American economy was hitting the skids.

The financial tremors had begun around the time Dickson went away for his health and culminated in a panic on the New York Stock Exchange in early May 1893. "It was cruel, cruel," reported the *New York Herald*. "[T]he men of Wall street trembled, for no one could say what crash would come next.... There was danger everywhere, danger of a general collapse." Down on the trading floor a frenzied mass of humanity struggled for survival. "Hats were smashed, coats torn and cravats ruined. Old men and young men grappled with each other until the weakest were forced outside of the ring. It was a question of financial life or death to many.... Many of the persons in the galleries of the Stock Exchange wept with excitement." The good news amid the financial wreckage was that the consensus among money men was that the worst surely was past.

It wasn't. It was only beginning. Companies went bankrupt, more than fifteen thousand by the end of the year; unemployment soared to levels never before experienced in America's agrarian past; banks collapsed by the dozen, then by the hundreds. Credit dried up and ready cash became so hard to find that by mid summer there was serious talk of closing down the New York Stock Exchange for a month. By the fall the country was mired in the worst slump of the post-Civil War era—what would be called the "Great Depression" until the greatest of all economic depressions superseded it in 1929.

This economic turmoil hit Edison hard and forced him to retrench. In Orange, the staff at the lab was greatly reduced and the neighboring Phonograph Works shut down completely. When a former employee wrote from Austria asking for a job, Edison responded via Al Tate that there was no work to offer him as "the Electric business in this country is perfectly dead, thousands of men being out of employment, owing to the panic which has prevailed here all summer. In Mr. Edison's opinion you had better remain in Europe.... Just now everything is at a standstill."

And so the Kinetoscope languished.

Although his time was largely taken up with ore milling, William Dickson continued to work part-time on the moving picture project during the summer of 1893, conducting tests, making adjustments and improvements—and securing a new supply of film, the Eastman Company having abruptly shut down production. The trouble went back to January 1892, when George Eastman fired his head chemist and plant manager, Henry Reichenbach, for plotting to leave and start a rival concern. It was an acrimonious parting that saw $50,000 in damage done to the company—a vast amount of emulsion spoiled and imperfect film approved for shipment to dealers—before Reichenbach and several other "conspirators" were pushed out the door. (The renegade outfit they started did not long survive.) For the rest of the year Eastman had difficulty maintaining quality with his product. The film came out with spots. Streaks appeared, caused by static. And worst of all, whole batches were losing their light sensitivity after only a few months, leaving eager Kodak users with photos of nothing. On November 6, 1892 it all came out in a *Chicago Tribune* exposé calling Eastman's film "worthless." "I can hardly find words to express my indignation at the disappointment and trouble I have suffered with those confounded films," one disgruntled Kodak owner was quoted as saying. "I became so disgusted that I sold my camera." Another customer recounted a tale of woe of having returned from the trip of a lifetime to Europe only to find that every photograph he had taken with his Kodak was blank. "Doesn't Do the Rest—Kodakers Press the Button and the Picture Won't Materialize," proclaimed the headline in the *Denver Republican* as the story made its way across the country. It was the worst kind of publicity, the press throwing Eastman's own slogan, "You press the button, we do the rest," back in his face. Unable to isolate and fix the problem, he shut down his celluloid film production line.

With Eastman no longer providing the film that he needed, Dickson was forced to turn to the only other outfit then manufacturing celluloid strips: the Blair Camera Company of Boston, which had recently come out with the Kamaret camera to compete against the Kodak. The first sample rolls that were sent were found to be insufficiently durable for the Kineto camera and viewer, prompting Dickson to press the Blair people for "a special film of leathery consistency" that was "<u>less</u> <u>brittle</u>." He eventually got what he needed and was able to proceed with making test films.

By this time Dickson's moving picture plans had outgrown the confines of the photography building. A larger structure that he had designed was in fact being constructed at the time of his nervous breakdown—yet another strain Dickson must have been feeling—and was ready for use in May 1893. Dubbed the "Black Maria" for its resemblance to the enclosed wagons used by the police, it was the first purpose-built movie studio in the world.

The Black Maria was an eccentric-looking building, long and narrow and covered with tar paper. At one end was a darkroom and a space for the Kinetograph camera. At the center was a fourteen-by-sixteen-foot stage, a high, peaked roof overhead. One entire side of this roof could be lifted back like a lid by means of ropes and pulleys to expose the stage to direct sunlight. Behind the stage, comprising the rear twelve feet of the building, was a deep empty space entirely covered in black felt—a light-absorbing void, what Dickson called a "black tunnel," to serve as a background for whatever was being filmed.

As odd as the Black Maria was in outward appearance, even more striking was the fact that it revolved. The entire fifty-foot-long building was balanced on a central pivot and had wheels at either end that rolled on a circular track. In this way it could be turned in any direction for maximum sunlight. When it was in position—this was done with muscle power, men pushing at either end—heavy posts were wedged against either side to keep it steady.

The interior of the Black Maria was no more refined than a barn or large shack, the wood frame and board cladding exposed and unpainted, the "stage" nothing more than an open space on the plank floor. A pair of rails were set in the floor, running from near the stage all the way to the darkroom at the rear of the building. The Kinetograph camera rested on these rails atop a wheeled table. It was housed in a trunk-sized box and was extremely heavy—purposefully so, Dickson having placed weights inside. This was done to make the device solid and steady to dampen the vibrations caused by the intermittent mechanism and ensure sharp images during filming. It ran on electricity, Edison's own direct current, wires running out the back of the box to connect to the lab's power supply. Batteries could also be used if an independent power source was needed. The camera was started by pulling on a lever on the side and was automatically stopped by a timing mechanism in a small box sitting on top, the timer counting down the twenty-odd seconds the film ran. When the camera needed to be loaded or unloaded, it was wheeled backward atop its table into the darkroom, the door was closed and the box opened up in the red light coming through the ruby filter-covered window.

Through the latter part of 1893 and into 1894, Dickson and William Heise made test films in the Black Maria, mainly impromptu subjects, most of them now forgotten or lost. They may also have tried to film moving images with synchronized phonograph sound, a futile effort to realize Edison's greater vision that would soon be abandoned. Toward the end of the year, with the first twenty-five Kinetoscopes still unfinished, the contract for their manufacture was given to Heise, who soon began turning them out. Dickson in the meantime was considering possible film subjects for the machine's commercial release, something to present to the public that was more than mere movement. It had to be interesting to the viewer even in the absence of sound; it had to fit within the confines of the Black Maria; and it had to last no more than twenty seconds, the running time of fifty feet of film.

Dickson's mind initially turned to the stage—to vaudeville acts and dancers and visual comedy gags. For the subject of his very first film of a commercial nature, he chose German strongman Eugen Sandow, then in New York on his American tour. It was a logical choice, for Sandow had what in vaudeville circles was called a "dumb act," a stage routine without any speaking. It was here, in the muscular showman's visit to the Edison lab on March 6, 1894, that the motion picture industry, the movie *business*, began.

Eugen Sandow arrived in Orange at eleven o'clock that Tuesday morning, traveling down on the train with several theater men from New York. The party was met at the station and taken to Edison's lab and shown the Black Maria where the filming would take place. The building had already been rotated into the optimal position for midday filming, the roof opened to expose the stage to the direct rays of the sun.

The strongman stripped off his clothes and donned the scanty loincloth he wore for posing. He rejected the skin-hugging tights preferred by other strongmen, who were not as handsome as he was nor as well endowed with such a perfect physique. A Sandow appearance meant Sandow uncovered, rippling muscles on full display, taut flesh, like polished ivory, exposed. In the *tableaux vivant* portion of his stage show, prior to the hoisting of weights, he usually stood inside an artfully lit cabinet and went through his poses at a leisurely pace, holding each for half a minute or more to give the audience time to gaze and admire. This of course would not do for Kinetograph work. After Dickson explained the time constraints of the camera, Sandow practiced a greatly abbreviated version of his routine, speeding it up to squeeze eight poses into twenty seconds. The curtain shielding the Kinetograph from the bright sunlight was then drawn back and the camera wheeled forward, positioned close to the stage to film Sandow from the waist up. The machine was set into motion, Sandow rushed through his poses and a roll of film was exposed, then the camera was pushed back into the darkroom for reloading. The process was repeated two or three times to provide multiple negatives from which to make copies. The intense noonday sun was not the best illumination to show off Sandow's muscles but Dickson would not have thought this a problem. He wanted bright, clear images and that's what he got, Sandow's milk-white body standing out in sharp contrast against the black of the tunnel behind the stage.

Thomas Edison was present to see Sandow's magnificence for himself, to feel his biceps and pose together for a photo. To demonstrate his renowned strength, Sandow turned to one of the men in his party and asked if he would mind being "chucked." The man was clearly not keen on chucking but Sandow seized him anyway and tossed him out the door. He then returned to the station to catch the train back to New York, pleased with the experience and satisfied with his payment. His usual appearance fee was two hundred fifty dollars but he had waived this for the pleasure of shaking Edison's hand.

The research and development phase of the Kinetoscope was now over. In the weeks that followed, Dickson and William Heise would shoot a number of other films of a commercial nature, their subjects ranging from the Spanish dancer Carmencita and the contortionist Bertholdi to Highland dancers, an organ grinder and his monkey, a trained bear, a cock fight and a comical barbershop scene. Preparations in the meantime were underway to convert an empty Manhattan storefront into the very first Kinetoscope parlor. The first ten machines were to be delivered on April 6, 1894.

The movies, in their nascent peephole form, were about to open for business.

PART TWO

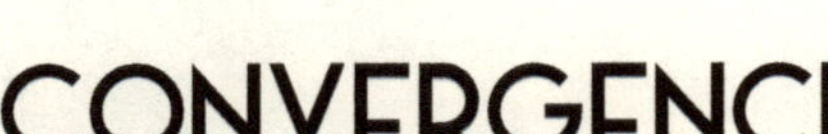

CONVERGENCE

CHAPTER 8

OPEN FOR BUSINESS

IT WAS A SUNNY AFTERNOON in New York in the spring of 1894, the streets alive with shouts and clangs and hustle and bustle, the aroma of manure and urine from the city's sixty thousand horses sharp in the air. Enoch Rector, a tall West Virginian recently arrived in Manhattan, was strolling up Broadway with his old friends Gray and Otway Latham, taking in the sights and looking for amusement. With so many diversions available it was difficult to chose. There was a variety show at Huber's Museum featuring the strongman Sampson and Wellon's cat circus; a matinee performance of *Amazons* at the Lyceum; the musical *Cinderella* at Abbey's Theater, the beautiful Ellaline Terriss in the lead; the *tableaux vivant* "living pictures" at Koster and Bial's and John Philip Sousa's band at Madison Square Garden. Or perhaps they should head over to Brooklyn for Buffalo Bill's Wild West Show at Ambrose Park. Or they could take the trolley uptown to the Polo Grounds to see the New York Giants take on the Boston Beaneaters. It promised to be an exciting game, for the Beaneaters were setting new standards for unruly behavior this season.

The three men continued to make their way up Broadway, past Madison Square, past Twenty-Third Street, past Twenty-Fourth, cable cars humming by at thirty miles per hour, the iron-bound wheels of carriages and wagons rattling loud on the granite slabs of the road. They had first met more than a decade before, when Enoch and Gray had been students at West Virginia University, studying under Gray's mercurial father, Woodville Latham, known as "Professor" or "Major" and to intimates as "Marse Woody." Gray had spent the intervening years mostly in the pharmaceutical business, first in a drug store in Nashville set up by his older brother Percy, then, after that business failed, as a traveling salesman with various drug-related concerns. It was an occupation that suited the handsome twenty-seven-year-old well, for he was charming and playful and less encumbered by the arrogance that tinged the rest of his family. He was profligate, yes, but he made people feel good, reading out passages from the little volume of *The Faerie Queene* he carried in his pocket, bursting into Negro spirituals at unexpected moments, dancing jigs when he ran into friends. He was, to use an electrical expression then catching on, a "live wire." As one business acquaintance would later comment, an encounter with Gray Latham was sure to set you right for the day.

Otway Latham was Gray's younger brother, twenty-five years old in 1894. After attending the University of Mississippi, where Woodville had gone to teach chemistry after WVU became too hot for him to stay, Otway had joined his brothers in the Nashville drug store, then had followed Gray into the traveling salesman game. Although gregarious and likeable and an excellent salesman, he was more prone than Gray to the stress and fatigue of life on the road and eventually settled down to work in an office. He was currently managing the recently opened New York City branch of the Tilden Company of New Lebanon, New York, manufacturer of liquid extracts, pills and elixirs such as the cannabis-laced, thirty-percent alcohol Uterine Sedative Tonic. His fun-loving nature, charm and pretentions of old family wealth made him popular in New York social circles, a Southern gentleman pet. He knew people and had connections beyond his relatively humble economic status in life.

As for Enoch Rector, "Nicky" to friends, he was at loose ends when he ran into the Lathams that spring. At thirty-one, he was the oldest of the three. He had worked as a civil engineer and more recently as an electrical engineer. Currently he was weighing his options, waiting for something to turn up.

It did, just a few steps further along, in the form of a handbill thrust into their hands. "Edison Kinetoscope," it read. "The most recent and marvelous production of the great inventor's brain. . . .

Now on Exhibition for the *First* time at 1155 Broadway, near 27th Street, New York." The trio continued on to the nearby address, a narrow storefront just off the corner of Twenty-Seventh and Broadway that until recently had been a shoe store. The sign above the door now announced "Holland Brothers" and a placard in the window "Edison Kinetoscope." The place was attracting a crowd.

There was not much to see through the window—a bust of Edison, potted plants lining the walls, two rows of chest-high wooden cabinets over which customers were stooped, peering into the top. These were apparently the Kinetoscopes referred to in the signage.

Curious, Rector and his companions joined the line shuffling into the shop. There was a booth inside the door with a pretty young woman selling tickets for twenty-five cents, one ticket to view five of the Kinetoscope devices, two for a look at all ten. After paying his money, Rector followed the strip of carpet to the first machine in the first row and, presenting his ticket to the attendant, lowered his head to the eyepiece. At first there was nothing to see, only blackness. Then the attendant pulled a rod in the back of the cabinet, a hidden mechanism began to stutter and the white torso of a superbly built man appeared.

It was a photographic image of Eugen Sandow, stripped almost naked, displaying his muscles—and *moving*. It wasn't just a single movement either, a half-second Zoetrope loop repeated over and over. This was twenty seconds of flowing, uninterrupted action: Sandow front view, flexing his biceps, crossing his arms, tensing his stomach; Sandow back view, arms outstretched, back muscles rippling. A two-inch-high representation of the renowned German strongman seemed to be startlingly alive inside the box.

Rector continued to the next Kinetoscope machine, resting his arms on the brass railing as he peered in. This time he saw an organ grinder's mischievous monkey snatch a boy's cap. The third Kinetoscope contained the contortionist Madame Bertholdi—somewhat erotic. The fourth: two men wrestling. Then Highland dancers, a cockfight, a blacksmith scene, a barber giving a man a hasty shave and a haircut. The living pictures were not perfect—they flickered somewhat and occasionally jittered about—but it took no great leap of imagination to envision what the great Edison would make of this new invention. Rector and the Lathams left the Holland Brothers' establishment greatly impressed.

It was Gray Latham who had the brainstorm when they were back outside on the sidewalk. "There," he said, "that's the business to get into. I'll tell you what—everybody's crazy about prize fights, and all we have to do is to get Edison to photograph a fight for this machine and we take it out and make a fortune on it."

His brother Otway and Enoch Rector both liked the idea. It made excellent sense, and on multiple levels. First, there was the obvious drawing power of prizefights. Championship battles made the front pages of newspapers all across the country and generated tremendous excitement and yet only a relative handful of people ever got to see them. Just imagine if the Sullivan-Corbett fight had been photographically captured and presented to the public. Or the Fitzsimmons-Dempsey middleweight matchup. Or Jack McAuliffe defending his lightweight title. Line-ups to see these Olympian battles surely would snake down the street.

And then there was all the morality-driven legal trouble dogging prizefighting, the city ordinances and state laws that made it impossible to hold a match in so many parts of the country. With the Kinetoscope, all these impediments would be neatly sidestepped. For it would not be a real prizefight being presented, but merely a photographic reproduction, a show of light and shadow, a mirage, an illusion. Kinetoscope parlors showing prizefights could be opened from New York to Seattle without fear of running afoul of the law.

The most immediate and most compelling attraction of Gray's idea, however, lay in its economics. A prizefight under Marquis of Queensberry rules, being divided into rounds, was perfectly suited to Edison's new invention, with a single round being presented on a single Kinetoscope machine. To see a ten-round contest, customers would have to pay for ten machines, for who would walk away from a fight before its conclusion? At a nickel per machine, that would be fifty cents each customer would fork over. What would that add up to in a day...two hundred dollars? Yes, it would easily be two hundred dollars, probably more. And if they charged a dime per machine—this would be a stimulating, blood-and-gore prizefight, after all, not some dancing bear act—that would be a dollar a head. And at a dollar a head, assuming, say, a mere fifty customers an hour and an eight-hour day, no, make that ten hours...

Oh, yes, this was the business to get into. And here, sent by providence, was Enoch Rector, a skilled engineer in need of employment. Who better to manage a Kinetoscope parlor than good old Nicky? The beauty of the idea may have sent Gray Latham to dancing one of his jigs.

That was how Enoch Rector stumbled into the motion picture business. His journey to this point had been a long one, traveling as he did by way of the American West, Cape Horn, Buenos Aires and the interior of South America. He liked to tell stories of his many adventures, going all the way back to West Virginia, where, he said, he had killed his brother.

There was something of a mystery about that.

Enoch J. Rector was born near Parkersburg in Wood County, West Virginia on October 9, 1863, three months after the Battle of Gettysburg where the tide of the Civil War turned against the South. The war had divided this border area on the Ohio River, even individual families like the Rectors, Enoch's grandfather, a well-known Baptist preacher also named Enoch, supporting the Northern cause, his uncle Ransom Rector favoring the South. Enoch's father, Thomas Rector, served in the Union Army in the enlisted ranks of the 113th Regiment Militia of Wood County. He appears to have survived the war uninjured but was marked by sorrow just the same. In April 1863, shortly before Enoch's birth, Thomas's firstborn, Waterman Rector, died in childhood, likely carried away by one of the epidemics—typhoid, smallpox, yellow fever—that regularly swept through the county. Then, in 1866, his wife Mary passed away at age twenty-nine.

Mary's death tore the Rector family apart. Enoch and his oldest brother Thomas Jr. were sent to live with their Aunt Elizabeth and her husband John Johnson in Briscoe Run in Williams Township, while brother James and sister Emma went to their maternal grandfather, James Hiett, in Parkersburg. The two homes were no more than ten miles apart so the siblings likely saw each other on occasion. They may even have attended the same school. But the sudden separation nevertheless must have been traumatic—particularly with their father no longer around. Thomas Sr., perhaps troubled following the death of his wife, went off on his own for the next decade. The 1870 federal census found him working and living with his younger brother George, a lumber dealer at Lockhart's Run in Slate Township, east of Parkersburg across the Little Kanawha River. In 1877 he was running the general store in Leachtown in Clay Township. Throughout much of his remaining childhood, Enoch would not have seen much of his father.

It was not until November 1877, when Enoch was fourteen, that Thomas Sr. remarried and the family was at last reunited. Thomas's new wife, Jane Sivey, was the widow of a surgeon and came to the family with a son of her own, nine-year-old William. Enoch thus found himself living with a step-mother and a step-brother who were strangers.

What happened next remains a mystery. The story Enoch told his granddaughter Sara Chermayeff toward the end of his life was that he accidentally killed his brother with a bow and arrow and ran away to join the circus. When he returned home some time later, the prodigal son, he was upset to find that the old half-blind family dog didn't recognize him as he walked up the lane. "Prince," Enoch said, "don't you know me?"

Neither of Enoch's two brothers died anywhere near this time. James succumbed to typhoid fever in 1882 and Thomas Jr. lived to old age. Did Enoch injure one of them, non-fatally, with an arrow? Or was step-brother William the victim? This latter scenario seems more likely. For Enoch and his full brothers, William would have been an outsider and competition for their returned father's attention. Was sibling rivalry at play? Did Thomas and James encourage younger brother Enoch to do something rash with a bow and arrow? Did Enoch do something on his own that resulted in William being sent away from the family and thus effectively "killed"? Whatever may have happened, by the time of the 1880 census William Sivey, then age eleven, was not living with the Rector family in Wood County. He was staying with his mother's parents in neighboring Wirt County. Jane Rector, formerly Jane Sivey, is listed twice in the census as living in both places.

In 1883, just short of his twentieth birthday, Enoch followed his older brother Thomas Jr. to Morgantown—no doubt the longest journey he had ever taken—to enroll in West Virginia University. It was then a small school, with one hundred fifty-odd students and a faculty of thirteen. Enoch would remain there for two years, primarily studying mathematics, chemistry and physics—foundational courses in electrical engineering, which was just starting to emerge as a specific field of study, MIT having established the first program in the country only one year before.

It was at WVU that Enoch first met the Lathams. Woodville Latham was professor of agriculture, chemistry and physics and taught many of his classes. Woodville's eldest son Percy and second son Gray were fellow students, while youngest son Otway, then in his mid-teens, frequently assisted his father in the lab. They were a colorful family of old Virginia stock, the Lathams of Culpeper County, as anyone making their acquaintance quickly learned. It may have been this Southern pride in past family glory that got Gray and Percy into a fight shortly after Enoch's arrival on campus, when another student dumped a pail of slop on Gray's head.

Professor Woodville Latham was by most accounts an irascible and insufferable presence on campus. A graduate of Virginia University in the 1850s, he fought for the Confederacy during the Civil War, a captain in the Nelson Light Artillery Regiment of Virginia, while his wife Eliza ran contraband across the front lines. Eliza was arrested for this in early 1863, the year their first child, Percy, was born. The post-war years found the family in a reduced state, the old wealth gone and two more children, Gray and Otway, to feed. Obliged to lead a workaday existence, Woodville settled into a career in teaching, first at a women's college in Kentucky and then, starting in 1880, at West Virginia University. It was here that Eliza died—a loss that may have contributed to Woodville's drinking and cantankerous nature.

Woodville was a leader of the "old Virginia crowd" that dominated the university at this time. The group's condescension toward West Virginian society added resentment to the many complaints already simmering about Woodville. In August 1884, at the start of Enoch Rector's second and final year at WVU, it all boiled over in spectacular fashion when a number of students signed a petition to have Woodville dismissed. In the Board of Regents' investigation that followed, affidavits were presented accusing the professor of all sorts of disreputable conduct. He had been seen drunk on numerous occasions. He used profane language and played cards for money. He was habitually absent from morning chapel, saying it was all "damned foolishness." He looked upon West Virginians as "bushwhackers and backwoodsmen" and went around with his nose in the air. He had a bad temper and was "harsh," "overbearing" and "abusive" to his students, driving them away and contributing to the recent precipitous decline in enrollment. Even the school janitor got in on the act, testifying that he had heard the scraggly-bearded professor exclaim in a moment of anger, "Botheration, dod burn the infernal god damned thing!"

The board of regents kept Woodville on but his days at WVU were numbered. He left the following year to take up a chemistry professorship at the University of Mississippi. It would be here at Ole Miss that Otway received his higher education.

Enoch Rector—who did not sign the petition against Professor Latham—finished his studies at WVU in the same year the Lathams departed, 1885. Like many of his fellow students, he left the university without earning a degree, staying only long enough to obtain the education necessary to embark on a career. For Enoch, with a solid foundation in the sciences, the way ahead led into engineering. He headed west to work as a surveyor for the Northern Pacific Railroad, the transcontinental line of which had recently been completed through Montana and Washington to reach the West Coast. Ending up in Seattle with two hundred dollars in his pocket, he left the United States in November 1886, taking passage to Buenos Aires via Cape Horn. There he secured a position as engineer in charge of a team of surveyors laying out the route for a proposed railway from Brazil to Bolivia through the Brazilian state of Mato Grosso. This was possibly the Mogyana Railroad, the central line that would eventually connect Rio de Janeiro to the remote interior town of Cuiaba. Enoch's older brother Thomas Jr., hired by the Argentine Meteorological Service, may have helped him get the job. Or perhaps it was Enoch who led the way south. In any event, April 2,

1890 found Enoch back in Buenos Aires applying at the American legation for a passport. He was twenty-six years old at the time, five feet eleven inches tall, "Nose: Large, Mouth: Small, Complexion: Dark, Face: Long." And written in the space on the application for specifying the reason for needing a passport: "Protection."

It made perfect sense that Rector, employed by the railroad in the forested heart of Brazil, would be more than a thousand miles south in Buenos Aires. The Argentine capital was the gateway to the Mato Grosso, the departure point for steamers heading north up the Parana and Paraguay Rivers, and the place of return for adventurers and workers to rest and recuperate, stock up on supplies and perhaps apply for a passport. Laboring in the interior would have been intensely hard work for Rector—and dangerous too, for the Mato Grosso was untamed, largely unexplored, and rife with rebellion. In early 1892 the state would in fact explode into open revolt, rebels declaring it the independent Republic of Transatlantica. Rector would tell his granddaughter Sara exciting stories of this time in his life—such as when there was a fight among the Indian workers in their forest encampment, resulting in one of the men being stabbed in the gut. Enoch sewed up the wound and thought he had saved him but the man never made it past morning. Someone cut his throat in the night.

Enoch returned to the United States in the latter part of 1891, to Chattanooga, Tennessee, where he became briefly reacquainted with the Lathams. The colorful family, father and sons, were sojourning in the city following the failure of their Nashville drug store, trying to make a go of it as dealers in mineral and timber lands. Rector, revealing an aptitude for mechanical invention, developed a "spring-motor" to power sewing machines and other light machinery and threw in with Woodville Latham, John Lang and James Roper in a newly incorporated concern called the Lang Motor Company. The venture soon fell by the wayside and Enoch moved on at around the same time Gray and Otway became traveling salesmen.

It was not a good time to be out of work and seeking employment, what with America on the brink of economic collapse. By spring 1894 sixteen thousand companies and more than six hundred banks had gone bankrupt and the country was mired in a crushing depression, with not even a glimmer of recovery in sight for another three years. For an engineer like Rector, the prospects must have been gloomy, for the railroads and related industries were among the first affected and hardest hit. It was therefore a stroke of luck when he ran into the Lathams in New York and Gray had his brainwave. He was possibly low on money and needed a job.

Although it had been Gray Latham who came up with the idea of photographically capturing prizefights for Kinetoscope exhibition, he was not free at the moment to take an active part in the plan. His presence in New York was only temporary, in large part to see Rose O'Neill, a young artist and magazine illustrator he was passionately courting. His job as a traveling salesman necessitated that he go back out on the road. It was therefore up to Otway Latham and Enoch Rector to get the business started.

There was a problem, of course, staring them right in the face. The films they had just seen inside the Holland Brothers' Kinetoscope parlor were not three minutes long, the length of a round under Marquis of Queensberry rules, nor were they two minutes, nor even one minute. They were barely twenty seconds. That wouldn't do. A more substantial length of prizefighting action would have to be photographically captured if the plan was to succeed.

Otway apparently did not consider this much of a hurdle, for he rushed ahead regardless. First he visited his employer, Tilden Company owner and president Samuel J. Tilden Jr., to secure backing and financial support. Then he headed down to Orange to meet with William Gilmore, Thomas Edison's new private secretary and business manager following the departure of Al Tate. Gilmore and in turn Edison were receptive to the idea of filmed prizefights. It seemed the sort of thing that would appeal to the public, yet was of such a specialized nature that it would not infringe on the North American Kinetoscope concession then being negotiated to exhibit Edison's own line of films. Samuel Tilden's backing also lent weight to the venture.

On May 16, 1894, Otway placed an order through Gilmore for ten Kinetoscope machines—the model that showed films of twenty seconds' duration, the only one then being made—at two hundred forty-five dollars each, batteries and film extra. In a hurry to start making money, he requested delivery by July 2 but had to settle for no later than the middle of the month. He returned to the Edison facility on May 25 to put down a deposit of one thousand dollars, drawn from Samuel Tilden, and to write out an authorization for the Edison lab "to buy and charge to me necessary strips of 100 or 150 feet in length, limiting you to $30.00 in cost." This is the earliest indication that he and Rector planned to make films one minute (one hundred fifty feet) long, triple Edison's current standard. The fact that Otway had gone ahead and placed an order for ten regular Kinetoscopes suggests that he assumed this expansion in capacity posed no particular problem.

All he and Rector needed now were premises in New York for opening their own Kinetoscope parlor. Oh yes, and two fighters to slug each other in front of Edison's camera. The biggest names they could get.

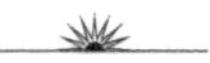

CHAPTER 9

UPS AND DOWNS

JIM CORBETT HAD BEEN RIDING HIGH since defeating John L. Sullivan to win the heavyweight title. He continued to fill theaters with his play *Gentleman Jack* after more than a year, pleasing audiences with his charm and stage presence, then thrilling them with the fistic display that came at the end. It was more popular than anything put on by John L. and was attracting a different kind of theatergoer, people from the "better" classes, the sort who were able to pay for one-dollar seats. They came to see Jim and they went away sated—even more so starting in 1893, when the play was rewritten to highlight Jim's comedic talent and beef up his lead role. "From the rise of the curtain on the first act until time is called at the end of the fifth, it is Corbett," observed the *Sunday Morning Courier* when the play hit Lincoln, Nebraska. "Corbett as a hero in white flannels, Corbett as a gentleman, Corbett as a banker, Corbett as a tremendous moral hero, and finally Corbett as Corbett. When the champion isn't on the stage the other people talk about him and when he is on the stage the support shrinks until it is hardly visible, leaving Corbett as a most conspicuous center piece." For Jim, who threw himself into every performance with gusto, it was all so much more pleasant than fighting that he began to entertain thoughts of abandoning the ring altogether. "I do not think I flatter myself when I believe I will make an actor," he said. "I never expect to be a Booth or a Salvini, but I think I can do light parts very creditably."

This was Jim's time in the sun, his chance to use the heavyweight crown to make money. By 1894 he owned a $20,000 house in New York City, a large property in Asbury Park, New Jersey, a "roadhouse" (drinking establishment) and other investments—including a half share in William Brady's theatrical business, which kept up to four plays on tour at one time. Jim was well on his way to becoming far richer than any boxing champion before him, his earnings reportedly in the vicinity of $100,000 a year.

Pressure in the meantime was mounting for him to hold his first title defense. The obvious challenger to take on was Charles Mitchell, the model for villain "Charles Twitchell" in *Gentleman Jack*. While Jim was generally called the heavyweight champion of the world after defeating Sullivan, the point could be made that he could not really claim that title until he met and defeated English champion Mitchell, thereby unifying the Old World crown and the New. There was an exciting personal element to the contest as well, the hard feelings that existed between the two men, the sense that they had a score to settle. It was largely feigned on the part of Mitchell, the challenger playing the game of getting the champion's goat, but for Jim it was real. He had loathed the loudmouthed Englishman ever since that drunken encounter in the theater and he dearly wanted to give him a "whipping." It all served to stir up tremendous interest in a Corbett-Mitchell matchup. As the *New York Press* ballyhooed in the lead-up, it would be "the greatest ring battle of modern times."

It took over a year to pull off the contest, Jim being tied up with theatrical commitments, Mitchell playing coy or out of the country and legal obstacles cropping up on all sides. By September 1893, however, everything appeared to be settled for it to be held at the Coney Island Athletic Club for the immense purse of $40,000. It seemed an unlikely venue, prizefighting being illegal in the State of New York. But Coney Island wasn't the state. It was "Boss" John McKane's private fiefdom. He and his cronies wanted the fight and the lucre it would bring and so passed an ordinance to host it, calling it "a scientific glove contest of twenty rounds or more" to deflect criticism. (If both fighters were still standing after twenty rounds, the referee would declare a draw and a second twenty-round fight would begin, followed by a third if needed.) Two months later, however, "Boss" McKane overplayed his hand in stealing the November election and ended up being indicted. The Corbett-Mitchell fight would have to be held somewhere else.

Bob Fitzsimmons in the meantime was struggling out of the hole into which he had fallen. His troubles had begun back in March 1892 when he parted ways with manager and trainer Jimmy Carroll. "I am done with Carroll forever," he fumed when asked if there was any chance of them getting back together. "He is small and mean. He tried to cheat me in every town that we traveled through and was jealous of every applause I received. I shared everything I made with him." Like most ring champions—Corbett being an exception—Bob was not good with money and matters of business. He preferred to hand everything over to somebody else so he didn't have to worry about it, which of course left him vulnerable to being taken advantage of and prone to misunderstandings.

Following Carroll's departure, a young acrobat who went by the stage name Martin Julian (real name Martin Samwells) took over the management of Bob's career. Although only twenty-three, Julian had long experience in the theater, he and his contortionist sister Rose having performed on the stage since they were children. Under Julian's guidance a new vaudeville show was organized featuring Rose and a variety of comedy numbers and culminating with Bob in a one-act play called *The Heroic Blacksmith* in which he shoed a horse, recited sentimental lines and gave a sparring exhibition. Bob's performance "fell very flat" when the show opened in Brooklyn. His voice was weak and the poem asserting his superiority over Corbett was hissed—although the couplet, "Though Corbett placed his blows quite well, we won't go back on our John L." got a big cheer. The company did mediocre business on its subsequent tour of the South and was disbanded after less than two months, following a disastrous engagement in fight-saturated New Orleans, playing to a nearly empty house. Returning to New York, Bob denied the show had been a failure, insisting in the theatrical press that it had merely been postponed until after the distraction of the presidential election.

Julian's involvement in Bob's affairs had by this time come to include the management of his career as a fighter. Assisted by Bob's older brother Bill, who had recently arrived in the States, Julian even took a hand in Bob's training despite having no experience in the fight game. Their first major fight together was the long-awaited middleweight title defense against Jim Hall, finally brought off in New Orleans on March 8, 1893, nearly two years after the attempt to hold it in St. Paul had been blocked. It would be Bob's third time to fight in New Orleans, where local politicians had all been properly bought and paid for and thus could be relied on to not interfere. ("The price of a member of the Louisiana Legislature," commented one observer, "ranges from $5 to a glass of beer.") This time, however, it would not be the reliable Olympic Club hosting the contest. With so much money at stake there had been a rift at the Olympic, President Noel and other key members breaking away to form a rival syndicate called the Crescent City Athletic Club. It was this new organization that rashly made the biggest offer for the Fitzsimmons-Hall fight in the fevered heat of bidding, promising the astonishing purse of $40,000.

On the eve of the contest Bob stopped in at the New Orleans courthouse to be sworn in as an American citizen, casting off his foreignness as a drag on his popularity in the United States. From now on he would be an American champ, just like Sullivan and Dempsey, just like Corbett. To hammer the point home, he waved the Stars and Stripes when he entered the ring, then revealed a belt of red, white and blue when he stripped off his robe. He was in high spirits, smiling and joking and not the least bit nervous. "Don't put a lump of lead in there now!" he called over to Hall's seconds as they laced on the gloves, earning a big laugh.

It would be a short fight. The two men mixed it up evenly for the first three rounds. The fourth began similarly, plenty of action, both men even, the audience on its feet roaring "Go it, old sorrel top!" and "That man can't put out a gas jet!" Then *boom*, Bob landed one on the chin. Hall's supporters would complain after that Fitz got lucky, that up to that point "it was $1,000,000 to a gooseberry that Hall would win." But knockouts didn't come any more unequivocal than this. Hall dropped like a stone, raising a little cloud of dust as his skull bounced off the hard boards of the ring, the hollow *thock* of the impact heard throughout the arena. His body stiffened into a bridge, his lips drew back into a ghastly leer, then he lay still, out cold for nearly a minute. After another patriotic display of flag waving, Bob retired to his dressing room and let loose the kid that was in him, hysterically laughing as he hugged Martin Julian and roughhoused with his brother Bill on the floor. Then he pulled on his clothes and rushed to the hotel where Louisa was staying, eager to break the news that the forty-grand purse was now his.

Or so he thought. As it turned out, the Crescent City AC had lost money on the fight and was in dire financial straits, with delinquent taxes owing. It was thus able to pay Bob less than a quarter of the purse, putting up the rest in notes that soon became worthless when the club went bankrupt. After paying everyone off—three thousand dollars to Martin Julian, eight hundred to his sparring partner, five hundred each to wife Louisa and brother Bill—Bob was left with virtually nothing. It was a catastrophic blow, for he had been counting on the purse. Not only was almost everything he had earned to date gone, poured into his vaudeville company, invested in San Francisco real estate that he had signed over to Louisa or otherwise spent, he had been borrowing freely and had creditors to pay. Suddenly, shockingly, he was facing ruin.

And then, just two weeks later, back on the road with *The Heroic Blacksmith*, things got worse. It started in Baltimore, where Bob noticed that Louisa and handsome young Julian were always together, that Louisa wouldn't even sit down to dinner unless Julian was there. Bob's suspicions were confirmed at the next stop in Philadelphia, when he and his wife had a room at the Continental Hotel adjoining Julian's and he heard things through the door. When he confronted his wife and his manager, they confessed they were in love, Louisa adding that she would "go to the end of the world" for Martin. When things became heated, Julian threatened Bob with a revolver.

Bob stormed out. That was the end of his first marriage. Louisa disappeared with Julian and Bob struggled on alone for a few more weeks with the show, then retreated to Newark, New Jersey, where he had previously lived. Wanting to get away, he said he was planning on going to Europe, that people wanted to see him over there. But he didn't go to Europe. Instead he hit rock bottom, broke after clearing his debts, then further shaken by the news that his mother in New Zealand was on her death bed and would soon pass away.

In the lowest depths of his troubles, Bob was helped out by Captain Charles Glori of the Newark Police Department, an avid sporting man whom Bob considered a friend. Glori, the son of German immigrants, had risen from patrolman to captain in the past ten years and had attained a certain social standing, his portrait appearing in an illustrated souvenir book on the city and on a cigarette card in the "Police Inspectors and Captains" collectible series. When Bob washed up in Newark without any money, Glori let him stay in his office at the Fourth Precinct, then moved him into his house.

It was Captain Glori who assisted Bob in initiating divorce proceedings against Louisa. He hired an investigator to track her and Martin Julian down—they were found in a boarding house in Brooklyn—then had them watched. When sufficient evidence of infidelity was collected, papers were served suing Louisa for absolute divorce. That meant no alimony.

What followed was messy. Louisa hired a lawyer and went on the offensive, denying the infidelity charge and claiming it was Bob who had ruined their marriage. He had neglected her and had tried to entrap her as he himself carried on with other women—including Julian's sister, the contortionist Rose, and a mistress he had consorted with in New Orleans named Florence, who had the boldness to give out calling cards printed up with the name "Mrs. Fitzsimmons."

Bob's suit was ultimately denied. He was ordered to pay Louisa alimony and legal expenses when their divorce was granted in April 1894.

With Coney Island's "Boss" John McKane on his way to Sing Sing for six years of hard labor, the Corbett-Mitchell contest spent a month in limbo, a fight in search of a home. The Duval Athletic Club in Jacksonville eventually got it by promising a $20,000 purse and coming up with a crafty plan to get around Florida's anti-prizefighting law, with a backup plan to pull off the contest on the sly, like Sullivan-Kilrain in 1889, using a portable ring set up in the woods. The complex legal maneuvering continued up to the eve of the battle, with the Duval AC's lawyers ultimately securing an injunction preventing the governor and law enforcement officials from interfering in what was merely a "scientific glove exhibition." It was something of a Pyrrhic victory, however. With so much uncertainty attached to the fight and with armed militia dispatched from Tallahassee, sporting men stayed away in droves and ticket sales were disappointing. Those who did show up, moreover, were such a riotous bunch of drunks and louts that the good people of Jacksonville soon regretted supporting the fight in the expectation of the flood of money it would bring to the town. "Some of us were over to New Orleans when Corbett fought Sullivan," said one shopkeeper, "and we thought the same sort of a crowd would come here, but, instead of that, we got a town full of loafers that are doing us more harm than good.... This town never saw such a crowd before and it never wants to see another like it, I tell you."

The fight took place on January 25, 1894, at the dilapidated fairgrounds on Jacksonville's outskirts, out past the shacks where the blacks lived. The arena, while capacious, was not much to look at, a rough construction of timber sided with recycled boards. Tickets cost early arrivals a whopping twenty-five dollars but soon dropped to fifteen, then ten, then five, as the Duval AC scrambled to fill up the bleachers. A sheepish contingent of the militia boys showed up without their weapons and were let in at a discount, the sight of their blue uniforms eliciting hisses as they took their seats. They never wanted to stop the fight, one of them said. "We came here to get drunk and have a good time." Down in the ring, Jack Dempsey, who would be working Jim's corner, was helping crush chunks on rosin into the springy pine boards that were the only superior thing about the arena. Overhead, workers were setting up the big gasoline lamps that would be needed if the fight extended into the evening. It was currently early afternoon.

The winter sky was overcast when Jim and Charley Mitchell stepped through the barbed wire enclosure, climbed into the ring and stripped off their robes. The sight of them facing each other for the first time was almost shocking, for Mitchell was several inches shorter and more than twenty pounds lighter, nowhere near Jim's physical equal as represented in the papers. He had clearly come to do battle, however. His face and hands were stained walnut brown from the liniment that had been used to toughen his skin. He had bandages wrapped about his middle to protect his stomach, and strengthening bands on his wrists. Jim had objected to stomach wrappings when he fought Sullivan but now, facing Mitchell, he let it go. The sight of the man's grinning face filled him with anger. Jim could hardly wait to rip into him, to smash him down, to tear him apart. "Hurry this thing up," he barked at the referee, "Honest" John Kelly. "It's getting cold in here." Kelly, his pockets bulging with money—Jim had insisted the purse be on hand in cash—called the two men to ring center and quickly went over the rules. When they separated, Jim refused to shake hands.

What followed was very different from Jim's battle against Sullivan sixteen months before. This time he was the aggressor, rushing at Mitchell from the opening bell, driving him against the ropes, shoving him away when they clinched. He kept it up through the first round and into the second, expending energy he would need if the fight went any distance. Luckily for Jim, it didn't. He dropped Mitchell in a latter part of the second, then closed in to finish it without giving the Englishman a chance to get up. "Foul!" bawled Mitchell's seconds, stepping into the ring, Corbett's following suit, Dempsey seizing Jim around the waist and pulling him back.

The bell sounded and Jim turned away to return to his corner. Mitchell, on his feet now, his grin gone, his nose streaming blood, lunged at Jim and delivered a blow that glanced off his shoulders. "Foul!" roared Jim's seconds. Jim shook his head and the referee let it go. Mitchell was already beaten. Everyone in the arena could see it.

Mitchell was still shaky when he answered the bell for the third. Jim immediately went at him, battering him against the ropes, then polishing him off with a right to the chin. Mitchell's legs gave out and he dropped face down onto the boards as the blinding explosion of a photographer's flash momentarily filled the arena. He made no attempt to rise. He was out cold, his seconds plying him with smelling salts, then the hundred-year-old brandy a friend had sent Mitchell to take into his corner for good luck. ("Brandy was not old enough," the friend was cabled after the fight.) In New York City, a white flag was hoisted by *World* staff atop the Pulitzer Building, the prearranged signal for a Corbett win, and the city erupted. The newspaper had planned to use its recently installed Electric Cloud Projector to flash bulletins onto low-lying clouds, but alas, the fight had taken place during the day. At Harry Corbett's pool room in San Francisco, Jim's father Patrick, who had hollered like a maniac as the fight cables came in, let out a final whoop and collapsed exhausted into a chair. Back in Jacksonville, Jim left the ring without expressing the slightest concern for his downed opponent. The overwhelmingly pro-Corbett crowd was similarly unsympathetic, hurling insults at Mitchell as he was helped through the ropes.

Jim came away from the Mitchell contest with the $20,000 purse plus $5,000 from the side bet. He and Mitchell also got promptly arrested, for by going ahead with the fight they had broken state law. They had to post bonds before being released, obliged to return later that year to face a jury trial that would see them quickly acquitted. It was at the courthouse, after fronting their bonds, that Mitchell made a little speech expressing his regret for past statements and Jim agreed to bury the hatchet and shake hands.

Having defended his title and satisfied the sporting world's expectations, Jim set out on a new tour with *Gentleman Jack*, the play reportedly clearing $20,000 in the first two weeks alone. "You could not be a gentleman and be a pugilist," his stage sweetheart mewed for the hundredth time in New York, Philadelphia, Chicago. "Oh, yes, I could," replied Jack, thrusting out his chest. "A gentleman at heart is a gentleman at anything!" Jim continued to throw himself into the part, his enthusiasm for the stage undiminished. Toward the end of March he confided to a newsman that he had personally come up with the idea for his next play, *Modern Society*, about prizefighting and New York's social elite. All that was needed was to hire a playwright to craft the dialogue and work out the "stage business."

On April 12, 1894, after ten weeks of mostly sold-out shows, Jim embarked with his theatrical company for England, his parents going along to visit their Irish home for the first time in twenty-five years. *Gentleman Jack* had its Old World debut at London's Drury Lane Theatre on April 21, the villain transformed from "Charles Twitchell" into Texan "Bat Houston" so as not to offend the English. It earned rave reviews in London papers, the *Daily Telegraph* calling the fight scene "nothing less than marvelous." The way the stage "audience" responded to the fight was singled out for particular comment, for "Each men in that vast assembly, each one of these individuals, seems to have a separate individuality, and to be acting not by rote, but by impulse. That is the great secret of the success. It is not theatrical, but natural.... No horse race, or fire, or shipwreck on the stage was ever so accurate and realistic, and in a measure so effective, as this prize fight."

The effect had been easily achieved by William Brady. He sent free tickets to London pubs and clubs, then seated people on stage when they eagerly showed up, first come, first served.

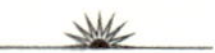

CHAPTER 10

THE MOVIES REACH A MINUTE

ENOCH RECTOR TOOK THE FERRY across the Hudson River to Hoboken and boarded the west-bound train on the Morris and Essex Railroad. It was the second week of June 1894 and he was heading to Thomas Edison's Orange, New Jersey lab. The journey was only twelve miles, nine short stops on the train, but for Rector it was momentous. For he was about to oversee the filming of the very first prizefight, the one that would launch the Kinetoscope venture that would hopefully make him and the Lathams rich.

The plan had been moving forward with remarkable speed, almost a headlong rush thanks to Otway Latham. Within days of their stumbling on the Holland Brothers' Kinetoscope parlor on Broadway, Otway had secured the backing of his employer, Samuel Tilden Jr., and had met with Edison's business manager William Gilmore. An enthusiastic young man with a big idea normally would not have gotten far with Gilmore. But Otway had the Tilden name behind him, a name attached to a large pharmaceutical manufacturer and one that commanded respect, Tilden's uncle, also named Samuel Tilden, having been the governor of New York and the Democratic candidate for the presidency in 1876. Gilmore and in turn Edison therefore gave Otway's plan to exhibit prizefights on the Kinetoscope serious consideration. A potential complication was that the North American rights for the Kinetoscope were about to be sold to Norman Raff and Frank Gammon, the investors who had wanted to exhibit the device at the Columbian Exposition in Chicago. A binding contract, however, had not yet been signed. And in any event showing prizefights seemed a separate matter, a specialty sideline, something that would not conflict with the interests of Raff and Gammon and their sub-agents the Holland Brothers, who would still have the exclusive right to show the films William Dickson was making, *Sandow, Carmencita, Cockfighting, Boxing Cats* and the rest.

On May 19, 1894, Gilmore wrote to Otway accepting his order of ten Kinetoscopes for delivery in early July. Otway visited the Edison lab on the 25th to make the deposit of one thousand dollars in person and give written authorization to purchase film in "strips of 100 to 150 feet." At the bottom of Otway's authorization Dickson jotted a note to Gilmore: "[A]m writing to Blair Camera Co. to find out cost of such strips and w[ould] like to have a talk with you about this. It will be a bonanza all round." This document, on Edison laboratory letterhead, suggests that Latham—and almost certainly Rector, for he was the technical brains of the outfit—consulted with Dickson on their visit and learned that not much more than one hundred feet of film could be used in the Kinetograph camera. Beyond that and the reels would be so heavy that the jerking of the intermittent movement would tear the celluloid strip. By using a slower camera speed, thirty frames per second instead of the optimal forty, this limited amount of film could be made to last longer without compromising image quality unduly. The duration of the rounds of a Kinetographed prizefight was thus determined by a combination of the camera's limitations and the amount of image flicker Latham and Rector were prepared to accept. They settled on one minute.

The question now was: Who would they get to fight in front of the camera? The name that would attract the most attention was of course heavyweight champion Jim Corbett, with John L. Sullivan a close second. Corbett, however, was not in the country. He was in Europe and not expected to return until the end of the summer. And even if he were available he was not the best option to start with, for he would certainly demand a big payday, too much to risk on a first filming effort. It would be the same with Sullivan. Assuming he was in presentable condition for fighting—which by all accounts he wasn't—he wouldn't come cheap.

Casting about for other options, Otway and Rector hit on the idea of a contest between undefeated Australian featherweight Albert "Young Griffo" Griffiths and Michigan fighter George Lavigne. The pair had fought to a draw three months before in Chicago. A rematch, presented to the public via a row of Kinetoscopes, one round per machine, would be sure to attract a great deal of interest. The fighters' modest size may have been an added attraction, a better fit inside the confines of the Black Maria. Lightweights also had the advantage of being generally faster than heavyweights—and movement was what the Kinetoscope was all about.

With a deal in the offing, Griffo and Lavigne were invited to the Edison lab around the end of May to see the proposed venue. The set-up in the Black Maria shocked them, the ring being only twelve feet across, the walls on either side looming in close. It was too small, they said, and promptly backed out.

Another pugilist invited to the Black Maria was lightweight champion Jack McAuliffe. It seems likely that Latham and Rector were involved in arranging the visit but this is not clear. In any event McAuliffe agreed to come to Orange with his sparring partner and box a few rounds for the Kinetograph camera. The demonstration was unimpressive, lackluster sparring with none of the blood-and-thunder look of a real prizefight, and was further marred by the fact that McAuliffe was badly out of shape, tipping the scales at more than one-sixty. He had stepped into the ring at his last fight "as fat as a prize hog," as one paper put it, and showed up in Orange looking no better. Whatever film was shot of the champion that day wasn't used.

In the end Otway and Rector set their sights still lower, arranging a six-round contest between lightweight contender Mike Leonard, a product of the tough Brooklyn neighborhood of Smoky Hollow down by the docks, and an unknown local scrapper named Jack Cushing. The upside was that the two men came cheap, Leonard costing one hundred fifty dollars plus expenses, Cushing only fifty. Cushing's obscurity also made it easier to arrange for the sixth round to end with a knockout—and it had to be arranged, for considering the brevity of the rounds a KO had to occur within a window of scarcely ten seconds. Neither Otway nor Rector are mentioned by name in any newspaper account of the event but they were clearly the ones referred to in the *New York Sun* write-up: "Two young businessmen conceived of the idea of having a prize fight reproduced by the kinetoscope, and in order to put the scheme to a practical test they made arrangements for the fight, and offered a purse of three hundred dollars for Leonard and Cushing to slug each other for. The fighters were informed at the time that if their 'go' wasn't on the level there'd be no money for them to divide." What Latham and Rector were after wasn't a fake fight or an overly stage-managed contest, but five rounds of hard-fought action followed by a sixth in which the lesser-known Cushing went down. That would be exciting. That would sell tickets.

With Otway tied up managing the Tilden Company's New York office, Enoch Rector would have taken the lead when the time came to film the Leonard-Cushing fight on June 11, 1894. The two fighters were ready to go that morning, the Black Maria was rotated into optimal position, William Dickson and William Heise were standing by to operate the Kinetograph camera—and the sun refused to come out. The first day thus proved a bust, as did the second and as did the third. As the little party continued to wait on the weather, Dickson and Heise experimented with filming under artificial illumination—arc lights and powerful magnesium lamps. The results were unsatisfactory. The Blair film they were using, coated with the most sensitive emulsion the company produced, required nothing less than direct sunlight flooding the subject.

Finally, on June 14, the day dawned clear and the fight went ahead. It was a private affair with just a few newsmen, Edison employees and invited guests present. Leonard, nicknamed "Beau Brummell" on account of his being such a snappy dresser, stepped through the door of the Black Maria wearing an expensive coat with velvet cuffs and carrying a walking stick, surpassing even Jim Corbett for resplendent dandification. "What d'ye think of the coat?" he had earlier said. "Gave up sixty for it.... I like to dress like a gentleman." He stood in marked contrast to the roughly dressed, working-class Cushing, who was noted to have "a very plain face." As Leonard would quip after the fight, "I generally hit 'im in the face, because I felt sorry for his family and thought I would select the only place that couldn't be disfigured."

The scene was stark, a low white platform, encompassed by a single rope, set against the Maria's black tunnel. The two men entered the ring. Leonard, stripped to a skimpy white breech cloth, took the left side. Cushing, in dark tights extending just below the knee, took the right. Their seconds, two for each man, positioned themselves on the apron on the back side of the ring. They all wore light shirts to be clearly visible against the black background. The referee wore a dark shirt and trousers so as not to distract from the action. To ensure that bulky padded gloves would not obscure the combatants' faces, small two-and-a-half-ounce gloves were used. There was no timekeeper. William Dickson, effectively the film's director, would serve that purpose. He would call for the combatants to commence after starting the Kinetograph camera and would signal the end of each round when the film ran out one minute later. There would be a seven-minute break between each round for the Kinetograph to be wheeled into the darkroom for the film to be changed.

What followed was a rough-and-tumble street fight in which Leonard and Cushing gamely swung at and wrestled each other—not much artistry but a lot of heart and big arcing right hands. As one observer noted, it was more like six separate fights than a single contest, the brevity of the rounds and the long rests in between ensuring that the two men came out fully refreshed and swinging each time. Edison himself was reportedly among the knot of onlookers, having come down from the Ogdensburg plant to attend. The inventor, whose tastes could run to the earthy, was said to have thoroughly enjoyed the battle, balling up his fists and punching along with the action.

If the film could be said to have a producer, it was Enoch Rector, looking on from behind the camera, his jacket stripped off as the interior of the Black Maria grew hot in the sunlight streaming in. At least five hundred dollars had been spent so far putting the fight together and Rector had to ensure that value was had for the money. That meant real fisticuffs, not tame sparring. According to one account of the contest, the fighters were instructed beforehand "to draw blood if possible."

No blood was drawn but the results were satisfactory just the same. Leonard and Cushing whaled away at each other for five rounds, no holding back, then in the sixth Cushing took an uppercut to the jaw and went down. This was probably cued by Rector or Dickson to ensure proper timing—*All right, boys, finish it up*—and involved a bit of playacting by Cushing in crumpling and laying still as the referee counted him out. It didn't matter. The important thing was that it looked real. And it did. As far as the average viewer would be concerned, the Leonard-Cushing contest was a genuine prizefight captured on film.

The Lathams and Rector now had a fight film but no way to show it, for the Kinetoscope in its present form held only twenty seconds of film. This was the duration of the productions Dickson was shooting, and for good reason, short films being cheaper for Edison to manufacture and cheaper to sell. With there being no commercial justification for Edison to develop a large-capacity Kinetoscope for exhibiting a full minute of film, Rector was invited to do the work himself. He did so starting in late June or early July, working at the Edison Chemical Works in Orange, where a manufacturing department for Kinetoscopes had just been established. It was here, in the shadow of the plant's three smokestacks, that Rector had his first good look inside the motion picture viewing machine.

The mechanical portion of the apparatus was crowded into the top of the cabinet. It consisted of a guide reel on the left and a toothed gear that advanced the film on the right, power coming from a belt attached to a small motor. In the center, under the film where it passed the eyepiece, was a wagon wheel-shaped rotating shutter that flashed the images intermittently to the eye and, underneath this, a light bulb for illumination. The rest of the cabinet, fourth-fifths of the interior space, was taken up with the looped strip of film. It was not fifty feet long as so often stated, but only around forty-two (which, if Rector had done a quick calculation, would have revealed that the Kinetograph's and Kinetoscope's real frame rate was substantially slower than the claimed forty-six per second). The film ran over a total of eighteen velvet-covered spools, nine at the top and nine at the bottom, back and forth and back and forth so that the celluloid loop would fit inside the confined space. All the spools were identical except the rightmost one on the bottom, which had a lever attached. Consulting the directions pasted on the inside of the cabinet door, Rector would have learned that it was for adjusting tension, which was very important. "Great judgment should be exercised in avoiding *over strain or slackness* of film," warned the paper, "as both are equally bad—when too tight the film is apt to tear, when too slack film is apt to ride up on reel edges and tear...."

After familiarizing himself with the machine's inner workings, Rector set about increasing its capacity nearly three and a half times so that it would hold one hundred fifty feet of film. He did this very simply by increasing to approximately sixty the number of spools over which the film had to travel, thirty at the top of the cabinet and thirty at the bottom. The resulting "Special Kinetoscope" was the same width and height as the regular model but three times longer, fully six feet to accommodate the increased number of spools. Rector built a prototype and prepared detailed drawings which he passed on to Edison's Kinetoscope Department to begin manufacture. He also wrote to the Edison Manufacturing Company to change Otway's earlier order of ten regular Kinetoscopes to "twelve Special Machines, similar to those which you are now putting through under our instructions.... It being understood that six of the above Machines are to be pushed right through."

Otway Latham in the meantime had leased a spacious storefront to serve as a Kinetoscope parlor, the first in what he and his partners hoped would grow into a chain. It was located at 83 Nassau Street near the southern tip of Manhattan, beside New York's first telephone exchange and near Brooklyn Bridge. It was not a prime location—not like 1155 Broadway in the heart of the entertainment district where the Holland Brothers opened the first Kinetoscope parlor. Perhaps Otway reasoned that locating their business in the male enclave of the financial district made sense, where men with a taste for prizefights and money in their pockets would be thick on the ground. Or perhaps it was simply a matter of convenience, 83 Nassau being literally just around the corner from the Tilden Company office he managed at 51 John Street. For Otway, impetuous and eager to get started, it may have been as simple as that.

A few miles to a west, in Newark, New Jersey, Bob Fitzsimmons was back on his feet, solvent again and his gregarious nature restored after his financial ruination and marital breakup the previous year. He had begun giving sparring exhibitions as he angled for his next fight, the earnings from which he hoped to use to form a new theatrical company to take on the road. He wanted that fight to be against Jim Corbett and in February 1894 he renewed his public call for a matchup—although he still lacked the wherewithal to post a hefty side bet to make the challenge official. He was not bluffing, he said. He wanted this fight, he was ready for this fight, and Jim could have it however he wanted. "I'll go into a room with him and fight him just for fun," Bob declared, "any way and under any rules."

Jim, busy with his play, had scoffed in return, dismissing Bob as a middleweight and not a legitimate contender for the heavyweight title. "Really, I wish people wouldn't mention his name to me," he said. "It makes me sick." When pressed, he issued a flat refusal, stating, "I will never fight Fitzsimmons unless he defeats some first-class man. Why doesn't he fight Choynski? If he defeats Choynski I will give him a chance." Then, after noting Bob's financial troubles: "Why don't he fight someone and get some money? I know that if I was flat broke I would fight for $1000. Why don't Fitz fight Dan Creedon? I think the latter is more than an even money chance and I will back him for $5000 against Fitzsimmons." Jim then put Bob entirely out of his mind and headed off for Europe.

Bob took Jim's pronouncements to heart and set out to satisfy his demands. On June 18, 1894, while Jim was touring England with *Gentleman Jack*, Bob faced Joe Choynski in front of three thousand spectators at a theater in Boston. It was only a six-rounder—a fight to the finish would not have been tolerated in Boston—but it saw plenty of action just the same, starting with Joe laying Bob out flat in the third. Bob was up and smiling at the count of nine and survived the round, then came out in the fourth to knock Joe down four times before the bell. The beating continued into the fifth, Joe gamely struggling back up after being dropped yet again, bloody now and hanging onto the ropes. He was one good shot away from being knocked out when the police sent to observe the contest decided it was too brutal and stopped it. Since Joe was technically still on his feet, the bout was declared a draw as per the pre-fight agreement. But it was obvious to everyone present that Joe had lost badly and that Fitz had won big.

With some real money at last in his pocket—his Choynski payday had been sixty-five percent of the four-thousand-dollar gate—Bob married Rose Julian on June 24, two months after his divorce had been granted and just one day after Rose gave her final performance and retired from the stage. She was startlingly changed from when Bob first met her when she toured with his show in 1892, having put on a great deal of weight. She had become a Rubenesque armful and Bob loved every pound. They were married in Newark with only a minister and maid of honor present and honeymooned at Asbury Park for two weeks. Some time thereafter, Bob's ex-wife Louisa and Rose's brother Martin Julian followed suit and got married, completing an eyebrow-raising arrangement that nonetheless resulted in two happy unions. Whatever bitterness Bob may have felt toward his former manager was now apparently forgotten. At the Choynski fight, it was Julian in his corner fanning him between rounds.

On August 11, an ad appeared in the *New York Clipper* seeking comedy acts for "Bob Fitzsimmons' Own Specialty Show" and soliciting inquiries from theater owners "wanting a Big Box Office Attraction." This new theatrical venture was a partnership between Bob and Captain Charles Glori, the Newark policeman who had helped him out the previous year. Listening to Bob's talk of the big money to be made from fighting and theatrical touring had inflamed Glori with visions of wealth. Convinced that the opportunity of a lifetime was camped in his spare bedroom, he lent Bob money to cover the Choynski fight expenses, then invested his savings in Bob's show, resigning from the police force to become his manager and partner.

It was a decision Glori and Bob would both come to regret.

"PRIZE FIGHT," the handbill announced under the photo of two pugilists squaring off. "Mike Leonard vs. Jack Cushing. 6 SLASHING ROUNDS. Faithfully Reproduced by THE KINETOSCOPE. Don't Fail to See It." And on the back, in case there was any doubt about the nature of the exhibition: "A Genuine Prize Fight Fought to a Finish by Professional Pugilists."

The Latham-Rector Kinetoscope parlor opened on Saturday, August 4, 1894, at eight o'clock in the morning, with Enoch Rector as manager, a barker bellowing outside—*Genuine prizefight! See the knockout!*—and handbills distributed throughout the neighboring streets. The shop window on the narrow street featured a display of a small prize ring and two chairs facing, a portrait of Leonard in one and Cushing in the other. Their Kinetographed fight was the sole attraction inside, in past the ticket window and red curtains, one round on each on the six massive Kinetoscopes that Rector had designed. Ten cents got you this far and a view of the first round. To see the rest of the fight cost a nickel per machine. It was an irresistible attraction—*Fiercest battle ever fought! Both men out for blood!*—and was good value, the same price as the Kinetoscope parlor uptown for films three times as long, a full minute rather than a mere twenty seconds.

One of the few critical reviews of the films, written by a supposed fight aficionado in the *New York Sun*, observed that the contest was a "disappointment" because it failed to demonstrate any of the finer points of boxing, the "hits and stops executed with the clearness and precision expected in the mechanical perfection of the imaginary prize fight...the theoretical blows from the shoulder aimed with the deliberate intention of a rifleman, and hitting squarely and truly as a bullet." Instead it was "more like a common street fight, a brachial rough and tumble.... The real hits...are scarcely perceptible and can be picked out from the general mass of punching only with difficulty. The final blow, the knock-out, isn't a long straight delivery as we read about, but a half-arm jolt partially shielded from the spectator, and the beaten man drops like a log while many will wonder why." The upshot wasn't that the fight appeared fake but rather that it was too real, with a "rough and blurred aspect" that obscured the artistry of boxing that the unnamed critic was evidently eager to see. Fortunately for the Lathams and Rector, this was a minority opinion. The fact that Leonard and Cushing were seen to be punching hard, mixing it up, was far more important. That, not a display of finesse, was what most people wanted to see.

The idea of exhibiting prizefights on Edison's Kinetoscope, conceived by Gray Latham just three months before, was off to a good start. With the parlor at 83 Nassau Street doing brisk business, it was time for the Lathams and Enoch Rector to think big, to aim for the top.

For their next film, they wanted Jim Corbett.

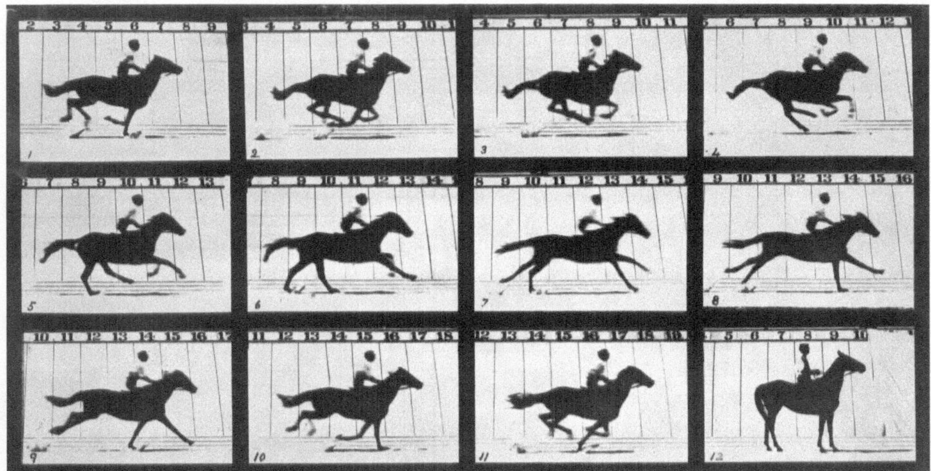

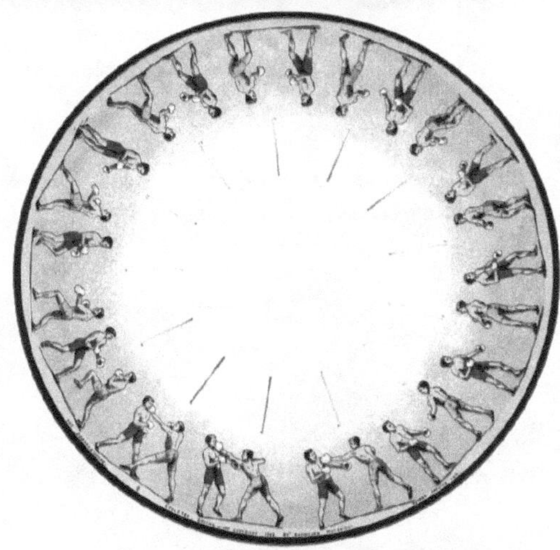

ABOVE: Eadweard Muybridge's "instantaneous photographs" of Leland Stanford's racehorse Sallie Gardner, 1878.
LEFT: Hand-painted disk, "Pugilists," 1893, used by Muybridge on his Zoopraxiscope to recreate motion.
BELOW: Muybridge's original "Pugilists" motion study photos, 1887, from which the images on the disk were traced.

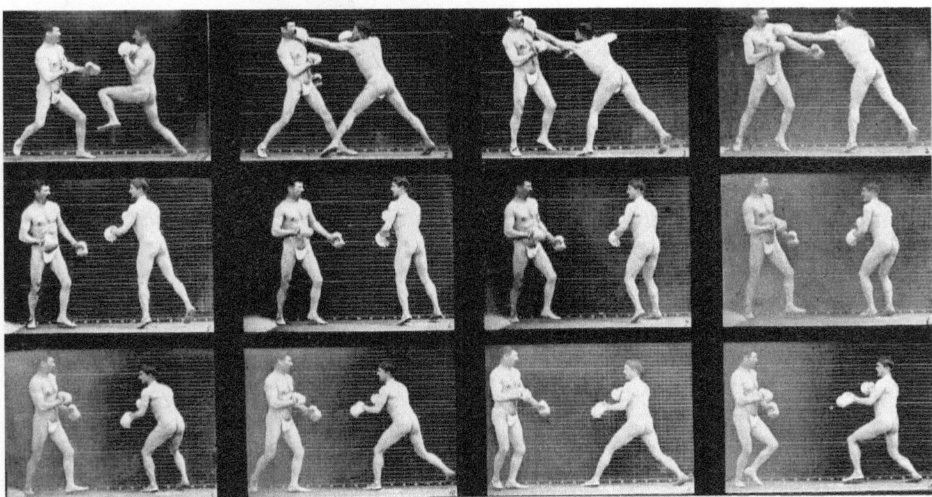

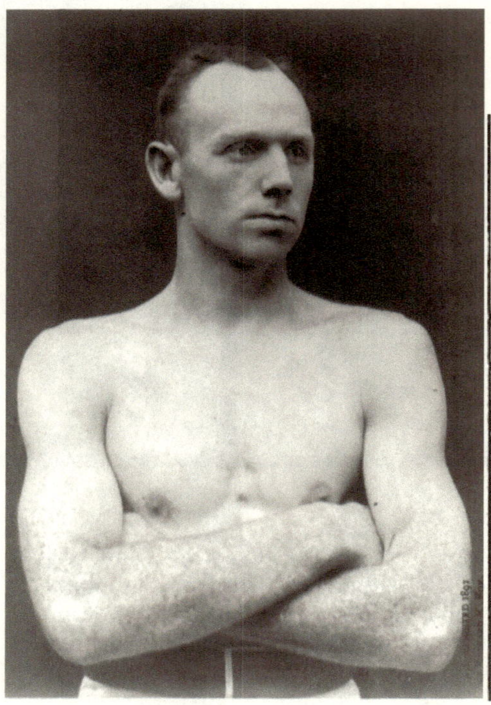

ABOVE: Bob Fitzsimmons in 1891; Dempsey-Fitz fight ad, *New Orleans Daily Picayune*, Jan. 9, 1891. RIGHT: Fitz, the new middleweight champion, in 1892. Note the superb development of his back, the result of his early years as a blacksmith.

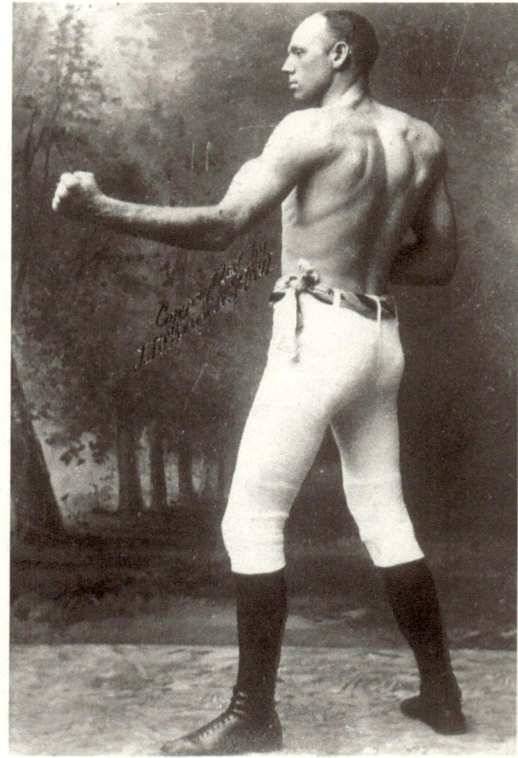

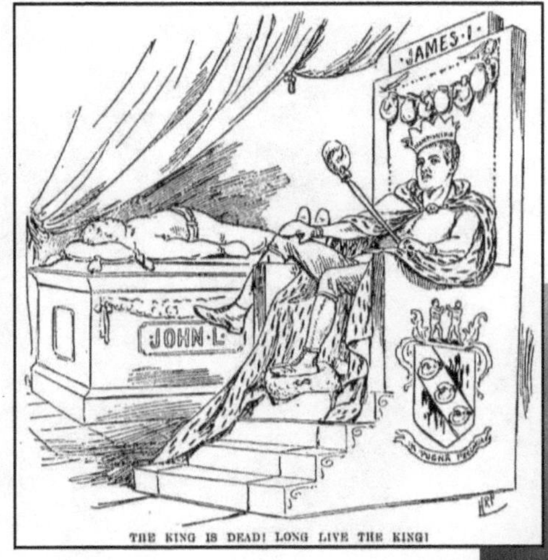

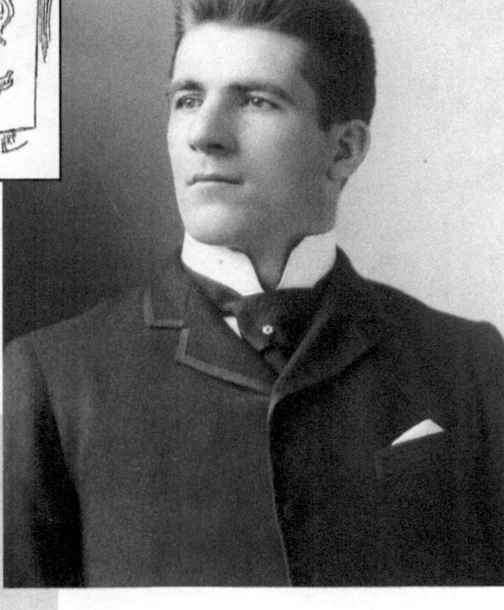

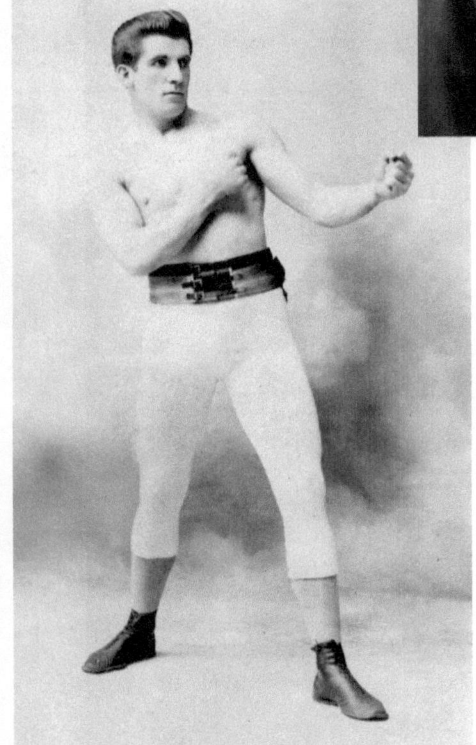

TOP: Cartoon celebrating Jim Corbett's defeat of John L. Sullivan to become heavyweight champ: "Long live the king!" (*Chicago Tribune*, Sept. 9, 1892) ABOVE: Corbett the well-dressed gentleman in 1892. LEFT: Corbett in 1894, sporting the hairstyle that earned him his second nickname, "Pompadour Jim."

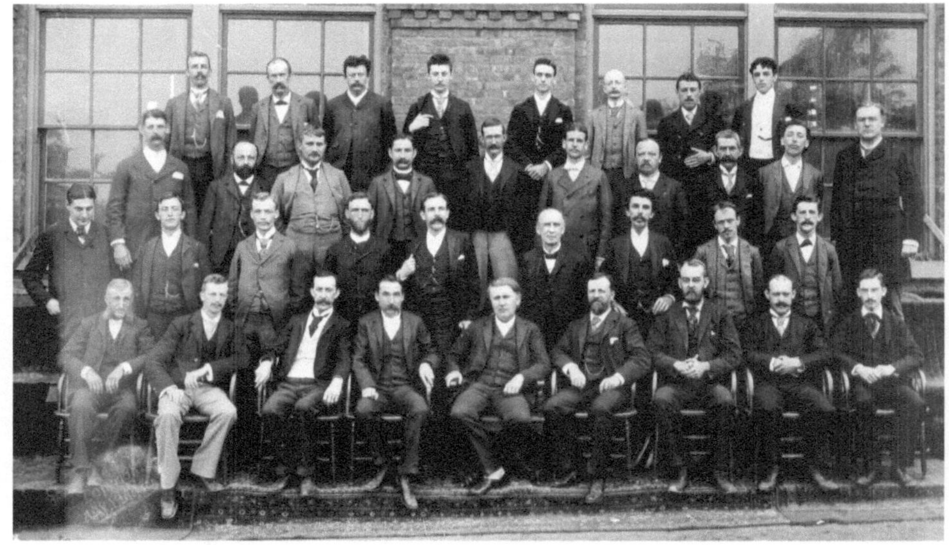

Edison's staff, 1893, with blowups below of W.K.L. Dickson (left), Edison (right), William Heise (bottom left) and Fred Ott (bottom right). Also in the photo: Charles Brown and John Ott (first row, first and fourth from left).

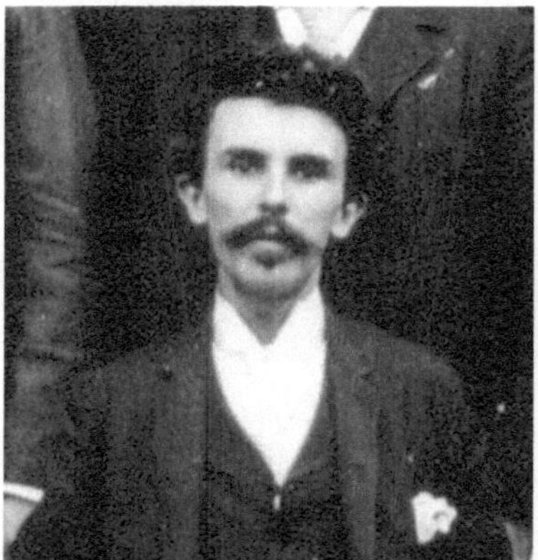

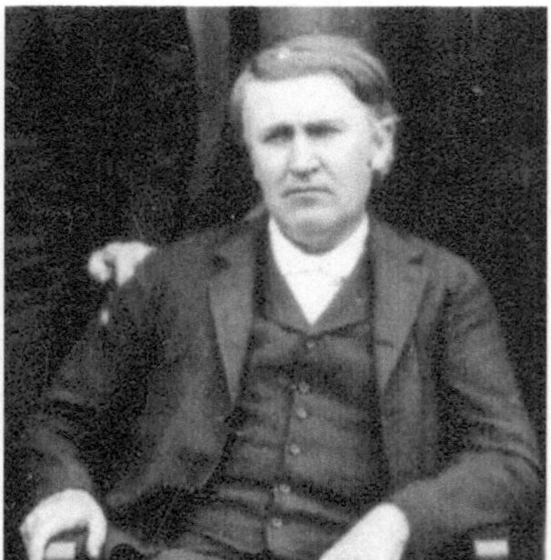

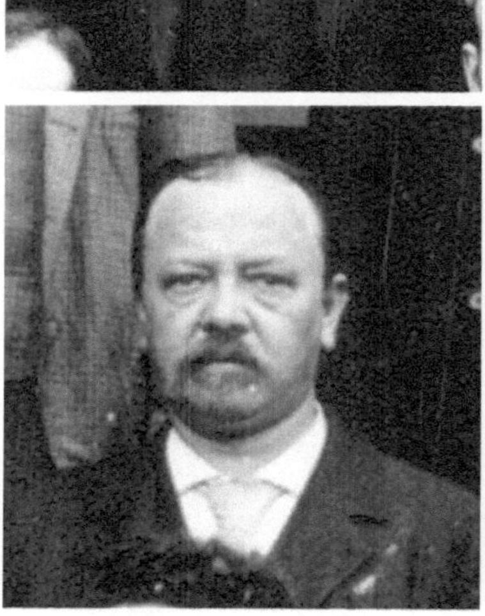

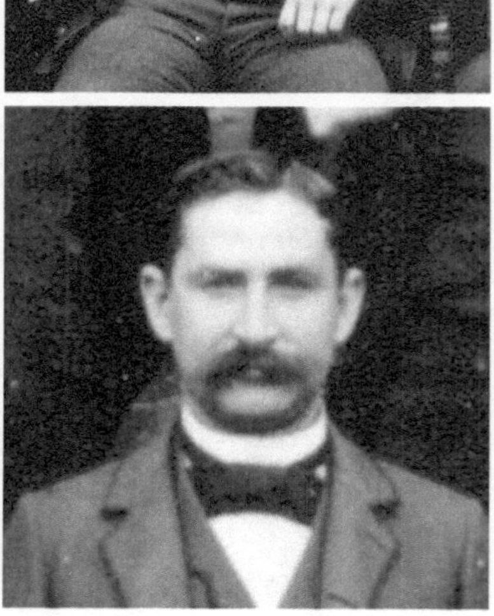

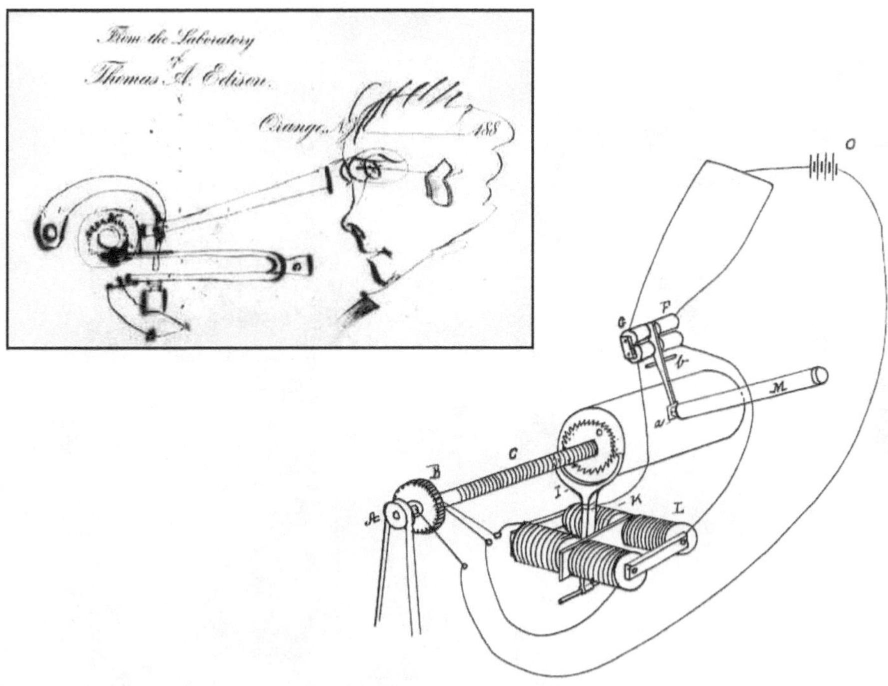

Edison initially planned to use a Phonograph-like device to record tiny images on an emulsion-coated cylinder. TOP: An undated Edison sketch showing how the images would be viewed. (TAED NA010A01) ABOVE: The cylinder Kinetograph, drawing from Edison Caveat 110, Oct. 15, 1888. (TAED PT031AAA) BELOW: "Cylinder 3," with which the cylinder design reached a dead end. The images on the attached celluloid film are Fred Ott's *Monkeyshines*. (Edison National Historical Park, photo by author)

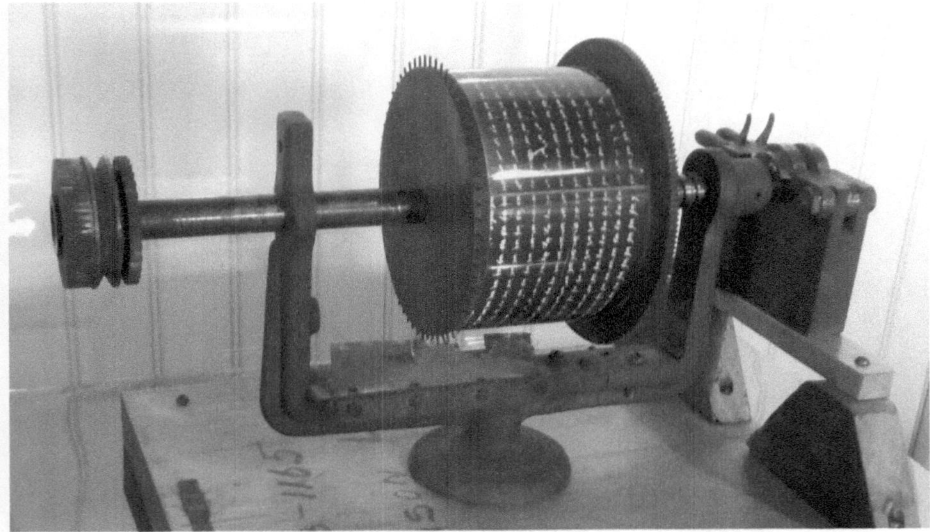

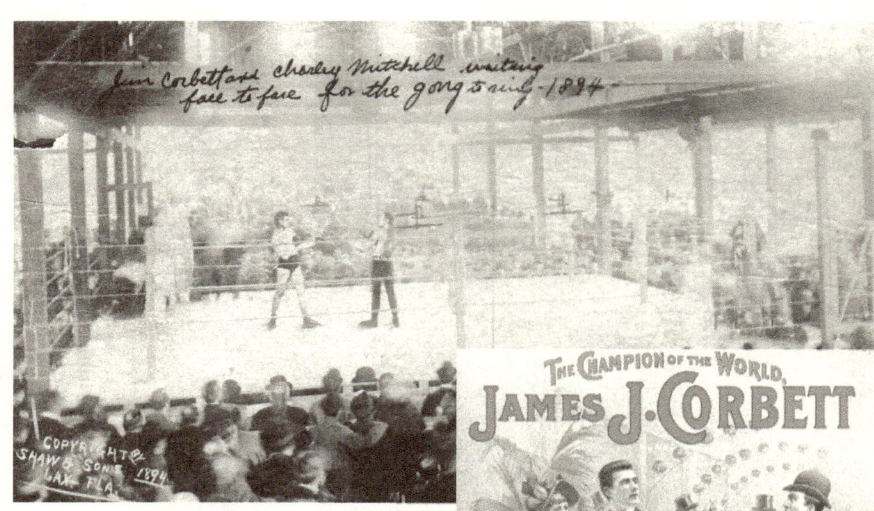

ABOVE: Corbett (left) defends his title against Charles Mitchell, Jan. 25, 1894. RIGHT: Poster for Corbett's play *Gentleman Jack*: "I'll defend the championship of America against the world!" BELOW: 1894 lithograph showing Corbett meeting the heads of Europe—which never actually happened.

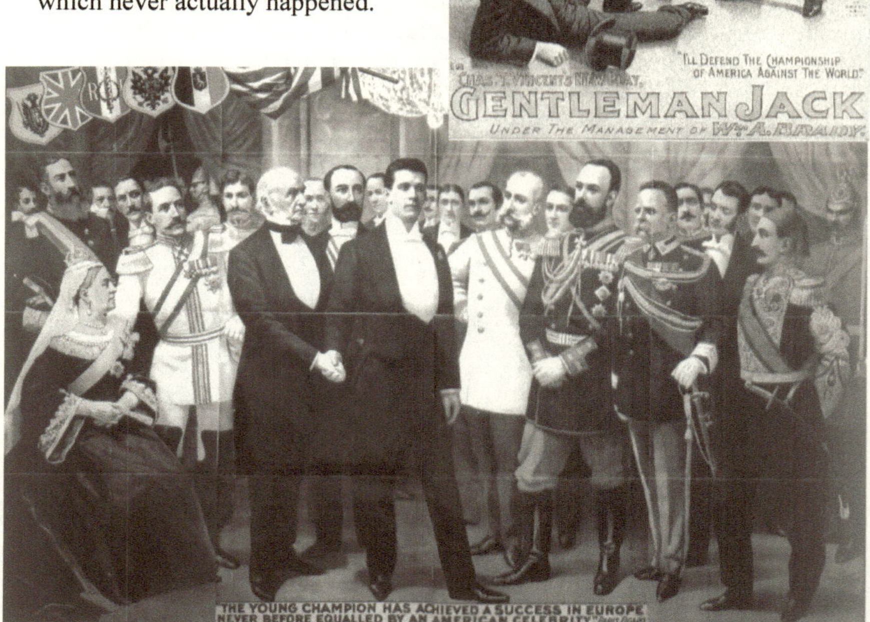

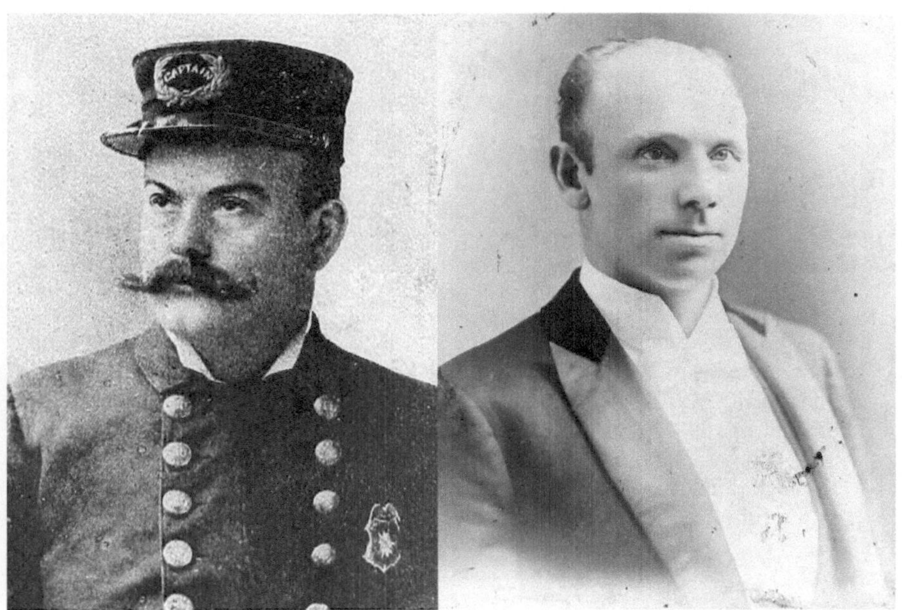

ABOVE: Bob Fitzsimmons (right) in the early 1890s; Captain Glori (left), Fitz's manager in 1892-93. BELOW: Fitz in a fight pose, 1892; an ad for his vaudeville show, *Philadelphia Inquirer*, April 9, 1893. Fitz's act included bag punching, sparring and occasional on-stage horseshoeing.

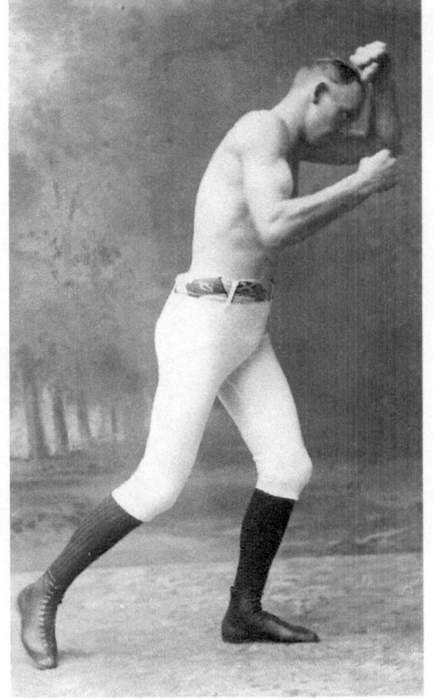

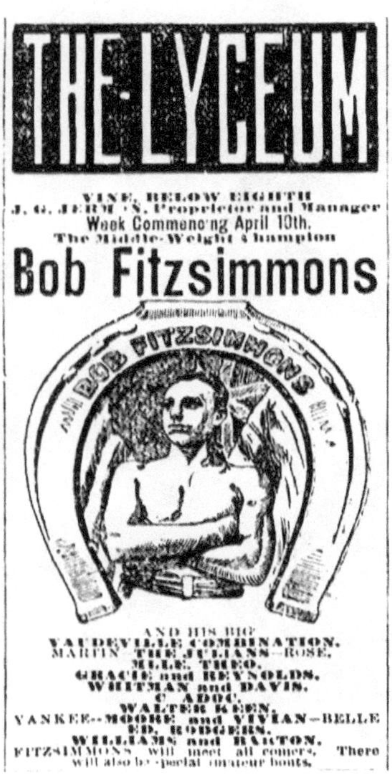

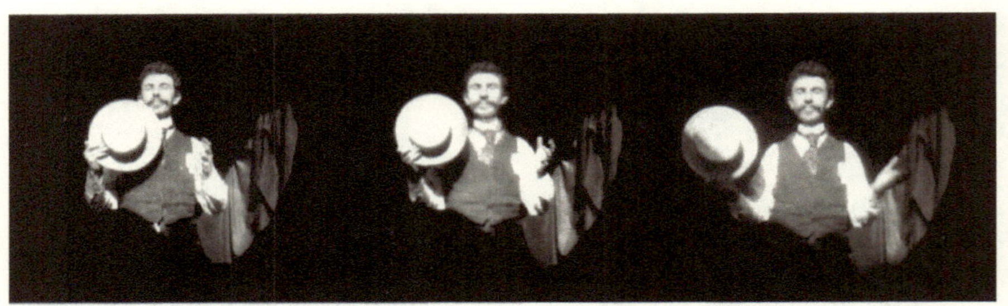

ABOVE: William K.L. Dickson in the first Edison motion picture shown to the public, May 20, 1891. The film ran horizontally and had a round frame. BELOW LEFT: Eugen Sandow in Dickson's first commercial film, shot Mar. 6, 1894. Film orientation was now vertical, with rectangular frames and sprocket holes on both sides. BELOW RIGHT: Edison's "Kinetographic Camera," patent application filed Aug. 24, 1891. Note how the film runs in a straight line—and under strain—from reel to reel.

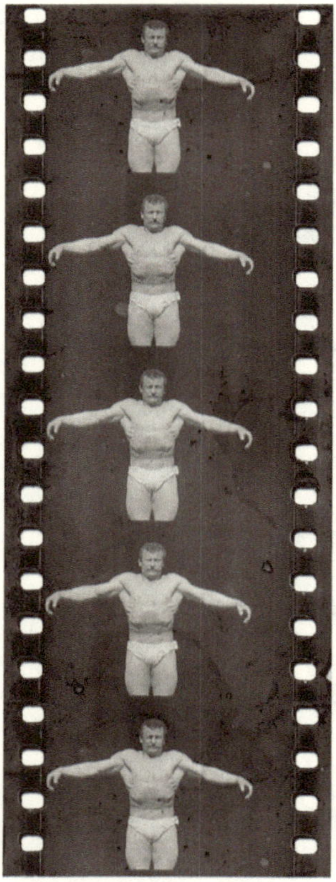

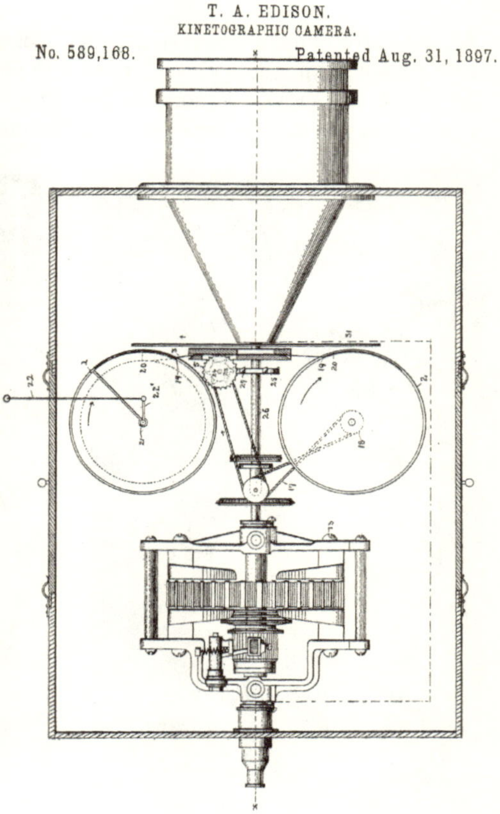

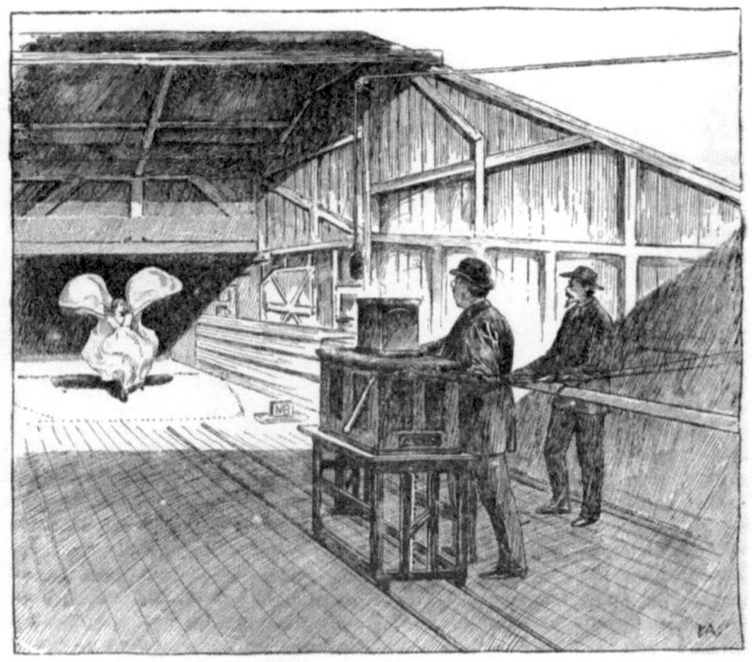

ABOVE: Filming dancer Carmencita in the Black Maria. William Heise operates the Kinetograph as Dickson looks on. (*Frank Leslie's Popular Monthly*, Feb. 1895) BELOW: Holland Bros. Kinetoscope Parlor, opened in New York in April 1894. The Edison films customers viewed were scarcely twenty seconds long. (*Electrical World*, June 16, 1894)

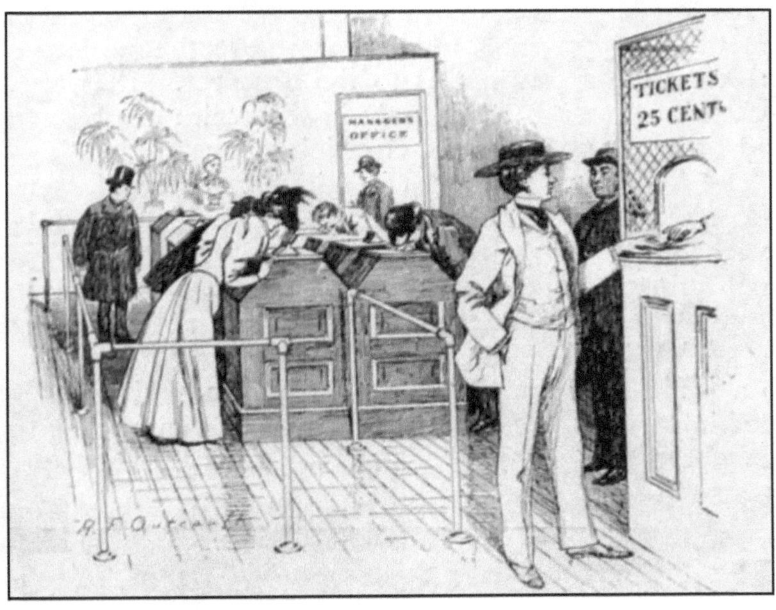

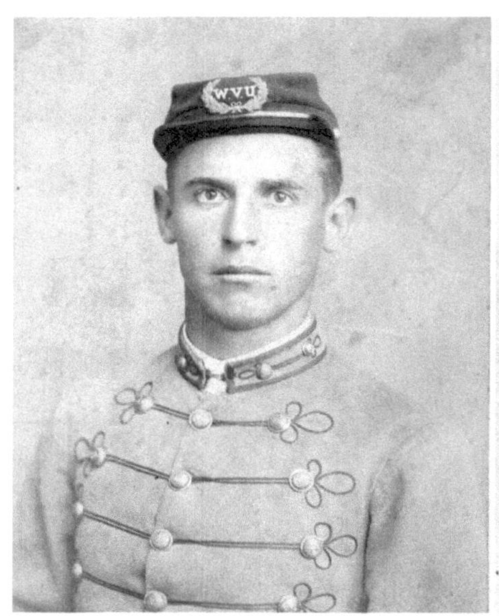
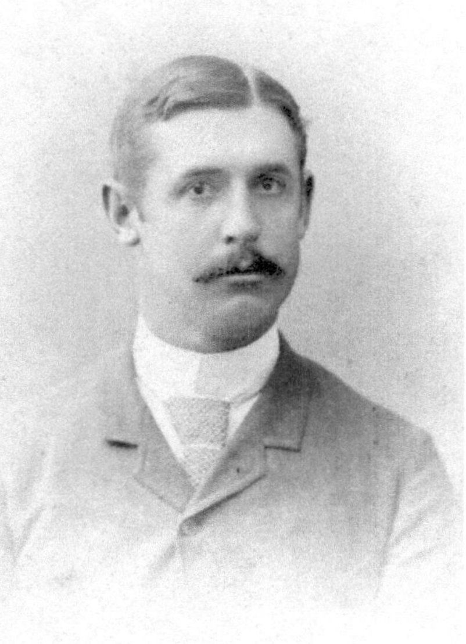

ABOVE: Enoch Rector in the cadet corps at West Virginia University, 1883 (left) and in Cordoba, Argentina in the late 1880s. (Courtesy Sasha Chermayeff) BELOW: Woodville Latham as a Confederate officer in the Civil War (left) and as he appeared in the 1880s when he taught at WVU.

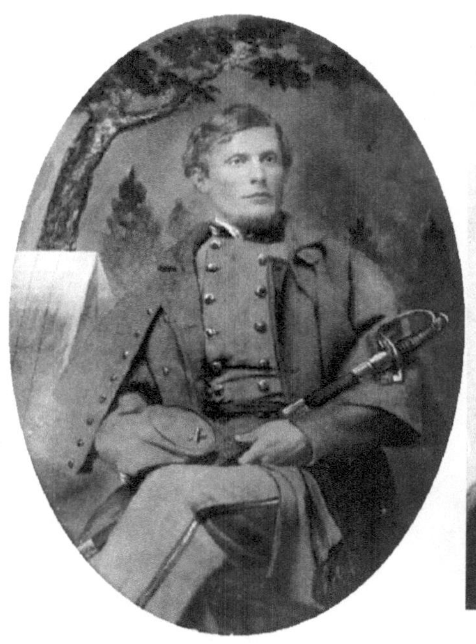
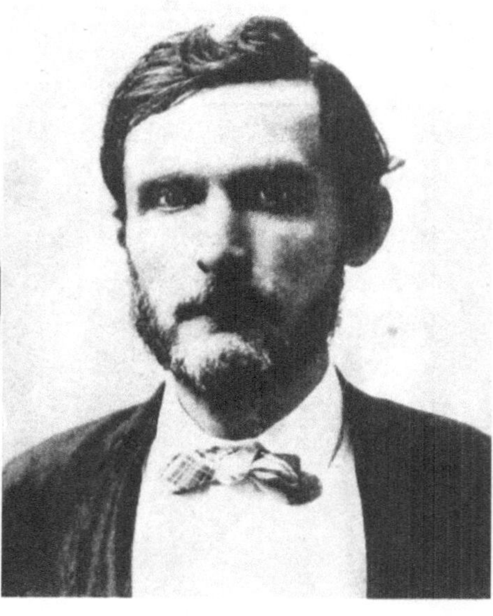

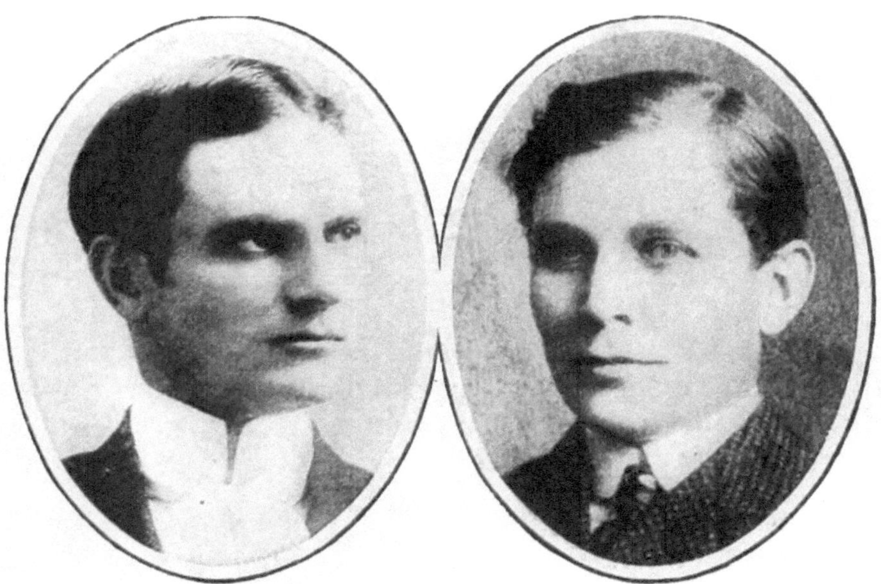

ABOVE: Otway (left) and Gray Latham (right). BELOW: Gray (left) in an 1896 watercolor by his wife Rose O'Neill; a young Otway (right) at the beach with an unidentified friend. (Both courtesy David O'Neill)

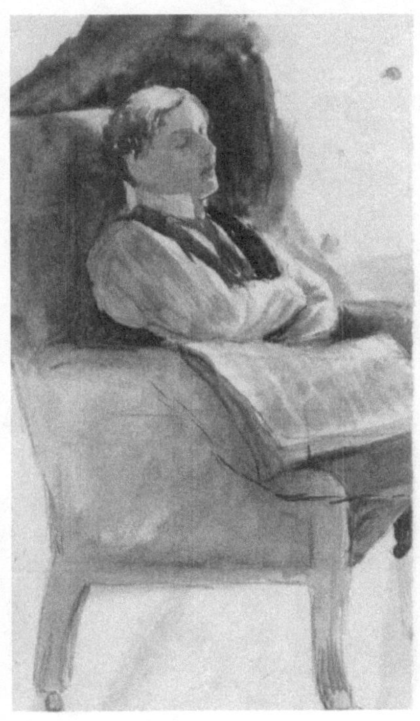

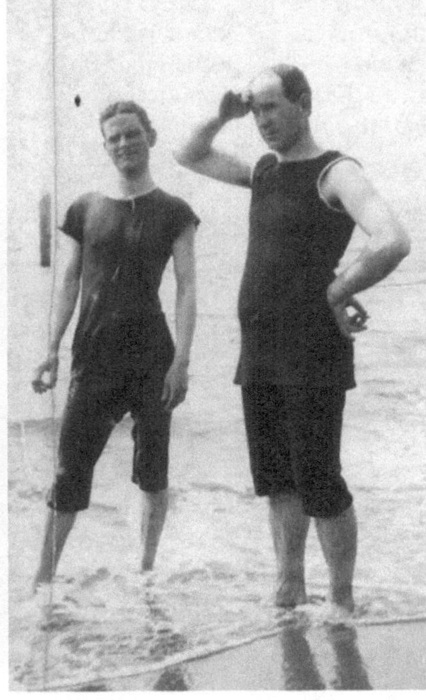

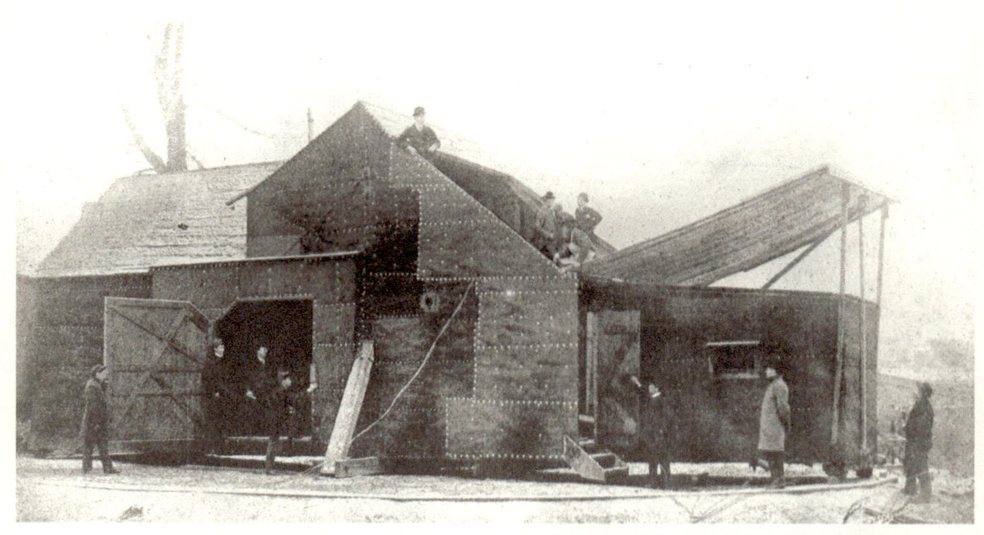

ABOVE: The Black Maria, Spring 1894. In the open roof, William Dickson is third from right, Otway and Gray Latham possibly first and fourth. (Edison National Historical Park) BELOW: Mike Leonard, hired by the Kinetoscope Exhibiting Co. for their first film. RIGHT: Frames from the Leonard-Cushing film, June 14, 1894, Leonard on left. It pushed the movies from twenty seconds to a full minute.

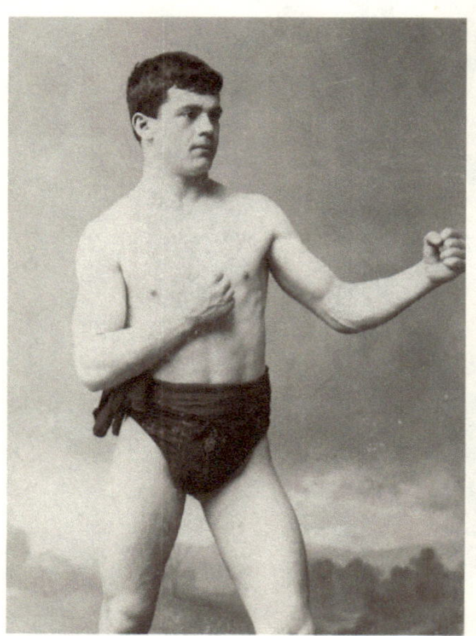

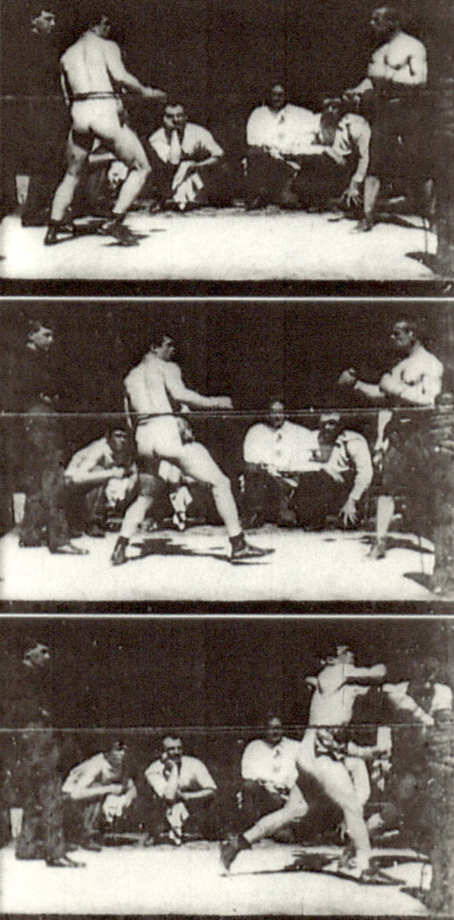

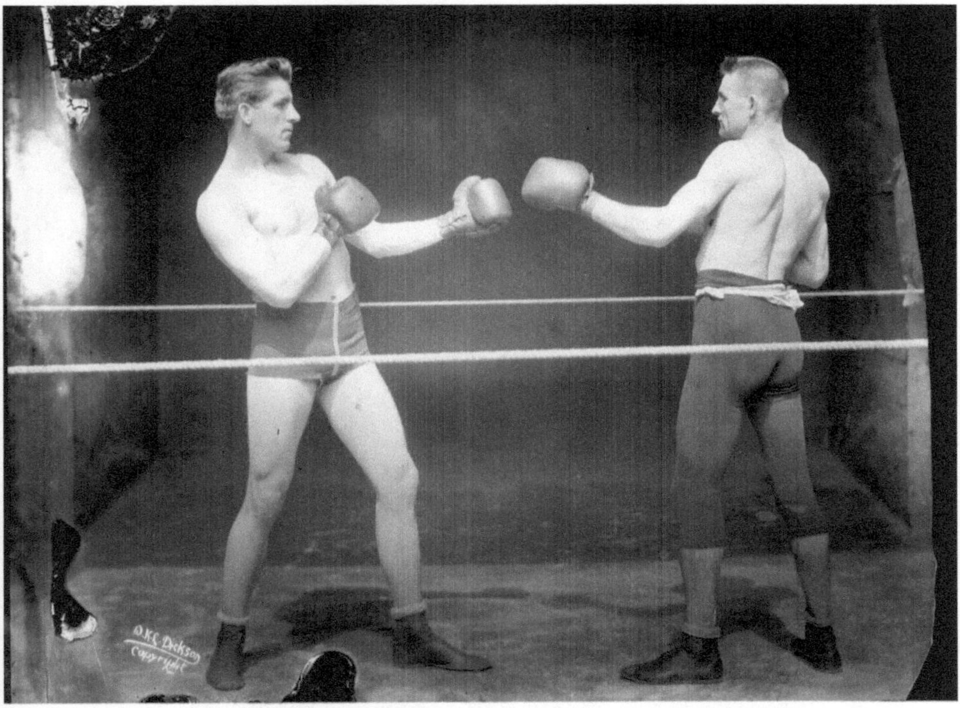

ABOVE: Jim Corbett poses for a still photo with Peter Courtney at the filming of the KEC's second fight film, Sept. 8, 1894. (Edison National Historical Park) BELOW: The large-capacity Kinetoscope developed by Enoch Rector, a six-foot-long behemoth that could accommodate films of more than one minute. The machine on the right is labeled "Corbett Fight, 1st Round."

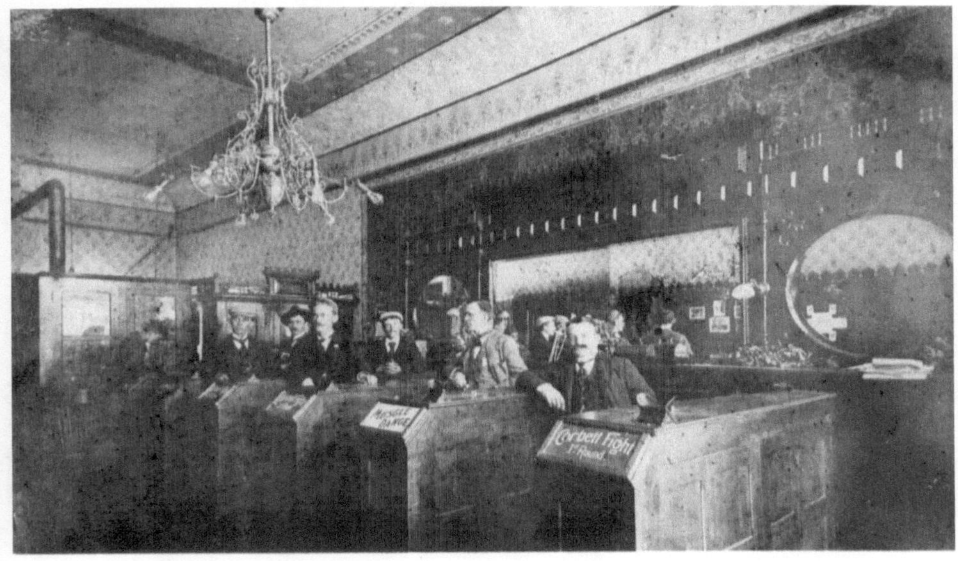

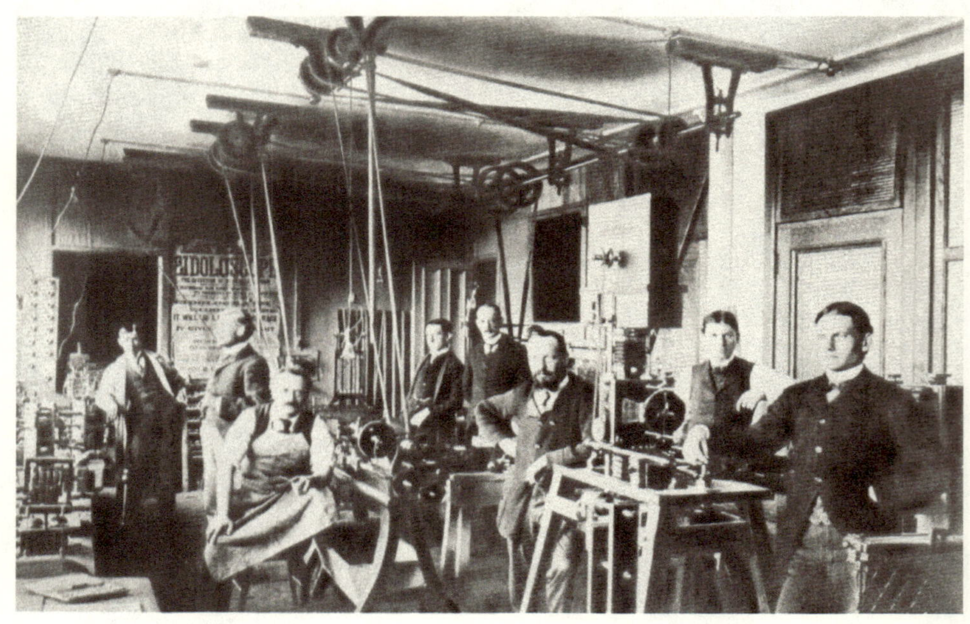

ABOVE: The Lathams' workshop, 1895, Gray and Otway Latham at right, Eugene Lauste at center with elbow on projector, Emile Lauste at far left, Woodville Latham gazing out window, Emil Kleinert seated.
BELOW: The Lathams' first film, shot in early March 1895, showing Emile Lauste (on ground) and Emil Kleinert sparring, Gray Latham (left) refereeing as Eugene Lauste (center) and Woodville Latham look on.

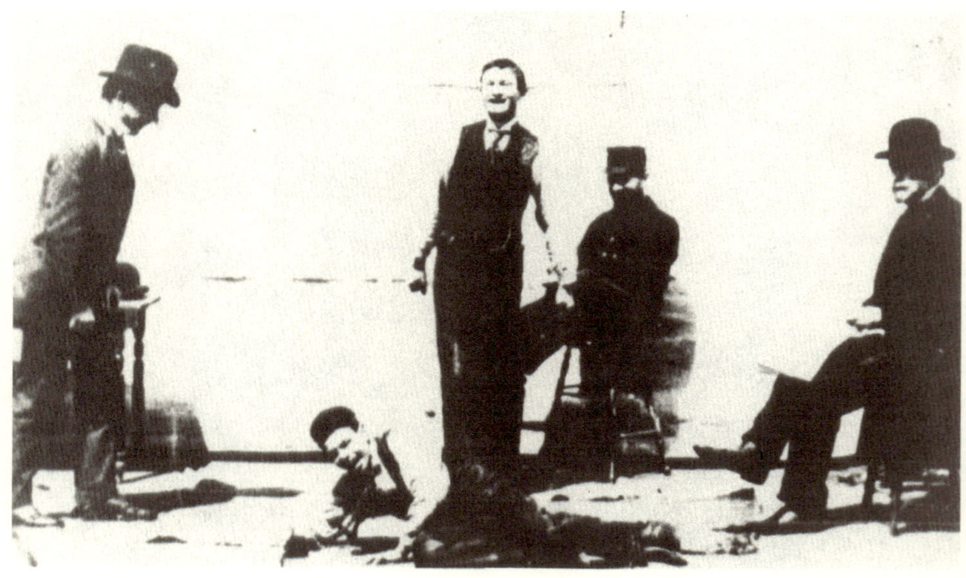

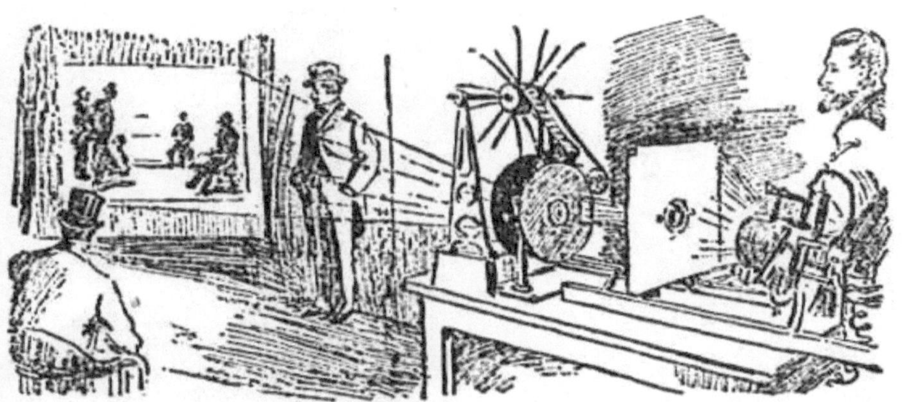

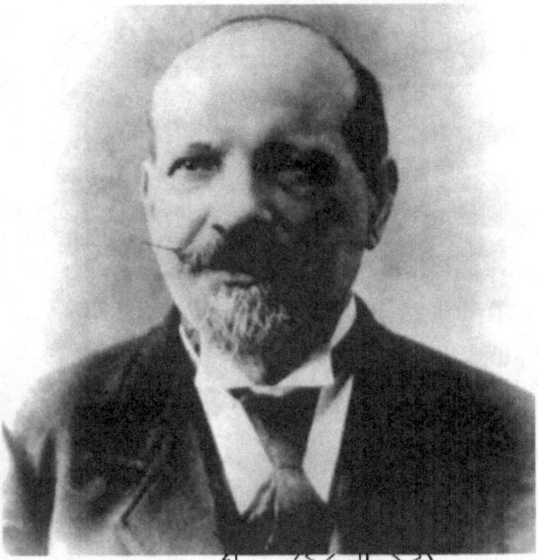

ABOVE: Woodville Latham unveils his projector, April 21, 1895, the first demonstration of film projection in North America. LEFT: Eugene Lauste, the man who built the machine. BELOW: The Lauste-built Eidoloscope projector, from Woodville Latham's June 1, 1896 patent application.

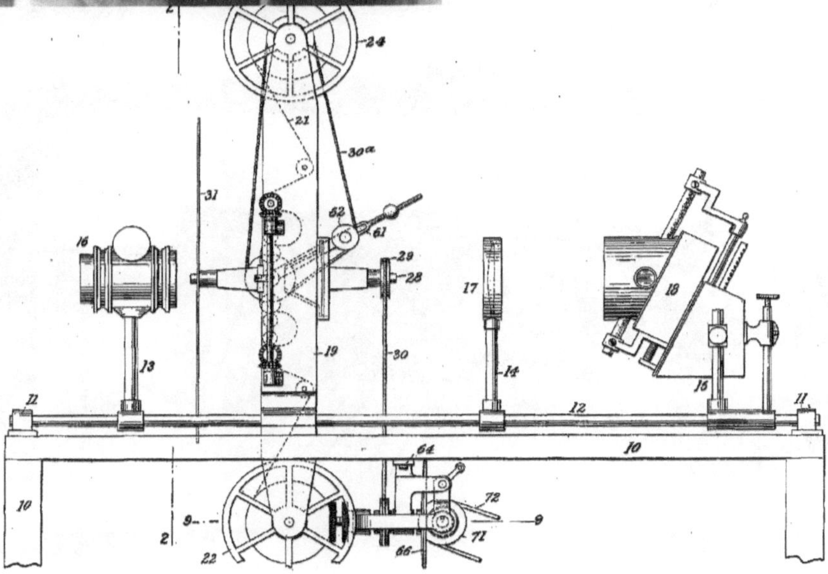

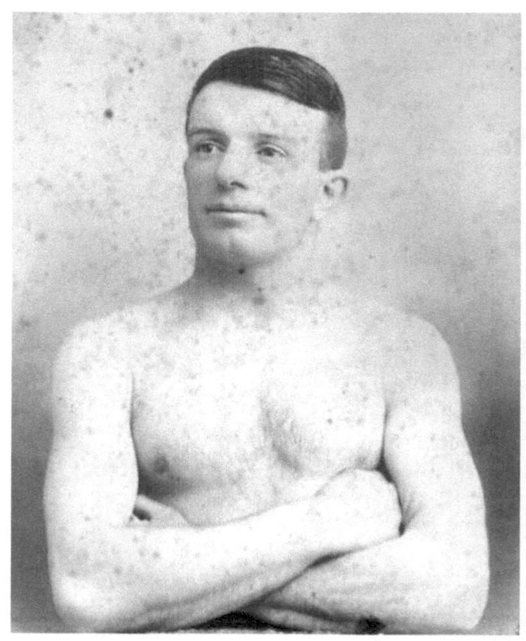

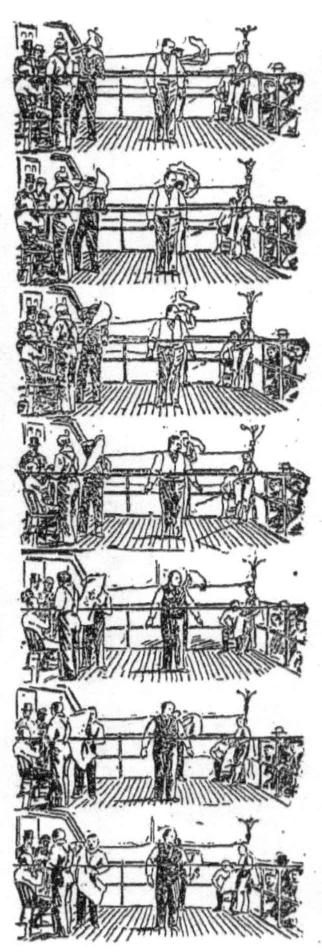

ABOVE: Albert "Young Griffo" Griffiths. RIGHT: Illustration of sample of Griffo-Barnett fight film, now lost. (*Brooklyn Daily Eagle*, May 8, 1895) BELOW: Illustration of the opening shot of the movie, as projected on a canvas sheet at the film's debut on May 18, 1895. (*New York World*, May 26, 1895) The eight-minute film was the longest made to date—and the first commercially projected movie in history.

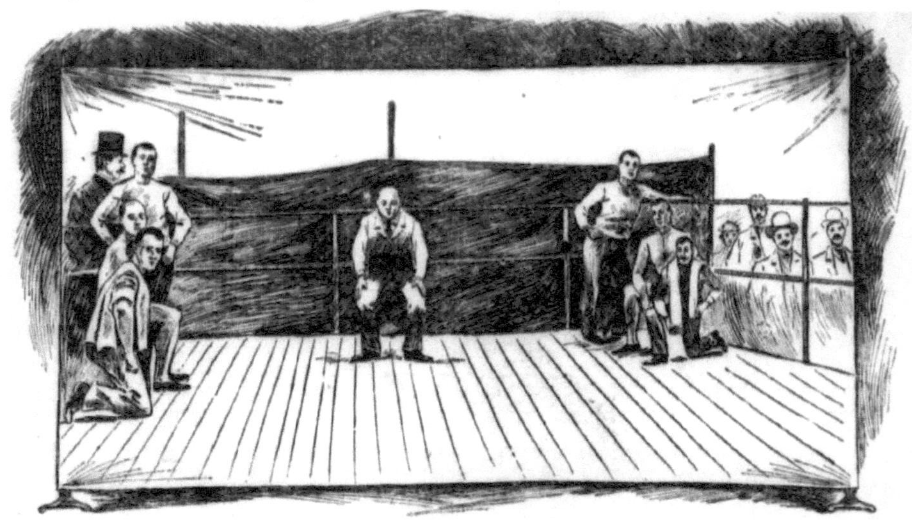

CHAPTER 11

CORBETT-COURTNEY

JIM CORBETT RETURNED FROM EUROPE on August 1, 1894, his ego bruised, his bank balance depleted and his plans for a new play of his own creation, *Modern Society*, permanently shelved. His Old World tour with *Gentleman Jack* had been a bust, the play turning into a money-loser soon after its successful opening night at the Drury Lane Theatre. The company was fifteen hundred pounds in the red when it left London after three weeks and the losses continued to mount as it toured Liverpool, Sheffield, Birmingham, Manchester and Leeds. "The English public was fight-minded enough," William Brady would later write in his autobiography *Showman*. "They'd stand round and gape at the man who had licked Charley Mitchell as blatantly as any yokels at an Iowa railroad depot. But they wouldn't pay money to see him in action on the stage."

Gentleman Jack wound up its European tour earlier than expected, Paris being the only bright spot, and the cast was bundled off home on a second-rate steamer. "Corbett made a mistake as to the English public," stated disgruntled actress Florrie West, who refused the substandard transportation and paid her own passage home. "He thought the people there would dance attendance on him as they do at home, but he was mistaken.... The English public were disgusted with the idea of a pugilist appearing at high class theaters. They did not, therefore, patronize Gentleman Jim liberally. The sporting fraternity also did not take to Corbett kindly, because he considered himself too much of a gentleman to associate with them."

Upon his return to New York, Jim made his way to his new home on East Eighty-Eighth Street for a much-needed rest. When *Gentleman Jack* opened for a new season in Trenton, New Jersey two weeks later, audiences were greeted with an immense full-color lithograph outside the theater showing Jim surrounded by admiring kings and queens and heads of state of Europe—none of whom he had actually met. At the bottom was the money quote: "The young champion has achieved a success in Europe never before equalled by an American celebrity—*Paris Figaro*." Corbett's European failure had been turned into a raving success.

Enoch Rector was seeing good business at the Nassau Street Kinetoscope parlor he managed, the six machines showing the Leonard-Cushing fight in steady use from eight o'clock in the morning until seven at night. A single attraction, however, would not draw in customers indefinitely. To keep the enterprise going and fuel expansion, follow-up fight films with bigger names had to be made.

On August 9, Otway Latham, identifying himself as the president of the "Photo-Electric Exhibition Co.," sent Jim Corbett's manager William Brady a letter informally offering a purse of $15,000 for a fight to the finish between Corbett and Peter Jackson, the one adversary in the champ's past that he had not bested. The contest would have to take place in front of the Kinetograph, Otway stated, at a location of the company's choosing and in a ten-foot ring. "[S]ome quiet nook in the North would suit us very well," he added when the offer was released to the press and reporters came calling. "We think the authorities would not interfere, as it is merely a business venture, and we would not violate any laws."

Although receptive to the idea of a Kinetographed contest, Brady rejected the specifics of the proposal, stating that the purse for a Corbett-Jackson matchup would have to be at least $25,000 and that a ten-foot ring was simply too small. Otway didn't attempt to negotiate or sweeten the deal—not surprisingly, for the whole thing was likely a stunt to drum up publicity and get Corbett's attention. Instead the two parties held more serious talks in private, during which the realities were no doubt explained of what fighting for the camera really entailed.

What Corbett and Brady learned was that a real fight wasn't needed, only a fight that *looked* real, much like the staged battle Corbett performed every night in his play. It would take only half a day of his time and scarcely ten minutes of actual work in the ring, and in return he would stand to make a great deal of money. A phony purse would be offered to build up the event as a prizefight but that wouldn't be the real payment. Corbett would instead receive a royalty check of one hundred fifty dollars a week for every set of Kinetoscope machines showing the fight, machines that would soon be appearing in parlors across North America and then around the world. A company was at that very moment being formed to make it all happen.

It was a lucrative proposition and Corbett seized it. He signed an agreement with Otway and assisted in rounding up a suitable opponent—not a legitimate contender, for this was not a genuine prizefight, but a compliant unknown who could be "knocked out" on command.

Peter Courtney of Trenton, New Jersey was the man who was chosen. He had been in the professional fight game for a year and a half, since moving east from his native Pennsylvania, but his nose was already smashed flat and he had the suitable look of a bruiser. His reputation consisted of beating a man claiming to be the heavyweight champ of New Jersey and surviving four rounds against Bob Fitzsimmons during Bob's recent stop in Trenton meeting all comers. (He did so, one observer noted, "by clinching and sprinting.") With his confidence boosted, Courtney had written to Corbett, appearing in Trenton with *Gentleman Jack* at the same time as Bob, asking for work as his sparring partner. His letter was received just when Corbett needed an opponent for the Kinetoscope venture. After a quick sizing-up by Corbett's sparring partner John McVey, Courtney was hired. His supposed payday would be two hundred fifty dollars, the loser's portion of the fictitious five-grand purse. In reality he would get only twenty-five dollars—still a large sum to Peter Courtney, who drove a freight wagon for a living and likely earned less than two dollars a day.

With Corbett signed, the fight film venture now took a major step forward with the incorporation in the middle of August of the

Kinetoscope Exhibiting Company of New Lebanon, New York, starting capital $30,000. Samuel J. Tilden would be president of the outfit; John H. Cox would be secretary; Otway Latham and Enoch Rector directors. Gray Latham also became fully involved in the enterprise at this point, quitting his salesman job to become vice president of the new company. Within days Otway placed an order with the Edison Manufacturing Company for seventy-two large-capacity Kinetoscopes, to be delivered in batches of six as new parlors opened. Anticipating booming worldwide business, company letterhead was printed listing branches in Boston, Chicago, St. Louis, San Francisco, London, Paris and Sydney—none of which actually yet existed.

The "quiet nook in the North" where the Corbett-Courtney fight would be held was of course the Black Maria at the Edison lab in Orange, where virtually all Kinetograph work to date had been done. William Dickson would have welcomed the chance to film Corbett in action, for he had planned that very thing months before as his second commercial effort following the filming of Eugen Sandow. "The next celebrities to be photographed," the *New York Sun* had reported on March 11, 1894, quoting an unnamed Edison source, "will be Corbett and Mitchell engaged in an exciting boxing contest. For taking prize fights and athletic contests, when movements are lively and the contestants do not have to leave a circumscribed space, the kinetograph promises great results."

The fight went ahead on September 7, 1894, after a one-day postponement on account of an overcast sky. Corbett and his entourage met Enoch Rector and Otway and Gray Latham at the Hoboken ferry shortly after eight o'clock in the morning. A handful of reliably credulous newsmen had been invited as well, foremost among them reporters from the *New York Sun* and the *World*. Corbett's presence at the ferry terminal soon attracted a crowd, including a curious policeman who inquired where he was going. "Oh, I'm just taking a little run out into the country," said Corbett, playing the part of the crafty, law-skirting prizefighter.

There were more gaping onlookers and more questions on the ferry and on the walk on the other side to the train. Jim just smiled and kept his mouth shut. If word got out that he was heading to Orange "to knock out a stiff," as he confided to the man from the *Sun*, the contest might be prevented and the whole party arrested. The possibility was reportedly making the Lathams and Rector nervous—so much so that they suggested they split up to leave the train. Half the party, Corbett among them, accordingly disembarked one station short of their destination and continued on by trolley car. The rest, including Rector and the Lathams, got off at Orange.

Here they met up with Peter Courtney, who had stopped off at a restaurant for breakfast. The twenty-six-year-old seemed cool and relaxed as they proceeded to Edison's lab, expressing confidence that he wouldn't be such an easy mark for the champ. When asked if he was afraid that Corbett would "knock his head off," he casually replied, "Naw! He's got to hit hard to do that, for me nut is well set."

They arrived at the Edison facility and, after some explanation, were admitted through the gate. After a stroll around to kill time, the cry went out of "Here he comes!" Corbett and his party had arrived.

"How do you do?" said Corbett, shaking Courtney's hand.

"Howdy?" replied Courtney.

"It's a nice day for this little affair of ours," observed Jim.

"Ain't it!" was the laconic reply.

It was eleven o'clock when the two fighters were told to get into their togs, Jim changing in the old photography building, Courtney in a nearby shed. When they emerged, stripped to the waist, Courtney appeared to be in somewhat better condition, his stomach hard and carrying no extra fat. Corbett had not trained seriously for nearly eight months, not since his fight with Mitchell, and looked a bit soft.

They made their way to the Black Maria. It had been recently enlarged, a fresh covering of tar paper secured to the exterior with gleaming rows of large-headed nails, and was "the most dismal-looking affair" the visiting sportsmen had ever seen, reminding them of a huge coffin. They stood by as the structure was rotated to get the sun shining in through the open skylight at the optimal angle. Then Dickson emerged—"a nervous little man with a black mustache, a slight goatee and a linen duster," the *World* reporter observed—and invited them to enter.

"My, but this is small," said Corbett, ducking though the side door to behold the ring. It was fourteen feet across, the sides extending all the way to the walls, which were padded. There was no raised platform as with usual rings. It was simply a space on the floor, the pine boards well rosined, a single rope demarcating the front and the back. Unlike in the Leonard-Cushing contest, the space visible to the camera behind the ring was not left empty. Several men were instructed to stand here to enhance the effect that this was a real prizefight with spectators looking on.

The fighters took their respective corners and their seconds laced on the gloves—five-ounce gloves, not the two-ouncers Corbett said he preferred. He and his second, Joe Vendig, had had a discussion about it earlier for the benefit of the newsmen, Jim saying that he needed the smaller gloves to be sure of knocking out Courtney— "doing the job clean," as he put it. "You will cut this man up awful, Jim," Vendig cautioned, "and then people would say it was brutal. Better wear the big mitts." Corbett, emoting deep concern, acquiesced.

They waited. And waited. Some problem had occurred with the camera. Dickson would be attempting this time to get nearly a minute and a half of action out of each roll of film, which meant a great deal of tinkering to push the Kinetograph to its absolute limit. As the minutes ticked by, the interior of the Black Maria grew hotter and Corbett started to sweat. Finally he shifted his chair out of the direct sunlight. Courtney, mirroring everything Corbett did, followed suit. Most of the fifteen-odd onlookers crowded inside had their jackets off now and were mopping their brows.

The problem with the Kinetograph was finally fixed. It was eleven-forty, the sun nearly at its zenith. "Are you ready?" asked Dickson, his hand on the lever. The fighters nodded and rose to their feet. Dickson started the camera and the referee called "Time!"

With the rounds so short and each second counting, there was no cautious circling, no preliminary feeling-out as the machine buzzed to life. Courtney threw himself at Corbett with both arms swinging, determined to give the Kinetoscope people the fight they wanted and earn his twenty-five dollars. Corbett slipped the clumsy blows with ease, laughing as he dodged and weaved, for Courtney was almost entirely unskilled as a boxer. To his credit, though, the wagon driver was game, flailing away and absorbing Corbett's return shots right up until the film ran out and the camera fell silent, signaling the end of the round.

A long wait while Dickson and William Heise pushed the Kinetograph into the darkroom to remove the exposed roll of film and load a fresh one. Then the second round began, Courtney resuming his wild rushes. Corbett let it go on through the second, then got serious in the third and dropped Courtney with a hard left and a right. He stood back as Courtney struggled to his feet and the film was used up.

"Did I hurt you?" Jim asked as they returned to their seats and the Kinetograph was wheeled back into the darkroom.

"Naw," said Courtney. "There's a buzzing sound in me head, but I guess it's the heat."

The fourth round saw Jim coasting to stretch out the fight, for six rounds had been ordered and so six rounds had to be filled. Then he laid on the mustard again in the fifth, softening Courtney up and this time drawing blood from his nose—just enough for authentic effect without being gory—then doubled him over with a pile driver into the gut. The wait for the Kinetograph to be reloaded was not long enough this time for Courtney to recover. He came out looking weak in the sixth and Jim quickly floored him. A feeble attempt to rise and Jim dropped him again, this time for good. As in the Leonard-Cushing fight, the knockout was perfectly timed and obviously coached, Courtney collapsing within a window of perhaps fifteen seconds. There was just enough film left in the camera to record the referee counting him out.

Immediately after the fight, Gray Latham—"a good looking young man with a very wide-brimmed straw hat," the *World* called him—made a show of presenting Corbett with a check for $4,750 and having him sign a receipt. It wasn't as much as he earned for defeating Sullivan two years before, Corbett observed, but "a nice little bit of cold turkey" just the same. He and Courtney then returned together to New York for a champagne lunch before Jim headed off to the theater for his nightly performance of *Gentleman Jack.*

"I tell you want it is, boys," said Courtney, guzzling the bubbly like beer, "this here stuff is liable to change your color if you take enough of it." He ended up thoroughly drunk—the first and only time that day, one observer dryly noted, that Peter Courtney was truly knocked out.

The five-ounce gloves hadn't helped at all. There was legal trouble just the same and it came within days. On September 11, 1894, a newly empanelled Newark grand jury was instructed by the judge to investigate reports that two prizefights had been held at Thomas Edison's lab and to issue indictments "against the principals and spectators" if it was determined that the law had been broken. The next day a deputy sheriff showed up at the lab in Orange to gather evidence and question Edison—who was fortunately not there, preoccupied as usual at his Ogdensburg mining operation. Alarmed, Dickson sent a warning cable to Enoch Rector in New York.

The story was promptly communicated to the press and appeared in the papers the next day. It was free publicity, after all, evidence that the Corbett-Courtney contest had been a genuine prizefight, an illicit, blood-stirring sensation that the public would certainly want to see. And what could the law do about it? Absolutely nothing. That was the beauty of the fight film idea. For all the laws against the staging of prizefights, the legal impediments that made it so difficult to hold a live battle, there was not a single law anywhere in the Union barring the exhibition of prizefights on film.

"I shouldn't be surprised if they tried to pull us all," said Rector when a *New York World* reporter stopped by the Nassau Street parlor to get his reaction. "However, I think it can be easily proven that we have violated no law. The affair was conducted for scientific purposes in every sense of the word, and was neither rough nor brutal in any of its details. Yet there are those who have curiously emphatic views on such matters and they may try to make trouble for us." Was he worried? Not at all. He had "no apprehension of the result of the Grand Jury investigation or prosecution."

As for the talk of Edison's involvement, Rector assured the reporter that the inventor "had nothing to do with the affair from beginning to end." This surely was not true. Edison may not have been present but he certainly knew of the battle. When Edison himself was questioned, however, he issued an adamant denial. "I was not there," he said. "I did not understand a prizefight was to take place.... I should certainly not permit any fight to a finish in my place under any consideration."

The not unwelcome controversy filled the Kinetoscope Exhibiting Company's sails as it prepared for the debut of its Corbett-Courtney fight film. Production commenced on the seventy-two additional Kinetoscopes that had been ordered, copies of the film were made and a second New York parlor was opened at 587 Broadway. Six new machines were delivered to this location on September 14, after being inspected by Rector, and the parlor quietly opened its doors the following week. The press remained silent on the opening—a wise precaution considering the looming threat of indictments—but the new film proved a hit just the same, the daily take regularly reaching one hundred eighty dollars according to Otway. *Corbett and Courtney Before the Kinetograph*, as the film would come to be called, would become the most successful film by far of the Kinetoscope era, featured in scores of KEC-owned and sub-agented parlors that would open in cities across the country, then in Europe and the Antipodes via the Continental Commerce Company, which secured the rights for overseas distribution. As for the grand jury investigation, it went nowhere. No indictments were issued and the matter was eventually dropped.

Down at the original Nassau Street parlor, meanwhile, things were not going well. First there was a rash of film breakages that necessitated closing the shop until the temperamental Kinetoscopes could be fixed. This would be an ongoing problem with the large-capacity machines used for fight viewing. It would eventually be solved by replacing their cheap Edison motors, which tended to generate fluctuating speeds, with more reliable units made by Perret. There was also an emerging problem with the shop itself. For the fact was that Otway had chosen the location unwisely, in a down-town business district that emptied of people at the end of the day. As curiosity in the Leonard-Cushing exhibition was satisfied, sales therefore dried up, for there was no constantly renewed entertainment traffic here as on Broadway, no visitors strolling about late into the night in search of amusement. By the middle of September, one month after opening, the Nassau Street parlor was seeing a major drop-off in earnings. By the end of the year it would be closed, replaced by a buffet restaurant, the Kinetoscopes moved elsewhere.

Finally, there was the matter of the Lathams. It was becoming clear that Otway and Gray, so likeable on first acquaintance, were not sound men of business. They were spendthrifts and playboys, more interested in carousing about town than attending to work—and possibly on occasion dipping into the till. Otway may have begun neglecting his duties as manager of the Tilden Company's office on John Street as well. On August 15 he stated in *The Pharmaceutical Era* that business at the New York branch was "picking up nicely." Six weeks later, the same publication noted that the office had recently closed.

Most troubling of all, though, was that the Latham brothers, joined now by their father Woodville, had begun talking about moving beyond the Kinetoscope to projecting films on a screen. It was a visionary idea that made perfect sense, for while a Kinetoscope moving image could be seen by only one viewer at a time, a projected image could be simultaneously shown to a whole theater of people. It conflicted, however, with the business they were currently involved in, the Kinetoscope Exhibiting Company business, which was investing more than $20,000 in single-viewer Kinetoscope machines. Considering the blithe character of the Lathams, they may not have even realized this, so focused were they on their next grand idea and on having a good time. But their old friend Enoch Rector did. And so did Samuel Tilden and John Cox when they found out.

On August 24, 1894, the five principals in the Kinetoscope Exhibiting Company—Tilden, Cox, the Latham brothers and Rector—held a stockholders' meeting to sign over to the company all rights in the Kinetoscope venture that they individually held. In the weeks that followed, with this new corporate authority, changes began to take place, Rector taking over from Otway in dealings with the Edison Manufacturing Company. When confusion inevitably resulted, Rector issuing one set of instructions and Otway another, Samuel Tilden wrote to EMC general manager William Gilmore that "for the future all business for us relating to the equipment, inspection, receiving, shipments, etc. of Kinetoscopes, will be conducted by Mr. E. J. Rector, whom I have appointed with authority to act."

Otway was being pushed aside. This made Gilmore and in turn Edison uneasy, for all their dealings had been with Otway, his signature most recently on the contract for the purchase of the seventy-two Kinetoscopes now being built. To avoid possible legal complications, Gilmore wrote KEC secretary Cox asking for written authorization from Otway transferring his Kinetoscope order, made in his own name, to the company. Cox responded the next day with a lengthy explanation—and no written authorization from Otway.

"My reasons for not desiring to ask him for any such paper at the present time must be obvious to you," Cox wrote; "it might be construed as an intimation that we thought Mr. Latham did still have some individual ownership in the contract and thus probably give him an idea of the matter which he does not entertain at present.... I write to you personally as you understand the matter from beginning to end and I also feel that you can arrange this matter with absolute safety to Mr. Edison's interest without asking us to do anything that might raise a question as to our rights in the matter." Cox then concluded with something cryptic: "There was an election in this State on the 6th. 'Nuf said."

The election in New York the previous week had been a Republican landslide, the Democrats losing the governorship and more than half their seats in the Assembly. Was Cox signaling to Gilmore that a similar shift was in the offing at the Kinetoscope Exhibiting Company—that Otway Latham and his brother Gray were about to be ousted by Tilden, Cox and Rector, three votes to two?

Because that is precisely what would happen before the end of the year.

CHAPTER 12

CHALLENGE ACCEPTED

BOB FITZSIMMONS WORKED HIS WAY along the row of big Kineto-scope machines, peering into one after another at the moving pictures of the boxers inside. They were in rich sepia tones of reddish brown and mahogany, beautiful to look at, and were wonderfully clear when the film wasn't too jumpy. Fitz could make out Corbett's grin and the play of the light on his milk-white torso, even the facial expressions of the spectators behind the fighters' seconds squatting at the edge of the ring. But the fight itself didn't impress him. It may even have irked him. For here was Corbett taking on the rawest of stiffs while continuing to ignore Bob's own repeated challenge.

Bob would subsequently refer to the film when asked if he really thought he could beat the heavyweight champ, so elusive with all his jabbing and ducking. "Think he will keep jabbing me back out of reach, eh?" he said. "Well, now I want to tell you Corbett is no jabber; if you don't believe it go look at his kinetoscope fight with Courtney. You won't see a jab in it. His blows are all side blows and ducks. I am the jabber . . . only twice the power that others put in it. It knocks out, the same as Sullivan's side swing used to do. As for ducking, I think I must know something about it myself, else how have I got through so many fights without a black eye or any mark about my face?"

In the middle of August 1894 Bob traveled down to the Olympic Club in New Orleans to face Dan Creedon, the second fighter Corbett said he had to beat to be considered worthy of a shot at the title. The articles stipulated a weight limit of one hundred fifty-eight pounds, undermining the fight's value for determining heavyweight contention—a possible indication of the dodging game Corbett was playing, for if Fitz won, the whole thing could be dismissed as a middleweight bout. "I've Fitz where I want him," Creedon crowed after the articles signing. "He can't whip me at 158 pounds. He will be too weak." He planned to soften Fitz up with kidney blows, Creedon revealed in the lead-up to the contest, then finish him off with his specialty, a right-hand smash to the heart. "I invented that blow.... As a knockout blow I consider it better than that for the point of the jaw."

Bob thought otherwise. Creedon, he said, "just cannot beat me; that is all there is to it. I am going to win, and will do it as quick as I can."

It was quick indeed, Bob forgoing his usual caution to send Corbett a message. He put Creedon to sleep in the second round, laid him flat out, arms outstretched. The sand of the ring saved Creedon's skull from the board impact that could make knockouts so severe in this era but it was still several minutes before he revived. He complained afterward that Bob had fouled him with something called a "wrist blow," a shot to the side of the head with the bare wrist, an old Australian trick that Jimmy Carroll had warned him was one of Bob's favorites. "Fitzsimmons worked this blow on me in the last part of the first round," claimed Creedon. "It was as if I had been hit with a club." No one paid much attention. It was just a loser "squealing."

Following the knockout, while Creedon was still being restored to consciousness in his corner, the referee called for quiet and Bob issued a fresh challenge to Jim Corbett, this time offering a serious side bet of $10,000. The Olympic Club, eager to host the contest, immediately cabled Corbett the challenge together with an offer of $25,000 for the purse.

Jim once again brushed the challenge aside. "I will say nothing about Fitzsimmons at present," he responded. "He must meet Steve O'Donnell first before I will notice him." He followed this up with an insulting letter, printed in newspapers across the country, stating that it was a "lie" that he had promised to fight Bob if he defeated Choynski and Creedon. Bob had yet to prove himself as a contender, Jim asserted, since the heavyweights he had faced so far, Choynski and Maher, were "second-class." "[T]here is no power on earth that will make me notice you, until you have defeated Steve O'Donnell, and all further talk from you I will consider simply a bluff."

It was now clear that the champ was playing a game, putting Bob off by throwing one name at him after another, first Choynski, then Creedon, and now Jim's current sparring partner O'Donnell. "He wants me to meet Steve O'Donnell, eh?" Bob angrily replied upon his return to New Jersey to open his new show at the end of September. "Let O'Donnell ship Maher, or Hall, or somebody I have done; then I will fight him. I shall put my fist in Corbett's face yet." He followed this up at the beginning of October with a more carefully worded letter that was published nationwide in the press.

"To James J. Corbett, Champion of the World," it began. "According to all customs and recognized rules of the prize ring, I believe I am entitled to challenge you for the world's heavyweight championship. I hereby do so in the most business-like manner possible by posting $1,000 as a forfeit for you to cover.... I have consulted all the best sporting authorities in America on this point and they all agreed that you are obliged to fight me or lose the championship by default.... I, however, pray you will not lose the championship by default, but will go into the ring and defend it like a man, as your predecessor, John L. Sullivan, did, who threw up his theatrical engagements to fight you. I certainly shall not allow any of my theatrical engagements to interfere with my defense of the honored title if it comes to me. [Signed] Robert Fitzsimmons, Champion middleweight of the world."

Jim shot back with a public letter of his own, dismissing Bob as having "no right to a place in my class. I propose to enter the prize ring once more and then retire, whether I win or lose. I want my next contest to be with the best man in the world. I do not consider you that man and I do not propose to meet you and then, after having defeated you, be told by your friends that you are only a middleweight after all. I care nothing for the past history of the ring or its obsolete rules. My future is in my hands and I do not propose to be told by you or any other man living what I am to do."

I care nothing for the past history of the ring or its obsolete rules.... This was arrogance of a whole new level. It added to the groundswell of anti-Corbett feeling now rising, a groundswell that Jim himself fueled with outbursts that included denigration of the revered former champ. "Sullivan had always more mouth than courage," he hotly responded when John L. stated the obvious that Jim did not want to put his title and in turn his big theatrical earnings at risk. "[Corbett] seems to be blind to the fact," the *New York Herald* thundered back, "that champions existed before he lived and will no doubt do so after he has been forgotten. With two battles to his credit Corbett now assumes the role of dictator. Custom and rules are kicked aside by him as he would an old pair of boxing gloves.... Nothing but ridicule would have been meted out to the champions of the past had their tactics been those of the present holder of the international title. When challenges were issued and deposits made as a guarantee of good faith satisfactory answers had to be given and fights arranged.... Fitzsimmons may be on the high road to abject pugilistic humiliation, but his challenge will have to be met, and met in the spirit of fair play, by Corbett, or the redoubtable 'Jim' will be compelled to announce his retirement from active participation in arenic displays."

Jim had gone too far. The press was calling him "childish," "foolish" and "yellow" and even his friends were speaking against him, making further belligerence unwise. And then, from the president of New Orleans' Olympic Club, came an alarming ultimatum: "It was in the Olympic club that both you and Fitzsimmons won your greatest honors, and it is now within the province and the duty of the Olympic club to declare Robert Fitzsimmons the champion heavyweight of the world should you persist in refusing to accept his challenge.... In the event that you do not answer and accept the challenge of Robert Fitzsimmons by Thursday, October 4, we will declare Robert Fitzsimmons the champion heavyweight of the world."

The cable must have made Jim livid. Who was the Olympic Club to unilaterally declare Fitz champ? There was every reason to believe it would actually do it, however, and that the sporting world, now against him, would go along. He therefore relented. On October 2, Jim sent a cable to the theater in Connecticut where Bob was appearing accepting his challenge. Captain Glori received the message and excitedly rushed it to Bob. "We have made him come off his high horse, and have brought him to his milk," Bob exulted after dancing a jig.

The meeting between the two fighters to discuss terms took place in the Manhattan offices of the *New York Herald* on October 11. Bob, formally decked out in a long-tailed suit, high collar and shiny silk hat, showed up first with Captain Glori. Jim swept in some minutes later, uncharacteristically attired in a casual sweater and jacket as if he had just come from training or a day's work in a warehouse. It was Brady's idea, to make him look like an everyday fellow, not the least bit proud—and to make Bob look like a "dude."

"Take the chair, Captain Glori," Bob said as they got down to business. He preferred to let his manager do the talking. "The Captain is my spokesman today."

The meeting began with Bob meek and quiet and Jim, speaking for himself, loud and rude and aggressive. "You have a thousand dollars!" Jim derisively snorted when Glori said they had placed that sum on deposit. "I thought you said you had ten thousand dollars." When Glori explained the thousand was merely to bind the match, Jim responded with a dig at Bob's recent financial troubles. "I suppose you want to go on the road," he said, "and make the $10,000 and put it up as it comes into the box office."

That got a rise out of Glori. "That isn't a fair statement. You are rich, you know, and we are not."

"Now listen!" Jim snapped, getting worked up. "Don't start that sort of talk. Don't start any sympathy gags. As far as I am concerned I want you people to distinctly understand that I would fight Fitzsimmons if it was only for a five dollar bill."

"You're a great stringer," said Bob, rising to Jim's taunts. "But I can string a bit myself."

Jim turned to face him. "Did you say you would shake your finger in my face?" He was referring to a comment attributed to Bob in the papers.

"No, I deny it," said Bob. "I'm too much of a gentleman to say any such a thing."

"Well, I wouldn't expect you to make such a crack."

"Nor would I expect you to."

"I'd make good if I did."

"So would I."

The situation was getting ugly. "Gentlemen—ge-e-e-ntlemen," cautioned the temporary stakeholder, stepping between the two men.

The matter of the $10,000 side bet was settled. Jim made a show of counting the cash out from a fat wad he had in his pocket. Captain Glori promised to put up Bob's share in four monthly payments. They moved on to the next item of business, Bob speaking up again to ask when Jim wanted to fight.

"When do I want to fight?" Jim again was being offensive. "That's a pretty question. Don't you know when I want to fight? Well, you're not up to date. I will fight after the 1st of July and not before. And another thing I want to tell you. I've got till next September. And if I fight next September I will have fought three championship battles in three years and you can take your book of rules and look that over. The champion before me didn't do that."

The following July was nine months down the road. Glori suggested the fight be held within six months but Jim wouldn't budge. "I am champion," he said, "and I have the right to dictate, and I will dictate, by ——. The man who fights me will fight me when I say so, and not when it suits him."

Glori let it go. The fight would be held after July 1, 1895, just as Jim wanted. All that remained was to decide on the venue. This would be done by open bidding by the three athletic club representatives present.

"We'll give $25,000," began William Scholl of the Olympic.

"On behalf of the Florida Athletic Club," said Joe Vendig, "I will give $30,000 for the fight." He produced a stack of bills. "Here is $5,000 to bind us."

Frank Williams, representing the Auditorium AC in New Orleans, spoke up. "I bid $35,000."

"Mine is $37,000," countered Vendig.

Scholl dug deeper. "Forty thousand."

"Forty-one thousand," said Vendig.

"Fifty thousand dollars!" bellowed Scholl.

Fifty thousand dollars. That would be the biggest fight purse ever paid. Bob, who thought highly of the Olympic, wanted to take it. Jim didn't. He insisted on seeing a cash forfeit up front, dismissing Scholl's promise to put up $5,000 the next day.

"I will give $41,000," repeated Vendig. "And there"—he tapped the five grand he had laid on the table—"is my money to back it."

Bob: "Isn't $50,000 more acceptable than $41,000?"

Jim: "But Scholl can't put up the money."

Bob: "Well, you didn't expect the clubs to make a big deposit today, anyhow."

Jim: "Oh, I didn't! How do you know? You must be a mind reader."

Bob acquiesced. And so it was settled. The Florida AC, a recently formed syndicate in Jacksonville, would host the Corbett-Fitzsimmons fight for $41,000, on a date of their choosing after July 1st. The contest would be held in Jacksonville and no doubt face church opposition, but according to inside sources the governor was unlikely to interfere after being chastened by his failure to stop the Corbett-Mitchell fight. Articles were accordingly drafted, the Corbett-Sullivan agreement serving as a template. The actual signing would have to wait until the principals were back on the road with their respective shows, Bob in Philadelphia and Jim in Springfield, Massachusetts, for even the arranging of a prizefight was illegal in the State of New York.

The reaction down in Jacksonville was not encouraging when it was learned that another championship battle was to be held in that city. "Allow us to remark right now," stated the *Florida Citizen* the next day, "that the preliminaries for this so-called scientific glove contest may as well be abandoned at once. Jacksonville is not a candidate for any further notoriety in this line.... As soon as the Legislature of next spring shall have been organized, and some member can get the attention of the Speaker, we shall have an iron bound anti-prize fight law that will cover every phase of this subject. There is no mistake about this, and Messrs. Corbett and Fitzsimmons may prepare to take their show to some less civilized and more lawless country."

"Don't fret about the next Legislature," soothed an anonymous sporting man and state politician. Legislators with their pet projects needed the support of the state's well-heeled sporting element, he said, and wouldn't dare antagonize them. "It's money that talks, and the next Legislature will be called upon to pay off some political debts recently incurred in Florida. No change in the laws affecting prize fights will pass. Mark my word."

Florida, anonymous assurances notwithstanding, looked like it might be a problem. Seizing the opportunity—and the publicity too—Kinetoscope Exhibiting Company vice president Gray Latham stepped forward on October 26 with a counteroffer, sent to the two fighters and simultaneously released to the press. Should the Florida club withdraw its offer, Gray stated, the KEC was prepared to put up a purse of $50,000 for the fight to be held in Mexico in front of the Kinetograph camera, with the stipulation that it be subject to postponement to a clear day with sufficient sunlight for filming. The offer would have been made earlier, Gray went on to explain, "but for the fact that we had learned nothing from our Mexican agent, and again, because the experiments of three-minute subjects with the kinetograph had not proven entirely successful. Now, however, we shall not only be able to take each three-minute round of the fight, but also the action of the seconds, and during the one-minute rest between the rounds. We have advice from our Mexican agent which is most favorable. There can be no interference with the fight, and he is assured by the authorities that everything will be done to protect those engaged in the contest as well as those who go to Mexico to see it."

It was a grand proposition, just the sort of big thinking that Gray was good at. The fact was, however, that the Kinetoscope Exhibiting Company didn't have $50,000. Almost all its starting capital of $30,000 was tied up in Kinetoscope machines. Nor had the technical hurdles been cleared for filming three-minute rounds. (It is possible, however, that the KEC was beginning to realize that manually operating the camera presented a possible way forward, as will shortly be seen.) As for the talk of "our Mexican agent" and amenable authorities south of the border, Gray's investigation of Mexico as a venue would have been cursory at best—a letter or telegraphed inquiry perhaps. The offer, in short, was entirely flimsy.

Flimsy or not, Bob Fitzsimmons was eager to accept it, for his confidence was waning that the Florida club would be able to pull off the fight. "Why, that just suits me," he enthused. "Just think of $50,000 for a fight. Cinch money, too. None of your worthless paper like the Crescent City unloaded on me when I whipped Hall.... They are willing to put up the money before we fight, and we will get it if there are only a half dozen people at the ring side.... I will sign with these people just the minute Corbett says it will suit him."

That minute never came. Corbett refused to fight in Mexico. "I can't see why Fitzsimmons keeps harping about the kinetoscope," said William Brady, speaking for the champ. "Fitzsimmons has never had any experience with kinetoscopes, while Corbett and I have." Edison's camera, Brady pointed out, was "absolutely useless for a finish fight," for it could only film for a minute and a half and was also prone to breaking down, as indeed occurred during the Corbett-Courtney contest. "Mr. Edison hopes to perfect the kinetoscope so that it can be regulated to suit any time," Brady concluded, "but it may take him a long time to do so, and Fitzsimmons and Corbett might be grayheaded before he succeeded."

Nothing came of Gray Latham's offer. For the time being Jacksonville remained the tentative venue for the Corbett-Fitz contest and the two fighters continued to tour with their shows. Jim was now in the middle of a hectic tour with *Gentleman Jack*, the company working its way through Massachusetts, New York and Ohio; west into Illinois, Kansas, Iowa and Missouri; south into Tennessee, Arkansas and Texas—all before the end of the year, full houses at almost every stop. "Corbett has improved in his acting," the *New York Dramatic Mirror* observed of one of the earlier performances in New York. "The scene at the Olympic Club, where Corbett appears in ring costume, set the gallery wild, and evoked enthusiasm in the lower part of the house."

Bob and his partner Captain Charles Glori, meanwhile, were on the road with Bob's new vaudeville entertainment, the Bob Fitzsimmons Specialty Company. It was not as successful as *Gentleman Jack*, rarely enjoying sell-out crowds as it bounced around from Bridgeport and New Haven to Philadelphia, Scranton and Newark. In early November, five weeks into the season, it was noted in the papers that Bob and his company were "doing a very light business on the road."

As with his previous show, Bob finished up the program with a sparring exhibition. He had a new sparring partner this season, Irish-born Cornelius "Con" Riordan, whom Bob had known in Australia. Riordan had been a respectable pugilist once, working as a boxing instructor alongside Jim Corbett at San Francisco's Olympic Club in the late 1880s and touring for a time as Peter Jackson's sparring partner. When Bob ran into him in September 1894, however, he had fallen on hard times, a dissipated drunk one step from the gutter. Wanting to help out an old friend, Bob hired him as his sparring partner for the show, making him promise first to straighten himself out. Riordan did for a while, for he was desperate for work. But it didn't last. Soon he was drinking again.

Riordan was in bad shape on November 16, 1894, the second of a three-night engagement in Syracuse, New York. It was a rare full house that evening, in part because a popular local fighter named Joe Dunfee would be joining Riordan to spar with Fitz. He was needed, for Riordan had been drinking all day. Con was observed vomiting before the show and downing a large glass of whisky, and when he came on stage at ten-thirty that evening he asked Bob not to hit him in the stomach or ribs. "Go easy a bit to-night, Bob," he whispered. "I'm not feeling well."

The round began slowly, Bob aiming at Riordan's head and pulling his punching, taking it easy as requested. They moved about the stage doing the tamest of sparring—so tame that Captain Glori, serving as timekeeper, was "disgusted." Two minutes in, Bob feinted and stepped in with a "monkey punch," a light, slapping blow with the back of the glove that he often used in theatrical work, "so light," he would say after, "that it would not have injured a ten-year-old child." It seemed to shake Riordan, however, for he half-turned to Captain Glori and asked him to call time, then his legs gave out and he collapsed. Now it was Bob's turn to be disgusted, for he thought that Riordan was either faking or drunk. So did some in the audience, who started to hiss. Bob helped Riordan up and two attendants rushed out from the wings and carted him off the stage.

Keeping the show going, Glori introduced Joe Dunfee and the sparring recommenced, this time a more lively exhibition, the audience loudly cheering for their local hero. As he fended off Dunfee, who was giving his all, Bob kept glancing at Riordan propped on a chair in the wings. He seemed all right at first. He was speaking with the property manager, refusing to have his gloves removed because he had to go back out for another round. Then he slid off the chair and into a heap on the floor. Distracted, Bob let his guard down for a moment and Dunfee dropped him with a shot to the chin. As the audience erupted with cries of "Dunfee! Dunfee!" the curtain was brought down and Bob scrambled to his feet and hurried offstage.

There was something wrong with Riordan. A doctor was summoned, then a second, police surgeon David Totman, who found his pupils fixed and dilated, suggesting a hemorrhage in the brain. Injections of ammonia were administered without result. Electricity was also tried, Riordan being hooked up to a battery and his body made to jerk. This too failed to revive him. At two o'clock in the morning, with the stricken boxer apparently dying, he was moved to a nearby hotel. Bob was taken to the police station.

It was there, around three-thirty, that Bob was informed that his old friend was dead. The news came as a great shock, for Bob was convinced that Riordan was merely drunk and would come round when he sobered up. The next morning, after spending the rest of the night in a cell, the emotion welled to the surface and Bob burst into tears. "Poor Conny!" he said. And to a reporter: "I feel as if at this moment, I would not care if I never put on a glove again."

Bob was released later that day after posting bail. At the afternoon and evening shows he appeared only briefly on stage to bow to the half-empty house. A small service was held for Riordan early the next morning and the saddened troupe boarded the train for Boston, their next engagement, under a cloud.

Back in Syracuse, an autopsy with several doctors present revealed a massive hemorrhage in Riordan's brain. With there being nothing to indicate that the cause had been a blow to the head, the coroner's inquest that was held a few days later cleared Bob of any criminal wrongdoing. District Attorney Benjamin Shove was not prepared to let the matter drop, however. There had been a ring death in Syracuse the previous year, involving none other than Joe Dunfee.

Dunfee had been exonerated for that killing, a knockout blow from which his opponent never awakened, but this time Shove intended to take it to trial. When the next grand jury was impaneled in the new year, he announced, he would seek an indictment for first degree manslaughter against Bob Fitzsimmons.

DA Shove would be aided in this by police surgeon Totman. Returning to the morgue for a private reexamination of Riordan's brain, now removed from the skull, Totman found lacerations which he ascribed to a blow to the head. This dubious finding, unsupported by the other doctors at the autopsy, was appended to the official report and served as the key piece of evidence against Bob when Shove got his indictment on January 19, 1895. Bob was responsible for the death of Con Riordan, the document read, because he "did unlawfully and willfully strike said Con Riordan and wound him in and on the chin, neck and face...and did thus unlawfully and willfully punch and strike the said Con Riordan down upon the wooden floor, then and thereby inflicting upon the base of the brain of said Con Riordan mortal bruises and wounds; and so the Grand Jury say that Robert Fitzsimmons did unlawfully kill the said Con Riordan...."

CHAPTER 13

EUGENE LAUSTE'S LOOP

WHEN HE MADE THE Kinetoscope Exhibiting Company offer for the Corbett-Fitz fight in late October 1894, Gray Latham was already involved with his brother Otway and father Woodville in a new venture to develop a system for motion picture projection. The plan had come into being the previous month, when Otway sounded out Woodville about the feasibility of projecting Kinetoscope moving images, as he had overheard a number of customers at the Nassau Street parlor say they would prefer this. It made excellent sense, and not just because the exhibition could be made life-sized and thus more interesting to look it. Purely in terms of making money, it would mean that a parlor could operate with just one machine, not six, and that dozens, even hundreds of paying customers could be accommodated at one time—in short, that costs could be slashed and profits greatly increased. It would also make the business much more mobile, easily shifted from one venue to another as opportunity beckoned, freed from the necessity of planting six bulky Kinetoscopes in one place. After considering all this, Woodville recalled later, "I said to my son that I had not the slightest doubt of my ability to do what he had suggested, and I immediately began to consider plans for the construction of such apparatus."

With the Corbett-Courtney film scarcely debuted and the Kinetoscope Exhibition Company only just getting started, Otway veered off on his own to bring this new idea to fruition. He took his plan first to William Dickson only to be informed that Edison had no interest. As Edison saw it, fifty projecting machines would be enough to serve the whole country, a negligible market not worth pursuing—unlike the one-viewer-at-a-time Kinetoscope, which was starting to bring in a handsome and much-needed profit. Projection, in short, did not pass the profitability test that for Edison indicated practical value. He remained more interested in improving the peephole Kinetoscope by adding sound, his stated intention from the beginning of his work on motion pictures. And indeed, in the following spring he came out with just such a device, the Kinetophone, one of the last inventions Dickson worked on at the Orange lab. It was a standard Kinetoscope with a Phonograph attached that the viewer listened to via ear tubes as he peered into the peephole—a large step down from the grand opera experience Edison had wanted to deliver. The sound was in fact unsynchronized and thus was limited to musical accompaniment to visual subjects like dancers and acrobats and comedy gags. Intended to spice up the Kinetoscope to prolong its novelty value, the Kinetophone would prove a failure and soon fade away.

Edison's lack of interest in projection did not deter the Lathams. They promptly decided to develop the technology themselves and start a new company, the Lambda Company, incorporated in Richmond, Virginia and based in New York. Gray would be president, Otway vice president and Woodville the treasurer and secretary. The trio wanted Dickson on board as well as technical expert and they worked hard to cultivate his friendship. It began cordially in September 1894 with wining and dining, Dickson warming to Woodville especially with his Southern manners. Then, in mid October, things took a serious turn when Woodville revealed their plans and asked Dickson to join them. He would be a full partner in Lambda Co., Woodville promised, and get a quarter of the stock, a nominal value of $125,000.

Dickson would vehemently deny to his dying day that he ever had any real intention of joining the Lathams. He associated with them, he insisted, to keep an eye on what they were doing and to probe for possible Kinetoscope patent infringements. In other words, it was an act of loyalty to Edison, not an act of betrayal. "If they [the Lathams] had only known the real object of my hanging around to spy out what they were doing," he would confide in a letter in 1932,

"I think they would have shot me. I kept this to myself all these years as I was not particularly proud of it." It is clear, however, that Dickson was genuinely interested in the potentially lucrative ground-floor opportunity the Lathams offered and that he gave them assistance in the beginning. And it is indisputable that he eventually received Lambda Company shares, holding them at arm's length through a lawyer. He may even have entertained thoughts of leaving Edison, for he was unhappy with the way things were being run at the lab. He was disappointed that Edison had vetoed the development of a motion picture projector and he was starting to chafe under Edison's new business manager William Gilmore, who was intent on imposing corporate discipline and reining him in. In June 1894, for example, Dickson was obliged to transfer to Edison the copyright for Kinetoscope films he had made and copyrighted in his own name. And in the following February Edison himself, likely prompted by Gilmore, objected to Dickson calling himself "co-inventor" of the magnetic ore separator, even though Dickson's name appeared on the patent. After years of steady advancement to a privileged status, Dickson was being pushed back down by Gilmore, treated like any other Edison mucker. And he didn't like it.

After helping the Lathams with preliminary experimentation, Dickson grew cautious and took a step back. As Woodville would later remember, Dickson "exhibited a morbid dread of having Mr. Edison learn of what he was doing." When pressed for further assistance, Dickson recommended that they hire a trusted old friend—a gifted machinist, inventor and former Edison lab employee named Eugene Lauste.

It was the castor oil his mother spilled while dosing the family's sick dog that gave eleven-year-old Eugene Augustin Lauste his first breakthrough in moving picture projection. After the messy job was done, while young Eugene was gathering up the newspapers that had been spread on the floor, he noticed that the spots where the oil had been spilt were semi-transparent. It was a eureka moment that seemed to solve a problem the inquisitive boy had been having: How to use his magic lantern to cast the images from his toy Zoetrope, printed on opaque paper strips, onto the wall. He soaked one of the picture strips in oil and dried it, then ran it past the lens in his oil lamp magic lantern. And *voilà*, there, projected on the wall were … blurred smudges. After a good deal of trial and error, holding onto the apparatus to keep it from falling off the table, Eugene discovered that by placing his hand in front of the lens so that the light passed through a gap between his fingers, the smudges clarified into a viewable image. "[I]t was one of my best attraction as well to other boys who assisted to my performances," he remembered toward the end of his life, writing in imperfect English. "I must add that the pictures was not very good, but good enough for me."

Eugene Lauste grew to manhood in Paris and became an inventor. One of his early efforts was a gasoline motor for road transportation, which he and his partner initially thought would make them a fortune. Eventually they abandoned the idea, discouraged by friends who insisted that something as dangerous as an internal combustion engine would never be allowed on the roads. Seeking new opportunities, Lauste emigrated to the United States with his wife and children in late 1886 and, despite speaking almost no English, found work with Thomas Edison as a machinist. It was here that he befriended William Dickson, with whom he could abandon the struggle of speaking English and communicate freely in French.

On April 13, 1890, Lauste encountered the first of the many bumps in the road that would make his life a vale of tears. His wife ran off with their boarder, taking his bank book and leaving him with their three children. Lauste pulled himself together and carried on, reestablishing himself in Orange to work at the new Edison lab. He did well here and soon found favor with the Edison family, called up to the house by Mrs. Edison to do little chores and even decorate the tree at Christmas—completely oblivious that this caused jealousy back at the lab, particularly with his immediate superior, John Ott. It thus came as a shock to Lauste when he was fired in March 1892 for recording hours worked when he was not at the lab. It was a simple misunderstanding, he having been reassigned to work elsewhere. Unable to defend himself in English, Lauste was forced to turn in his tools and leave before the end of the day.

After a period of hardship in Newark, with destitution looming and jobs scarce due to the deepening economic depression, Lauste returned to Orange to confront Edison and managed to convey something of the injustice that had been done him. Edison, wanting to put things right, offered him a job at the Ogdensburg mine when it opened. Taking the inventor at his word, Lauste waited until the appointed day, then spent the last of his money on train fare to Ogdensburg for himself and his eldest child Emile only to find Edison in a bad mood and the job offer forgotten. Without money for return fare, the unlucky Frenchman and his son set out to walk back to Newark. It was a two-day journey in the pouring rain, a slog through the mud with nothing but hopelessness, poverty and real hunger awaiting. And it was all due to what Lauste perceived as the treacherous hand of John Ott. "I am not a Phrophet [sic]," he wrote years later, "but regarding my vengeance against the man who was a traitor, I wish him to be paralyse [sic] for his life, which at last, I heard that my wishes came true for what he deserved." He was referring to the crippling fall Ott suffered in 1895, putting him in a wheelchair for the rest of his life. It was divine retribution.

It was at this low point in his life that Lauste received a letter from William Dickson with a possible lead on a job. He seized the opportunity and was soon seated in Woodville Latham's room at New York's Hotel Bartholdi, listening with quiet surprise as Woodville explained his ideas for motion picture projection. It was something that Lauste himself had investigated in the late 1880s, pursuing his childhood interest. While his knowledge of photography was limited, he had a deep understanding of optics and mechanics and had even made sketches for an intermittent movement that would work equally well in a motion picture camera or projector. Yes, Lauste assured Woodville, he could build the machines the Lambda Company required, and he named his modest price, twenty-one dollars a week. The meeting concluded with Woodville producing a jug of whiskey, the likely source of his poor health. Lauste waited for a glass to be offered, then, when one was not forthcoming, raised the jug to his lips.

It was not long after this meeting that Gray and Otway Latham were ousted from the Kinetoscope Exhibiting Company. Their careless and erratic management style; their profligate ways and excessive carousing; and now their forming of a rival venture instead of attending to KEC business—it was all too much to let pass. Toward the end of 1894 Enoch Rector sided with Samuel Tilden and John Cox to vote the Latham brothers out of the company.

This marked the end of Rector's friendship with the Lathams, who had involved him in their projection idea and possibly wanted him to join Lambda Co. As Terry Ramsaye, who interviewed Rector in the mid 1920s, would delicately describe the breakup in his cinema history *A Million and One Nights*, "Rector continued yet a while in the background of Latham affairs but he was planning a course of his own." That course would be with Tilden and Cox, not with the erratic Latham brothers and their mercurial father. In the reorganization of the KEC that followed, Tilden remained president and Cox secretary, while Rector, replacing Otway as the company's front man, was elevated to vice president, the position Gray had previously held.

Gray and Otway responded with a lawsuit, naming Rector as a defendant along with Tilden and Cox. They claimed that the three had defrauded them into signing over their rights to the company in exchange for being made KEC employees and getting between them two-fifths of the stock, which they claimed was worth at least $125,000. They had never received that stock after being booted from the company and now they wanted compensation.

The lawsuit went nowhere and was eventually dropped.

Eugene Lauste tramped around downtown Manhattan for several days after being hired by the Lathams, accompanying Otway in a search for premises to rent for a workshop. They settled on a room on the third floor of a crumbling old building at 35 Frankfort, traffic rattling by outside up the Brooklyn Bridge. A lathe, drill press, vise, grinder and tools were purchased and on December 10, 1894 Lauste went to work. For the next several months he would labor with an intensity that not even Thomas Edison could surpass, working twenty hours a day, seven days a week, eating his meals at his workbench and sleeping on a cot when he grew exhausted, his son Emile running errands, doing the shopping and preparing his meals. It would be an astonishing period of productivity and invention.

And unlike Edison, who had a whole staff of muckers, Eugene Lauste would do it largely alone.

His first task, guided by a general description provided by Woodville, was to adapt the Kinetoscope peephole viewer for projection so that they could quickly start making money. This posed a fundamental challenge, one that Dickson had first confronted in 1889 in his own experiments with projection. Unlike the Kinetograph camera, which used an intermittent mechanism to advance the film, in the Kinetoscope the film moved continuously, a rotating disk shutter flashing glimpses of passing frames to the eye. This worked sufficiently well when the device was used as a peephole machine because the images the viewer saw were very small and thus required little illumination. When these same images were projected onto a screen, however, blown up to many times their original size, the flashes of light passing through the slits in the spinning shutter faded almost to nothing. The obvious solution of building a projector with intermittent movement did not seem practical for the reason that such a mechanism was brutally hard on the film. With a camera this was acceptable because the harsh passage through the machine had to be endured only once by the film. With a projector, on the other hand, a film had to endure hundreds of showings without sustaining damaging. To do that, a continuous movement thus had to be used.

The first device Lauste built projected a very dim image, little better than what Dickson had achieved in his aborted projection experiments years before. To improve it, Lauste claimed that he convinced the Lathams to increase the width of the film they were using, thereby increasing the amount of illumination cast onto the screen. This meant that a new camera would have to be built to handle specially ordered two-inch-wide film. The idea was appealing to the Lathams because wider film with a more rectangular frame would be better suited for filming genuine prizefights in a regulation-sized ring, which they remained convinced was the road to riches. The concept may indeed have predated Lauste and come out of discussions with Dickson and Enoch Rector back in the summer of 1894. Whenever it arose, the Lathams now instructed Lauste to set the projector aside and proceed at once with building a camera—then they obliged him to waste time on a useless intermittent mechanism design they had coaxed out of Dickson. It was a simple Geneva movement such as used in a watch, far too slow and delicate for advancing celluloid film and certain to break when run at high speed; a meaningless nothing Dickson had sketched to put off the Lathams with their incessant prodding for tips. Lauste dutifully built the camera as ordered and proved to his employers it didn't work. He then proceeded to build one that did. It was tested for the first time on the night of February 26, 1895, Dickson present to supervise and develop the film. The simple experiment, the camera pointed at a swinging light bulb, was a success, the negative strip showing a black spot moving across a white background. A second test was made a few days later on the roof of the Frankfurt Street building, this time with Otway operating the camera as young Emile Lauste wrestled and boxed with recently hired shop assistant Emil Kleinert, Gray acting as referee, Woodville and Eugene Lauste looking on.

The atmosphere in the workshop by this time had become tense. Lauste had not asked for an assistant and did not like having the new and "very lazy" man Kleinert around. Neither did Dickson on his regular visits. He feared that Kleinert, a former Edison employee, might reveal his secret that he was associating with the Lathams. As for the Lathams, they were becoming uneasy about Dickson. He kept dropping by the shop and expressing interest, yet he remained unwilling to commit himself in any meaningful way to the venture. And then there was his habit of conversing with Lauste in French, which Otway, always present to keep an eye on them, did not understand. Did Dickson have something to hide? Was he really there spying? The Lathams began to regard him with suspicion.

On April 21, 1895, a handful of reporters were invited to the Frankfort Street workshop and shown the short film of Emile Lauste play-sparring with Kleinert up on the roof. It was the first public demonstration in North America of projected moving pictures, coming one month after the Lumière brothers' inaugural private screening in Paris of their superior Cinématographe camera-projector, of which the Lathams and Lauste were likely unaware. The images were cast onto a screen four feet across using the new machine Lauste had just completed after another marathon work session, Woodville Latham introducing it as the "Pantoptikon" and his own invention. The *New York Sun* published the fullest report of the event and included Thomas Edison's dismissive reaction. "The throwing of pictures on a screen was the very first thing I did with the kinetoscope," said the inventor. "I didn't think much of that, because the pictures were crude, and there seemed to me to be no commercial value in that feature of the machine.... If they [the Lathams] exhibit this machine, improve on what I have done, and call it a kinetoscope, that's all right. I will be glad of whatever improvements Mr. Latham may make. If they carry the machine around the country calling it by some other name, that's a fraud, and I shall prosecute whoever does it. I've applied for patents long ago."

Woodville, incensed, responded in a letter to the editor of the *Sun* the next day. "I am not acquainted with the interior structure of Mr. Edison's kinetoscope," he wrote, "and am unable, therefore, to tell whether there are points of similarity between his apparatus and mine or not. I have, however, seen the outside of his, and I do know that mine is not half as large, though it includes an appliance for projection, which his does not. Another obvious difference is that my machine can carry thousands of feet of film as well as shorter lengths, and can be used for making long exhibitions, while, as I am credibly informed, his larger machine (first made, by the way, on the order of one of my sons), can carry no more than about one hundred and fifty feet of film, and can afford an exhibition of only about one minute. These facts would seem to indicate a very material difference of make-up...."

"As to Mr. Edison's threat to 'prosecute' anybody that exhibits my machine under any other name than one he chooses to call it by, it is something a great deal worse than puerile. I prefer not, at this time, to characterize it more pointedly.... If Mr. Edison can project pictures of moving objects on a screen, as he says he can, why does he not do it as publicly as I have done, and do it at once?"

It was a valid challenge. For while Edison had talked about projection for the past four years, he had yet to come out with a projecting machine. More important, though, was that while Edison's

Kinetograph camera and Kinetoscope viewer system was limited to one hundred fifty feet of film lasting not much more than one minute, the Latham's new system, as Woodville asserted, "can carry thousands of feet of film." This was a crucial advance. It had been made by Eugene Lauste, a simple but inspired design change to his camera's film feed mechanism that would come to be credited to Woodville as the "Latham Loop."

With Edison's Kinetograph camera, the celluloid film traveled from the feed reel and past the lens to the take-up reel in a taut state. This meant that as the intermittent mechanism advanced the film frame by frame, it pulled it directly off the feed reel. So long as this reel contained only a small amount of film and was thus not too heavy, the strain placed on the film was not too great. If more than one hundred fifty feet of celluloid was used, however, the feed reel became so heavy, like a dragging anchor, that the film could not stand the strain as the intermittent mechanism jerked it forward. It would inevitably tear and break.

Lauste's solution was elegantly simple. He removed the strain by adding an extra gear in front of the intermittent mechanism so that the film formed a loop—or "slack" as Woodville called it in his subsequent patent application. Now, as the intermittent mechanism advanced the film, it jerked on only this slack loop, a mere few inches of film, not on the entire weight of the film reel behind it. With this modest design change it suddenly became possible to make films that were five minutes, ten minutes, even twenty minutes long—whatever sized reel would fit inside a camera. Build a camera big enough and you could theoretically film for hours using Eugene Lauste's little loop.

The Lathams were now ready to commercialize their projection system. But first William Dickson had to find himself out of a job.

The crash had come on April 2, 1895, when William Gilmore summoned Dickson into his office and accused him of going behind Edison's back to double-deal with the Lathams. Outraged at being called disloyal, Dickson stormed over to Edison's house and demanded that his employer choose between Gilmore and himself, for one of them had to go. When Edison refused to support him and fire

Gilmore, telling Dickson merely to get back to work, Dickson angrily resigned on the spot. The sudden, acrimonious parting—indeed, the entire episode with the Lathams—would be the greatest regret of Dickson's life. He would try repeatedly in later years to get back into his former employer's good graces. But by then Edison was convinced that Dickson had betrayed him. He would never trust him again.

How Dickson's involvement with the Lathams came to Gilmore's attention is unclear. It is possible the information might have come from Emil Kleinert. Dickson himself, however, would blame the Lathams. Their pressing Lambda Company stock on him while he still worked for Edison, he claimed, had been an underhanded scheme "to compromise me and force me to join them." And: "The Lathams did work hard to get information from me, but failing, turned their bitter enmity on me for refusing." And: "I soon became disgusted with their business methods.... Had they behaved as gentlemen I most likely should have thrown myself heart and soul into the work."

Although he would not say so outright, it appears that Dickson thought the Lathams set him up with the gift of Lambda Company shares and then somehow leaked word to Gilmore to drive him out of Edison's orbit and into their own. If so, it didn't work. By June Dickson had severed his ties with the Lathams and returned all the stock.

CHAPTER 14

※

GRIFFO-BARNETT PROJECTED

THE ONLY SCHOOL ALBERT GRIFFITHS attended was the school of hard knocks in the rough dockside neighborhood of The Rocks in Sydney, what one paper called "a perfect garden of ruffianism." He didn't see much of his father, a taciturn, affectionless coal shoveler and seaman, and nothing at all of his mother, who died when he was an infant. Foisted off on others to raise, young Albert was put to work before the age of ten, hustling pennies selling newspapers, then driving a produce cart and working as a racehorse trainer as he grew up to become a "larrikin," Australian slang for a hoodlum. By sixteen he had taken to the prize ring, honing his natural ability as a street fighter with almost weekly bouts in Larry Foley's "Iron Pot," starting with bare knuckles, then moving to gloves. He picked up a cauliflower ear along the way and also started bathing, gentlemen patrons seated at ringside having complained that he was "anything but aromatic when he got warm." By 1890 the stocky, thick-necked Griffiths, popularly known by his newsboy nickname "Young Griffo," had established himself as Australia's premiere feather-weight despite the increasingly dissolute lifestyle he led with his Rocks gang. He was no knockout artist but incredibly shifty and fast, standing in place and jabbing his opponents to pieces while dodging and slipping nearly everything thrown in return—"as elusive," according to one admirer, "as a pickled onion under a blunt fork."

After more than a hundred fights in Australia, Griffo was coaxed to embark for greater ring glory in America in May 1893, three years after Bob Fitzsimmons made the same journey. He was seen off, the *Sydney Truth* reported, "by one of the liveliest crowds of blackguards Sydney ever produced—which is saying something." The *Sydney News* wasn't sorry to see him go and predicted failure in America if Griffo didn't change his ways. "[O]ur joy at his departure," the paper noted, "is tempered by the sad reflection that he leaves the 'Rocks' and other 'pushes' [gangs] behind him. We could well spare them also."

It would be said of Young Griffo at the height of his fame that he out-Sullivaned John L. Sullivan himself. This was not a reference to his dominance as a fighter but rather to his legendary carousing and lackadaisical approach to training. Beefing up on a diet of American booze and hard living, Griffo earned a second nickname, "The Alderman," on account of his paunch and neglected physique, and he was frequently observed to be drunk or hung over when he entered the ring. On the very day of his big fight with George Dixon in June 1894, for example, he was found unconscious in a saloon after a three-day bender. His manager dragged him to a Turkish bath and sweated him sober, then pushed him through the ropes that evening to fight Dixon to a twenty-round draw. It was performances such as this that left Griffo's fans shaking their heads as they wondered: *Just think what he could do if he took care of himself.*

Among those fans were Gray and Otway Latham. They had tried to get Griffo back in May 1894 for the first Kinetoscope Exhibiting Company film before settling on Leonard and Cushing. Now, rushing to commercialize their Lauste-built camera and projector so that the undercapitalized Lambda Company could start earning money, they approached Griffo again.

First contact was made at the Manhattan Athletic Club on the night of March 26, 1895, after a typical Griffo performance in which he dominated a much fitter opponent for six rounds despite being in horrible shape. According to the *Brooklyn Eagle*, Griffo and his manager were approached by "a stranger, . . . an agent for the kinetoscope," with an offer "to fight at catch weights before the wonderful camera at Llewellen [sic.] park," the opponent to be later determined. This "stranger" was almost certainly Gray or Otway, who freely mentioned Edison's name and place of work in their dealings even though they no longer had any connection with the inventor. An agreement was reached whereby Griffo would receive the lion's share of an unspecified sum and the three men came away from their meeting "looking mightily pleased." It didn't hurt a bit that, just five days later, Griffo's latest drunken escapade made the newspapers. It was publicity for the Lathams, good advertising. This time Griffo had accosted Jim Corbett in a New York restaurant, bawling "It takes us Australians to do up you chumps" before taking a swing. Corbett, nearly a head taller, slapped him to the floor.

The opponent chosen to face Young Griffo was New York featherweight Charley Barnett. Twenty-four at the time, the same age as Griffo, Charley hailed from Cherry Street in the Fourth Ward, a tough Irish-American neighborhood down by the East River docks in the shadow of Brooklyn Bridge. His father was a porter and his mother soon would be dead, used up at age forty-four, and all three Barnett brothers, Florrie, Jerry and Charley, had gone into the ring. Charley made regular appearances at New York clubs in undercard bouts and had a respectable but mainly local reputation, his biggest fight to date having been a recent slugfest against an out-of-shape Mike Leonard that ended in a draw. He was in prime condition and skillful and game enough to test Griffo, bringing out all that wonderful dodging and weaving. And best of all, he came cheap.

The fight took place on May 4, 1895, on the roof of Madison Square Garden, just behind the bicycle school where newcomers to the recent craze practiced riding their "wheel." It would be a four-round contest with five-ounce gloves, the plan being for one-and-a-half-minute rounds with thirty-second breaks in between. Unlike the previous two fights recorded by the Lathams and Rector, the flow of the contest would not be interrupted after each round for the film to be changed. Eugene Lauste's camera, capable of handling more film, would run continuously from the opening bell to the end.

The machine itself was a rough prototype and looked it, a conglomeration of disparate parts that did not neatly match, a corner filed down here, an edge bent there. The *New York World* reporter called it "old-looking." Wires ran from it to five bulky batteries that would deliver the power. Lauste was certainly present, fussing over the apparatus, making last-minute adjustments, but was overlooked by the newsmen. "Professor" Dickson's presence was noted, however. No longer obliged to keep his involvement with the Lathams a secret, Dickson took the train up from Orange to attend, arriving a half hour late and keeping everyone waiting. He would not play an active role in the proceedings beyond checking things over and observing. Instead it was Otway who presided behind the camera, Lauste no doubt hovering nervously nearby.

Things got underway at eleven-twenty in the morning, the sun near its zenith, the improvised ring flooded with natural light. Charley Barnett, seconded by his brothers, occupied the left side of the ring in the foreground as seen through the lens, Griffo and his seconds the right, referee Charlie White in the middle. When everything was ready, Otway threw the switch and the camera buzzed to life, photographing at a claimed rate of fifty frames per second. Time was called, White directed the two fighters forward and the action commenced.

The first round saw Barnett the aggressor and Griffo slow to warm up. Then Griffo took command, employing his famous slipping and jabbing. It continued this way through the second round and the third, Griffo dominating, Barnett receiving punishment but acquitting himself well. With everything going smoothly up to this point, an impromptu decision was made to extend the final round to two minutes. Griffo spent it very aggressive but was unable to put Barnett down, the two dancing around the ring right up to the bell. No decision was announced by referee White when it was all over and Otway switched off the camera but it was clear to the sporting men present that Griffo had won. More than a thousand feet of film, meanwhile, lay exposed in the camera, far more than Edison's Kinetograph could handle. Thanks to Eugene Lauste's loop, motion pictures had just made the leap from not much more than sixty seconds to eight full minutes.

The Griffo-Barnett fight ended without a knockout or even a knockdown. It had been a legitimate, unscripted sparring contest, without the stage-managing that gave the Leonard-Cushing and Corbett-Courtney fights perfectly timed KOs at the end. From a theatrical standpoint this was a major shortcoming, for it meant that audiences would be denied a satisfying climax, the finishing blow that many visitors to the KEC's Kinetoscope parlors made a beeline to see. The fact that Otway and Gray were willing to pass up this dramatic denouement indicates that they were committed now to filming real fights. When Gray attempted the previous October to get the rights to record the upcoming Corbett-Fitzsimmons contest, William Brady had rebuffed him with the comment that the two fighters would be "greyheaded" before motion picture technology was up to the task. Now the prospect had radically changed. The ability to film a championship prizefight, full three-minute rounds with one-minute rests in between, was no longer years away, but just a matter of months.

As the film of the Griffo-Barnett fight was being developed and everything made ready for its commercial debut, Woodville Latham came up with a new name for the continuous-movement projector that Lauste had been hired to build. Henceforth the machine would be known as the "Eidoloscope," from the Greek root "eidolon" for a phantom-like image.

The film was publicly shown for the first time on Saturday, May 18, 1895, in a converted storefront at 156 Broadway, not far from the Frankfort Street workshop. "Eidoloscope," announced the pasteboard tickets sold to the curiosity seekers who lined up upside. "Exhibition No. 1. The Lambda Co. Admit One." To commemorate the event, Otway wrote an inscription on the back of the first ticket sold, "May 18, 156 Broadway, 1st paid admission," and signed his name. For him, the significance of the event was partly personal, for it marked the first money earned in a venture that would hopefully restore the Latham family to wealth. He, Gray and Woodville were also clearly aware of the greater historical significance, however, as evidenced by the advertising posters that had been printed. Beneath the title proclaiming "Latham's Eidoloscope. Exhibition of Living Moving Pictures (Life Size)," was the following statement: "This is the first practical exhibition of subjects showing Actual Life Movements on a screen ever made in the world."

To be more precise, it was the world's first projected movie shown to paying customers, predating by seven months the Lumière brothers' first commercial screening in Paris. And that pasteboard with Otway's notation on the back—that was the world's first movie ticket. The person who purchased it, the world's first projected movie patron, is unknown. The ticket itself survived at least into the 1930s, when it was in the hands of a former chinaware shop owner from Cincinnati named Charles Braunstein, then retired in California. It may still exist out there, forgotten in a box or tucked in a book.

What this first movie patron experienced may have been something like this. After entering the nondescript storefront and buying his twenty-five-cent ticket, he passed through curtains into an open space arrayed with rows of folding chairs, the sort that could be rented from a funeral parlor. He took a seat and was soon joined by a few dozen others, facing a rectangle of white canvas approximately eight feet across. The lights went out, a muffled clatter started up in the makeshift projection booth at the back of the room and a ghostly image, like a familiar old magic lantern show but with movement, came to life on the screen. The picture was somewhat dim and had a flicker that was hard on the eyes, and it tended to wander about on the canvas. But that did not detract from the stunning novelty of the thing. For there were two pugilists, Griffo and Barnett, squaring off and swinging at each other as real as life. The silent action was exciting and looked entirely authentic, eliciting exclamations from audience members of "Mix up there!" and "Look out, Charlie!" It continued for eight uninterrupted minutes, six times longer than the longest film on a Kinetoscope machine, then the screen went black, the clattering apparatus fell silent, the lights were turned on and the show was over. As our anonymous patron rose and left the room, he might have glimpsed the man in the booth, sweat beaded on his brow from the heat of the projector's intensely bright lamp. He was beginning to rewind the reel of film on his machine, getting ready for the next show to the next group lined up outside.

The Griffo-Barnett fight film presentation, soon lengthened to twelve minutes by the addition of unrelated footage of dancing street urchins, enjoyed several weeks of moderate success at 156 Broadway, the Lathams doing little advertising, relying mainly on roping in passersby. By July it had moved to a tent on Coney Island, middleweight Tom West hired to punch a bag outside to attract a crowd. An engagement in Chicago followed, then back to New York, then down to Atlanta, Gray and Otway taking their projector wherever opportunity beckoned, a week here, a night there, wrestling matches and vaudeville dancers and other entertainments being filmed along the way to add spice to the show. Money was coming in now but it was far from a flood, not enough to keep the free-spending Lathams and their Lambda Company out of the red. The company would in fact soon disappear, folded into a new entity called the Eidoloscope Company incorporated in the latter part of 1895 with a new group of investors. The Eidoloscope Company would follow the Edison Kinetoscope business model going forward, selling territorial rights for their projector and films. Woodville's nephew LeRoy Latham would make the first purchase, acquiring the rights for the state of Virginia for three thousand dollars and opening an exhibition in Norfolk.

Gray and Otway, meanwhile, continued to dream and scheme of filming the ultimate prizefight, the upcoming Corbett-Fitz championship bout. To succeed at such a tremendous undertaking, they put Eugene Lauste to work building two additional cameras so that a total of three machines would be ready at ringside. This would allow one camera to be kept in constant operation while the other two were being loaded with film. What Lauste came up with was something he called a "twin camera"—two cameras housed inside one body and activated by a single switch. This would act as insurance against film breakage or mechanical mishap, for if one of the temperamental machines ceased to function, the second would continue to film. The matter of reloading these cameras does not appear to have been given much thought by the Lathams. It was a complicated and delicate procedure and would require a darkroom at ringside. It would also have to be done quickly, before the film in the other cameras ran out, for at a genuine fight there would be no chance to pause the action or try again.

As Lauste slaved at his workbench for what he would later estimate was less than fifteen cents an hour, a draughtsman was hired by the Lathams to make drawings of his projector and camera for patent applications. Woodville Latham's name would appear on the documents as the inventor, Lauste receiving compensation of two hundred shares in the company. Arrangements such as this were common in the world of invention, nowhere more so than at Edison's lab, where Edison frequently received sole credit for inventions such as the Kinetograph and Kinetoscope that had been largely developed and perfected by his employees. Woodville Latham, however, was no Edison—as would become abundantly clear during preparations for a New York Eidoloscope screening.

The venue was the spacious barroom in the closed and soon-to-be demolished St. James Hotel, the windows covered with heavy black curtains. The projector was set up far back from the screen, resulting in a very large and very dim image. The problem was that the continuous-motion machine as designed could not project enough illumination to allow for so much enlargement, its rotating disk shutter with its quarter-inch slits blocking ninety-five percent of the light. Eugene Lauste tried to explain this to Woodville, but Woodville had other ideas. Since the problem was lack of illumination, he reasoned, the solution was to increase the amount of light hitting the screen. He therefore ordered that a separate beam of light be shone onto the canvas. Lauste was taken aback by this ludicrous notion and sarcastically suggested that they might as well throw open the curtains and let in the sunlight. Woodville, the imperious professor, insisted it would work.

A light was accordingly set up, pointed at the screen and turned on. Woodville signaled to the projection booth: "Go!"

Nothing appeared on the screen.

"Let go!" cried Woodville, thinking the projector had not been turned on.

Still nothing.

"Go ahead! Are you not ready? Go ahead!"

Still nothing.

Woodville stormed back to the booth to see what was holding things up only to find that the projector had been running the whole time. His idea had not worked. Still not satisfied, he insisted that Lauste run the reel again. This time Woodville scratched his head as he stared at the blank screen, puzzling over why his auxiliary lighting was dimming the image to the point of invisibility instead of making it brighter.

The Griffo-Barnett fight film never enjoyed the wide circulation of *Corbett and Courtney Before the Kinetograph*. Printed on uniquely sized two-inch-wide film, it could only be shown on the Eidoloscope projector and thus faded away with the demise of that apparatus, while the Corbett-Courtney film, on standard Edison stock, went on to continuing success as a projected movie. The footage shot by Otway Latham, generally known today by the title *Young Griffo vs. Battling Barnett*, is a lost film. The hand-drawn illustrations of snippets of the film published in the *New York World* and *Brooklyn Daily Eagle* in May 1895, thirteen frames in the former and seven in the latter, are all that remain.

Charley Barnett did not enjoy any time in the sun as a result of his filmed encounter with Griffo. He sank back into obscurity for a few more undercard bouts, then left the ring to earn his living as a junk dealer. As for Griffo, he would go on to become the archetype of the down-and-out fighter, the aging, cauliflower-eared, broken-down bum.

His troubles began in earnest with his arrest for an "unmentionable crime" committed just days after his fight with Barnett—and indeed, the crime was never mentioned in the papers, although the fact that the victim was a nine-year-old boy and the possible sentence twenty years in prison left little doubt it was child molestation or rape. Griffo was eventually convicted in August 1896 on the lesser charge of assault and spent a year in prison, then did a stretch in an insane asylum starting in 1899. By 1906, after a few more years in the ring, he had sunk to what one paper called "a common loafer, existing by the generosity of former friends and cronies." When that wasn't enough, he hung around bars and demonstrated his old skills in exchange for drinks, planting one foot on a handkerchief and inviting people to try to hit him. When the bars closed with Prohibition, he panhandled in the streets.

Young Griffo spent his final years sitting on the steps at the side entrance to Broadway's Rialto Theater, broke and fat and unwashed and clad in old clothes, his health destroyed by more than two hundred fights and the booze he could no longer get. He was a regular fixture on the steps, and passersby, even celebrities like Al Jolson, would often stop for a chat. They would ask him, *Why do you sit here, Griffo?* And Griffo, who was no longer young, would murmur in answer: "I don't know...Just watching...just watching...It all goes by and it never stops. It's always changing and it always keeps me from being lonely. It keeps bringing me back. I don't know why...Just watching it go by."

The sun would go down and the streetlights come on and Griffo would continue to sit on the steps. Just watching. Then he would get up and shuffle off into the night.

CHAPTER 15

ENTER DAN STUART

JACKSONVILLE, FLORIDA WAS OUT. The Corbett-Fitzsimmons title fight could not be held there or anywhere else in the state. The move to kill the contest had started with the Jacksonville city council repealing its ordinance allowing prizefighting and ended with the Florida legislature passing an anti-fight law. On May 21, 1895, engaging in any kind of fistic contest became a felony in the state, punishable by a heavy fine or up to five years in prison.

Joe Vendig, secretary of the Florida Athletic Club, remained unperturbed. As he put it, he still had "a cast iron cinch on the fight," for the agreement Corbett and Fitz had signed did not specify that it would be held in Jacksonville or even in Florida. "So long as the Florida Club complies with the agreement," Vendig stated, "and puts up the amount of the purse and stake as stipulated in the articles, Corbett and Fitzsimmons will have to fight where the club says." Corbett agreed. He had long since concluded that Jacksonville was a bust and the fight would have to take place somewhere else. Fitz balked at first, threatening to claim the forfeit money the club put up, but eventually relented.

So, where would it be? The obvious fallback was the Olympic Club in New Orleans, which had forced Corbett to put his title on the line in the first place and had wanted the fight all along. But New Orleans was no longer an option. Louisiana was at that moment in the grip of its own anti-fight backlash and New Orleans had ceased to be a pugilistic safe haven, the Olympic reduced to hosting exhibitions of wrestling and billiards. A syndicate in Canada made an offer to hold the contest near Montreal but that possibility was immediately squelched by Quebec's attorney general. "It will certainly not take place in this province if I can help it," he said. And then, on the very day that Florida passed its anti-fight law, Corbett and Fitzsimmons each received a telegram that read simply, "Will be in New York before June 1st ready to talk business." It had been sent from Dallas by a man named Dan Stuart.

Entrepreneur, investor, sporting man and visionary—Daniel Albert Stuart was solid in every sense of the word. Physically, the forty-nine-year-old bachelor was well over six feet tall and weighed three hundred pounds, towering over all who entered his Dallas saloon and gambling house or the stock exchange and pool room he presided over next door. Financially, he had reportedly amassed a half million dollars since leaving Vermont in his teens to seek his fortune in Texas. And in terms of character he was the proverbial rock, "a man whose word is his bond," according to one admirer, "stand[ing] ace high in sporting circles in the West and South."

Stuart made a good impression upon his arrival in New York. He was affable, confident and exquisitely mannered and seemed just the man to rescue the Corbett-Fitz fight from a quagmire of legal obstruction and doubt. He met with both fighters and soon won them over. He also won over Joe Vendig and the Florida AC, persuading them to elect him president and treasurer of the club and relocate it and the heavyweight title bout to Dallas, where there were no anti-fight laws and where the citizenry was ready to welcome them with open arms.

The Corbett-Fitzsimmons fight was back on. And this time it seemed a sure thing, unstoppable by "nothing short of a revolution," Stuart proclaimed as he revealed his Texas-sized plans. He would hold a "fistic carnival" in Dallas, an entire week of big-name bouts culminating with the Corbett-Fitz battle. Visitors would flood into the city from all surrounding states to attend, enjoying special excursion rates arranged with the railroads. They would spend their dollars in hotels and restaurants and saloons and shops, which was what Dallas wanted, and they would fill the amphitheater that Stuart had already designed. "It will be a mammoth structure," he stated, lighting a massive cigar, "built in octagonal shape. There will be four entrances. The seating capacity will be 40,000. There will be 250 boxes with ten chairs in each. The prices for boxes have not been determined, but the admission will be $10, with reserved seats $20."

While all this was going on, a struggle was taking place behind the scenes to secure the film rights for the contest. It had begun in October 1894, shortly before the Lathams' ouster from the Kinetoscope Exhibiting Company, with Gray's widely publicized offer of $50,000 to hold the bout in Mexico. In the following May, after the successful filming of the Griffo-Barnett fight, one of the Latham brothers, likely Gray, tried again. This time a personal approach was made to Corbett and Fitzsimmons, appearing in Cincinnati at the same time with their shows.

"[A] gentleman named Latham called on me," Bob revealed a few months later, "and unfolded a scheme for the reproduction of the coming fight. We talked the matter over thoroughly, and to say that I was much pleased at the idea is putting it mildly. We parted with the understanding that we were to meet the next day and agree as to what I should receive for the permission of being eidoloscoped the world over. Well, to make a long story short, Mr. Latham never came back the next day, nor did any one connected with him or his invention."

This may have been just another example of the Lathams' impetuous, flighty nature, exciting Fitz with talk of a film contract and then leaving him hanging. It is possible, however, that something more calculating was going on. For as the Lathams were well aware, the Kinetoscope Exhibiting Company had an exclusive contract with Jim Corbett, signed the previous summer when Gray and Otway were still directors, in which Jim agreed to perform only for the KEC's camera. It was therefore a forgone conclusion that if the Corbett-Fitz fight was to be filmed, the KEC would be doing the filming. In approaching Corbett in May 1895, the Lathams were thus knowingly treading on KEC ground. They almost certainly believed, thanks to Lauste's little loop, that they had the only camera in existence capable of filming three-minute rounds and thus that the KEC would be open to some sort of arrangement presented through Corbett. The private meeting with Fitz, however, suggests a second, darker motive. In filling Bob's head with visions of film riches, the Lathams may have been trying to sabotage the KEC and derail the fight.

If so, they nearly succeeded. In the lead-up to the contest Bob railed against the private film deal he suspected Corbett had with the "eidoloscope people" and threatened to pull out unless he got $20,000. "Some people may think that my figure is high," he said, "but I don't. Stop for a moment and think that when this fight was being arranged the Edison Kinetoscope company [sic.] bid $50,000 for the contest to be fought for them in private, and their kineto-scope will only permit for one person viewing the fight at one time, while this eidoloscope can portray the battle to 10,000 people if they can get into the building where it is exhibited." Bob said this in September, no doubt repeating what he had heard from the Lathams. And he was still complaining in October: "I will insist on President Dan Stuart's word when I get south that these people can't bring their photographic instrument into the building unless I am paid for their transferring me to canvas.... If Corbett gets nothing, why I am satisfied to get nothing. I want an even break, however, with him in everything, eidoloscope, choice of referee and fair play. I will stand for no 'hog combine.' Brady, Corbett & Co. might manage that in theatricals, but they can't in fighting, at least where I am concerned."

Bob never got a piece of the Eidoloscope action, for as Joe Vendig tried to make clear, there wasn't any to get. The Florida AC was "not interested in that invention," he stated, "and the eidoloscope will not be permitted to be brought into the building on the day of the fight." But Bob and Martin Julian didn't trust Vendig. They still suspected that there was a plan to film the fight. And they were correct.

It was instead the Kinetoscope Exhibiting Company that would undertake the filming. This should have been a hopeless endeavor, for Enoch Rector had only Edison's Kinetograph cameras to work with, which were capable of handling no more than a minute and a half of film, the limit already reached with the recording of the Corbett-Courtney fight. In talking with film historian Terry Ramsaye many years later, Rector explained this away by claiming that the Kinetographs he had custom made were equipped with the "Latham Loop"—and that he himself was the loop's inventor. But this was not true. There was no strain-eliminating loop in Rector's new cameras. He was likely unaware of the loop at this time. He had devised a different way to remove tension from the film as it passed through the camera so that the dragging weight of bigger film reels didn't tear it to pieces. All that was in fact needed was to remove the electrical drive from the reels and turn them by hand, thereby ensuring that the film was kept constantly slack. There was just one problem: the men who would do the turning, one rotating the feed reel and other the take-up, had to be sealed inside the camera. Fortunately for Rector, that accorded perfectly with his plans.

Rector's new Kinetographs, four altogether, would be custom-made by the Edison Manufacturing Company, which handled Edison's motion picture business now that it had moved out of the lab. After meeting with Rector to hash out the details, William Gilmore acknowledged the order on September 10, 1895, manufacture to begin at once, the cost for each camera to be six hundred dollars. The KEC would own the machines but their use was to be greatly restricted. "We will send a competent man to operate the machines, with one assistant," Gilmore specified in his letter, "the former to have entire charge of the handling and disposition of said apparatus, all the way through, and to supervise the taking of the subject properly, you to provide all necessary assistance.... [T]he machines and appurtenances shall always remain in his possession, and be in no way molested or removed without his sanction."

The four cameras were intended to handle five-hundred-foot rolls of film, enough to record four minutes of action with fifty feet extra (suggesting a photographing speed of around thirty frames per second). Rector's plan was to be prepared to film twenty-five rounds— one hundred minutes—in duplicate, two cameras constantly running. To do so would require fifty rolls of film, which was additionally ordered, an immense and unprecedented total of 25,000 feet.

The resulting footage would be exhibited to the public on a "new Kinetoscope, or apparatus," Gilmore specified in his letter, "to be gotten up by ourselves, in conjunction with your Mr. Rector." This new machine, built to accommodate four hundred fifty feet of film, would have been massive, around fifteen feet long, with five peepholes arrayed down its length so that multiple customers could view the film at the same time. Its purpose was ultimately to keep the Kinetoscope business alive by presenting longer films to the public and by providing a new viewing experience that could be shared. Rector's gigantic apparatus, which in the end was never built, would have pushed the peephole Kinetoscope as far as it could go. It was, in effect, an evolutionary dead end.

To produce a more rectangular picture, Rector decided to use two-inch-wide film rather than Edison's standard one-and-three-eighths. This was the same film width being used by the Lathams. A major reason why the Lathams went to wider film, at least according to Lauste, was to increase the size and in turn the brightness of the image when projected on a screen, their Eidoloscope projector using continuous movement and thus being inherently dim. This would not have been a concern for Rector, who was still thinking in terms of peephole Kinetoscope exhibition, which required less illumination. As for the more rectangular frame, this was specifically to facilitate the filming of prizefights, the common goal of the Lathams and Rector. It is indeed likely that they discussed this with Dickson going back to the latter half of 1894, when they were partners in the KEC, which would explain how they now came to adopt the same film format. Whereas previous filmed fights had been held in under-sized rings to squeeze the action into the almost square dimensions of the Edison film format, Corbett and Fitz would do battle in a regulation-sized ring twenty-four feet across, a comparative vista. With Edison film, the camera would have to be positioned much further back to take it all in, reducing the ring to a narrow sliver in the center of the frame. Using a horizontally elongated frame had the advantage of allowing the camera to be moved much closer, the increased width a better fit for the ring and the fighters inside, leaving no wasted space above and below. So it was that the widescreen film dimensions familiar to moviegoers today came into being to encompass a boxing ring.

By using four cameras to record the Corbett-Fitz fight, Rector hoped to keep two machines running at all times while the other two were being reloaded with film. This reloading step posed another problem. Unlike filming in the Black Maria, where there was plenty of time, it would not be practical at ringside to disconnect each Kinetograph in turn from it batteries and wheel it into a darkroom; to close the door and open the camera and remove the exposed film and seal it in a can; to load a fresh roll of film and close up the camera and open the door and wheel the machine back into position and reconnect it to its batteries and turn it back on. The process was much too cumbersome to be completed with any reliability, again and again, in under four minutes.

The idea Rector came up with once again required that the camera operators be sealed inside the camera. He would call this gigantic apparatus, large enough to accommodate a whole team of men, the "Kineto-Multiscope." It and its successor, Rector's "Veriscope," occupy an overlooked branch in the evolutionary tree of motion picture technology, a developmental dead end that has been forgotten.

They are the Neanderthal at the beginning of cinema history.

As Jim Corbett and Bob Fitzsimmons went into training for their upcoming battle, set for Dallas on October 31, 1895, both were struggling to recover from a turbulent year in their personal lives. Bob's problems had begun the previous November with the ring death of sparring partner Con Riordan and his subsequent indictment for manslaughter. With a trial looming and a possible prison sentence hanging over his head, he soldiered on with his vaudeville show, which was doing poor business. The mounting financial strain soon soured his already troubled relationship with his manager and business partner Captain Glori, resulting in violent arguments over money and accusations by Bob that he was being "robbed right and left." The tension between them became so extreme that Bob disbanded his theatrical company, severed all ties with Glori and returned to his former manager and now brother-in-law, Martin Julian. When an advertisement was placed in the *New York Clipper* on March 30 seeking theater engagements for Bob's new, "thoroughly reorganized" show, the disclaimer was included that "Capt. Chas. Glori ... [is] in no way connected with Bob Fitzsimmons or this organization."

This of course led to a lawsuit, Glori calling Bob an "ingrate" and suing him over their broken partnership agreement. Hiring lawyers and reaching a settlement left Bob with almost nothing. He was back to where he had been in 1893 when he washed up in Newark and slept in Glori's station house—a story that Glori now repeated in the press. "That stationhouse story... was another one of Glori's lies," Bob shot back. "I was not broke at the time, and only stayed at the stationhouse at his earnest solicitation." He was certainly broke now, however—"financially crippled" by Glori's "mismanagement," as he put it. And he had yet to pay the law firm that was defending him against the manslaughter charge.

The trial began in Syracuse on June 24, 1895, Bob looking nervous, District Attorney Shove determined to make an example of him and strike a blow against boxing. The case hinged on the damning testimony of police surgeon Totman—and it was here that it all fell apart. For it came to light that the lesions on Riordan's brain supposedly caused by a punch to the head had not been noted in the official autopsy but had been added to the report later by Totman himself, after a second examination of the body conducted in private. With other medical men testifying that Riordan had been a physical wreck and that the lesions had likely been caused during the autopsy when the brain was removed from the skull, the jury quickly reached a verdict of "not guilty." Bob leaped to his feet as the words were read out and seized every juror in turn by the hand. He then went back on the road with his show, desperate for money to cover his legal expenses and the $10,000 stake for the Corbett fight, which was still only half paid.

Jim Corbett, meanwhile, was having trouble of his own. It was not financial. He was rolling in money, prospering like never before from his investments and theatrical ventures, *Gentleman Jack* continuing to attract big crowds wherever it played. Jim's problems instead were marital. His womanizing had reached the point where his wife Ollie, from whom he had been living apart for some time, could no longer ignore it. The last straw was a blonde beauty named Vera Stanwood, otherwise known as Jessie Taylor, formerly a waitress from Omaha, Nebraska. Jim had met her at the World's Fair the previous year and took her on the road, registering in hotels as "Mr. and Mrs. Corbett" as the rest of the *Gentleman Jack* company pretended not to notice. It all came out in the papers, the scandal of the day, when Ollie filed for divorce and the suit went before the court in July 1895, her lawyers threatening that further evidence of Jim's infidelity could be presented. But there was no need. Jim offered no defense and the divorce was granted, Ollie awarded alimony of a hundred dollars a week. Jim married Vera in Asbury Park less than a month later in a ceremony attended by three witnesses and his old cook.

It was against this backdrop, Bob struggling financially and Jim publicly embarrassed, his image as a gentleman tarnished, that the nose-pulling incident occurred in a Philadelphia hotel on the night of August 11. Jim and William Brady were seated in the dining room with Jim's brother Joe, who was about to make his Major League debut as a pitcher, when they noticed Bob at the front desk registering for a room.

"Well, you are up to your old tricks again, I see," said Jim, striding over to confront him, angry over comments attributed to Bob in the press. "Been saying you would pull my nose and all that sort of thing, I hear."

"I don't know that I have," replied Bob, nonchalant, "but what of it anyway?"

Jim didn't answer. Instead he made a grab for Bob's nose and gave it a yank, then spit at him as Bob jerked free.

"Gentleman Jim! Gentleman Jim!" Bob sneered as his friends pulled him away and seated him at a table. "Oh, yes; Gentleman Jim! I think this shows how much of a gentleman you are."

"I can lick you myself, you red-headed chump," said Joe Corbett, who had followed his brother over.

Bob seized a carafe from the table and threw it at Joe, missing him and hitting Brady in the chest as a barrage of insults erupted on both sides. The two parties were separated and order restored but the feud was by no means over. It would continue hot in the papers, Corbett claiming that Fitz had been "beastly drunk" and that he would make "this foreigner take his medicine or crawl," Fitz responding that "Jim simply lies" and that "Corbett doesn't know how to infight, and he won't until I teach him something."

By September the two antagonists had gone into training, Corbett at Asbury Park and Fitz down in Corpus Christi, Texas, Fitz claiming to be in the best shape of his life thanks in part to "a course of electric treatment" he was receiving. Over in Dallas, Dan Stuart's amphitheater was under construction, gangs of workmen hammering together whole trainloads of lumber for what was claimed to be in terms of seating capacity the second-largest arena in history, surpassed only by the Coliseum in Rome. Anti-fight fever, meanwhile, was rising across the state, religious groups drawing up petitions and applying pressure, Texas governor Culberson threatening to introduce legislation outlawing pugilistic displays. None of this particularly worried Dan Stuart, not with his fistic carnival less than two months away and the legislature not even in session. He was betting that everything would be over and done with before state lawmakers ended their long holiday and reassembled in Austin and got around to cobbling together some sort of bill.

He was wrong. On October 2, in a special session called by the governor, a bill was rammed through the legislature making prizefighting a felony in Texas punishable by up to five years in prison. It was a seemingly fatal blow but Stuart remained unshaken. This was due in part to his strong stubborn streak, his determination to overcome all obstacles and complete what he started. Just as important, however, was the insurance he had quietly arranged for himself when he was laying his plans, the fat sum a consortium of Dallas businessmen had agreed to pay should anything prevent him from holding his fight-fest in their city. The necessity of relocating the fistic carnival was thus not as big a financial disaster as it appeared, at least not for Stuart. "I have been arranging for this emergency for some days," he stated, nonplussed, following the passage of the new law, "and have three places in view, each within convenient distance to Dallas. I will decide on the place within the next twenty-four hours."

The new venue Stuart selected was the resort town of Hot Springs, three hundred miles northeast in neighboring Arkansas. The citizens there, hard-hit by the economic depression, were eager to host the fight and welcome the flood of visitors it would bring—unsavory types, perhaps, but with good money to spend just the same, money that Hot Springs' languishing hotels and restaurants and shops desperately needed. With prizefighting only a misdemeanor in the state and no town ordinance in Hot Springs barring such contests, the legal opinion was that the battle could be pulled off without interference and fines paid after the fact, as had been done in Florida after the Corbett-Mitchell bout.

Corbett and his party, just arrived in Texas, continued on to Hot Springs and set up a training camp in a hotel outside town. Fitz and Martin Julian remained in Corpus Christi, seething with resentment that Fitz was getting the short end of the stick from Corbett and the "hog combine." Stuart's request to postpone the fight until November 11 to allow time for a new amphitheater to be built was just the opportunity they needed to make a stand, and they made it, Fitz stating that he would fight on October 31 as per the agreement or not fight at all. Julian was invited up to Hot Springs for a parlay with Stuart and Corbett but it did no good.

"Will you kindly withdraw your objection, Mr. Julian," Stuart pleaded, "and agree to November 11?"

"I will do nothing of the kind," Julian snapped. "Fitzsimmons will only fight on October 31."

"You are very severe, considering the circumstances. Don't you think we are entitled to some consideration?"

"No, sir, we have not been fairly treated, and, therefore, we refuse to give way an inch."

That was it. Stuart withdrew the purse and declared the fight off. "It is all over with us," moaned Joe Vendig. "The Florida Athletic Club has shut up shop and temporarily gone out of business." They both put the blame squarely on Fitz and Julian for taking such an unreasonable stand. William Brady went further, stating that Fitz purposefully sabotaged the fight because he knew he would lose. "[N]ow that he is compelled to either fight or crawl," Brady said, "he chooses the latter course." Corbett put it even more strongly, calling Fitz a "cur," a "yellow dog" and "the biggest coward ever put on record." Julian shot back that it was Corbett who did not want to fight; that he had not bothered to properly train for the contest and now wanted to give Arkansas governor Clarke more time to intervene, which Clarke was threatening to do.

Fitz and Julian departed Texas for Hot Springs on October 29, planning to either fight Corbett on the agreed-upon day or claim the title and the forfeit money pledged by the Florida AC. Just as the train was crossing the Arkansas border, two sheriffs entered the car to confront them. One had been sent from Hot Springs to escort them to town—protection to get them to ringside so that the fight still could be held for the stake money alone. The other had come from Little Rock with warrants signed by the attorney general for their arrest. In the standoff that followed, the Little Rock sheriff prevailed and took Fitz and Julian to the state capital to face charges. With there no chance now of a fight, Corbett turned himself in, stopping off first at the ring in Hot Springs on fight day so that he could claim the forfeit money that Fitz would be denied. "I want you men to understand that I have nothing against you personally," Governor Clarke told the two fighters after their appearance in court, "but you may as well understand that I will have no prize-fighting in Arkansas. I will exhaust every legal means to prevent it, and I am as sure of succeeding as that the sun will rise tomorrow. That's all. Good evening."

As the courtroom drama played itself out and Corbett retreated to New York and Fitz back to Texas, a faint glimmer of hope continued to flicker that the fight might still be somehow pulled off. The more exotic venues suggested included a barge towed out into the Gulf of Mexico, a platform floated up into the air by balloons and—most unlikely of all—Connecticut. Then, on November 12, Dan Stuart received a telegram from William Brady that seemed to completely extinguish any chance of a fight. "Corbett surrenders championship and belt to Maher," it read, "and will back Maher for $10,000 against Fitzsimmons."

It was no stunt. Corbett really was giving up his title to Peter Maher, who had just defeated Steve O'Donnell by knockout in the first round. "I was so disgusted with Fitzsimmons' dunderheadedness in going to Little Rock with the Governor's deputies," Corbett would recall in *The Roar of the Crowd*, "and so angry at being chased around the country from state to state, that I publicly announced my retirement from the ring and handed over the championship to Peter Maher.... This, of course, I had really no right to do, for you cannot *hand* a championship to a man; he has to win that with his own hands in the ring."

Corbett did it anyway. Henceforth he would devote himself fully to the stage and his new play, *A Naval Cadet*, now in rehearsal.

With Fitz loudly claiming the abandoned title for himself, Dan Stuart set out from Dallas to either talk Corbett back into the ring or find another way forward. His remarkable tenacity was being wondered at now, one rumor attributing it to the shadowy "eidoloscope people" who had supposedly offered $50,000 to film the fight. Arriving in New York, Stuart met first with William Brady to propose a Corbett-Fitz meeting in Mexico for a purse of $20,000, "confidential agents" south of the border having assured him there would be no trouble holding the fight there. When this offer was rejected, Stuart turned to Maher's manager John Quinn and arranged a Fitz-Maher matchup for a purse of $10,000.

The articles were eventually signed after Fitz got through playing coy and making demands. It would be Bob Fitzsimmons vs. Peter Maher on February 14, 1896, ostensibly for the heavyweight championship of the world.

"I am sure," Dan Stuart confidently announced as he headed back to Texas, "that nothing but an earthquake can disturb the men this time."

CHAPTER 16

STANDOFF IN EL PASO

STUNG BY THE EXPERIENCE of being run out of Texas and Arkansas, Dan Stuart decided to abandon the United States altogether and hold the Fitzsimmons-Maher fight in Mexico, in the border town of Juarez. It was close to El Paso, an easy walk or mule-drawn street-car ride across the bridge spanning the Rio Grande river, and it had a bullring that would do as a venue.

Stuart's plan once again was for a sporting extravaganza lasting several days. It would kick off with the Fitz-Maher bout on February 14, 1896, with bullfights thrown in as an added attraction, and would be followed on successive days by title fights in lower weight divisions. There would be Joe Walcott vs. Scott "Bright Eyes" Collins for the welterweight crown, George Dixon vs. Jake Marshall for the featherweight title and lightweight Jack Everhardt battling Horace Leeds. Leeds' inclusion added an interesting wrinkle to the affair, for he would be accompanied by his manager Captain Glori, a name near the top of the list of people Fitz most despised. Another person on that list, Fitz's first manager Jimmy Carroll, would also be present. Carroll was hoping to see his former fighter, whom he regarded as an ingrate, "good and thoroughly whipped."

Fitz stepped off the train in El Paso leading his pet lion Nero on a chain. He liked oversized pets. Nero was certainly his biggest to date. Also in tow were two trainers, a cook and sparring partner, and Martin Julian. Rose would follow later with their newborn son Bob Jr. After paying Dan Stuart a visit, the party proceeded across the river to the dusty, flea-bitten town of Juarez. Fitz would make his training quarters here in an empty warehouse off the town plaza. "It will be all over in less than eight rounds," he predicted. "I know Maher's style of fighting like a book. I will put him to sleep so quickly that he will never know how it happened."

Maher was equally bellicose as he set up his own training camp at Las Cruces in New Mexico territory forty miles north of El Paso. He claimed he was no longer the inexperienced, poorly conditioned, overly nervous fighter who had lost to Fitz three years before, and his recent first-round demolition of Steve O'Donnell seemed to prove it. "Things are different now," Maher stated. "I have not tasted liquor in two years, I have now the confidence and experience which I was so painfully lacking in then, and I never enjoyed better health in my life. Fitzsimmons will find in me an entirely different man than he fought in New Orleans. I expect to defeat him inside of four rounds."

The two fighters set to work, Fitz throwing himself into it with his usual vigor. He began each day early with roadwork, either a jog or a hike in the mountains, or for variety a ride on the new-fangled bicycle that had come down in his baggage. After breakfast there was the heavy bag to hone the renowned power of his punches, a go on the wrist machine to strengthen his forearms, then, in the afternoon, eight rounds of sparring—sparring that had to be curtailed after he broke his sparring partner's nose and a replacement could not be found. The training sessions were open to the public, admission twenty-five cents, fifty dollars taken in on a typical day. Fitz would end the afternoon session by wrestling with Nero, giving the spectators a bonus scare for their money by pretending to set the beast loose. Then it was off to a shower, a big supper, an evening of relaxation and early to bed.

Maher for his part preferred a less structured approach, doing whatever struck his fancy, his trainers having to nag him out of bed every morning. He had the excuse of a case of boils but in this game there was no room for excuses. Particularly worrisome was the Irishman's John L. Sullivan-like disdain for roadwork. "That man had better fix his wind in good shape," Fitz warned when he heard the rumors. "He will need the best pair of lungs he can build up."

The fighters slated for the undercard matches were in the meantime arriving and work was underway at the Juarez bullring, where extra tiers of benches were being installed. It was not nearly as grand or as spacious as the amphitheater Dan Stuart had originally planned for Dallas, but if he could even half-fill it at ten and twenty dollars a head the take would still be impressive. After his many trials and tribulations, he could still come out of this making money on the deal.

Then came the figurative earthquake.

Governor Miguel Ahumada of the Mexican state of Chihuahua, which encompassed the town of Juarez, was the cause. He had had a change of heart since assuring Stuart that he would not oppose the fight being held in his jurisdiction. Personally, he would enjoy seeing a prizefight, Ahumada admitted. Publicly, however, he did not want to undermine his American neighbors, who were clearly opposed to such a fistic display. The fight therefore would not be allowed on Mexican soil. "[I]f its promoters come onto our side of the line," the governor said, "our soldiers will have orders to shoot without discrimination between combatants or non-combatants. Principals or spectators, everybody has been given fair warning, and if they disregard it, then it will be at their own peril."

So Juarez was out. It was a hard blow for Stuart, a loss of tens of thousands of dollars, for with the loss of the bullring went any chance of selling a large number of tickets. To go ahead now, his fistic carnival would have to be held in some out-of-the-way place.

Undaunted, Stuart pushed ahead. There was now more than money at stake. There was his reputation, his image as a mover and shaker who could put together big events and attract big investors and see big schemes through to completion. He would simply have to make new arrangements. Again.

New Mexico seemed his next best option. Holding his fistic carnival there would drastically limit ticket sales but that was inescapable no matter which way he turned. At least there would be no legal interference. For New Mexico was a territory, not yet a state, and thus was subject only to federal laws, which had nothing to say about prizefighting.

And then New Mexico was off limits as well. In the first week of February a bill prohibiting prizefighting in United States territories, proposed by New Mexico representative Thomas Catron, was rushed through both houses of Congress and signed into law by President Cleveland before he set off on a duck hunting trip. "Be it enacted," the bill read, "that any person who in any of the Territories or the District of Columbia, shall voluntarily engage in a pugilistic encounter between man and man, or a fight between a man and a bull, or any other animal...shall be deemed guilty of a felony, and upon conviction be punished by imprisonment in the penitentiary not less than one nor more than five years." The *El Paso Daily Times* responded with hot indignation, calling the local "Ministerial Element" that had pushed for the legislation a "puffed toad...posing as a martyr to the public welfare." A number of prominent El Paso businessmen renounced their memberships in local churches, promising that those meddling institutions would not see another cent from them. But it was already too late. The damage was done.

It seemed that every public official in the country was now against Dan Stuart and his heavyweight championship prizefight, everyone from state and territorial legislators to Congress and even the president himself. Yet none of it seemed to discourage the Dallas promoter. The Fitzsimmons-Maher fight would go ahead, he reassured newsmen and concerned sports almost daily. The bout would be held just as promised.

But where?

Two thousand miles northeast in New York City, Enoch Rector was preparing for the expedition down to Texas to film the battle. It would be a costly but necessary gamble, for it was clear now that the Kinetoscope business was in decline. Filming a real title fight and exhibiting it on a massive new peephole machine where the viewing experience was no longer solitary, but could be shared by five people, would give the Kinetoscope Exhibiting Company an exciting new novelty that would keep it alive.

Rector himself was now a man of substance, on the rise after two years in the city—vice president of the KEC, trusted agent of Samuel J. Tilden, resident of a good address at Gramercy Park and, for the past nine months, respectably married. He had returned to Parkersburg, West Virginia in May of the previous year to wed Jesse

Fremont Leech, of the Leech family he had known since childhood. He had been thirty-one years old at the time, Jesse twenty-two. They would have one child together, Anne Elizabeth, born in 1899.

After saying goodbye to Jesse, Rector took the train to New Lebanon for a final consultation with KEC president Tilden. The company was investing heavily in the venture, $17,000 in cameras, batteries, film and related expenses—and possibly also the purse for the fight, it was rumored, in return for permission to film it. Dan Stuart vehemently denied this, calling it a "malicious falsehood in toto. No man or company in any way has given one cent or has any interest in these fights except myself. I am alone, financially and in every way, responsible. The kinetoscope people will try and photograph the fight, and if successful will pay for it." The KEC was still taking a big gamble, the fate of the company resting on Rector's prospects for success with his Kineto-Multiscope. It was now public knowledge that the apparatus would be set up at ringside, the official program just put out by Dan Stuart noting that it would be on hand to "reproduce" the fight. The program went on sale almost the very day a cable arrived at Stuart's El Paso headquarters from the Lathams. They were interested in filming the battle with their Ei-doloscope, it said, and they wanted to know if they could acquire the rights. At this point the Lathams likely thought that they had the only camera in existence capable of filming for more than a minute or two.

From New Lebanon, Rector proceeded to Orange to pick up the four Kinetograph cameras the Edison Manufacturing Company had custom-made for him the previous September and the fifty reels of two-inch-wide film he had ordered, nearly five miles of it altogether. Although the machines were KEC property, the Edison company had insisted that they remain on its premises when not in use. Another stipulation was that an Edison technician with one assistant "have entire charge" of the cameras when Rector took them into the field, "[a]ll expenses of whatever nature, with the exception of the salaries of the two representatives above mentioned, to be borne by yourselves." Rector thus acquired two traveling companions in Orange. The technician who would operate the Kinetographs, William Heise, was known to him going back to the filming of the Leonard-

Cushing fight. Heise was Edison's main moving picture man now, in charge of filming in the Black Maria following Dickson's departure. He would be assisted by his twenty-one-year-old son Theodore Heise. Theodore had acquired enough skill with the Kinetograph by July 1895 to be sent to Europe by Edison to film subjects for Maguire and Baucus, who owned the Kinetoscope rights there. That excursion had not turned out well, Maguire complaining that he was "unable to get any satisfaction out of Mr. Heise" and questioning the Edison bill for services not satisfactorily rendered.

It took a little over four days for the trio of filmmakers to make the journey to Texas: the Royal Blue Line from the Central Railroad Terminal in Jersey City to Washington DC; change to the Southwestern Vestibuled Limited heading to New Orleans; transfer to the westbound Texas and Pacific for the rest of the way. They arrived in El Paso on February 7 at nine-thirty in the morning to find the city in the grip of a cold snap, the temperature not much above freezing and fresh snow on the ground—not a good sign for the outdoor work that lay ahead. They were in the real West now, dusty, wind-blown streets and desert all round and a genuine Boot Hill cemetery on the outskirts. There were cowboys and sombreroed Mexicans wandering around, in town for a steer-roping contest; Indians and weathered ranchers and scowling toughs and ruffians and decent folk sharing the streets, all mixed together. And at the courthouse, a sensational trial underway of the assassin of John Wesley Hardin. The infamous gunslinger, who once killed a man—accidentally—for snoring, had been shot in the back of the head in the Acme Saloon, just over there.

By far the biggest sensation, of course, was "The Fight." It was causing more excitement than ever before seen in El Paso, a constant source of conversation, gossip and rumors. A company of Texas Rangers under Adjutant-General Mabry was now on the scene, sent by Governor Culberson to enforce the state's anti-fight law. They were watching Dan Stuart and they were following the fighters. And with the "kinetoscope man" now in town, they started following Enoch Rector. A Ranger named Edwin Aten—Winchester rifle, two revolvers—was assigned to tail him.

All this outside interference had El Paso's city leaders fuming, resentful that the governor and the Rangers were preventing them from conducting local affairs as they wished. They expressed their indignation in a resolution unanimously passed by the city council. "We regard and characterize the action of the Governor and the adjutant general," it concluded, "as an outrage and an insult to this entire community, and to all other law abiding and liberty loving people of Texas, and a shameful attempt on the part of the Governor and adjutant general to gain cheap notoriety under the guise of enforcing the laws." The situation was so heated that a hopeful rumor began circulating that Bat Masterson was coming to town with a hundred "bad men" to run off the Rangers. It was half true. Masterson indeed would soon be arriving, but alone. He had been hired by Stuart to oversee security for the fight.

Across the border in Juarez, Bob Fitzsimmons was feeling the pressure, his every move now watched by a company of Mexican soldiers. Governor Ahumada had also informed him and Martin Julian that they had to register at the mayor's office any time they left town. When Julian asked for the reason, the governor declined to explain. Well, persisted Julian, what if we want to leave late at night, when the mayor's office is closed? In that case report to one of the men guarding your house, replied Ahumada. We have three of them there watching you round the clock. To make a trip into El Paso, which he did almost daily to pick up his mail, Fitz therefore now had to go a half mile out of his way to stop first at the mayor's office. And when he crossed the bridge into Texas, there were Rangers waiting to take over from the Mexican troops in dogging his every step.

It was thus not surprising that Fitz and Julian were tense and fractious at the meeting on February 10 to make final arrangements for the fight. After the gloves had been examined and the rules and choice of timekeeper and referee settled, Stuart made a request: Would the two sides accept a lesser purse should something more crop up to prevent Stuart from bringing off the fight? He had a new venue lined up which he was keeping a secret, but in light of all the present trouble he felt it necessary to prepare for the worst.

Julian, his eyes bulging out of his head, indignantly refused to even consider the idea. He then stalked off and hunted up Rector and vented his and Fitz's simmering grievance.

"I understand that you are the proprietor of the kinetoscope," Julian said, "and that you expect to photograph this contest?"

Rector nodded. "That is my intention."

"Well, I want you to know that you've got to pay Fitzsimmons $10,000, or you won't be allowed to take a picture. We have agreed to fight for Stuart's $10,000, but we have not agreed to pose for you, and we won't do it unless you pay this money."

"I have nothing to do with you," Rector replied, taken aback. "My business is with Stuart. Go talk to him."

Julian did. The last-minute demand for more money pushed Stuart over the edge.

"I have done all that I intend to do in this matter," he growled at Julian and Fitz. "If you are not satisfied with the way things stand, we will call the whole thing off." He then no doubt reminded them of the contract they had signed, in particular article eight granting Stuart "all privileges appertaining to the contest." *All* privileges. That included making arrangements for the fight to be filmed.

The pair had no choice but to back down. They returned, angry, to Juarez. When Peter Maher heard of the matter he suspected that Fitz had secretly arranged a cut of the Kinetoscope deal for himself. He contented himself with merely grumbling about it.

By this time Gray Latham and Eugene Lauste had arrived in El Paso, Lauste's "twin camera" and a Daimler gasoline engine to power it in their baggage. Rector would have known that Gray was in town, for El Paso was not large and the arrival was noted in the paper. Gray was clearly there to do more than just take in the fight. He was competition, probably nosing about for an opportunity to film the contest. If an encounter occurred between the former friends, it must have been tense.

With Gray now hovering about, posing a vague threat, Rector assembled the exterior components for his Kineto-Multiscope apparatus—the base, sides and top that would form its rectangular body. The next step was to get it to the secret location Stuart had found and to set everything up without anyone knowing. To confuse the Rangers watching the station, the railcar bearing the Kineto-Multiscope parts and ring materials was sent down the line in the wrong direction, west and out of the state and Ranger jurisdiction, then was switched to a freight train heading the opposite way. Rector and the Heises, father and son, meanwhile slipped out of El Paso by road, late in the evening on February 11. After a long ride through the night they arrived at an outlying depot and quietly boarded the train.

It was a long, slow ride to get to where they were going. An old man—white hair, full beard, sombrero and chaps—was waiting to meet them at the depot in the middle of nowhere. He led them out across the desert, south through a landscape of desiccated earth and low shrubs, to a bluff overlooking a river.

Right there, he said, pointing to a sandbar on the opposite side.

It was a desolate place, no sign of life about, definitely private. Rector gazed back at the wagon track they had followed out from the depot, then down the steep path that dropped from the bluff to the river. Everything would have to be carried down. And a bridge would have to be built.

I'm going to need men, he said. Three or four dozen.

The grizzled old-timer nodded. I can get you Mexicans, he replied. As many as you need.

More trouble for Dan Stuart. It was never-ending, as if God had marked him as a latter-day Job.

This time it was Peter Maher. A swirl of dust and sand had blown into his eyes during a run across the mesa. The pain from the scratched corneas and inflamed tissues—the locals called the condition "alkali eye"—was so intense that Maher lay awake moaning all night and had to stay in bed the next day, a drug-soaked handkerchief over his eyes. The doctor who examined him said he needed at least a week to recover.

There was nothing for Stuart to do but arrange a postponement, Fitzsimmons and Julian blustering about calling a forfeit and claiming the thousand-dollar guarantee that each side had put up. After they had been quieted down, a new fight date was set for Monday, February 17. This then had to be extended to give Maher's eyes more time to heal. At the meeting in Stuart's office to negotiate this second postponement, Julian again threatened to call a forfeit and this time nearly came to blows with Maher's manager, Buck Connelly. Fitz, enjoying the heated exchange, offered to bet a thousand dollars that Julian could beat Connelly inside four rounds.

"I'm no fighter," said Connelly, fingering a heavy paperweight on Stuart's desk.

"No," snapped Julian, "you're a welcher."

So now the fight was to be held on Friday, February 21, positively the last delay the Fitzsimmons camp would allow. "I am tired of waiting around here, making concessions in behalf of other people," Julian ranted after the meeting. "It was the same way in the Corbett fiasco. Fitzsimmons always gets the worst of it."

Sunday came, February 16. There were bullfights scheduled for Juarez and the visitors in El Paso crossed the bridge to see them, eager to sample this new sport. All the fighters were in attendance, including Fitz with his wife Rose, Horace Leeds with Captain Glori, and John L. Sullivan, who had just arrived. What they saw left them thoroughly disgusted: four bulls tormented to exhaustion, then slaughtered; four skinny horses gored to death; the arena left thoroughly covered in blood. It was the mistreatment of the horses especially that upset the Americans in the stands, prompting curses and sending some storming out. After yet another disemboweling, the pathetic, blindfolded creature galloping about in a panic, its entrails dragging, Fitz jumped up and strode over to Governor Ahumada seated nearby.

"Ask him how he likes that sort of thing," he demanded, addressing the interpreter at the governor's side. Ahumada's reply amounted to a shrug. "Well," Fitz tried again, "ask him if he thinks fighting with gloves is anywhere near as brutal as this bloody thing he is looking at." Another bland response, the governor observing that it was the custom in his country. Fitz turned away and stalked back to his seat, scowling. "Fighting is golf to this blooming, bloody game," he was heard to say.

On the following day the exodus from El Paso picked up. Visiting sports, fed up with the postponements, were leaving. On February 19, with his plans for a fistic carnival in ruins and potential spectators departing in droves, Dan Stuart canceled the undercard matches and released all the fighters.

It was now down to just one fight, the main event between Fitzsimmons and Maher.

Enoch Rector had by this time slipped back into town from parts unknown, worn out with worry and work. The postponements only added to the stress he was feeling, for every extra day made it more likely that the secret location where his Kineto-Multiscope was to be set up would be found out and Mexican troops arrive on the scene. When asked by a *Galveston Times* reporter for a comment, he revealed his frustration by replying, "You may say for us that we do not care now whether the fight comes off or not. I perspired blood until I am tired of it."

An additional worry was the public filming experiment Rector had arranged for the evening of February 17, a long shot to get something out of the Texas venture should the Fitz-Maher contest fall through. It would take place at the Myar Opera House at the final performance of the play *The Wicklow Postman*, an attempt to film the John L. Sullivan sparring match that had been added to the show for its El Paso engagement. For this to have been possible, given the lack of sunlight normally needed for filming, suggests that Rector and the Heises intended to use powerful arc lamps to illuminate the stage. Unfortunately, Sullivan showed up at the theater falling-down drunk—"loaded to the gunnels with booze" as the *El Paso Times* put it—and could do little more than stagger about the ring. Whatever film Rector may have shot that evening, whether it turned out or not, was never shown.

And then, two days later, Peter Maher was causing a fuss, supposedly threatening to pull out of the fight unless he was paid to be filmed. The rumor, which turned out to be overblown, swept aside whatever equanimity Rector had left. "Both Maher and 'Fitz' may make all the claims they care to," he angrily stated, "but they shall not get a cent. I am already a $17,000 loser on this venture, and I am sick of it. If it were not for the forlorn hope of next Friday, I would throw the whole thing over and go home."

The announcement appeared on the door of Dan Stuart's office at mid-afternoon the day before the fight. "Persons desirous of attending the prize fight," it read, "will report at these headquarters tonight at 9:45 o'clock. Railroad fare for the round-trip will not exceed $12."

Twelve dollars. That and the twenty-dollar admission to the fight amounted to nearly a month's wages for many in the crowd that had assembled. They were forced to give up on the adventure, grumbling that the affair had been arranged for millionaires. The rest with the wherewithal plunged inside to lay their cash on the counter. Be at the railway station at a quarter past ten this evening, each man was quietly instructed. And don't ask any questions.

Fitz and his entourage and the Maher party arrived in town a few hours later. In the interval before the appointed hour of departure, Fitz and Julian dropped by Stuart's office to deliver a last-minute demand. They wanted the $10,000 purse presented to the winner in cash at ringside. "Checks don't go," Fitz said, wary from his experience of worthless paper at the Hall fight. "No cash, no fight."

Stuart had no choice but to agree. Stakeholder Tom O'Rourke was summoned and, after a private word with Stuart, went to the bank and returned with a wad of hundred-dollar bills to waft under Fitz's and Julian's noses. With the pair satisfied, O'Rourke returned to the bank and converted the money back into checks. He had no intention of heading into the unknown with so much cash in his pocket. Carrying the checks would give him enough to worry about.

There were some two hundred fifty men waiting at the station at ten o'clock in the evening: spectators, newsmen, the two fighters and their parties, pickpockets busily working the crowd, Texas Rangers seated against the wall with rifles across their knees. Many had come with picnic baskets of food for what was expected to be a two-day excursion. Others were content with a bottle and the promise of whatever could be scavenged from station dining rooms along the way. Everyone had a $11.65 train ticket for a destination as yet unknown.

Maher appeared recovered from his affliction, a slight redness about the eyes all that remained. He had resumed training three days before and seemed in fine fettle. "I understand that Fitzsimmons characterized me as a cur a few days ago," he announced to the correspondents hovering about for a comment. "Wait till I get a crack or two at him to-morrow, and he will see who is a cur. He is a great, big bluffer, but bluffs won't go in our argument." Down the platform Fitz was making similar declarations, assuring listeners that it was a "dead cinch" he would win.

Ten-fifteen. A conductor led the motley gathering to five cars parked on a siding. The Rangers ensconced themselves in the first. The Texas and Pacific Railroad had insisted that each buy a ticket. The next two cars were filled with spectators and newsmen. Maher and his seconds and supporters took car number four, the Fitzsimmons party car number five. Dan Stuart and right-hand man Joe Vendig kept a low profile so as not to be peppered with questions. George Siler, who had been chosen to serve as referee, stayed with them. Bat Masterson, in charge of security and showing no visible signs of a weapon, stuck to Tom O'Rourke and the purse.

The cars were hooked onto the regularly scheduled San Antonio-bound train, a heavy freight locomotive doing the pulling. A blast of the whistle and they were away at ten-thirty. But where to? Stuart still wouldn't say.

A long night followed as the train made its way east, many of the sports sitting up to play poker and trade fight stories and puzzle over their destination. They were a subdued bunch, uneasy about not knowing where they were heading, blindly trusting Stuart and his secret plan. At least one thing was clear: there was no way the fight would take place in Texas, not with General Mabry and his Rangers aboard. A barge in the gulf off Galveston remained an outside possibility despite Stuart's laughing denials, for they were certainly heading in that direction. It's bound to be Del Rio, others opined. It's right on the border. From there we can slip into Mexico and have the fight there.

This led to speculation about what would happen if they were caught on Mexican soil. "They won't throw us in prison," spoke up one man with the voice of authority. "No, we'll be drafted straight into the army."

This seemed to cause Tom O'Rourke some additional worry. "How many years do you have to serve in this army?" he wanted to know.

"Five," pronounced the voice of authority. "And they shoot you if you try to jump."

Finally, in the wee hours of the morning, as the train continued on through an endless landscape of cactus and mesquite and dry desolation, Dan Stuart leaked word of their destination. The news was met with the same question in all the cars:

Langtry? Where the hell is Langtry?

CHAPTER 17

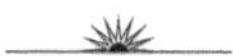

THE MEN INSIDE THE CAMERA

LANGTRY WAS ON THE Texas and Pacific Railroad two thirds of the way from El Paso to San Antonio, within eyesight of the Rio Grande river and the Mexican border. It consisted of a single street running parallel to the tracks and a crossroad heading north to a scattering of ranches. The handful of structures included the train depot, a grocery store that doubled as the post office, a few private dwellings that took in occasional boarders, and Judge Roy Bean's unpainted, plank-built saloon. Known as the Jersey Lilly, the saloon additionally served as Bean's home and the courthouse and was Langtry's most prominent feature. "Law West of the Pecos" proclaimed one of the signs affixed to the low roof of the porch that tall men had to duck under. And, just above it: "Ice Cold Beer."

Enoch Rector and the two Edison technicians, William and Theodore Heise, had arrived in Langtry around February 12, following their discreet departure from El Paso. After eluding the Rangers, they had boarded the train some ways down the line and proceeded east on the long ride to Langtry. It had been Judge Roy Bean who led them to the bluff overlooking the river and pointed out the sandbar where the fight would be held.

The first step was to get the lumber unloaded from the railcar and hauled to the edge of the bluff in a wagon. The forty-odd Mexican laborers Bean rounded up were needed to carry it the rest of the way on their backs, down the steep path descending to the floor of the canyon. Here Rector oversaw the construction of a footbridge over the river. It was a makeshift affair, seventy-five feet long and the walkway two feet wide, but adequate for the job, for the Rio Grande at this point was little more than a stream. After the bridge was completed, the necessary equipment was muscled across to the sandbar on the Mexican side. The ring would be erected here, Rector's Kineto-Multiscope beside it.

Putting the ring up was work for only a day, for that was all there was to the venue. There would be no seating for spectators, no covering against the weather; just a wooden platform set up on the sand, four feet high and twenty-four square. When it was finished, a covering of unpadded white canvas was stretched over the boards and the ring posts and ropes were installed. The final touch was to erect a length of circus-tent canvas all round to block the view from those who hadn't bought tickets.

All that remained now was for Rector to erect his Kineto-Multiscope apparatus, hammering together the platform, top and sides that he had preassembled back in El Paso. Completed, it looked like a shack, twelve feet long, seven feet wide and seven feet high, the whole thing elevated on stilts to command a view of the ring. On the ring-facing side were two ample-sized windows, each with a smaller opening just underneath. An additional opening, some sort of skylight, was cut in the roof.

There was nothing particularly notable about the interior of the structure, just four bare walls and the two windows and skylight. Once the glass was installed, however, its true purpose emerged. The windows and roof opening were fitted with glass tinted a deep red, the light passing through them painting the inside a ruby hue familiar to anyone who had worked in a photographer's darkroom. This impression was confirmed by the rolls of tar paper that were next put to use, every interior surface lined with the material so that no light could penetrate inside. Shelves were then built against the front-facing wall, directly beneath the smaller openings beside the red-tinted windows. The four custom-made Kinetographs would be installed here on fight day, set up in pairs, their lenses flush to the openings, the big batteries to power them placed underneath.

When the work was done, Rector checked the structure for soundness. It had to be solid. Any vibration would be imparted to the Kinetographs and blur the images captured on film. He then blocked up the windows, skylight and lens openings and sat in the darkness, searching for any stray light getting in through overlooked crannies and gaps.

This was Enoch Rector's Kineto-Multiscope. It was in effect a huge camera body, big enough to accommodate himself and the Heises and a half-dozen or more assistants. Being itself light-tight allowed for the Kinetographs to be removed from their cases and installed on their shelves "naked," film run through them like on a projector, entirely exposed. The film would not be affected by the red light in which Rector and his team would work because it was orthochromatic, sensitive only to the blue and green side of the spectrum. (Panchromatic film, sensitive to the full spectrum and thus requiring handling in complete darkness, would not be introduced by Eastman until 1913.) With his Kineto-Multiscope Rector thus did away with the need to move the Kinetographs in and out of a darkroom to change the film. The camera was itself a darkroom, with the operators sealed inside. Film could be removed from and loaded onto the machines right where they sat.

With the apparatus now set up, Rector and the Heises made their way back to El Paso for the attempt on February 17 to film John L. Sullivan sparring on stage. Their subsequent failure was not a good omen. Nor were the clouds that rolled in the next day. The fifty rolls of Blair film they had brought with them required bright sunlight for a good exposure. Overcast skies wouldn't do.

Conditions remained unchanged on February 19, warm and no rain but thick clouds overhead. The day after that, the eve of the fight, dawned the same way. Rector had come down from New York believing that the Texas climate would be perfect for filming, dry and clear skies for most of the year. The *El Paso Daily Times* promised as much in an advertorial printed in every single issue. "El Paso's Climate," read the headline, "Health Restoring Qualities of our Atmosphere." But there was nothing healthy, cinema-wise, about these lingering clouds. They spelled death for filmmaking—and possibly for the Kinetoscope Exhibiting Company too.

With fight day, February 21, approaching, Rector and the Heises returned to Langtry ahead of the main train to make final preparations for filming. Anxiously scanning the sky, praying for a glimpse of blue, must have been a tremendous strain for Rector after all the effort he had expended. The prospects for a favorable outcome were not looking good.

The train carrying the fighters and spectators rumbled on through the night, traveling east through the desert. With the coming of dawn Bob Fitzsimmons and Peter Maher took the opportunity of station stops to jog up and down alongside the tracks, swinging their arms to keep themselves limber. The sports and correspondents along for the ride were content to stand around watching, collars turned up against the drizzle, glad to be in the fresh air after the smoke and stink of the cars. Gray Latham was probably among them. If his cavalier conduct during his subsequent trip to Mexico City was anything to go by, he likely had left Eugene Lauste behind in El Paso without any money while he went off to see the fight and have a good time.

By now the story of Fitz's antics in the middle of the night had reached every man on the train. He had apparently spotted a bear chained up by the tracks where the train stopped to take on water at three o'clock in the morning and had leaped out to wrestle with it. It was typical of Bob. He was always clowning like that.

A report was circulating, meanwhile, that the fight might have to be postponed until the next day, something to do with the Kineto-scope man having telegraphed up the line about not being able to take pictures. This prompted a rush to accost Dan Stuart and Joe Vendig, the travel-weary passengers making it clear that any such postponement would be very unwelcome.

"And where do we sleep?" asked one. There were no hotels at a rough depot like Langtry.

"Sage brush isn't half bad," joked another, "when you haven't anything else."

Rector and the Heises set out across the desert from the Langtry depot, leading a procession of porters back to the Rio Grande sand-bar where the ring and the Kineto-Multiscope were set up. In the crates and padded boxes distributed on backs down the line were the four Kinetograph cameras, the heavy batteries that would power them, fifty cans of film, an assortment of tools and miscellaneous gear.

It was no good trying to ignore the gray sky, not with occasional sprinkles of rain now falling. With such dark clouds overhead, there would surely not be enough light for filming. The realization must have left a sick feeling. Rector had sent a telegraph down the line asking Stuart for a postponement but there was not much chance the request would be granted. The fight was now moving inexorably forward. It would take place whether Rector could film it or not.

The party arrived at the sandbar and began the final installation work inside the Kineto-Multiscope. The four Kinetographs were hoisted up the ladder and secured to their shelves in two pairs, their lenses flush to the openings, batteries positioned underneath. The plan was to keep one machine in each pair constantly going to make a double record of the fight, insurance against technical mishap. Would it be worthwhile even to bother, considering the lack of sunlight? This question must have been assailing Rector, for the miles of film he had brought had cost the Kinetoscope Exhibiting Company thousands of dollars. Should he use it, even though the chances of getting pictures were slim? Or should he scrap the whole plan and return the film for a refund so as not to further increase the KEC's already great loss?

No, surely an experimental attempt had to be made. After all, there was still a glimmer of hope. To begin with, the adjustable slots in the Kinetographs' rotating disk shutters could be opened all the way to let in maximum light. This would mean sacrificing picture sharpness but that could not be helped. The exposed film could then be chemically pushed to the limit, left in the developing solution longer to coax out an image. Between the two, something usable might yet be salvaged from the whole sorry affair.

It was time to test the machines. William Heise loaded a short strip of film onto the first Kinetograph, hooked the machine up to its case of batteries, and turned on the switch.

Nothing.

He checked the connections at either end and played with the wiring. He tried again.

Nothing.

Batteries had been a major concern for the Kinetoscope Exhibiting Company from the very beginning. The first Kinetoscope machines they purchased, the ones installed at the Nassau Street parlor, had come with Edison batteries that proved unsatisfactory, delivering an unsteady electrical current that ran the machines sometimes too fast, sometimes too slow. In opening subsequent parlors the KEC therefore acquired batteries from elsewhere, more expensive units that delivered a steadier current. This practice had continued with the Kinetographs. The batteries were not an Edison product—and now they didn't seem to be working at all.

Heise disconnected the dead batteries and ran the Kinetograph wires to a second array. A deep breath, he threw the switch and the intermittent mechanism buzzed to life. He let it run for a few moments, turned it off, waited, then tried again. Yes, it was working. He tested the second machine. It whirred to life without trouble. So did the others.

Everything was now ready—everything except the weather, which showed no sign of clearing.

Rector set out to hike back to the depot. He would meet the train and beseech Dan Stuart to delay the contest until the return of the sun.

The train pulled into Langtry with a squeal of brakes and torrent of steam at half past three in the afternoon. It had taken sixteen hours to cover the nearly four hundred miles from El Paso. The town's entire population of fifty was on hand to gawk at the big-city sports and Texas Rangers as they descended from the cars and stretched the stiffness out of their limbs. Judge Roy Bean, sombrero, full white beard and big belly, stood at the forefront of the greeters, shaking hands and directing attention to the Jersey Lilly Saloon as the only place to obtain a cool drink. The locals behind him were looking every which way, taking it all in, the most exciting thing ever to happen in Langtry. Which one is Bob Fitzsimmons? they wanted to know. Which one is the Irishman Maher? And is that Bat Masterson over there, the one in the derby?

Fitz and Maher for the moment remained on the train. With no proper dressing room facilities at ringside, they were putting their fighting togs on under their clothes.

There was Dan Stuart, looking haggard from the long journey. Enoch Rector went over to confer with the portly promoter, stating as he had in his earlier cable that there was insufficient light for filming the fight and adding that the batteries were also acting up. Stuart was sympathetic. If the film venture failed it wouldn't be just Rector and the Kinetoscope Exhibiting Company that would lose. Stuart himself would be deprived of the substantial sum the KEC had promised him if the filming succeeded, plus twenty percent of the profit from every Kinetoscope that showed the films. There was simply no way, however, that he could put off the fight now. He had worked too hard to get to this point to risk having everything fall apart—one or both of the fighters storming off in a huff, the spectators growing fractious and demanding a refund, Mexican troops arriving to stop the contest and haul them off to prison now that the secret was out. No, they would just have to go ahead and hope for the best.

A thin cheer rose behind them, the crowd greeting Fitz and Maher as they stepped off the train. With their seconds clustered about them and local guides leading the way, the pugilists set off on foot for the river. Rector hurried on ahead.

It was an incongruous procession that headed out across the dry Texas scrubland, Fitzsimmons and Maher with their respective parties in front, then Bat Masterson and Joe Vendig who would be collecting the tickets, then the sports from El Paso in their suits and their derbies and a sprinkling of cowboys in Stetsons, then the contingent of Texas Rangers with their pistols and carbines. The party had spread out in a long straggling line by the time it reached the bluff overlooking the river, heavier men gravitating to the rear, huffing and puffing. The way forward took them down the path into the canyon, slipping and sliding on the wet stones, then along a muddy stretch beside the river to the bridge leading to a sandbar on the Mexican side.

The Rio Grande had risen with the rain, the brown water flowing forcefully now under the makeshift bridge and making it appear none too secure. The sports, already deeply invested, scurried across and handed their tickets to Masterson to gain admittance to the canvas enclosure. After all the big talk in El Paso and on the train, no one tried to push his way past the former lawman without paying. No one asked to buy one of the spare tickets either that Masterson had come prepared to sell at twenty dollars a head. There was no need, what with the hillside behind commanding an excellent view of the ring, right over the top of the canvas. The citizens of Langtry, joined by Mexicans and cowboys and the Texas Rangers, settled on this high ground to watch. The bluffs on the Mexican side of the river remained entirely deserted. No one lived over there for miles around.

One hundred and eighty-two, Masterson announced after the last man had been admitted and he had counted the tickets. It was a miserable take, a dead loss for Stuart. The gap in the canvas was closed and Masterson joined the spectators encircling the ring.

You would think, someone groused, that for twenty dollars we would at least get a seat.

Go ahead, said Masterson, motioning to the wet sand. Make yourself comfortable. Sit down.

It was a quarter past four. The sky remained a thick blanket of grey and it was drizzling again. As Fitzsimmons and Maher stripped off their clothes and slipped on their flannel robes, Rector and the Heises and their assistants climbed up the ladder into the Kineto-Multiscope and closed the door. Working in the safe red light coming through the windows and skylight, they removed four five-hundred-foot rolls of Blair film from their light-tight container, releasing the smell of camphor, and loaded them onto the completely exposed Kinetograph machines. A final check that the disk shutters on the machines were wide open. A perusal of the wires running to the batteries. Everything was all set.

They were ready. Rector peered out the red-tinted glass, waiting for the fighters to enter the ring.

Fitz, wrapped in his bathrobe and with a blanket thrown over his shoulders, was the first to duck through the ropes. He took the corner facing the bluff on the Texas side of the river. Maher followed a few moments later, occupying the corner facing the Mexican side. After shuffling about and bouncing on the canvas-covered boards to test the footing, they retired to their corners and sat on folding camp stools. Referee George Siler positioned himself in the middle.

"Siler," called out Martin Julian. "Where's the purse money?"

Siler turned to the crowd.

"Where's O'Rourke?"

Dan Stuart dropped his head. He had been dreading this moment.

Tom O'Rourke, not much taller than the ring, withdrew two certified checks from his wallet. "It's here," he replied, holding them up.

The sight of the insubstantial slips brought a frown to Fitz's lips. "I said I wanted cash," he said. "How do we know what those are worth?"

O'Rourke appeared offended. "Do you think I was fool enough to bring $10,000 with me into such diggings as these?" Then: "It's the first time that my honesty has been questioned."

"Nobody ever questioned your honesty," said Julian, "but we want the money. We will take no checks."

The crowd was starting to grumble. "It's not our fault," Julian said, turning to the assembly. "We notified the responsible people several days ago that Fitzsimmons would not fight unless the money was in the ring."

"They said it would be," Fitz chimed in from his stool.

"Go on with the fight!" yelled the spectators. "Stop wasting time!"

Julian, bridling, suggested that the complainers keep their mouths shut. That only served to stir things up further, putting Bat Masterson on alert. His strong-arm services might still be needed.

Rector could see through his window that something was up. He could hear little through the Kineto-Multiscope's walls but it was evident that Fitz and his people were upset.

Ah, it was the purse. There was O'Rourke waving the checks. Stuart had indicated there might be trouble about Fitz wanting cash. Could there still be a postponement?

"All right," roared Fitz, leaping to his feet. "We'll take the checks. I give in to every bloody thing they want."

He threw aside his blanket and yanked off his bathrobe. Maher did the same. The crowd responded with a cheer, relieved that the fight was going forward. Rector's glimmer of hope died.

It was nearing four-thirty when George Siler called the two men to the center of the ring. Fitz strode forward in navy blue trunks and Stars-and-Stripes belt, bare legs, socks rolled down to his boots. He was in fine condition, rock hard muscles, no excess fat. Maher, comparatively doughy about the middle, wore a green belt and black tights reaching just below his knees, scars visible on his calves from his years in Ireland playing football. He appeared nervous, licking his lips, mouth slightly open. Fitz, exuding confident aggression, remained menacingly still, his gaze locked on Maher.

"All right," said Siler, "by the articles of agreement this is to be a fair up-and-up fight. When there's a clinch and I call for a break-away, each of you take a step back. I don't want to be seizing you and getting between you. If there is a knock-down the man must be on his feet before he can be assailed. Now shake hands and get ready."

The combatants clasped gloves. They held the pose as a photograph was taken by a still camera William Heise had set up, manned by an assistant. They then retired to their corners.

A pause. The warning whistle. The call from the man holding the watch:

"Time!"

Inside the Kineto-Multiscope, Rector gave the signal. William Heise threw the switch on the first machine. It whirred to life, took a few feet of film, then died. He switched it off and turned on the second machine. It worked. As the long strip of celluloid stuttered its way past the lens, assistants turning the reels by hand, keeping the film slack, Heise began trying to get the first machine working, Rector anxiously looking over his shoulder and watching the fight through the window at the same time.

Fitz sprang forward, unleashing a flurry of blows that backed Maher into his own corner, a hard right getting through his defenses. Maher threw his arms around Fitz, tying him up in a clinch.

"Break!" Siler commanded. Fitz dropped his arms to break clean according to the agreed-upon rules. Maher, arms still on him, delivered a right to his ear.

"Foul! Foul!" cried Julian from Fitz's corner.

"How's that, Siler?" Fitz sneered. "He breaks his word the first chance he gets."

Siler issued a warning to Maher. "If you do that again I will decide the fight against you."

A minute of the film feeding through the first Kinetograph was used up. Three minutes to go. William Heise continued to tinker on the stalled machine as Theodore and the second pair of assistants stood ready at the next one. It would be switched on toward the end of the coming break between rounds, just before the film in the first machine was used up.

The two fighters came together again. Another flurry, Maher landing a left on Fitz's mouth, bloodying his lip. The Irishman seemed to be finding himself after an uncertain start. He closed to land a left and a right on either side of Fitz's head. The blows seemed to shake the Antipodean. He backed up. Sensing advantage, Maher stepped in with a hard left that Fitz sidestepped and countered with a right—a short driving right, a full-bodyweight right, a right that landed on Maher's jaw and dropped him to the canvas, his head striking the boards with a loud thud.

Fitz stepped back, looking down at his opponent, a smile playing across his face. Then he abruptly turned and strode back to his corner.

William Heise was still tinkering. Rector's eyes went from him back to the window. He saw that someone was down. It was Maher. A glance at the one working Kinetograph. Not even half the roll of film was used up.

Maher's seconds were hanging over the ropes, pleading with him to rise. "Get up, Peter. Get up. Get up. Get up." One of them reached into the water bucket and withdrew a dripping sponge, evidently intent on flinging it at the downed fighter to revive him.

"Foul!" cried the ever-vigilant Julian, pointing an anticipating finger from the opposite corner.

Maher, legs trembling, managed to raise his head off the canvas, vacantly staring at Siler relentlessly counting. Then he slumped back. He was done.

The fight had lasted ninety-five seconds.

Fitz slipped his bathrobe back on and looked on as Maher's seconds revived him and planted him on a chair. Then he strode across the ring and extended his hand, remarking, "Well, Peter?"

Maher, beaten and still woozy, was in no shape to feel resentful. He gave Fitz his hand but did not meet his gaze.

There was cheering now, desultory calls from some of the spectators at ringside, more vigorous hooting and handkerchief waving from the people on the hillside behind. Fitz responded with bows all round, then joined Julian at ring center for the customary announcement, formulaic but nonetheless sweet.

"Gentlemen!" Julian cried, motioning to the timekeeper to strike the bell. "Gentlemen! Mr. Fitzsimmons has worked his way up to the top of the ladder and is now champion of the world. He is ready to defend his title against all comers at any time or place. No man is barred and all comers will receive recognition."

The declaration was applauded. Then the crowd began to disperse, heading across the bridge for the hike back to Langtry. Few were pleased. Twenty dollars for a ticket and thirty-two hours round-trip on the train to witness a ninety-five-second prizefight was not much of a bargain. And then there were those who had traveled from New York, San Francisco, Philadelphia, Boston, spending weeks of their time and incurring considerable expense on the journey. "The whole affair," complained one of the disappointed, "was a case of wallop and out."

Filming inside the Kineto-Multiscope had now ceased. One roll of film had been enough to record the whole fight with two minutes to spare—if indeed anything had been recorded, which was doubtful. The exposed reel was removed from the machine and returned to its can and Rector opened the door. He wasn't done yet. He scrambled down the ladder and hurried over to Fitz getting dressed and laid a desperate offer before him: to remain in Langtry until tomorrow for a six-round exhibition match with Maher, this time just for the camera, for a purse of five thousand dollars.

Fitz had been waiting a long time for this, for others to do the begging and for him to play coy. He replied that he would be glad to knock Maher out in six rounds, but it would have to be at a time and a place of his choosing. And five thousand dollars wouldn't do it. He wanted ten grand. In advance.

It was a lot to ask for, but hopefully a starting point for negotiation. When Maher's people were consulted, however, they took Fitz's knockout-in-six talk as an insult and his demand for ten thousand dollars as gross hogging. An argument ensued, insults were exchanged and any chance of a deal was soon dead.

Six o'clock. It was time for the return trip to El Paso. Fitz and his party were in high spirits, Martin Julian giggling like a schoolboy as he downed a drink in the Jersey Lilly. The Maher group was subdued, Maher himself now sunk into a post-fight depression. He had remained a bit dazed for some time after the fight, asking one of his corner men as they walked back to Langtry, "Was it one round or two?" The knockout blow had left only a small mark on his chin. More noticeable was the egg-sized bump on his head where it had struck the boards when he fell.

The whistle, the conductor calling for everyone to board, Texas Rangers firing off their carbines by way of a send-off. "Three cheers for Mexico, boys!" cried one of the sports as the train lurched forward and gathered speed, leaving Langtry to its sleepy quietude after just two and a half hours.

"It was a chance blow," Maher told reporters as the train trundled westward and the sun disappeared into the desert. "I did the best I could under the circumstances. My eyes were in worse condition than I believed them to be."

"It was dead easy from the start," Fitz crowed one car behind. "I could have put him out with the first punch but did not reach him hard enough."

What about the offer to fight again for the camera? a newspaperman wanted to know.

"I don't care about fighting before the kinetoscope," replied Fitz. "Every time they want me to do anything they want to give the other fellow all the money and I want some of it. I don't fight before that machine unless I get $10,000 cash and fifty percent of the receipts."

Gray Latham and Eugene Lauste left El Paso the day after the fight, as soon as the train got back from Langtry. They were bound for Mexico City, there to film a bullfight and other Mexican subjects—and for Gray to do some serious carousing, leaving Lauste for days without money for food while he roved through "not very respectable" places. "The worst," Lauste wrote years later, recalling his disgust, "was that I found that he had some troubles which I could not describe here, and instead of attending our business my mission was to nurse him, and keep getting medicines." One can only imagine what "troubles" Gray had picked up.

Enoch Rector arranged upon his return to El Paso with the Heises to film a bullfight for himself—a coincidence, or either he or Gray stole the other's idea. He paid two hundred fifty dollars for one to be staged in the Juarez bullring for his Kineto-Multiscope on February 25, a sunny day at last. He thus would not be returning home entirely empty-handed, for he now had footage of what he called "the most bloody and exciting bull fight." Optimism bolstered by this last-minute success, he cabled home to Samuel Tilden, "We will get there yet," before setting out for New York.

Bob Fitzsimmons in the meantime had converted the checks for the purse into cash, rousting the El Paso bank manager out of his home to open the bank even though it was a holiday, Washington's birthday. With the wad of bills stowed in his pockets, he proceeded to the Grand Hotel and the welcoming arms of Rose and Bob Jr.

A telegram was awaiting Fitz upon his arrival. It was from Jim Corbett, in Chicago with his play. "Come to Chicago as soon as you possibly can," it read. "I will make a match with you for any amount to fight any place on earth.... Name the day you will be here between the 1st and 6th, and we will have no trouble agreeing on terms."

Gentleman Jim was back in the game.

PART THREE

THE FIGHT THAT STARTED THE MOVIES

CHAPTER 18

✳

NEW FIGHT, NEW MACHINES

So, GENTLEMAN JIM WAS BACK in the game? Bob Fitzsimmons said he didn't care. "I shall completely ignore that fellow Corbett," he announced before leaving El Paso. "It was $1000, American money, to 1 cent, Mexican coin, that Pomp Jim would get in his oar just as he has. I shall ... tell him to get a reputation. Let him go whip Peter Maher and Joe Choynski before he opens his head to me." The shoe was on the other foot now and Fitz was enjoying it immensely. He would keep it up for the next several months, throwing Corbett's own words back in his face.

Upon his return to New York at the end of February 1896, Fitz put together a new vaudeville show to take advantage of his contentious claim that he was now the heavyweight champion of the world. The headline acts would be him sparring with Dan Hickey and a display of wrestling by Ernest Roeber, plus musical numbers and comedy acts, a "Host of Pretty Girls" and "New Electrical Effects" and a "Spectacular Phantasy" imagining a trip to the North Pole. The show worked its way through several cities in the East and Midwest, then packed up and on May 26 sailed for England, Martin Julian traveling ahead to book music halls. Corbett had had his English tour back in 1894. Now it was Fitz's turn to reap Old World accolades.

Fitz's pet lion Nero didn't make the trip. It had died in Cleveland the previous month, on the roof of the gymnasium where Fitz kept it chained during his stop in that city. When Fitz came up to feed it late in the evening, Nero made a playful lunge at him and dragged its heavy chain over an electrical wire that was lying about, stripping off the insulation and giving himself a shock. Frightened, the animal leaped off the edge of the roof and was strangled by its own collar.

Jim Corbett, meanwhile, was touring with his new play *A Naval Cadet*, a light comedy with plenty of action and fighting but no formal ring scene. It was proving just as successful as *Gentleman Jack*, earning Jim a great deal of money, and Jim was continuing to improve as an actor. When the play closed out the season in Kansas City on May 2, there was no question that it would be good for another year, maybe two.

Jim's plan now was to take six months off to pursue "that coward Fitz" and reclaim the title. "It's this way," he stated. "My 'Naval Cadet' has had wonderful success, the people have accepted me as an actor and it makes no difference whether I ever have another fight or not. Fitzsimmons, as several others have done, kept at me while I was on the road making money, and I couldn't break my engagements. Now I'm free, or rather I've taken a holiday for six months for the purpose of following him and make a fight.

"Did I hand the championship over to Maher? Well, rather not. What right had I to do a thing of that kind? I never signed my name to any such an agreement, and the newspapers were too dense to see through the joke."

As William Brady made his way to England to keep an eye on Fitz and respond to any open challenges that might be made, Jim proceeded to San Francisco to spend time with his parents, who he had not seen much of during the past several years. His mother Catherine was still in good health, cheerful, hale and hearty, and his father Patrick continued relatively unaffected by the madness that was feared to run in the family, a periodic condition that had sent Patrick's sister to the insane asylum four years before. Every morning during his stay Jim went out to the old family home over the livery stable to have breakfast with them, then returned downtown to bask in the glow of being Frisco's most famous son.

On June 3 Jim attended an evening of boxing at Mechanics' Pavilion headlined by a tough and immensely strong brawler named Tom Sharkey, hailed as the champion of the Pacific Coast. When asked afterward if he thought he could finish Sharkey in four rounds,

Jim casually replied that he could. This resulted in a challenge being issued by Sharkey and his backers for Jim to prove it. "[C]an't a person crack a joke once in awhile without having his meaning misconstrued?" Jim responded, annoyed. After such a long layoff from the ring, however, a tune-up bout wasn't a bad idea. He therefore agreed to a four-rounder against Sharkey, payment to be half the gate. Jim regarded it as a sure win and an easy payday, for Sharkey, while impressively built, was not particularly skilled as a boxer. "Sailor Tom's" cauliflower ear and crooked nose would be good targets for Jim to use to knock off the rust.

It was a colossal miscalculation. After three weeks of lackadaisical training, Jim squared off against Sharkey on June 24 in nowhere near prime condition and was soon puffing hard and struggling to keep down his supper, fending off bull rushes and wild swings and being wrestled about. Sharkey was "the foulest fighter that ever stepped into the ring," he complained after. "He disregarded all the rules under which we were supposed to be fighting, and he bounced me about the ring giving me hiplocks and throwing me around as if he had a hold of a brawling sailor in a barroom fight." Jim was close to exhaustion in the final minute of the fourth round when Sharkey seized him again and threw him down. The police captain at ringside stepped in at this point and halted the proceedings—ostensibly on the grounds that it was getting out of hand, although some would claim Corbett asked him to do it. The referee declared the fight a draw and all bets off due to the stoppage. But to the eight thousand spectators looking on in Mechanics' Pavilion, Jim's disappointing performance had been tantamount to a loss.

It was a chastening and ultimately valuable lesson for Jim, a wake-up call that he had grown complacent. If he was going to reestablish himself as champ he would need to train in deadly earnest. No more fooling around. In the meantime he agreed to a rematch with Sharkey to assuage the humiliation, this time a proper fight to the finish, to take place within six months. Toward the end of the summer he headed east to Asbury Park, intent on recovering his lost stamina and power and getting into top shape. If Jim succeeded in doing so, John L. Sullivan opined, "he would simply butcher Sharkey. I have no doubt on this point at all."

Whatever film Enoch Rector may have shot of the Fitz-Maher fight, all ninety-five seconds of it, did not turn out. There had not been enough light to make a usable exposure on the insufficiently sensitive Blair film. The consolation footage Rector shot of the bullfight emerged from the developing bath in satisfactory shape but it was not enough to save the Kinetoscope Exhibiting Company from ruination after all that had been spent. The end came two months later, in April 1896, when the Supreme Court of New York ordered the struggling company to pay Jim Corbett royalties from the Corbett-Courtney fight film that had fallen into arrears. This cost the KEC another six thousand dollars, plus two thousand in a personal judgment against Samuel J. Tilden. Burned by his foray into motion pictures, Tilden retreated from the field and concentrated thereafter on running his family's pharmaceutical firm.

Not Enoch Rector. As the KEC faded from the scene he partnered with Dan Stuart to launch a new fight film venture, the Kineto-Multiscope Company, incorporated in New Jersey on April 9, 1896 with Stuart as president, William Wheelock as vice president and Rector as nominal treasurer and the technical brains. The purpose of the company was to further develop Rector's Kineto-Multiscope concept to film the fight between Corbett and Fitzsimmons that Stuart was still determined to arrange. The promoter was convinced now of the tremendous financial potential of a filmed record of the battle for the heavyweight championship of the world. As a live event, nothing could rival it in terms of gate earnings, spectators in the thousands willing to pay up to twenty dollars for a view of the action. Now imagine if the same could be presented on celluloid to the whole country, from Maine to Kansas to California, using the new projecting machines that were now entering the market. It would be an audience of hundreds of thousands, of *millions*. And it would sidestep all the anti-prizefight backlash, for it would not be a real fight that was being presented but merely a show of light and shadows. A film.

To pull it off, Stuart would pursue Corbett and Fitz for months, trying to get them to sign articles for a fight to the finish, the only kind of fight to determine true supremacy in the ring. Rector in the meantime addressed the problems that had prevented him from filming the Fitz-Maher bout. The first of these was insufficiently sensitive film stock. He would turn to Eastman Kodak for this. The company had recently come out with a new "Ciné" film specifically for motion pictures—a more light sensitive negative film for use in cameras and a more robust positive film to stand up to the wear and tear of projection. It was also better equipped than Blair to manufacture the huge custom order Rector intended to place. Rector additionally addressed what he felt were the shortcomings of Edison's Kinetograph camera as adapted for Kineto-Multiscope use. When William Gilmore refused his request to alter the apparatus further to make it easier and more reliable to use, Rector parted ways with Edison and set out to build a camera of his own.

The core of Edison's inventive genius was electric. Electricity was modern, the way of the future and thus the way he chose to power his machines. As Rector had experienced on that Rio Grande sandbar, however, electrically-powered machines could be temperamental. They required wiring and connections that could break or malfunction and bulky batteries when no electrical hookup was nearby—batteries that could go dead or otherwise fail for any number of reasons. He therefore decided to eliminate electricity entirely from his Kineto-Multiscope apparatus. Not only would the reels be turned by hand to keep the film slack and thus prevent breakage, the intermittent mechanism itself would be manually operated by means of a hand crank. No batteries, no wires, just a movement of the wrist to move the film past the lens. To Edison this would have seemed a colossal step backward, but for motion pictures it in fact pointed the way ahead. Until the advent of synchronized sound in the late 1920s, which required the precise film speed only electrical power could provide, reliable and portable hand-cranked cameras would be the industry standard, employed by every filmmaker from D.W. Griffith and F.W. Murnau to Charlie Chaplin and Sergei Eisenstein.

Rector built his hand-cranked camera in a workshop on Pearl Street in lower Manhattan. This was not the wide-format camera he would need to film the Corbett-Fitz fight but rather an intermediary device that used standard Edison film—a first step to figure out how to fabricate such an intricate machine. He then built a projector to screen the results, for it was clear now that exhibiting films by means of projection was the future. Thomas Edison himself had recently surrendered to declining Kinetoscope sales and come out with his own projecting machine, the Vitascope, commercially debuted in New York on April 23. Although billed as the "Edison Vitascope," it was in fact not an Edison invention. With his Orange lab muckers unable to come up with an acceptable apparatus and Edison himself preoccupied with ore separation, the patent for an invention by Charles Jenkins and Thomas Armat called the Phantascope was instead purchased and the device renamed and marketed under the Edison name. Over the next several months two other major projecting machines would hit the market as well: the Lumière brothers' Cinématographe, imported from Europe to debut in New York on June 29, and the Biograph, co-invented by William Dickson and unveiled in October. Both were considered superior to the Vitascope in terms of picture quality, the Biograph decidedly so. These would soon be joined by a host of lesser-known projectors, the Kineoptikon, the Cineograph and the Theatrograph, the Projectoscope, the Graphoscope and the Rayoscope to name but a few.

And then there was the Eidoloscope, which had led the way into the commercial projection market back in May 1895. The machine's technical shortcomings—it used continuous rather than intermittent movement and thus cast a dim image—was offset by the impressive length of the films that it showed, most recently the bullfight Lauste and Gray Latham had filmed in Mexico City, which was being screened during performances of the opera *Carmen* with great success. This bullfight was in fact yet another first for the Lathams, for at seventeen minutes it was the longest film ever made up to that time, double the length of their landmark Griffo-Barnett fight film. The Lathams were nevertheless destined to disappear from the scene following the bankruptcy of the Eidoloscope Company in August 1896. Their projector would linger on for a time before similarly fading away.

This was the increasingly crowded field that Enoch Rector was about to enter with the hand-cranked camera and the projector he built. One of the first things he filmed was presidential candidate William McKinley's "Sound Money" parade up Broadway on October 31, 1896, the camera pointed out a window in the Flatiron Building. He also shot a fire brigade turning out and a New York ferry arriving at the dock. A touring exhibition was then put together to start earning money, to be taken on the road by a man named Frank Clifton. By the time Clifton set out for the West Coast at the beginning of December, the Rector projector in his baggage had acquired a name.

It was called the "Veriscope."

Bob Fitzsimmons returned to New York from his overseas tour on August 22, earlier than expected, dressed like a dandy and looking pleased with himself. "Some people may think that I hastened home because I lost money in England," he told newsmen. "Not on your natural! I didn't make a barrel of money, but I had a good time and got enough cash in the bargain to lay idle for a couple of months if I want to." He had also met the Prince of Wales, something Corbett hadn't done, the fanciful lithograph of Jim with European heads of state notwithstanding. When asked if he would now fight Corbett, Fitz said he wouldn't. "Let him go and get a reputation," he replied, trotting out the line he took such delight in. "I am champion now and will dictate terms just as he told me once to get a reputation."

But the game was up. Fitz had been playing coy with Corbett now for six months and the sporting world was growing impatient, just as it had grown impatient with Corbett when he was fending off Fitz. A matchup between the two was expected. It was needed, for Corbett had not been properly dethroned as heavyweight champ. And if it wasn't soon arranged, public opinion would turn against Fitz.

Fitz kept up the "get-a-reputation" line for another three weeks. Then he relented. At a banquet in New York on September 10, he issued a challenge to Corbett and posted five thousand dollars in stakes money to show he meant business. The two men met that weekend at the Hotel Bartholdi to reach an agreement—another acrimonious session, Corbett acting rude and aggressive, insisting on dealing directly with Fitz and refusing to speak to Martin Julian, whom he loathed.

"I read of your challenge in the newspapers," Corbett began. "Don't you think it a rather cowardly piece of work in view of the fact that I am matched to fight Sharkey?"

"No," Fitz replied placidly, "I don't."

Julian cut in to say that they had already posted their stakes. This made Jim angry. "Keep quiet," he snapped. "If you don't, I'll leave the room and there will be no match."

Things grew heated, friends on both sides ready to step in, but in the end the two men reached an amicable agreement. They would fight to the finish within sixty days of Corbett's match against Sharkey, the venue to be decided by whatever club offered the biggest purse. The articles of agreement would be signed later, in Jersey City, to avoid violating New York's stringent anti-fight laws.

Indictments were issued a few days later just the same. According to the district attorney, the fact that Corbett and Fitz had arranged a fight, even without affixing their signatures to a document, had broken state law. And so another round of court appearances ensued, the wearisome legal dance that was an integral part of the fight business, a hassle and expense that simply had to be borne. For Fitz, it meant being arrested while eating his breakfast and being taken to the courthouse to appear before a judge and post bail.

Indictments or not, the long-awaited Corbett-Fitzsimmons battle was on. And Dan Stuart was going to get it. He had been pursuing the two pugilists since February, trying to coax them together, and was among the spectators at their Hotel Bartholdi meeting to see a fight at last taking shape. Now, with an agreement in place between the two fighters, he stepped forward to offer a purse of $15,000, nowhere near what might have been had a few years before but top-dollar now in the anti-prizefight climate pervading the country. The sum placed Stuart at the top of the diminished list of promoters still willing to take on the legal challenges and financial risks of a championship bout in the hope of a payoff. That he was willing to do so was due to the fact that he did not need to make much on the actual fight to come out ahead. For with the moving picture record he and Enoch Rector were planning to make, revenue would continue flowing long after fight day, people paying fifty cents or even a dollar to see a film of the battle, a thousand tickets or more sold every day, week in and week out, in theaters across the country—a veritable river of money that would make the profits of the biggest fights in the past look like the nickels earned by a peanut vendor on Broadway. The "privileges" that fight organizers previously reserved for themselves, the beer stand and souvenir concessions, for example, were thus no longer a little side bonus, a bit of gravy. With the advent of film rights, the profit to be earned through privileges potentially outweighed ticket sales. It was here that Stuart planned to make real money—and hopefully keep the lion's share for himself.

Stuart quickly secured Fitz's preliminary agreement. Nailing down Corbett would take longer, the main stumbling block being Jim's upcoming rematch with Sharkey. As it turned out, however, that fight fell apart. Instead it was Fitz who would step into the ring against Sharkey—Fitz who had stated shortly after his return from England that "I will gamble all I am worth that I can whip Sharkey in four rounds." The comment, no doubt intended to show up Corbett, was seized upon and a bout arranged, San Francisco's National Athletic Club taking advantage of the fight-friendly atmosphere still prevailing in the city. It would be a gentlemanly eight-rounder—Fitz thought better of limiting it to four—and there would be plenty of police on hand to ensure that it remained within the bounds of propriety. And if there were still moral concerns on the part of church leaders... well, it would be a shame if the largess of Frisco's sporting fraternity, which donated such large sums to charity, should suddenly dry up.

The fight went ahead, unopposed, on December 2, 1896. It was a fiasco. The first sign of trouble came earlier in the day, when it was announced that retired lawman Wyatt Earp would serve as referee. As soon as word got out, the betting odds took a suspicious lurch toward Sharkey. The fix seemed to be in. More troubling evidence arrived in the form of whispered warnings delivered to Fitz's dressing room before the fight, including a rumor that Earp had been promised twenty-five hundred dollars to decide the contest in Sharkey's favor. It was too late now for Fitz to back out, what with Mechanics' Pavilion crammed to the rafters with more than ten thousand people, the biggest sporting crowd ever assembled in Frisco. He made his way to the ring, sniffling and congested with a cold.

Wyatt Earp ducked through the ropes prepared for trouble, a Colt .45 sticking out of his coat. The chief of police confiscated the weapon but missed the second pistol Earp had on him, better concealed. As the fighters settled into their corners, Martin Julian stepped forward to raise a protest, announcing that Fitz would accept any man in the house as referee, but not Earp. This elicited hisses and cries from the audience of "Earp! Earp!" With a whole army of people baying for the bout to begin, Fitz relented. "I have given in to everything in all my fights," he announced, "and I give in to this." He would just have to allow Earp no chance to decide things unfairly. He would have to knock Sharkey out.

And he did. After beating on, wrestling with and bloodying Sharkey for seven rounds without much effect, Fitz finally cracked the hard shell and dropped him in the eighth, a left hook to the chin followed by a right to the stomach. Sharkey lay flat on his back for the ten-count, the crowd erupting with cheers as Fitz strolled back to his corner for Julian to unlace his gloves.

And then Earp was saying something. He was declaring that Fitz had delivered a low blow and that Sharkey was therefore the winner—Sharkey who was only just coming to. By the time the crowd understood what had happened and raised a howl of protest, Earp had slipped out of the ring and disappeared.

The decision was widely condemned as crooked, so obvious that it would ruin fighting in Frisco for all time. An injunction was placed on the ten-thousand-dollar purse and Fitz took the matter to court, and for a while it looked like he would win, two of Sharkey's trainers testifying that there had been no foul blow from Fitz; that Sharkey had been fairly knocked out and that Earp had been bought. Then the judge did something unexpected. He declared that since the fight had been in technical violation of the law, a dispute over the purse was not a matter for the court to decide. The case was thus thrown out and the money handed to Sharkey. If there was any consolation in it for Fitz, it was that in the court of public opinion he was seen as the winner. There was also justice in the fact that there would be little of that ten grand left over for Sharkey after Earp and everyone else had been paid off.

Ninety miles northeast in Sacramento, Enoch Rector's Veriscope projector was about to have its commercial debut, an attraction to follow the play at the local opera house, prime seats thirty cents, a spot in the gallery going for a dime. In addition to the parade and fire brigade and ferry films Rector had made, advance publicity for the show promised boxing—likely a round of Leonard-Cushing or Corbett-Courtney—and a bullfight, trumpeted as having been recently filmed in Madrid.

The initial presentation, on the evening of December 7, was a bust, Frank Clifton being unable to reduce the voltage in the theater to run the lamp in the Veriscope projector. For the following evening he switched to an oxycalcium lamp that could handle the current, installing a "water bath" between it and the film so that the intense heat would not cause the celluloid to burst into flames. The result was satisfactory but by no means perfect, the flickering of the images on the screen causing eye strain, a common problem with early projectors. Clifton managed to largely eliminate this by the second week by making careful adjustments to the delicate machine.

After a month in California, the Veriscope set sail for Hawaii. Projected moving pictures had never before been exhibited on the islands and this was reflected in the prices charged, the best seats in Honolulu's Opera House going for a dollar. "Edison's Veriscope!" the advertisements announced. There was little risk now in commandeering the inventor's valuable name—not at a distance of five thousand miles from New Jersey.

"Edison's Veriscope! It Produces Life! It Baffles Analysis! It Amazes All!"

Having both now been shaken by their encounters with Sharkey, Jim Corbett and Bob Fitzsimmons at last settled down with Dan Stuart to sign a formal agreement to fight. Jim was the first to affix his name to the paper, on December 17 in Jersey City. Bob would sign in a later meeting with Stuart. This suited Jim fine, for it meant that he didn't have to put up with Fitz's and Julian's "song and dance" and hours of "chewing the rag."

"We, the undersigned," the document read, "do hereby agree to fight to a finish, under the Marquis of Queensberry rules, for the heavy weight championship of the world and for a purse of $15,000...." The contest would take place on March 17, 1897, at an unspecified location that Stuart would name one month before, ten thousand dollars to be forfeited if he failed to bring it off.

Jim continued listening as the terms were read out, then jumped to his feet at the penultimate clause, the one in which Stuart reserved all privileges for himself.

"Wait a minute, there," Jim said, pointing his finger at Stuart. "This does not mean any picture business, old Mr. Foxy. No kinetoscope game, because if it does, I want to be in with it—that is, if Fitzsimmons is in with it. I want as much as he is getting and no more. I think if there are to be photographs of the fight the principals should get some of the proceeds."

"I know nothing of any pictures," Stuart replied with a straight face, "but that is one of the privileges allowed by the club if there is such a thing. I can assure you, you will be treated exactly the same as Fitzsimmons. I suppose that if some man comes along with a hot tamale contract you think you would be entitled to a piece of it."

"No, I don't," Jim replied. "But if there is any kinetoscope business, I shall want to know something about it, and I shall be sure to find out if Fitzsimmons is interested in it.... If there is any kinetoscope business the purse gets larger."

"No picture business will stop this fight from coming off," Stuart said, ending discussion on the point. "Of that you can rest assured."

Stuart had a separate conference with Fitz in Jersey City two weeks later. The fighter and manager Martin Julian perused the articles with Corbett's signature for some minutes in silence. Then Julian spoke up, objecting to the privileges clause. "This, of course, means the kinetoscope or vitascope," he said, "whatever machine is used to take instantaneous pictures of the fight. Now, we want a share of the profits from the pictures, or no pictures will be taken."

Stuart asked if Julian wanted to buy the film rights.

No, Julian replied, he didn't. Stuart could keep all the privileges, "from peanuts to shamrocks," if he wanted, "but if a photographing machine is on the ground we want a whack at the profits. I don't care to sign away anything of that kind, as I believe it to be a very valuable property if successfully managed."

Stuart tried to downplay the value, observing that a film of the fight might turn a comparable profit to the Ferris wheel he hoped to put up near the arena. But Julian knew better. So did Fitz. Gray Latham had awakened him back in May 1895 to the earning potential of a projected film of a championship battle; how a moving picture of Fitz in action could be shown in theaters over and over, in city after city all across the country. That would amount to much more than hot tamale or Ferris wheel money. It would be a gold mine. It would be riches.

"As regards the picture privilege," Stuart concluded, trying to quell the concerns, "I will say this: That should there be any bids or offers for such a privilege, I will come to some arrangements with both Fitzsimmons and Corbett about their disposal, and if we can come to a mutual agreement, then the privilege shall be sold, but if we cannot agree, then no pictures of any kind shall be taken, and the fight proceed, rain or shine."

Fitz signed the articles. The fight was on.

It was now up to Dan Stuart to find a venue. Pundits said it would likely be Mexico, a fight on the sly just across the border. Stuart, however, was directing his gaze elsewhere. He had been lobbying officials in Nevada for some time and the possibilities there looked good. Nevada had fallen on hard times after the silver rush in the 1860s and '70s, the population sinking to sixty thousand and public coffers left correspondingly bare. The authorities were willing to consider just about anything to reverse the state's flagging fortunes, and Stuart made a good case that hosting fights would do that very thing. The licensing fee that could be charged was just the beginning—a nice fat sum to keep out all but the biggest, most respectable contests. And after that there was the army of well-heeled spectators that would descend on the state, filling hotels and restaurants and spending freely. And would there be bums and hobos mixed in? No, there would not. The cost of traveling all the way to Nevada would keep out the riffraff, Stuart assured.

Most Nevadans looked favorably on the proposal, especially when holier-than-thou criticism started appearing in newspapers back East. "The fights of the present day ... are not as brutal as football and not as dangerous as baseball," declared the *Carson City News*, taking a knock at the East's two sporting passions. "Let us have what benefits there are from it," added the cold-eyed *Carson City Morning Appeal*. "We are after population." Even some members of the local clergy came out in support of prizefighting, the chaplain at Nevada State Prison pointing out that the Bible mentioned fighting hundreds of times and turning the other cheek only once.

"I do hate to see a man what has morals so shaky," summed up Carson City personality McSwarthy Murphy, "that he is afraid all the time something is going to spoil 'em."

A bill to legalize prizefighting was easily passed by the lower house of the Nevada legislature on January 26, 1897 and by the senate two days later, whereupon it was signed into law by Governor Sadler. The Silver State was now open for ring business. The stipulations: fights were to be confined to an enclosure to exclude those not in attendance; they were not to be held on Sundays; and no intoxicating liquors were to be served. The licensing fee: one thousand dollars.

Dan Stuart was elated. He was now free to promote the event for all it was worth and sell masses of tickets, the figure of fifteen thousand being widely quoted. "Nothing less than the death of one of the principals will stop the fight," he crowed. It would be "the greatest the world has ever seen."

All that remained was to finalize the exact location, Carson City, Reno and Virginia City all vying for the historic event. Stuart was only too glad to sit back and let the three cities compete, upping their offers of guarantees and incentives. As the days passed a fourth option presented itself, a syndicate in Utah offering Stuart a deal to hold the contest on Nevada's eastern border nearest Salt Lake City. Then reports surfaced that Wyoming was planning to steal away the fight by secretly passing a prizefight bill of its own.

That was the last straw for the backers of the Nevada prizefighting bill. They publicly demanded that the contest be held in their capital city of Carson. If it wasn't, they would repeal their bill "so quickly it would make Stuart's head swim."

That settled it. The Corbett-Fitzsimmons fight would take place in Carson City.

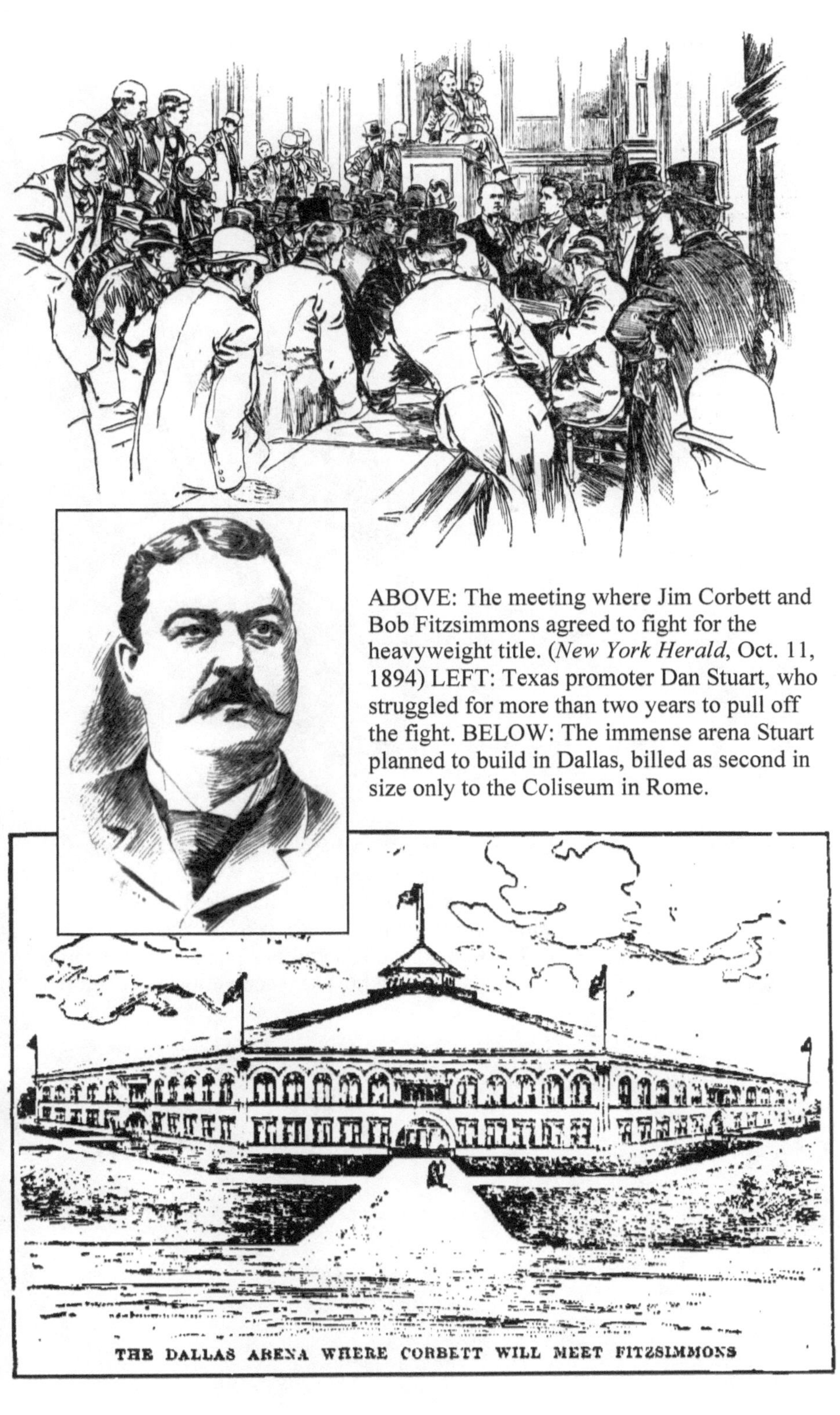

ABOVE: The meeting where Jim Corbett and Bob Fitzsimmons agreed to fight for the heavyweight title. (*New York Herald*, Oct. 11, 1894) LEFT: Texas promoter Dan Stuart, who struggled for more than two years to pull off the fight. BELOW: The immense arena Stuart planned to build in Dallas, billed as second in size only to the Coliseum in Rome.

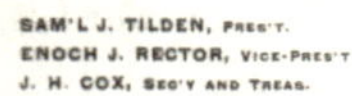
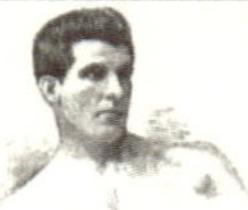

The Kinetoscope Exhibiting Co.

NEW LEBANON, N. Y.

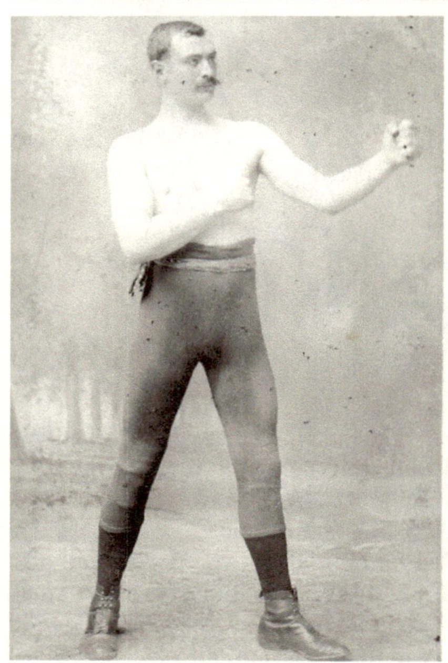

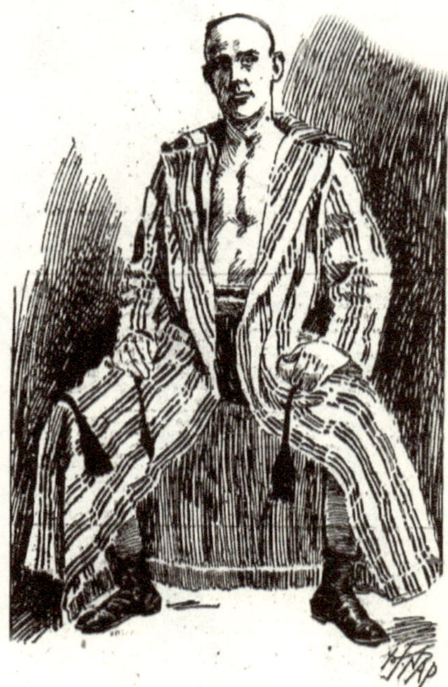

TOP: KEC letterhead, Enoch Rector elevated to vice president following the Lathams' ouster. (Edison National Historical Park) ABOVE: Peter Maher (left), who fought Fitz after Corbett vacated the title; Fitz (right) taking a break during training for the battle. (*San Francisco Examiner*, Feb. 10, 1896) BELOW: The five-person Kinetoscope planned by Rector for exhibiting full-length rounds of the fight. The machine was never built.

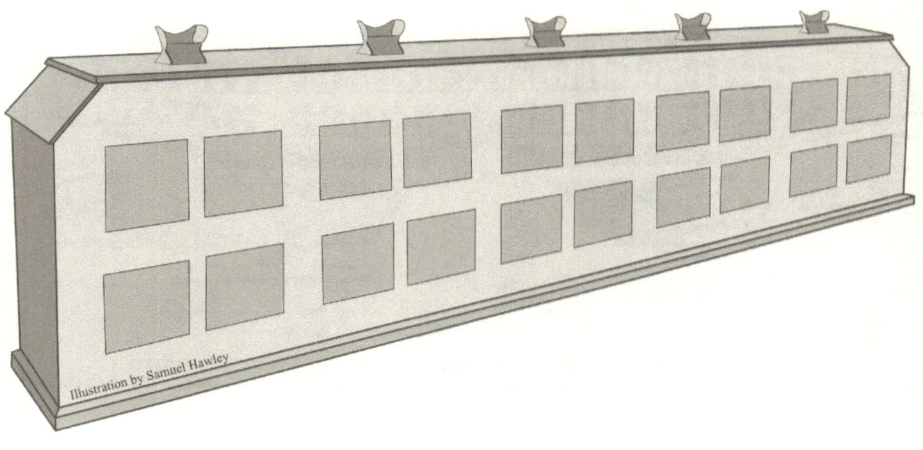

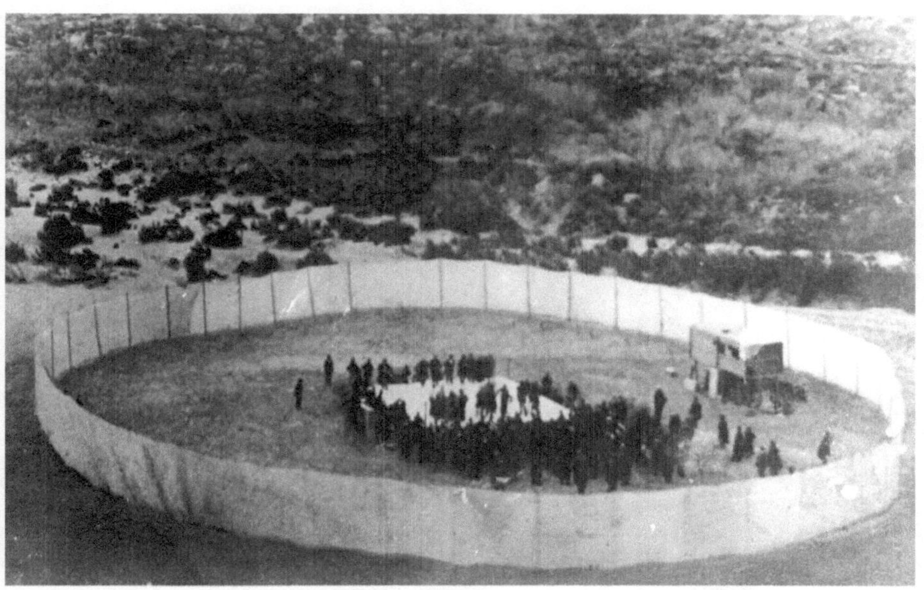

ABOVE: The Fitzsimmons-Maher fight on the Texas-Mexico border, Feb. 21, 1896, Enoch Rector's Kineto-Multiscope on stilts on the right. BELOW: The bridge across the Rio Grande leading to the ring, Rector in foreground, William Heise at left on the bridge, son Theodore possibly beside him. (both University of Oklahoma Library, Western History Collection)

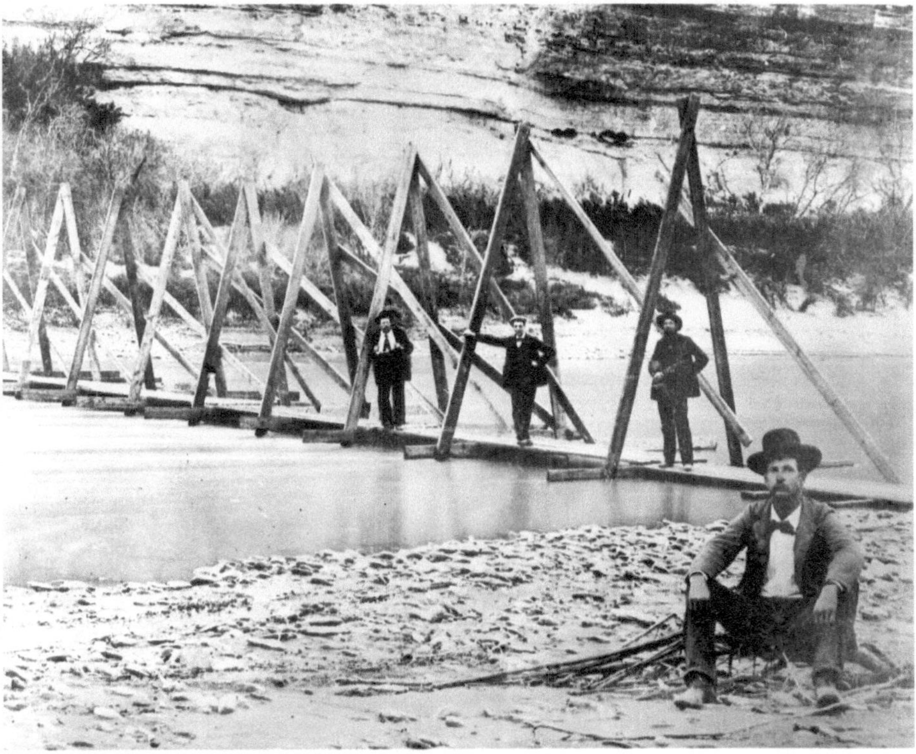

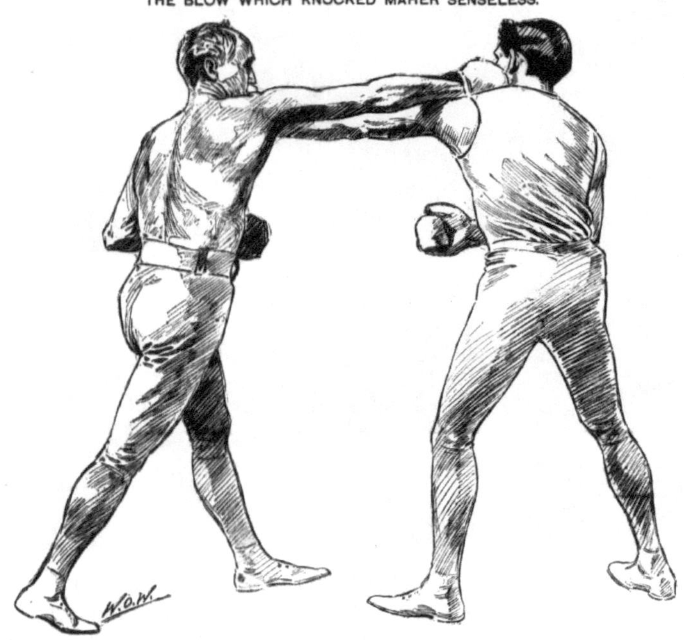

ABOVE: Fitz demonstrates the blow he used to stop Maher. (*New York World*, Feb. 22, 1896) BELOW: Kineto-Multiscope Co. vice president William Wheelock (left); Jim Corbett in his new play, *A Naval Cadet*, 1896 (right).

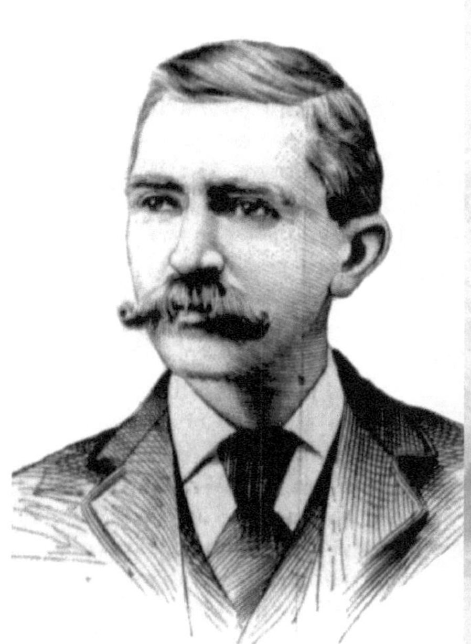

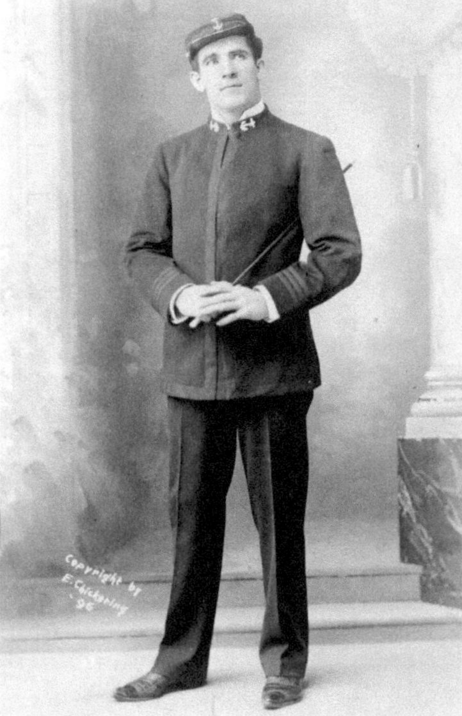

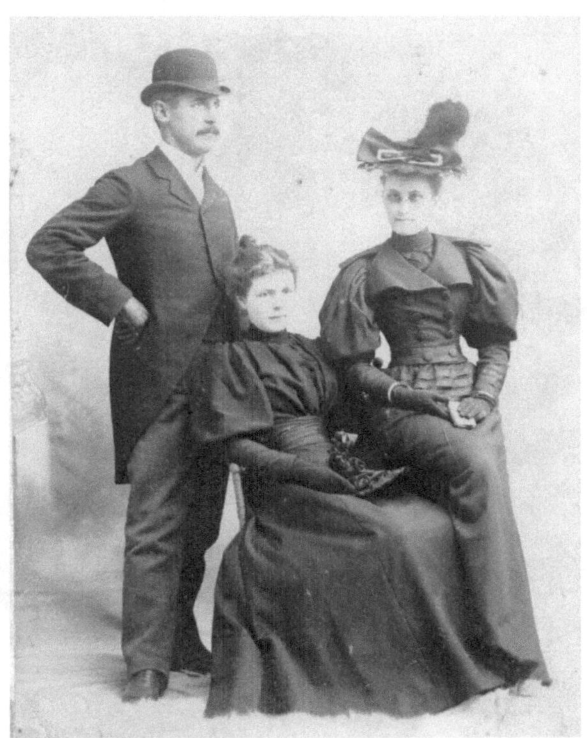

ABOVE: Enoch Rector and wife Jesse (seated), late 1890s. (Sasha Chermayeff)
BELOW: Rector's first version of his Veriscope projector, completed in late 1896. (*Phonoscope*, Jan.-Feb. 1897)
LEFT: Veriscope ad, *Hawaiian Star*, Feb. 8, 1897, Edison's name freely used.

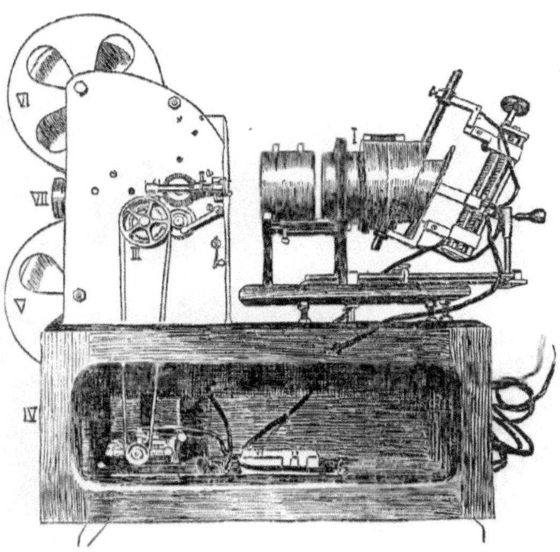

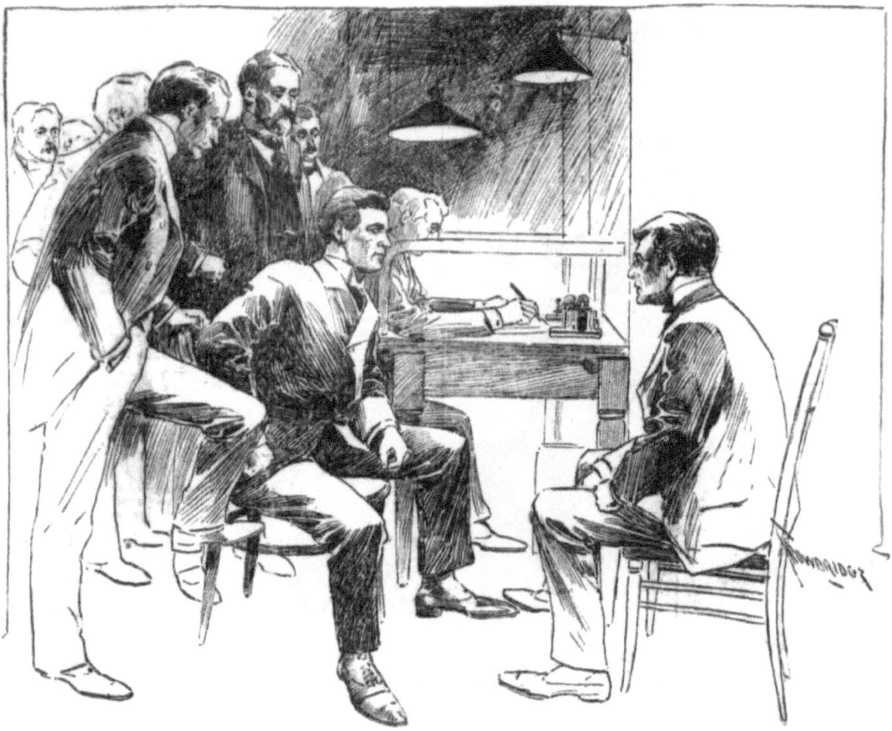

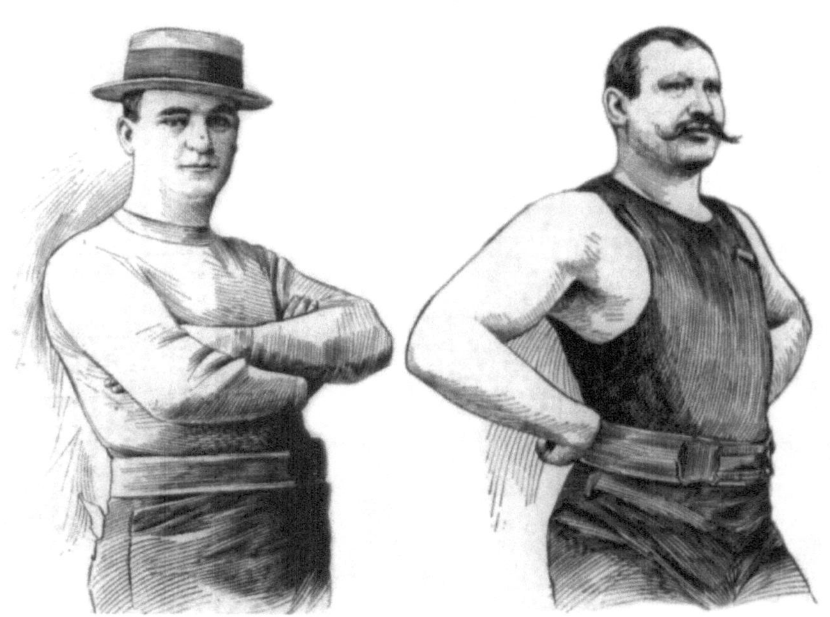

ABOVE: Corbett following the Fitzsimmons-Sharkey fight by tele-graph. (*New York World*, Dec. 3, 1896) BELOW: Corbett trainer Billy Delaney (left); Fitz trainer Ernest Roeber (right).

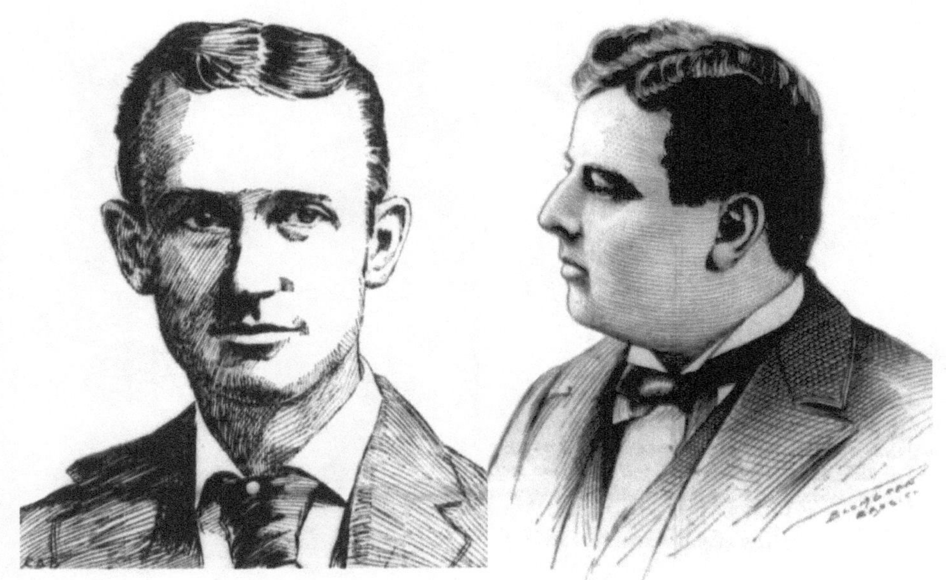

ABOVE: Corbett's manager William Brady (left); Fitzsimmons' manager Martin Julian (right). BELOW : William Muldoon, timekeeper for the fight (left); referee George Siler (right).

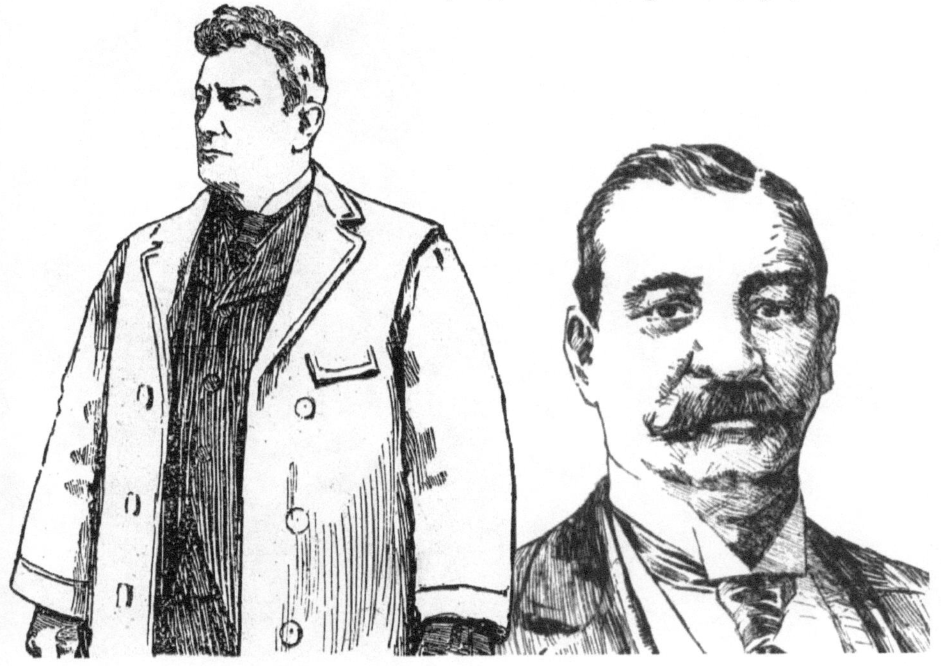

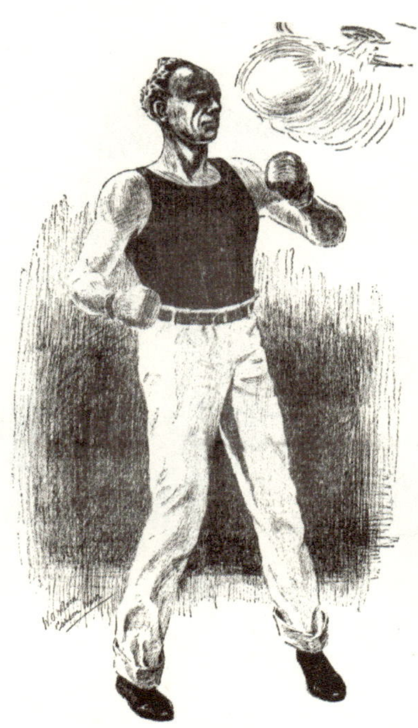

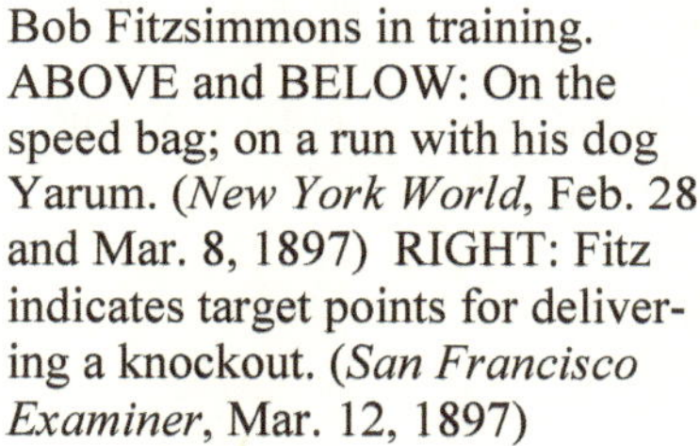

Bob Fitzsimmons in training. ABOVE and BELOW: On the speed bag; on a run with his dog Yarum. (*New York World*, Feb. 28 and Mar. 8, 1897) RIGHT: Fitz indicates target points for delivering a knockout. (*San Francisco Examiner*, Mar. 12, 1897)

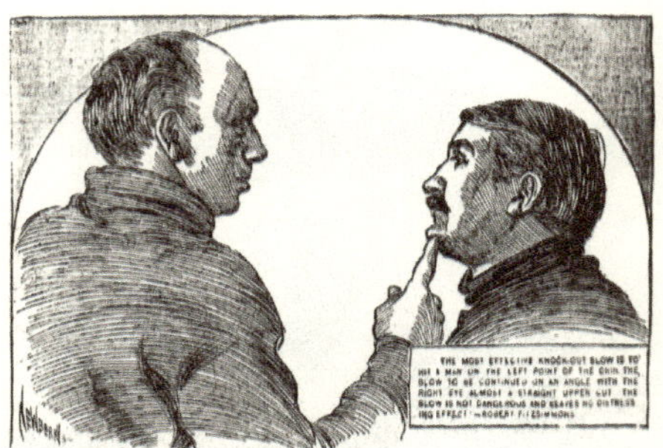

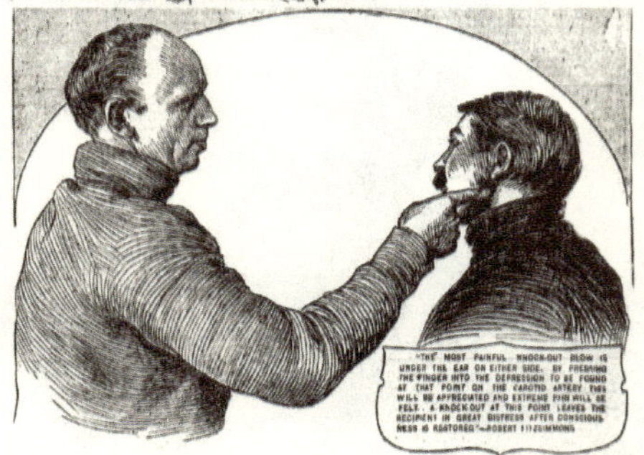

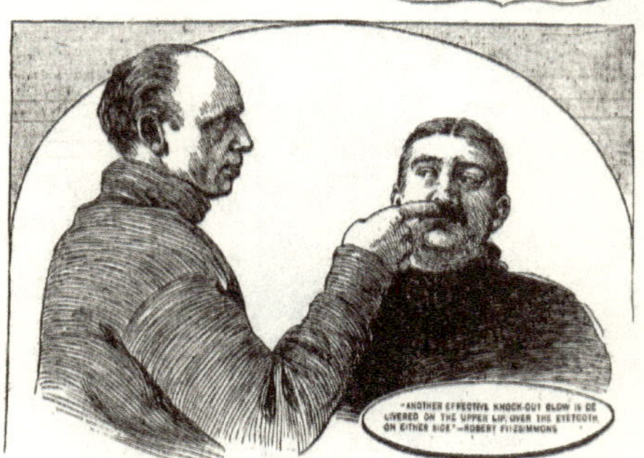

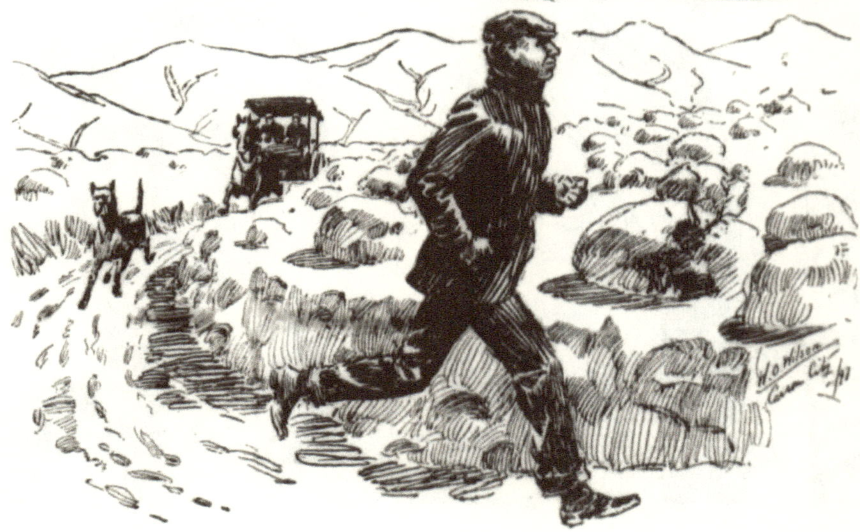

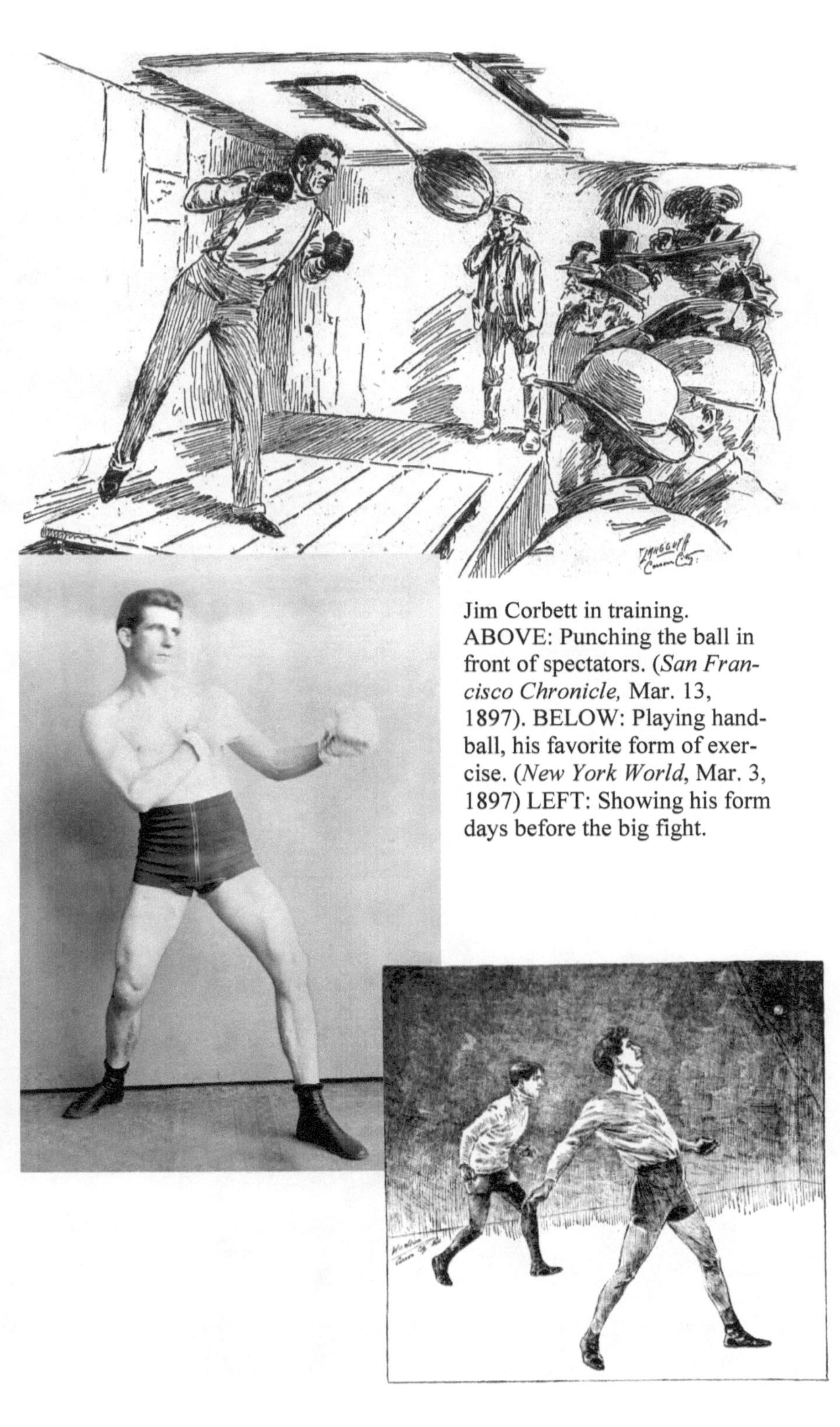

Jim Corbett in training. ABOVE: Punching the ball in front of spectators. (*San Francisco Chronicle,* Mar. 13, 1897). BELOW: Playing handball, his favorite form of exercise. (*New York World,* Mar. 3, 1897) LEFT: Showing his form days before the big fight.

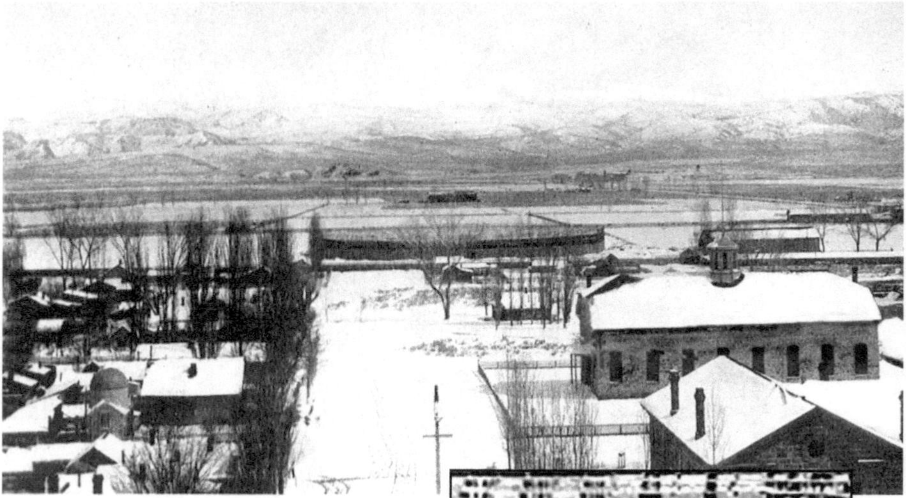

ABOVE: The arena on the outskirts of Carson City, Nevada.
BELOW: Photo of the fight taken
by Hugh Castle with a camera he
snuck into the arena. Enoch Rector's Veriscope is visible on the
right. RIGHT: Close-up of the
Veriscope, the arena still under
construction.

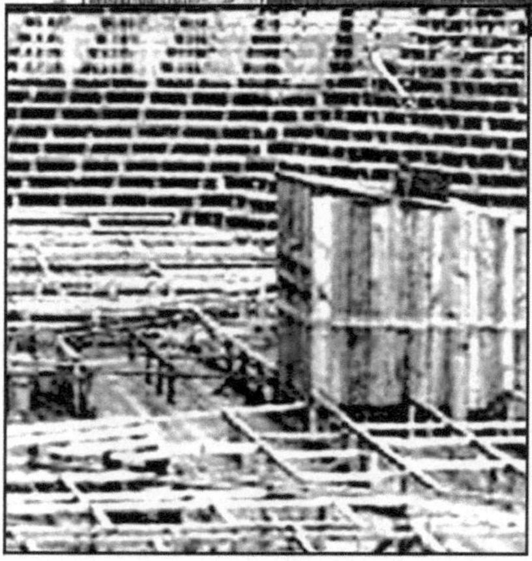

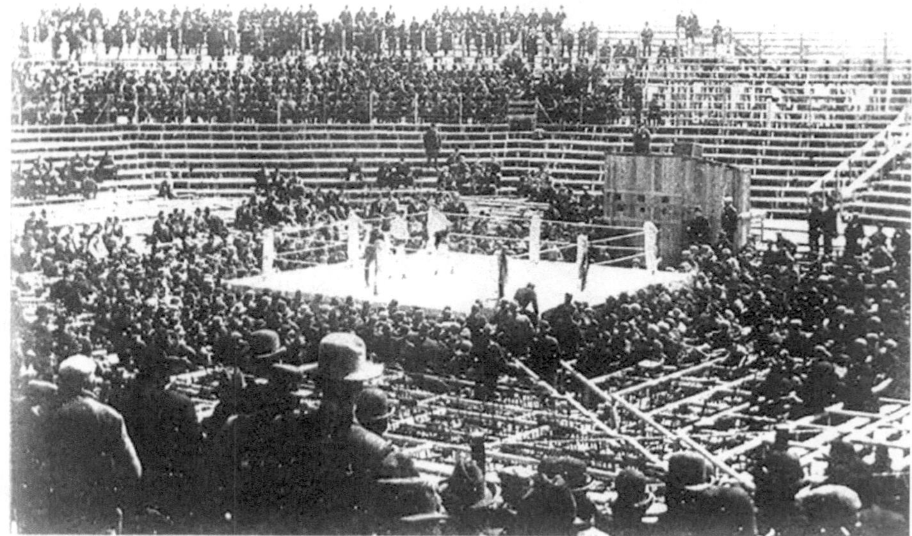

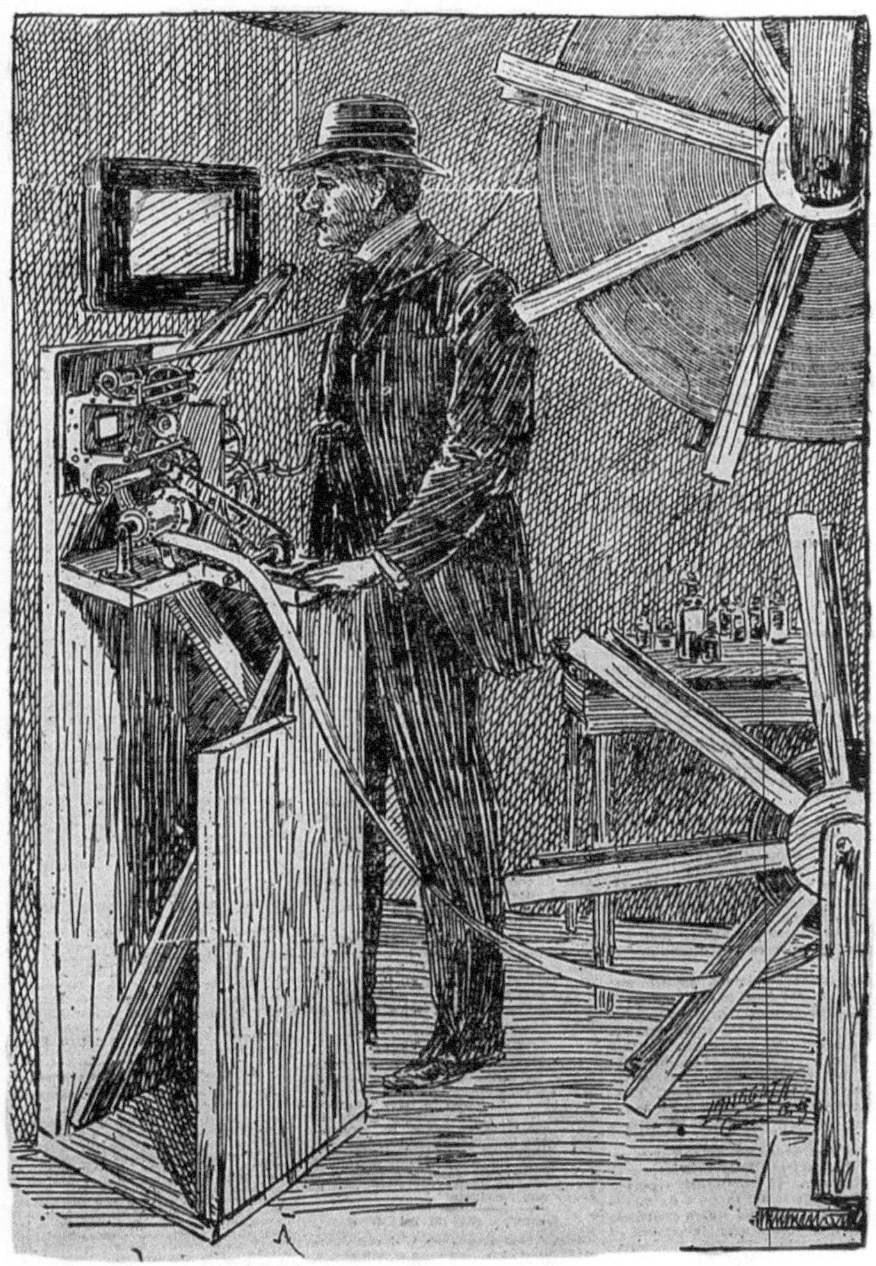

Enoch Rector looking out one of the Veriscope's red-tinted windows. (*San Francisco Chronicle*, Mar. 16, 1897) The Veriscope was a giant camera which Rector and his team of assistants operated from the inside as its human motor, cranking the photographing machines and turning the film reels by hand.

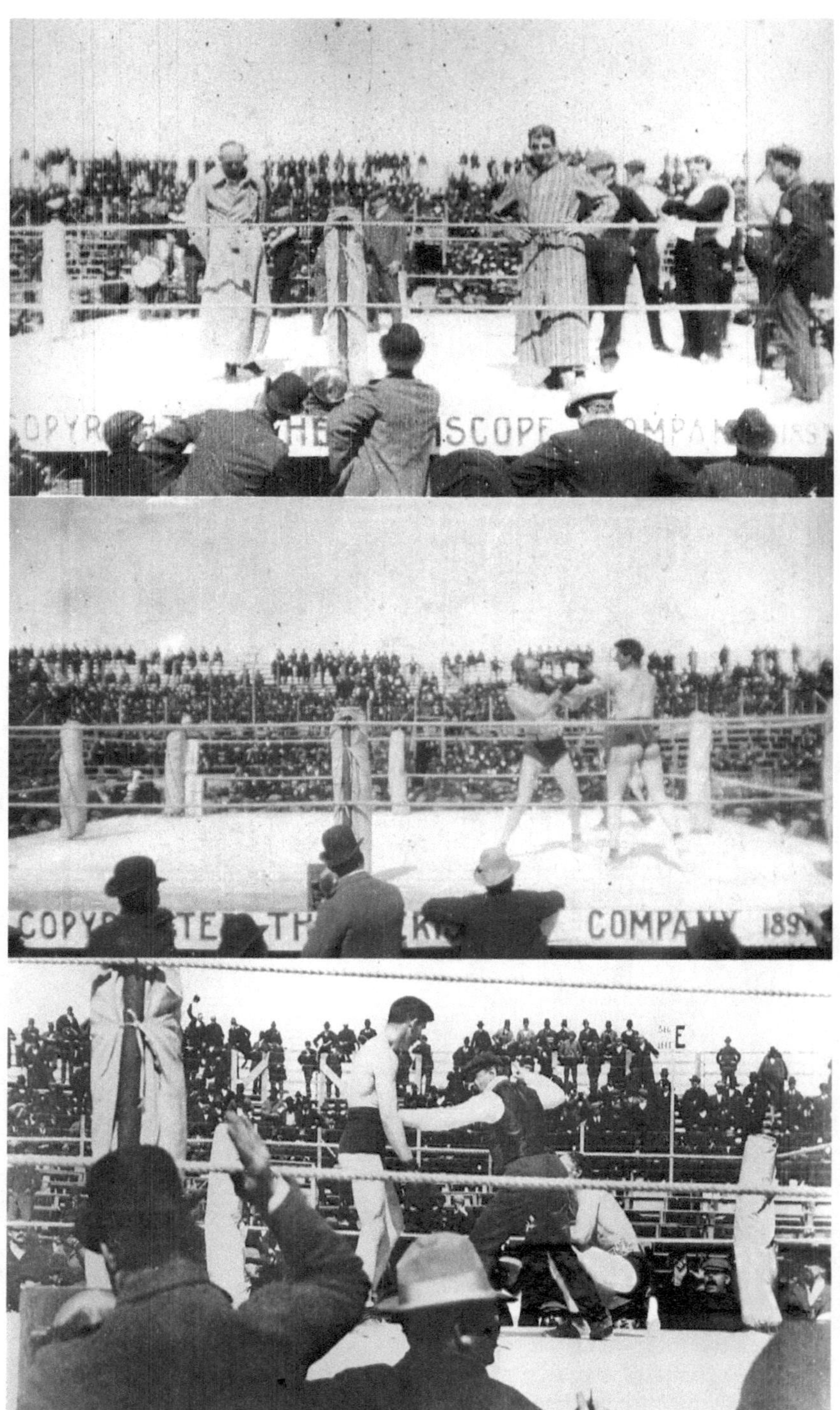

Rector's film. TOP: Preliminaries, Corbett and Fitz posing for the camera. MIDDLE: An unidentified round. BOTTOM: Fitz down in Round 6, referee Siler pushing Corbett back, timekeeper Muldoon's hand raised as he counts.

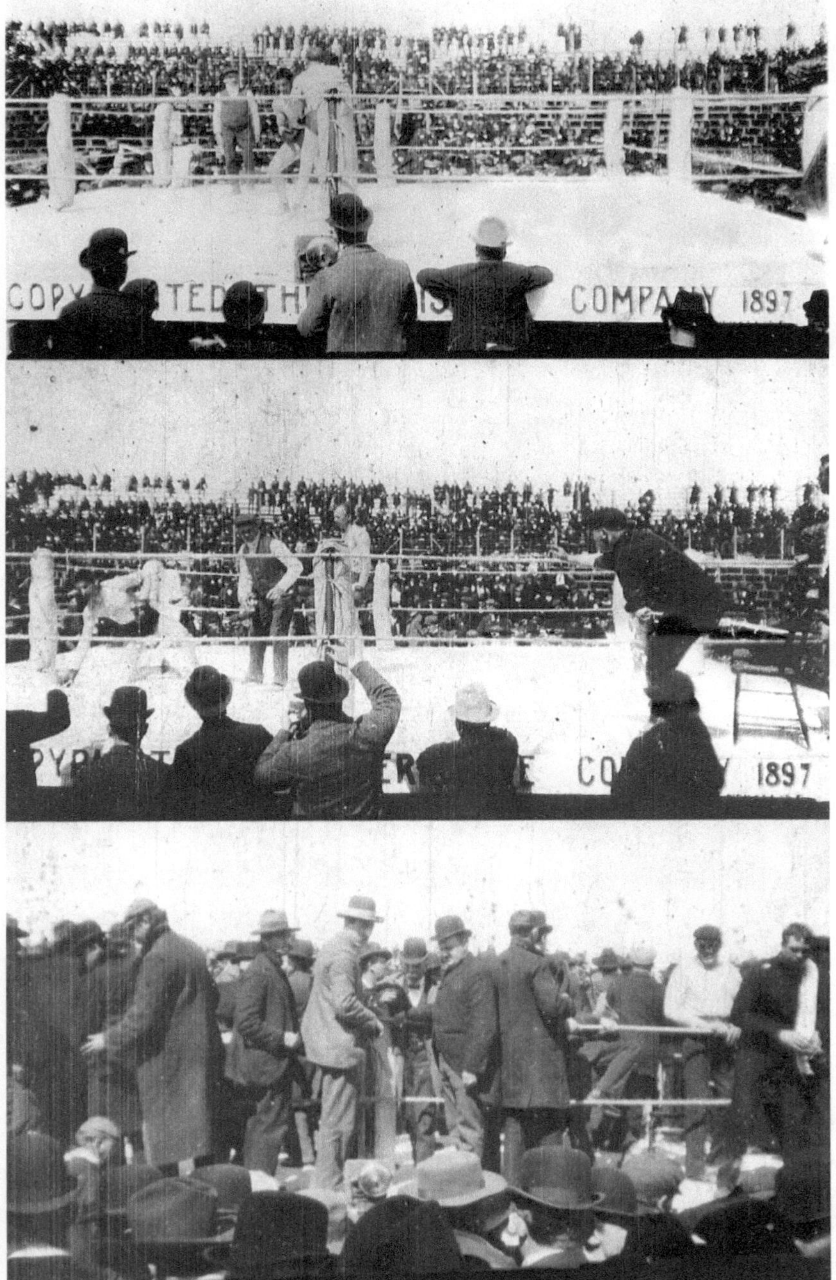

TOP: Fitz delivering the "awful blow" in Round 14, Corbett sagging.
MIDDLE: Corbett down, one of his seconds on the apron, Muldoon, clutching stopwatch, hand raised. BOTTOM: The crowded ring after the fight.

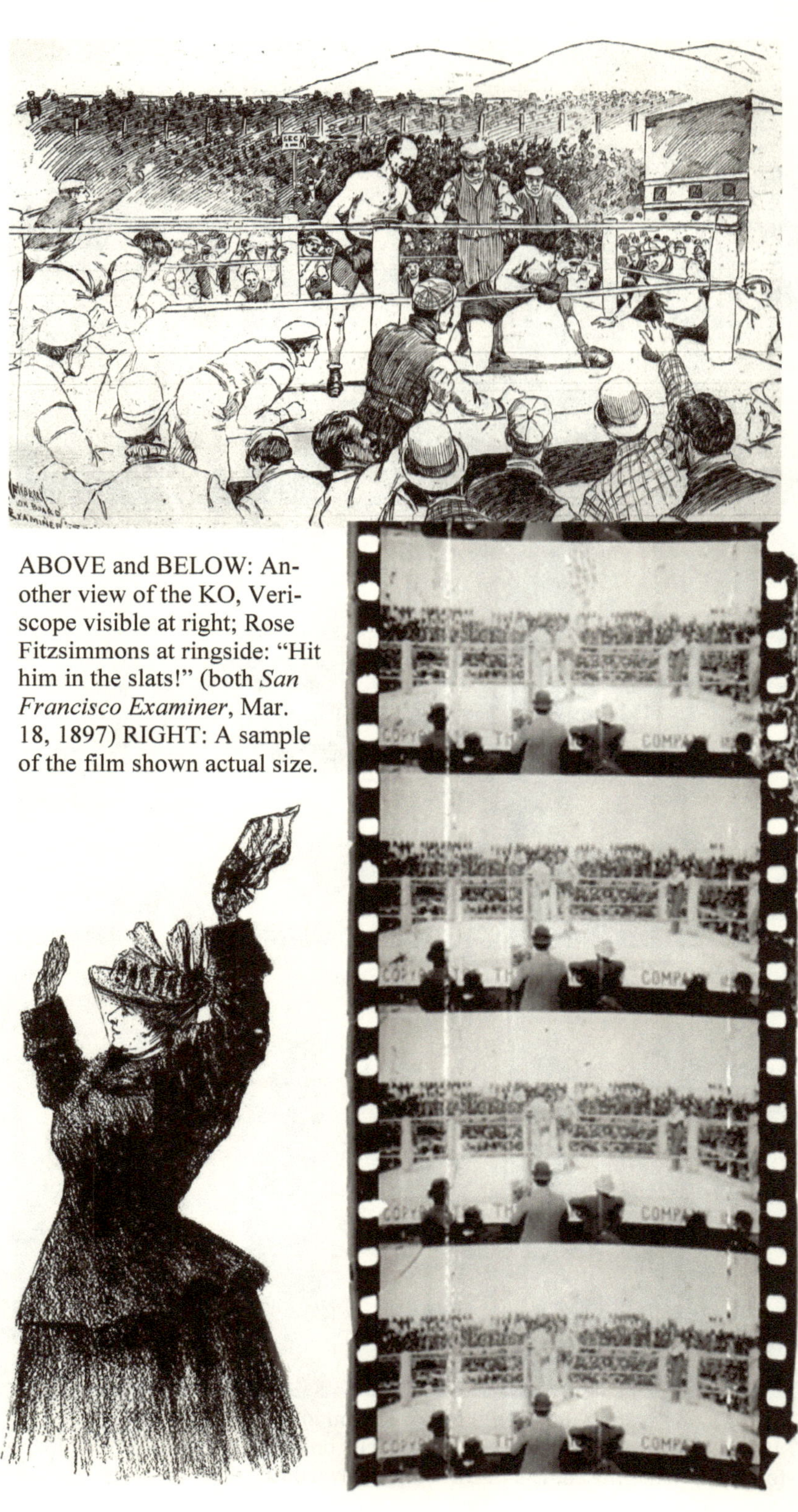

ABOVE and BELOW: Another view of the KO, Veriscope visible at right; Rose Fitzsimmons at ringside: "Hit him in the slats!" (both *San Francisco Examiner*, Mar. 18, 1897) RIGHT: A sample of the film shown actual size.

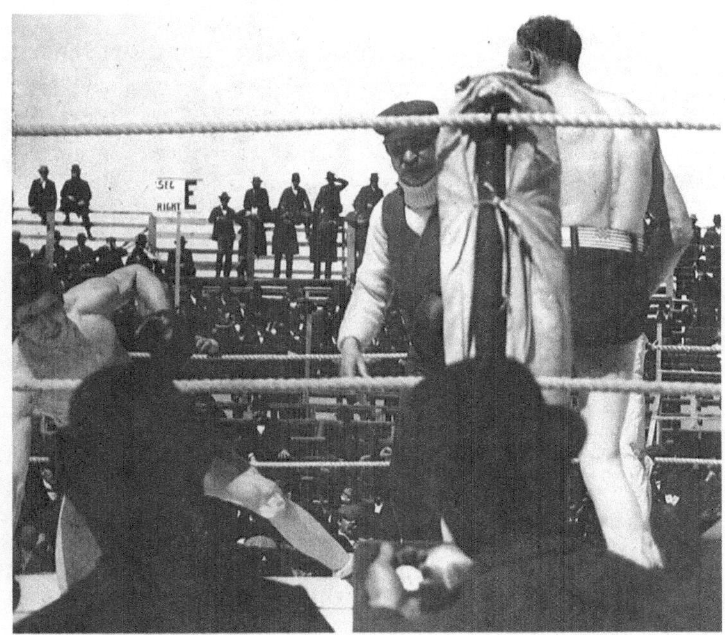

ABOVE: Detail of the knockout, showing the clarity of the Veriscope film. BELOW LEFT: Competing ads for the premiere of the real Corbett-Fitz film at the Academy of Music and the Lubin fake "reproduced by counter-parts" at Huber's Museum. (*New York World*, May 23, 1897) BELOW: Rector's film opens in Chicago. (*Chicago Tribune*, June 6, 1897)

ACADEMY OF MUSIC.
14TH ST. AND IRVING PL.
E. G. Gilmore & Eugene Tompkins....Props & Mgrs
THE VERISCOPE
PICTURES OF THE

CORBETT-FITZSIMMQNS

SPARRING CONTEST,
PRODUCED BY THE VERISCOPE CO.
DAN. A. STUART, PRESIDENT.
PRICES 25c., 50c., 75c., $1.00
Afternoons at 2 30.   Evenings at 8.45.
Seats four weeks ahead.

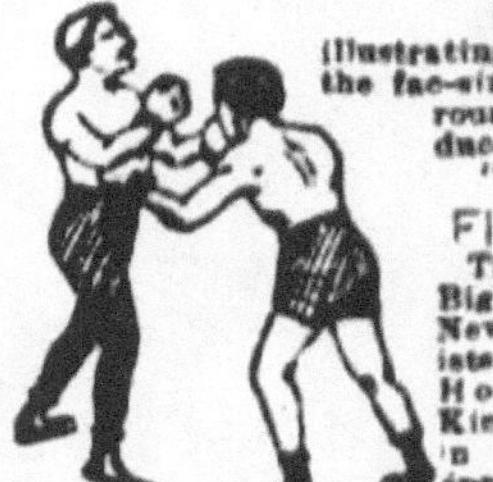

HUBER'S
14th St. $1 SHOW FOR 10 CTS
MUSEUM.

The Kinematographe illustrating life-size pictures of the fac-simile of the great 14-round fight of 1897; reproduced by counterparts of "CORBETT & FITZSIMMONS." The Knock-out Show. 3 Big Co's. Minnie Schult New Songs. 20 other Artists. Curio Ha lei Capt. Holtum. Cannon-Ball King Wills' Comedy Co. in "Two Old Cronies." Special attractions at Sunday Concerts.

GRAND OPERA HOUSE.
EXTRA
Announcement Extraordinary!
THE SENSATION OF THE SEASON
BEGINNING WEDNESDAY NIGHT

VERISCOPE

PICTURES OF THE FAMOUS

FITZSIMMONS CORBETT CONTEST...

A lifelike Reproduction of the Great Struggle from Photographs Taken on the Spot.
A TRIUMPH OF MODERN SCIENCE
Beginning Wednesday Night, June 9.
Every Night at 8:30.
MATINEES DAILY AT 2:30.

Seats and boxes may now be secured at the box office for any performance. The theater will be closed Monday and Tuesday evenings.

OPERA HOUSE AND THEATRE ROYAL.
Management of E. G. Cooke and G. M. Welty.

THE TALK OF THE TOWN.
THE MARVELLOUS
VERISCOPE REPRODUCTION
Of the

FITZSIMMONS-CORBETT

BOXING CONTEST
For the Championship of the World,

THREE MORE NIGHTS ONLY.

NOTE.—The Veriscope is on tour round the world, and in view of dates already arranged, the Brisbane Season must positively close on TUESDAY Next. The Management have, therefore, to announce the

LAST THREE NIGHTS
LAST THREE NIGHTS

Of the

FITZSIMMONS-CORBETT

INTERNATIONAL GLOVE CONTEST
For the Championship of the World.
SPECIAL ANNOUNCEMENT.
The Season at the Opera House Closes TO-NIGHT, reopening at the

THEATRE ROYAL

For
POSITIVELY TWO NIGHTS ONLY,
MONDAY, and TUESDAY,
8th November. 9th November.
Positively
THE ONLY OPPORTUNITIES
Of Witnessing
THE GREATEST ATHLETIC CONTEST OF MODERN TIMES
As Reproduced by the Veriscope.
Box Plan at Paling's. PRICES.—Dress Circle and Reserved Stalls, 3s.; Stalls, 2s.; Family Circle, 1s.; Pit, 1s. Doors open 7.15. Commence 8.15.

GUSTAV WALTER'S ENTERPRISES

OLYMPIA

S.W. Corner Mason and Eddy Streets.
THIS AFTERNOON! THIS EVENING!
THE ONLY AUTHORIZED
VERISCOPE PICTURES
—OF THE—

CORBETT-FITZSIMMONS
14-ROUND CONTEST,
Under the Management of DAN A. STUART.
SPECIAL POPULAR PRICES!
RESERVED SEATS.................25c
A Few Extra Choice Seats, 50c.

ABOVE: The Veriscope film in California. (*San Francisco Call*, July 20, 1897) LEFT: Veriscope world tour ads from *Brisbane Courier*, Nov. 6, 1897 (top) and *Johannesburg Standard and Diggers' News*, Feb. 15, 1898 (bottom). BELOW: Enoch Rector in 1899. (Courtesy Sasha Chermayeff)

AMPHITHEATRE.

E. G. COOKE and G. M. WELTY Lessees.

COMPLETE & INSTANTANEOUS
SUCCESS
OF THE WONDERFUL
VERISCOPE REPRODUCTION
OF THE

FITZSIMMONS
CORBETT

GREAT INTERNATIONAL

BOXING CONTEST

EVERY

Movement, Incident, and Detail as it actually occurred watched with breathless interest by an intensely-excited Audience.

THE VERISCOPE
WILL BE
EXHIBITED EVERY EVENING
AT 8.15
Until Further Notice.

POPULAR PRICES:

Boxes, £2; Single Box Seats, 7s 6d; Stalls, 5s; Gallery, 2s 6d.
Plan at Bonamici's, Jeppe Arcade.

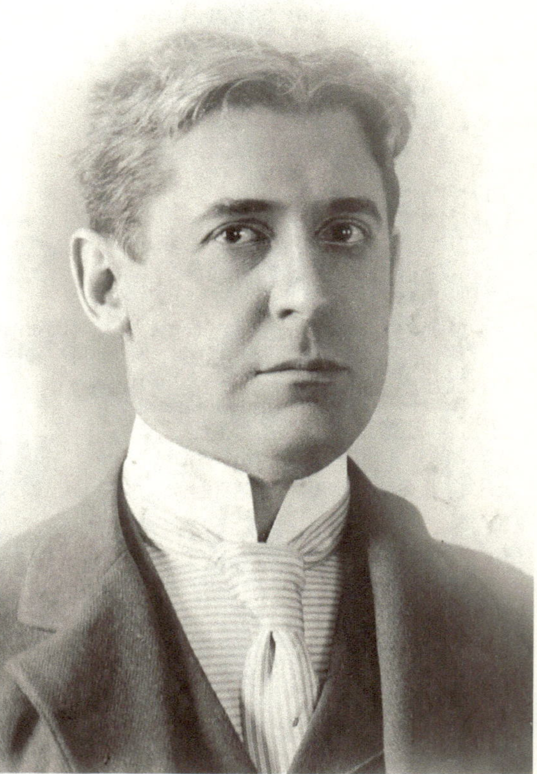

CHAPTER 19

CARSON CITY

THERE WAS SNOW ON THE GROUND in Carson City. The wintry mantel accentuated the depressive look of the place with its abandoned storefronts and empty houses, left behind by all the people who had moved on after the surrounding hills were mostly mined out.

Behind closed doors, however, clustered around their woodstoves, Carson's remaining citizens were buzzing with excitement. It was February 1897 and the Corbett-Fitzsimmons championship battle was coming. The spectacle promised to be the biggest thing to hit town in years, assuming one could afford a ticket to see it. And more important, it would bring a flood of visitors to the city, sporting enthusiasts with wallets full of money to spend. Carson, it was glowingly predicted, was about to enter a new era of prosperity with legalized prizefights. The Corbett-Fitz contest would mark the start of a return to good times.

All those visitors would need accommodation, of course. Some townsfolk were planning to rent out spare rooms. Others would be setting up dormitories in empty shops. A local furniture dealer was getting in a shipment of beds to rent out to homeowners wanting to pack them in like sardines.

Then there was entertainment and food. Abandoned storefronts would be turned into saloons, pool halls, Kinetoscope and Phonograph parlors. Eateries to feed the multitudes would also be set up, from a cafeteria in the agricultural pavilion to a barbecue joint in the old Salvation Army barracks serving ribs and beans, freshly baked bread and hot tamales. An old-timer living up in the hills was being brought in to make the beans. He had the best recipe in the county.

Other residents were eyeing the souvenir market, laying in supplies of commemorative spoons and buttons, novelty canes, decorative trays, bottles of Trib water from the nearby mineral springs. The local Piute Indians were going to stage a ghost dance and charge admission. One canny businessman, sensing opportunity in soft Eastern bottoms planted on hard wooden benches, had the convicts at the Nevada State Prison turning out ten thousand cushions stenciled with: "Corbett-Fitzsimmons, Fight of the Century." Even those with no capital to invest could get in on the act with the St. Patrick's Day angle, March 17 being the saint's day. Scrounge up some cheap green fabric, cut out four-leaf clovers, stick a pin on them and you had something you could sell for a dime.

And then a rush for the station. Jim Corbett was here!

Jim arrived in wet snow on February 16, the whole of Carson City seemingly turned out to see him. With members of his entourage distracting the crowd, he slipped out the back of the train and made his way to Shaw's Hot Springs, a spa resort a mile north where his advance agent and right-hand man Eddie Cooke had set up his training camp. The facilities consisted of a hotel with a communal dining room and bedrooms for Jim's trainers, a private cottage where Jim would sleep, a coach house with punching bag and pulleys and other apparatus and a specially built handball court with a removable canvas roof. Within a couple of days regular food shipments were arriving from San Francisco: the thick porterhouse steaks and chops that Jim liked, fresh vegetables and plenty of potatoes, Bartlett water for his constitution, two barrels of Russet apples for the baked apples-with-cream dish he habitually had for dessert.

Corbett had only just begun his training when another storm rolled in off the Sierra Nevadas. It left more than two feet of snow on the ground and ruled out any roadwork. Confined indoors, Jim threw himself into his work under the stern eye of long-time trainer Billy Delaney: an hour of handball with his brother Joe after breakfast—Corbett preferred handball to roadwork for stamina-building— then punching the bag and working the pulleys and strengthening his arms with dumbbells, then a hard session of sparring in the afternoon, brother Joe, John McVey and Billy Woods providing the opposition.

Joe, a pitcher now with the Baltimore Orioles and no mean boxer himself, was useful as a sparring partner for his incredible hand speed. With him Corbett worked on his dodging and weaving, blocking and counterpunching. Corbett would then go straight into a round of close-in work with McVey, a strong, big-bellied wrestler. This was good for overall strengthening and to practice clinching and hitting on the break—essential skills, Corbett insisted, because Fitz "is like a rat. When cornered he fights hard, and this is what I have to look out for."

Billy Woods would then take over in the "pneumatic armor" Corbett had purchased, thick pads covering his torso, an inflated ring protecting his face. With Woods, Corbett would let loose with everything he had, his full-force blows sometimes getting through the cumbersome face mask. "That was a peach," Woods would say in his thick Scots accent as he picked himself up off the floor, rubbing his jaw or his ear or feeling his nose.

Two additional men arrived at the Hot Springs training camp a few days later. The first was a new sparring partner, twenty-two-year-old Los Angeles boilermaker Jim Jeffries. Two hundred and twenty pounds of solid muscle and as durable as an ox, he had been brought in to give Corbett a seriously weighty challenge that would make handling Fitzsimmons, at least fifty pounds lighter, seem easy.

The second arrival was trainer Charlie White, who had previously worked with Fitz and knew all his tricks. In the following weeks White would secretly show Jeffries Fitz's various feints and shifts and punches to use in his sparring sessions with Corbett. Particularly dangerous were the Antipodean's pivot blows. In the rope pivot blow, for example, Fitz would lean against the ropes, feigning fatigue, turning away from his opponent like a rank beginner, then he would whip around and land a hammer fist—and maybe just a bit of an elbow. Corbett quickly clued into what his trainer and Jeffries were up to and took pleasure in evading the sneak attacks when they came. "You didn't get away with it," he would crow after evading Jeffries' latest. "You'll have to try again."

By early March Corbett was rounding into fine shape, the best of his career according to insiders. William Brady attributed it to the Sharkey encounter, that close call having done Jim a great deal of good. He was leaner and more powerful-looking now than ever before, his neck like a tree trunk, his legs sinewy and lithe, his stomach muscles standing out as sharply as Eugen Sandow's.

Corbett's stamina was also impressive. He would work out with dumbbells before stepping into the ring to force himself to cope with arm fatigue. Then he would work through his sparring partners, one man after another, round after round of nonstop action for nearly an hour. On one memorable occasion, Jeffries, on instructions from White, went at him full force. After two rounds of serious fighting Corbett knocked the bigger man out. "They told me in Frisco that you couldn't hit hard," Jeffries mumbled after being revived. Corbett then proceeded to batter his way through John McVey and Billy Woods, smashing Woods in his pneumatic armor so hard to the floor that all the snow slid off the roof with a *whooph*.

"I'm glad those pads don't fit me," McVey quipped.

"Me too," said Jeffries.

Charlie White and Billy Delaney looked on with approval. "Have you ever seen Jim in better condition?" said White.

"Never," said Delaney with an emphatic shake of his head.

But there were still things to worry about. There always were in the run-up to a big fight. For Delaney, there was the fear that Corbett was overdoing his training, working himself down too early to too fine an edge. He urged him to cut back but Jim wouldn't listen. For others at Shaw's Hot Springs, the irritability of "The Champ"— that was what they all called Corbett—was a worrisome sign. He was tense and snappish, visibly annoyed when he got clipped in sparring sessions or missed with one of his punches.

And what if The Champ got sick? What if he picked up that Carson City cold that was going around?

Back east in New York City, Enoch Rector was getting ready to film the big fight. He would do so with an updated version of the Kineto-Multiscope apparatus he had used at the Fitz-Maher contest. It had been rechristened the Veriscope, like the projector Rector had built the previous fall and now had on exhibition in Hawaii. Unlike the Kineto-Multiscope, which contained four Kinetographs grouped in pairs, filming two on and two off, the Veriscope would be fitted with three machines filming in sequence. These three machines would also be simpler and thus more reliable to use, for Rector had now done away entirely with electrical power. There would be no wiring, no mass of batteries such as caused trouble at the Fitz-Maher fight down on the Mexican border. None of this was needed because the Veriscope would rely entirely on human power. The photographing machines housed inside it would be cranked by hand. The reels of film would be manually turned to keep the film constantly slack. The Veriscope, in short, would be a living, breathing, thinking camera.

For film, Rector had decided to go even wider, to two and a half inches (63mm). He had negotiated the purchase of 300,000 feet of custom-made stock from Eastman Kodak at the end of December, enough to film the fight and make prints, after a morning of haggling with company president Henry Strong. The first two shipments had now been received and hand-cranked through a perforating machine to punch sprocket holes. Rector also had decided to use an even more rectangular frame. This would allow his apparatus to be placed closer to the ring and had an incidental but important benefit as well: The unique width, coupled with the use of five sprocket holes per frame rather than the Edison standard of four, would deter pirates from making and exhibiting illicit copies. The result would be images an inch and a quarter high by two inches wide—a widescreen format decades ahead of its time. Audiences would not see films this wide again until the 1950s.

To build this wide-format, hand-cranked camera, Rector turned to the New York firm of William T. Gregg, manufacturer of cameras and precision optical instruments used in engineering and mining. Three machines would be crafted to Rector's specifications in Gregg's Fulton Street workshop, an exacting job that would cost more than three thousand dollars. The film they would use, sixty thousand feet or nearly eleven and a half miles, was more than double what Rector had taken to Langtry. Half was coated with Eastman's most light-sensitive emulsion for use under an overcast sky.

The rest was of somewhat lower sensitivity for filming in direct sun. Whatever the weather, sunny or cloudy, Rector would have enough of either stock to film twenty-five rounds of action in duplicate, including the one-minute rests in between.

Dan Stuart in the meantime had dropped the coy act about the "picture privilege" and promised Corbett and Fitzsimmons each fifteen percent of the profits to get their agreement to be filmed. The money would be paid by a new venture called the Veriscope Company that Stuart spoke of forming, to supersede the Kineto-Multiscope Company or exist alongside it, it was not clear. Rector was assured a quarter share of net profits after Corbett and Fitz were taken care of. Stuart and his partner William Wheelock would get the rest. None of this was made public at the time. The details would only come out later, when things got contentious.

Bob Fitzsimmons arrived in Carson City on February 20, four days after Corbett. His wife Rose wasn't with him. She had stayed in New York to look after her sick mother and would follow later. The crowd waiting at the station cheered when Fitz descended from the carriage with his huge dog Yarum, the pet he had acquired to replace his hanged lion Nero. They wanted a speech and to shake his hand but he didn't oblige them, pushing his way through the throng to disappear into the Arlington Hotel. He had a cold and was not feeling well.

Martin Julian stayed behind to satisfy the newsmen with something salacious. He had received word, he said, that Corbett's backers were planning to rush the ring to stop the fight if their man looked to be losing. "I have taken care to prepare for just such an emergency," he said, "by sending for a 'push' of my own and you will find the toughest lot of citizens from New Orleans and Texas near Fitzsimmons' corner that ever landed in this state, and Corbett's gang will have a lovely time getting into the ring." Julian also spoke of the particular care that would be taken with Fitz's meals to prevent poisoning attempts. Oh, and he had booked Mechanics' Pavilion in San Francisco for March 19, two days after the fight, for the public would be eager to see the undisputed heavyweight champion of the world.

"I am sorry to see that Julian has been making an ass of himself again," was William Brady's withering response. "Julian seems to get more Julian as the years go on." The Mechanics' Pavilion booking was admittedly a nice touch, however. Brady shot off a telegram to reserve the place for the day before, March 18.

Fitz headed out to his training camp the next morning, a summer picnic site three miles south at a place called Cook's Ranch. The main house had bedrooms for Fitz and his people, a sitting room with an organ and well-stocked bookshelves, and a kitchen where Fitz's Chinese cook Sam would prepare his meals. Training would be done in a dance pavilion nearby, a big drafty structure that needed fixing up before they could get down to work. Fitz pitched in alongside the boys to get the place ready, tacking strips of barley sack over the gaps in the walls. The joke of the day was when he got the ice-cold tack hammer stuck to his tongue—and then yanked it away, howling like a banshee while everyone doubled over with laughter. When they had all the drafts sealed off, a wood stove was dragged in to heat the adjoining room, which would be used for rubdowns.

His lingering cold and the poor condition of the roads did not keep Fitz from his jogging. He owed his ring advantage of unsurpassed stamina to his years of intense roadwork and he was not going to let a little slop and sniffle get in the way. Starting in the last week of February he ran almost daily into Carson City and back, splashing through the slush and mud and puddles and getting back to the ranch a splattered, bedraggled mess. If the day was especially cold he went out running just the same with a sponge in his mouth to filter out the minute ice crystals that hung in the air. The locals called this frosty mist, reputed to cause all sorts of lung ailments, "pogonip."

After a clean-up and a meal—like Corbett, Fitz's appetite was enormous in training—it was off to punch the bag and get down to the serious work of sparring. Fitz had brought along three men to assist him: Dan Hickey, his sparring partner on his recent theatrical tour; Jack Stelzner, who had helped him prepare for the Maher fight the previous year; and the immensely strong German wrestler Ernest Roeber, who would be useful for building up strength in the clinches. There was no trainer. Fitz would be directing himself.

The daily sparring sessions at Cook's Ranch were brutal—not just for Hickey, Roeber and Stelzner, but for Fitz too. That was what he wanted. He wanted his partners to come at him full-force to toughen him up; to accustom him to delivering telling blows, finishing blows, while under fire. March 17 was going to be a *fight*, not a gentlemanly exhibition. He wanted to be ready for whatever Corbett threw at him and still be able to smash him down.

By the beginning of March the rigorous training had taken its toll. Fitz was sporting a black eye, a cut lip, two smashed ears and a bump on his head—Hickey, Roeber and Stelzner were equally battered—and his arms and wrists were so sore that he could not stand to have them massaged. In the Corbett camp there was talk that the Cornishman was wearing himself out. Fitz didn't see it that way. He started wearing pads on his wrists to ease the strain of blocking punches. And he kept at it. News arrived that Aimee Julian, Martin Julian's mother and Fitz's mother-in-law, had died. Training stopped for a day of mourning. Tears were shed. Then Fitz went back to work.

What about the knuckle you injured fighting Sharkey? one concerned visitor to Cook's Ranch wanted to know.

"Oh," replied Fitz matter-of-factly. "I knocked it flat on Roeber's head."

The William T. Gregg Company had completed the custom fabrication of Enoch Rector's three cameras. The machines had been delivered to Rector's Pearl Street workshop for final testing and were now ready to go, packed in padded boxes for the journey out to Nevada. The Eastman film was also ready, safely stowed in cans; men had been hired to assist with the filming; train tickets had been purchased and suitcases were packed.

And then there was trouble. A deputy sheriff showed up with a judge's order against the Kineto-Multiscope Company to seize Rector's cameras and all related equipment. As the stunned engineer looked helplessly on, the machines that he needed to film the fight were hauled outside, loaded onto a wagon and carted away.

The attachment order had been issued in response to a complaint from the Gregg Company. Rector still owed the firm for the manufacture of the cameras and other services rendered and it wanted the bill paid before the machines were taken out of the state.

Rector appeared in New York County Court to plead for the release of his cameras, pointing out that if he didn't have them at ringside for the upcoming contest, he and his partners would be ruined and thus unable to pay anything to anyone at all. The lawyer for the Gregg Company insisted that a bond be posted before the machines were released, his client reserving the right to increase the amount sued for to include damages for breach of contract.

The judge expressed little sympathy for the embattled inventor. "I cannot change the laws of the state to suit a prize fight," he said. "The plaintiff has three days under the law to examine the sureties."

Rector posted the required bond. And then he waited. He had more than twelve thousand dollars worth of film on hand, ready for shipment out west—and no cameras to feed it through.

Dan Stuart was facing challenges of his own in Carson City. First he had to select a site for his great arena. He chose the race track on the outskirts of town. An architect was hired, a design was selected and lumber purchased and shipped in from a distance, bypassing the local sawmill with its inflated prices. The structure would be a twelve-sided, open-air amphitheater with a twenty-four-foot ring in the center, reserved seating close in and an outer ring of general admission bleachers rising up in twenty-five rows. Total cost: fifteen thousand dollars.

Workers were just beginning to lay out the structure when Stuart fell ill with a near-fatal bout of pneumonia. He spent seventeen days in bed, dosed with quinine and morphine, then forced himself back to work and off the morphine cold turkey, suffering what he called "the tortures of the damned." Ticket sales had to be attended to, transportation arranged and attempts to stop the fight thwarted.

In Washington, a bill introduced in Congress to prohibit the transmission of fight news over telegraph lines had just been defeated. Further attempts to throw up legislative roadblocks were expected. In Reno, an organization calling itself the Law and Order League was seeking an injunction to bar the contest. It was nothing more than sour grapes from a town bitter over not getting the fight,

Carsonites retorted, but it added just the same to the negative publicity swirling around the contest—publicity that might discourage even more people from attending than those already put off by the high train fares the Southern Pacific was proposing to charge.

And then an even more immediate threat: Carson City District Attorney Jones announced his intention to swear out a warrant to scuttle the fight. It was an ironic twist, considering that Jones was the very lawyer hired by Stuart to draft the bill making prizefighting legal in Nevada. Jones was angry because his fee for that essential service had not been paid. Stuart blustered for a few days, complaining that the sum was grossly inflated. Then he paid it and the DA backed down.

The Odd Fellows Hall, meanwhile, was being fixed up as a Western Union telegraph office, thirty operators to be stationed on the second floor, above the scores of desks set up below for the press. Extra lines were being strung up to carry news of the fight, making for a total of eight lines leading from Carson, each equipped with Edison's quadruplex so that four messages could be sent simultaneously in either direction. The lines would be guarded by Pinkerton men, one every mile all the way to Reno. This was in response to rumors that powerful gamblers were scheming to tap into the wires to delay fight news and manipulate betting.

Another rumor had it that thieves were planning a raid on fight headquarters to steal the ticket receipts (which would be the scenario, incidentally, for the 1953 film *City of Bad Men*). "I'd like to see them get out of Carson," Stuart quipped when he heard the story, for half the men in town were packing revolvers. The promoter nevertheless assigned extra guards to stand at the entrance and watch the safe, just in case.

Over at the post office, mail was pouring in for both fighters, a good-sized stack of it every day. There were letters pledging support and offering advice and packages containing good luck charms of every description: rabbits' feet, horseshoes, a lucky wishbone, four-leaf clovers—even pieces of ear snipped off an unlucky bulldog who "never whimpered when he gave them up," the sender proudly wrote.

Corbett was receiving the strongest show of support. He was

seen as America's champion and Ireland's favorite son and had the additional appeal of being gentlemanly in manners and speech, at least in the public's imagination. Cornwall-born and New Zealand-raised Fitz was generally seen as more foreign. Perhaps not surprisingly, he received most of the hate mail. "That's hot stuff," said Fitz of a particularly vicious poison pen letter. Julian usually screened them out but this one was so good the boys passed it around. "I wish I had that fellow here to spar with for a few minutes."

"Dear Mr. Fitzsimmons," read a more sympathetic note sent to Bob from Philadelphia. "I am a little boy 11 years old and take much interest in your coming fight with Jim Corbett. I hope you will succeed in whipping him, as he is nothing but a big blow."

"Dear Sir," read a typical missive received by Corbett, this one from Montreal. "Please beat Fitzsimmons as fast as you can, because we Irishmen can't live in this town if you don't."

Also in Corbett's mail was a printed leaflet describing two runaway boys, forwarded by a police constable in Iowa. "Said to have started for Carson," read the constable's scrawled message. "Give them a good swift kick and send them home."

March 10, a week to go to the battle, and the two fighters were rounding into splendid condition. Visitors would pay a dollar for the old-time stagecoach ride out to see Corbett, admission included, and return to Carson convinced he would win. Then they would visit Fitz and come away equally impressed. Betting was running ten to eight in Jim's favor but mainly for sentimental reasons. When it came to a hard-eyed physical assessment, most agreed that the two men were evenly matched.

In the absence of any clear advantage, the mental state of each fighter was probed and debated. Corbett definitely was showing the most visible signs of strain, a brief visit from his wife and sister providing only momentary relief. His anxiety went beyond worry about losing his title and with it possibly the theatrical drawing power that was his real source of wealth. There was the awful thought of losing specifically to an unrefined, ungainly, working-class fighter like Fitz—"the wild man of Borneo," Corbett witheringly called him. Fitz also wasn't as good a boxer, his punches admittedly dangerous but his movements lacking Corbett's finesse and precision. And worst of all, he was nearly twenty pounds lighter—practically a middleweight, for God's sake. Corbett therefore *had* to win. Anything less would mean humiliation.

As for Bob, he continued to come across as a overgrown, carefree kid, delighted to have his wife Rose and young Bob Jr. now with him. Rose was even planning to attend the fight, something she had never before done, for Dan Stuart had just announced that women, if properly escorted, would be allowed into the arena. She would sit in the dance pavilion lovingly watching Bob train, Bob occasionally pausing to chat or to romp with his son, then turning back to seize Roeber by the neck or to give Stelzner a wallop. He seemed to be having the time of his life.

It wasn't an act. Fitz was fun-loving and easy-going by nature. But he was also clever. The out-of-character drinking spree he went on in Carson, for example, was likely a put-on, an attempt to manipulate the odds for the benefit of his backers. (The rumor of Corbett's supposed liver complaint may have served the same purpose.) And then there was the March 10th incident on the penitentiary road. Fitz was the instigator, almost certainly paid by the Hearst newspaper chain to stage an encounter with Corbett, *San Francisco Examiner* sports editor Bill Naughton conveniently present.

It began shortly after Corbett and a few friends had left the prison, having stopped in to view the prehistoric human footprints preserved on the grounds, a local attraction. Fitz and Dan Hickey, out for a training run with Yarum, came up behind on the road. Wanting to avoid an encounter, Corbett picked up the pace when he saw them. Fitz and Hickey ran faster to catch up, Naughton following behind in a buggy.

"Good morning, gents," said Hickey when they were all walking along in a bunch. The greeting was returned. No reaction from Corbett. He called his collie Ned away from Yarum. The two dogs suspiciously eyed each other.

"Good morning, everybody," chimed in Fitz.

Still nothing from Corbett. Fitz moved in closer until their shoulders were almost touching.

"Good morning, Jim."

"Good morning." Corbett drew out the syllables in a theatrical manner.

Fitz extended his hand. That did it.

"Oh, no," said Corbett. "I'll shake with you if you lick me over there on the 17th." He motioned toward Carson. "Not before."

Fitz stopped in his tracks, feigning amazement. "What was that?"

"I said I'd shake hands with you if you lick me on the 17th."

Fitz kept it up. "What?"

"The 17th, the 17th," repeated Corbett, getting in Fitz's face now, temper flaring.

Naughton was scribbling away on his notepad. This was just what was wanted. Then one of Corbett's companions led Jim away and spoiled all the fun.

"Oh I see," Fitz called after him. "There will be a live one there on the 17th."

"I'm glad of it," Corbett called back. "I'd hate to have to go against a dead one. You thought I was about dead or you would not be here now."

"You are nearly dead as it is," Fitz shouted after him. "You'll be a regular dead one after St. Patrick's day."

"Look at him," Corbett sneered, glancing over his shoulder. "He looks like a lightweight."

The game of course could be played both ways. It was turned on Fitz a few days later when Bat Masterson and Wyatt Earp arrived in town. Fitz liked Masterson. He had him out to Cook's Ranch and they played horseshoes together. But he hated Earp for the Sharkey fight fix. He was therefore intensely annoyed when a New York reporter brought Earp out to the ranch in the hopes of creating a scene. Fitz scowled and glared daggers at the famous gunslinger. Earp just sat there quiet, his gaze unwavering, an amused smile on his face. Nothing more happened. When the reporter tried to strike up a conversation, Fitz turned away

"For a man to speak to me when he is in company with Wyatt Earp is a little more than I care to stand," Fitz said. His boyishness was momentarily gone. He was clearly upset.

———— ✳ ————

Enoch Rector's cameras were released by the sheriff after the bond he had posted was accepted by the Gregg Company. He immediately proceeded to Carson City with his entourage of assistants, the Veriscope and film following in a freight car one day behind.

It was late in the evening of March 11 when Rector stepped off the Southern Pacific vestibuled sleeper and proceeded through the station to a waiting buggy. Carson was still very much awake, music and laughter filtering from the saloons and pool halls and restaurants, men strolling about and gathered in groups debating on corners, hawkers pushing their wares even at this late hour, sharpies with their games of chance set up in corners. A short ride and Rector was dropped with his baggage at the house where a room had been reserved for him through Dan Stuart's office. The average price in Carson for private accommodation had shot up to five dollars a night, more than a room at the best hotels in New York. For that you got clean sheets and breakfast and blast-furnace heat from a woodstove. It was no wonder every visitor here seemed to catch cold, what with the sweltering temperatures indoors and the freezing weather outside.

The crates containing the film and equipment arrived on schedule the next day. After verifying that the cameras with their delicate mechanisms were undamaged, Rector proceeded to the arena to examine the space that he had requested set aside for his Veriscope. It was to go in Section A, facing north, the front wall twenty-five feet from the ring. To his chagrin, he found that tiers of bleachers surrounded the ring on all sides, with no space at all left for his giant photographing machine. A mistake had been made, Dan Stuart having been unable to oversee construction due to the illness that had confined him to bed.

The first task in installing the Veriscope was therefore to tear up a section of arena seating. When this was complete, Rector explained his plans to the foreman and a work crew was set to the task. They would have the apparatus nailed together and light-sealed with tar paper in just a few hours, ready for the installation of the three cameras and red-tinted glass in the three windows facing the ring.

Reporters who dropped by the arena were drawn to the structure as it neared completion and came over to pepper Rector with questions. Rector was guarded with his replies, denying that Corbett and Fitz had any share of the film rights and stressing that the whole undertaking was "purely experimental." The *San Francisco Chronicle*, likely misled by Rector with a twinkle in his eye, stated that the Veriscope used eight-inch-wide film and operated at the fantastic speed of sixty frames per second. This report was accompanied by an illustration of Rector inside his apparatus, an oversized film reel more than three feet across loaded onto one of his machines.

The *New York World* was savvier. Its reporter got Rector to admit to being confident in his ability to successfully photograph the contest, the superior film he had brought greatly reducing the risk of being foiled by an overcast sky. "I don't think there will be any bad weather," Rector stated. "Although I don't consider myself the luckiest man in the world by any means. It cost me about $15,000 to have a lot of cameras and things down to Langtry, Texas, last year, but it poured there."

A snowstorm was of course another matter. His cameras could not be employed in a snowstorm. To guard against a calamity of that nature, Stuart got Corbett and Fitz to agree to a one-day postponement in the event of bad weather.

Rector had his apparatus fully outfitted and ready for testing on the afternoon of March 14, three days before the battle. Conditions were far from ideal, a light snow falling and the sky the color of lead. If usable images could be obtained in such poor light, the Veriscope with its supply of Eastman film would have proven itself capable of photographing in just about any sort of weather, with or without sun.

Rector locked himself inside the apparatus and threaded a small spool of the more sensitive film onto one of the cameras. The view through the lens nicely encompassed the ring platform, the posts and ropes not yet erected. He signaled to his assistant standing at the center of the boards, a German referred to in the papers as "Herr Heinrich," and started cranking the machine as Heinrich jigged about to give him something to film. The mechanism worked smoothly, the film passing through without tearing or catching. The exposed footage was then developed—the Veriscope was also a darkroom—in the chemical baths set up along the back wall.

There was a long pause, then muffled cheering and laughter that suddenly grew loud when the door was flung open.

The strip of negative had turned out fine, each frame sharp and clear despite the poor light. Sunny skies were no longer needed to make movies. "I was a little fearful about the clouds, but am agreeably surprised at the outcome," Rector exulted. "The machine is in perfect working order, and stood the trip West in great style. Nothing but Egyptian darkness can now prevent a perfect photograph of the fight. With a clear sky and a sharp sun the possibilities are unlimited."

Heinrich's cavorting figure was also amazingly large in each frame. This was thanks to the extra-wide film and widescreen format Rector was using, allowing him to place his cameras just twenty-five feet from the ring instead of the ninety feet that would have been required to encompass the whole thing using standard Edison film. It was comparable to moving the viewer from the cheapest seat at the back of the arena into a premium ringside box.

Rector set another of his assistants to work painting a sign in big black letters across the side of the ring facing the lens. It was the final touch before filming. "Copyrighted The Veriscope Company 1897," it read.

An important meeting took place in Dan Stuart's office the next morning. It involved Fitz's manager Martin Julian, Corbett's manager William Brady, Enoch Rector and Stuart himself, on the mend now after coming close to dying from pneumonia. The purpose was to finalize the matter of the "picture privilege"—specifically to placate Corbett and Fitz by putting their agreement with Stuart in writing. If it wasn't in writing, Julian and Brady threatened, their men wouldn't fight.

Contracts were drawn up and signed guaranteeing the two fighters fifteen percent cuts of the film's profits. If the thing could be pulled off, and it still seemed a long shot, that would earn them substantially more than they stood to gain in prize money and side bets if they won the fight, even after subtracting the many expenses Stuart reeled off.

Rector, standing quietly by, did not similarly insist on getting his promised share put in writing. His agreement with Stuart remained verbal. He continued to take the big Texan at his word.

March 16. The eve of the battle. The arena was finished, black numbers painted on all the seats, white canvas stretched over the bare planks of the ring. The gloves had been scrutinized and weighed; the fighters had been examined by doctors and declared fit; the rules referee George Siler would enforce had been agreed to, managers Brady and Julian putting on the usual show of getting upset in meetings, proclaiming that they were perpetually giving in to the other side's unreasonable demands. It was such an act that it was hard at times to keep a straight face—like when Julian insisted when they were arguing over whether to allow hitting in clinches that Fitz knew no more about in-fighting than a newborn babe.

Hitting in clinches would be allowed. So would shots on the break. Fitz's famous pivot blow would not. "We give way as usual," Julian moaned. When Julian sarcastically shot down the idea of Corbett wearing an undershirt and long johns if fight day proved chilly ("Why don't you put him in furs?"), Brady fumed right back: "You have had everything your own way, and now you want more!"

Jim had ceased training two days before, conserving his energy now for the contest. He spoke of having the utmost confidence of winning but it was clear he was stressed. Nerves before a fight were natural. It focused a man's mind, stoked his fighting spirit. But it was nevertheless distressing to have the champ so bad-tempered and snappish, and to see the tears in his eyes when he met his father at the station. Was it business as usual, the same old nerves that had beset Jim before his fights with Sullivan and Mitchell? Or was this something more? Did he perhaps have too much to lose?

"Now look here," Jim barked, annoyed at the anxious looks he was getting from everyone in his camp. "Just quit on this sizing-up business. I don't like it."

At Cook's Ranch, Bob Fitzsimmons was resting as well. He was doing only light work now to keep limber, spending more time with Rose and the baby and wolfing down the chops and chicken and calf's foot jelly that Sam sent out from the kitchen, all of it slathered with the special hot sauce that Bob made himself. In between he chatted and read the papers and stood beside the organ in the parlor singing his favorite ballads, not letting the wretchedness of his voice keep him from enjoying himself. He continued to seem relaxed, as if tomorrow was a hundred years away.

He had been dreaming, he said. He always had dreams before his big fights. Before defeating Dempsey in 1892 he had dreamed it would happen. Same thing in '93 before his victory over Jim Hall; twice before the Maher fight in '96.

It was as vivid as life, Fitz said of his latest dream of Corbett. "He fiddled around for a few rounds trying to get a lead and leave an opening. Well, I did let him get in on me a few times, but he did not hurt me, and in the fifth round I caught him a hook on the jaw and he went down and out."

In his bedroom in Carson City, Dan Stuart left the curtains open when he heaved his bulk into bed after midnight. He wanted to see the sky as soon as he opened his eyes in the morning. He had seen an immense flock of geese flying north two days before, supposedly a sign of sunny skies to come. The weather was not looking good at the moment, however: heavy overcast, a freezing wind and snow flurries. If it continued he would be forced to push the battle back one day and likely lose a thousand or more last-minute ticket sales, further depressing his already disappointing take. What he needed was a warm, sunny day and for Rector to capture the fight on film, which was looking like his best hope for financial success.

Down the street in his own room, Enoch Rector retired with the same feeling that his fortunes hung in the balance. He was confident that he could film in cloudy conditions, and if the weather became truly awful he was assured that the fight would be postponed. His biggest concern now was whether he would be able to capture the whole thing. The Corbett-Courtney fight film, made less than three years before, consisted of six separate films each recording a single, truncated round of action lasting not much more than a minute. The Griffo-Barnett fight film, made less than two years before, had raised the bar for filming continuous action to around eight minutes. Both were cinematic milestones—and both shrank to insignificance alongside what Rector would attempt tomorrow. He would be trying to capture a live prizefight that could easily last for over an hour, perhaps even two. And he would have only one chance to get it. If he made any mistake; if there was any mechanical failure that prevented him from filming, the fight would carry on and he would miss it and another whole year of effort would have been wasted. Again.

But if he succeeded ... a quarter share of the net profits awaited. Enoch Rector could emerge from this a rich man.

CHAPTER 20

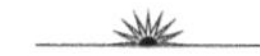

PRELIMINARIES

MARCH 17, 1897. Bob Fitzsimmons was out of bed at six o'clock in the morning. He had not slept well. He rarely did before a big fight. He tried to be quiet as he dressed and laced on his boots, Rose and Bob Jr. still sleeping, then he went into the kitchen for some of the coffee that Sam had hot on the stove. The Chinese cook was hard at work on breakfast. Martin Julian, Dan Hickey, Jack Stelzner and Ernest Roeber were sitting around the table, dressed and shaved and anxiously waiting.

How did you sleep, Bob? they wanted to know.

Like a baby, Bob replied. Ten straight hours.

A hot drink, a piece of toast and Fitz stepped out the front door into the most beautiful morning he had yet seen in Carson. It was still cold but the sun was warming the valley, burning off the frost that covered the ground. By fight time there would be no need for long johns in the ring.

He untied Yarum and took a turn through the nearby stand of cottonwoods to loosen up his muscles and distract his mind before breakfast. The Great Dane had viciously turned on him twice lately but now obediently followed, the pitchfork marks from the disciplining Fitz had administered still visible on its side.

Fitz was back at the ranch house by seven o'clock for breakfast, a hearty roast chicken meal to sustain him through the trial ahead. He ate quietly, his usual boisterousness gone. He had stopped talking about Corbett several days before, about how he'd wipe up the ring with him, and was now hardly talking at all. He didn't seem unduly nervous, just subdued, closed down within his own mind, as if the upcoming battle didn't interest him much. The meal finished, he went back outside to give a few comments to the newsmen who were arriving. "This is the day I've waited for for three years," he said. "If I lose you won't hear me whimper. I weigh 156 pounds and feel like a fighting cock."

One-fifty-six? That seemed unlikely. Of course, fighters lied about their weight all the time. Although there would be no official weigh-in, those in the know were saying that Fitz was tipping the scales in the low one-sixties, making him fifteen or twenty pounds lighter than Corbett.

Out at his training camp at Shaw's Hot Springs, Jim Corbett stayed in bed until seven o'clock, his room filled with flowers sent by well-wishers. "He's sleeping like a babe," his father Patrick informed the newsmen who began showing up at sunrise, contradicting reports that Jim hadn't been sleeping at all. The old man had absolute confidence in his son, his former concerns about the propriety of prize-fighting at last set aside. "Of course Jim'll win," he said. "How can a man lose a fight when the other man can't lay his glove on a vital spot?" But what about the lines under Jim's eyes? "Those lines about the eyes are perfectly natural," Patrick retorted. "I had them when I was his age."

Here was Jim at last in a tweed suit and turtleneck sweater. He looked relaxed and was acting cheery, greeting the boys waiting in the sitting room outside his door.

"How do you feel, Jim?" It was the inevitable first question out of Charlie White's mouth.

"Fine as silk, Charlie." Corbett gave his stout trainer a slap on the back. "Never better."

White led him over to the window to look him over, peering into his eyes, scrutinizing his skin, inquiring about the state of his lungs and his throat, Corbett submitting in remarkably good humor. White finished the examination and pronounced his charge in prime shape.

Corbett left the cottage and strolled over to the hotel for break-fast, chatting and shaking hands with the fans and sporting men and journalists gathered outside before disappearing into the dining room. After the meal—three lamb chops, two boiled eggs, some tea—he returned to his bedroom with trainers White and Delaney and manager Brady for a pep talk. White did most of the talking, warning Corbett to be patient, to take his time, to not lose his temper. "Just be cool and careful every minute you are in front of him," White said. "Fitz is expecting you to go at him like a bull at a red blanket and you must fool him."

"Jim," added Delaney, "he hasn't got a chance to lick you. I have trained you for all your fights, and I want to tell you right now—and it's no joke, either—that you never looked more fit for a fight than you do now."

Corbett reassured them that he had never felt stronger, and that he would take his time. The private session ended with them all solemnly shaking hands.

The hotels, boarding houses and Pullman cars on the sidings at the depot were emptying in Carson, the four thousand visitors to the city heading out for breakfast. Soon the restaurants, the lunch counters and the agricultural pavilion eatery down at the track were all filled.

With the meal taken care of it was time for a stroll, taking in the many interesting sights the city afforded. The visitors alone crowding the plank sidewalks were good of hours of staring. There were celebrities like portly John L. Sullivan; heavyweight contender Tom Sharkey, dressed to the nines; former lightweight champ Jack McAuliffe, never defeated; political heavyweights Senator Ingalls of Kansas and Nevada's own Governor Sadler; Wild West legends Bat Masterson, Wyatt Earp and brother Virgil. There were clusters of visiting Piute and Washoe Indians standing about in picturesque, inscrutable groups, their chests decorated with an indiscriminate mix of Corbett and Fitzsimmons medals. There were cowboys who had ridden in from outlying ranches, looking as exotic as Cossacks in their chaps and dusters and Stetsons, quiet and intense when sober, roaring and throwing money around when drunk. There were miners from the mines on the Comstock lode that were still open, given the day off to attend the fight. The many Cornishmen among them were grimly earnest in their support of Fitzsimmons, wagering little bars of gold and silver at even money, contemptuous of any mention of odds.

There was a less desirable element present as well, starting with the scores of hobos leaning against walls looking for handouts. Dan Stuart's assurances that riffraff wouldn't descend on Carson hadn't panned out. The police kept rounding them up and shipping them off in boxcars—to Reno, of course, just like that city deserved—along with the pickpockets and second-story creepers and confidence tricksters, the back alley grabbers and flimflammers and two-finger Petes. But more kept coming.

And then there were the souvenirs of the Fight of the Century to pick over. Hawkers had dozens of items to choose from: commemorative coins and medals; miniature boxing gloves; stenciled cushions; horseshoes à la Bob Fitzsimmons; St. Patrick's Day shamrocks in two- and four-inch sizes; canes with Corbett's or Fitz's profile carved on the handle; illustrated fight-day programs; turtleneck sweaters like the fighters wore; life-sized replicas of Corbett's right fist.

Need a haircut and shave? Itinerant barbers were open for business all across town. A dress shirt made up in a jiffy? Gee Hing was your man. A case of Trib mineral water, that virtuous beverage? Stop by any drugstore. A spin at the wheel of fortune? Step right over here. A corn neatly trimmed off your heel, perhaps? An ingrown toenail? Let Dr. Franklin, "The Homeliest Man on Earth," tend your feet.

By mid-morning the Arlington Hotel was the center of action. It was the best place to catch sight of the big names in town for the fight and to follow the betting taking place in the pool room across the street. The odds were still running in Corbett's favor, eight to ten. For those wanting to make a more sophisticated wager, there were chances to bet on the winner within a certain number of rounds ("Jim finishes Lanky Bob inside six") and mutual tickets offering various combinations of winners in the main event and the undercard battles to take place later that afternoon: "Mysterious" Bill Smith of Boston vs. George "Young Corbett" Green of San Francisco; Massachusetts fighter Martin Flaherty vs. Frisco's Dal Hawkins.

A crowd was also gathered at the ticket counter inside Dan Stuart's headquarters and spilled into the street. Late arrivals were selecting their seats from the big blue diagram of the arena and buying their tickets for the main event. The cheapest five-dollar bleacher seats were proving the most popular, so much so that Stuart raised the price to ten dollars; twenty- and forty-dollar reserved seats were more than most could afford. Admission to the afternoon undercard fights would require a second ticket, five dollars and up.

Stuart, looking weak and haggard from his recent illness, was putting a good face on things, swallowing his disappointment over ticket sales, smiling as he watched the proceedings. "It is the best we can do," he said. "There is no use of making any fuss. Carson is a long ways for lots of the boys to come and the hard times have made it impossible for many men to spend $200 to come here to see the fight and get home again."

He would be lucky to break even on the actual fight. His only chance now to make a profit, possibly a huge profit, was if Enoch Rector's film turned out.

Rector was already at the arena, pleased with all the blue sky and sunshine. He could not have asked for better weather for filming. He would of course be using the less sensitive film stock. This was preferable, for it would result in a sharper, more detailed image, the silver nitrate grains in the emulsion being finer than in the film that would have been used under an overcast sky.

Eastman Kodak employee George Kellogg was on hand to confirm this decision. The thirty-seven-year-old technician and photographer had been sent out from Rochester, New York to assist with handling the film and to offer guidance on matters of exposure—the amount of light that should be allowed to strike the film to get the best image. This was done by adjusting the width of the slits in the rotating disk shutter in front of the lens on each camera, taking into account the sensitivity of the film and the speed at which the machine would be cranked.

Inside the Veriscope apparatus, the three photographing machines were screwed down onto their wood bases, four feet between them, spanning eight feet in total from the first to the third. There were no heavy batteries underneath, no tangle of wires to contend with, just the hand crank on the right side of each machine, nice and simple. The film in its light-tight cans was stacked against the back wall, a supply of empty take-up reels beside it.

Rector took another sighting through the lens of one of the cameras. Yes, the left corner of the ring was definitely cut off. It had been a mistake requesting that the platform and ring be built slightly undersized to better accommodate the Veriscope, for the discrepancy had been noticed and had led to a protest. To keep the Corbett and Fitz parties satisfied, the platform had been extended on one side and the posts and ropes repositioned, making the enclosure now twenty-four feet by twenty-two—not quite regulation but close enough to let go. The result, as seen from the Veriscope, was that the near left corner, a neutral corner, was out of view.

There was nothing Rector could do about it now. Hopefully the action would stay out of that corner.

Spectators began gravitating toward the arena at eight o'clock in the morning. By nine o'clock five hundred were waiting outside, growing impatient. Some were starting to call out, "Open up!"

The gate was at last thrown open at nine-thirty, sparking a rush among those holding unreserved tickets, the blue ten-dollar pasteboards that had been most in demand. The press of bodies passing through the turnstile was so intense that the ticket-takers had difficulty collecting. Hold them up, they urged as spectators surged in. Once through the gate, each man was halted and searched. Pistols were forbidden inside the arena. So were cameras. Infringement on the Veriscope Company's exclusive right to record the contest would not be allowed.

The reserved ticket holders followed the initial rush in a more dignified manner, confident of their seats and thus able to stroll. There were ushers waiting to show them to their "boxes," little railed-in pens of chairs at ringside. By ten o'clock one thousand people were seated in the boxes and on the tiers of benches rising behind. They chatted and looked about at each other and admired the weather and the clearness of the mountains as they waited. Over the next hour their numbers would rise to three thousand.

A stir back at the gate. A drunk had just been apprehended trying to sneak in without paying. Carson teenager Hugh Castle took the opportunity of the commotion to slip past the distracted guards who had just turned him away on account of his Kodak camera. He made his way to the bleachers, no one noticing the bulge under his jacket. Sitting there, guiltily red-faced—perhaps this was why Dan Stuart called gate crashers "lobsters"—he could see a number of tough-looking security men under Bat Masterson's charge patrolling the aisles, each armed with a cane. Young Castle would have to be careful if he wanted to snap a shot on the sly.

The challenges started just before eleven o'clock. John L. Sullivan's was the first to be announced, supposedly backed by five thousand dollars. "I think there is one more fight left in me," the big man hoarsely bawled from the ring, looking stout and out of shape but apparently recovered from his recent drunken fall off a train. "I am here for business." It was of course a sham, a way for Sullivan to keep his name in the papers, but it delighted the fans just the same. Billy Madden, master of ceremonies for the day, followed with legitimate challenges on behalf of Australian heavyweight Joe Goddard and Tom Sharkey. The announcements did not attract much attention, the audience more interested in calling Sullivan back for one of his famous speeches. Sullivan turned and tipped his hat but remained seated, smoking a cigar, holding court at ringside. When it became clear that he would not oblige, the call went up for something from Sharkey. Sharkey said his piece about how he deserved a shot at the title only to be greeted with derisive cries of "Foul! Foul!" as he left the ring.

The crowd was starting to have fun. They wanted more speeches. Where's One-Eye Billy Connelly? they demanded. Give us a speech, One-Eye! The sporting character and self-styled world's champion gate crasher obliged. He was here to challenge the winner, he began, his parody met with hoots of laughter. He was a little disfigured, he continued, having lost an orb from one of his sockets. But he was ready just the same to meet the—

One of Bat Masterson's men collared One-Eye and hustled him out of the ring. Dan Stuart was not about to have his fistic carnival turned into a circus.

Bob Fitzsimmons by this time was on the scene. He and Rose had arrived at ten forty-five, Hickey, Roeber and Stelzner following behind. They had received word that the fight would not get underway much before noon in order to wait on final trains and so had delayed their departure. Bob Jr.—Fitz's usual term of endearment for the toddler was "You big stiff"—was left behind with a nurse.

The party made its way to the north side of the arena where a dressing room had been prepared, a cramped, low-ceilinged shed underneath the bleachers, plank walls, poorly lit, chilly. The boys got the woodstove going while Fitz huddled in his overcoat. He was talkative again but his comments seemed disjointed, his mind going in every direction. He was feeling it now.

When the little room had warmed up he lay on the cot that had been provided, still in his overcoat, and closed his eyes. Rose was with him. She leaned down and gave him a kiss. At the touch of her lips, Fitz opened his eyes and took her hand.

"It's all right, Rose," he said. "Be calm. That is needed more than anything else."

But it was hard to be calm. After a few minutes Fitz was up again, heading out into the sunshine with Rose on his arm to take a look at the arena. "Small crowd," he observed. He returned to the dressing room and lay back down on the cot but couldn't stay still.

Eleven-twenty. Dan Stuart appeared at the door and asked Bob how he was.

"First rate, Dan," Fitz replied, raising up on an elbow and extending his hand. "Never better."

"Good, good. We should be ready in another thirty minutes. Be through the ropes at ten minutes to twelve."

Fitz stood up and bid Rose farewell, sending her out to her seat at ringside. He then stripped and lay back down for a massage. "Okay, boys," he said, "let's get to work."

Stelzner and Hickey each took an arm, Roeber the legs. As they kneaded his muscles, Fitz closed his eyes and massaged his hands, still sore from training. Tension was mounting now. The two or three reporters allowed to be present felt it and became more subdued. One of them quietly asked Fitz if he had any thoughts on how long the fight would last.

"Something tells me I will win in three rounds," Fitz replied, still massaging his hands. "I don't know why, but I feel pretty confident it will be all over then."

The Corbett party was quiet on the trip into town from Shaw's Hot Springs, attempts at conversation going nowhere and soon petering out. The champ wasn't chatty. "I'm glad it will soon be over," Corbett remarked more than once.

They arrived at the arena at a quarter after eleven. Corbett's father and brothers Harry and Frank soon vacated the dressing room on the south side of the arena to take their seats, leaving Corbett alone with his trainers and seconds and a few trusted newsmen. He continued to express absolute confidence in his ability to whip Fitz—in seven rounds, he ventured when pressed.

"Six," chimed in Brady.

Corbett changed and the boys went to work rubbing him down. White, Delaney, John McVey and Jim Jeffries would work his corner. Corbett's younger brother Joe was to have been there as well but had pulled himself out. He was feeling too much anxiety over the fight, he confessed, to be of any use. His place had been taken by retired fighter John Donaldson, Corbett's long-time sparring partner in *Gentleman Jack*.

Brady went out to look over the arena and check on the ring. He found the ropes a little too slack for his liking. Referee George Siler ordered them tightened up.

It was now nearly two hours past the scheduled start time and the crowd was growing restive. There were perhaps four thousand present and they wanted a show. Sullivan! some of them tried again, the call being picked up all around the arena. We want Sullivan! Give us a speech, John L.!

The excited roar was salt in the wound for the thousand or more people gathered outside. They did not have ten dollars to gain admittance but were hanging around anyway hoping for a last-minute discount. They would be disappointed.

The door of the Veriscope apparatus was now closed, a security man standing guard outside to keep curious spectators from trying to enter. That would be a disaster once film was out of the can. Sealed inside with Enoch Rector were approximately ten assistants, each assigned to a specific location to avoid excessive moving around that might impart vibrations to the structure that could blur the film. There were three men to each camera, one to operate the hand crank, two to manually turn the feed and take-up reels and to change the film when it was used up, a task that had to be completed in under four minutes. At the back of the structure another assistant stood ready to hand out fresh film and to seal up and label cans of exposed footage. Finally, someone was needed to keep track of the fight through the red-tinted windows, using a stopwatch to time each round and calling out the minutes to keep the team informed of its progress.

Eastman employee George Kellogg was among this crowd squeezed into the twelve-foot-square space, one of the human cogs that would make the Veriscope work. So was Herr Heinrich who had jigged for Rector's film test three days before. Also present were Eddie Cooke, the short, plump theatrical agent who had been working as Jim Corbett's right-hand man for the past several weeks, and thirty-year-old Canadian actor and repertoire company owner Edward Houghton, who went by the name Edwin Houghton—as in Edwin Booth, one of America's greatest actors—when he appeared on the stage. That Houghton was included in such a technical undertaking may have been due to the fact that he understood moving picture machinery, having worked as a projectionist in Toronto the previous fall, screening some of the first projected movies ever seen in that city. His and Rector's shared interest in Brazil may have additionally served to bring them together. Houghton had written and starred in a play set in that exotic locale, entitled *In Darkest Brazil*, while Rector had spent years building a railroad in the actual country and relished telling stories about his experiences there.

Before filming could begin, test strips were made to check that the slits in the rotating disk shutters were properly set. A few feet of film was cranked through the first camera and developed—probably by Kellogg—in the pans set up against the back wall, the acrid smell of chemicals mixing with the aroma of closed-packed bodies. The negative strip were then examined in the red light. Dark sky, rows of light figures seated on bleachers, dark ring—the exposure looked good. The second camera was tested, then the third. A few final adjustments and the three machines were ready to go.

The first can of raw film stock was opened. It contained a roll of celluloid twelve inches across, twelve hundred feet of film all together. This was more than double the length of the reels Rector had taken to Texas for the Fitz-Maher fight, enough for eight minutes of filming, two rounds of action with the rests in between. The reel was removed from the can and loaded onto a sturdy arm projecting down from the ceiling behind Camera One. With it secured in place with a stout pin, Rector threaded the end of the film through the series of gears comprising the camera's feed mechanism and onto the take-up reel affixed to the floor. A few slow turns of the handle to advance the film—*ticka-ticka-ticka-ticka*—eyes on the gears for signs of catching or tearing. The film was passing smoothly by in front of the lens, the disk shutter rotating in synchronization.

Camera One was now loaded. Cameras Two and Three were prepared in similar fashion. When filming began, the three machines would work in sequence, Camera One, then Camera Two, then Camera Three, then back to One, the cycle repeated for however long the fight lasted, with enough film on hand for twenty-five rounds. By starting the cameras at intervals of four minutes, when half the film in the preceding machine was used up, two cameras would be in operation at all times, giving Rector the insurance of a duplicate record of the fight. To pull it off, the men locked inside would have to perform with smooth precision, camera operators cranking at an exact speed for eight-minute stretches, assistants manually turning the feed reel and take-up reel and loading on fresh film in under four minutes, the man in back keeping the exposed film in order and everything properly labeled.

Rector and his assistants, in short, would have to work together like a machine. For that was what the Veriscope was, a machine—a huge, three-lens camera with its human operators, its flesh-and-blood motor, sealed inside.

A cheer filled the arena a few minutes before noon, starting at the east side and circling around, for here was Fitzsimmons and his people at last. Martin Julian, in a red turtleneck sweater and cap, led the way. A step behind was Fitz, swathed in a "wonderfully and fearfully spotted bathrobe," according to one observer, "which no visitor at ringside will ever forget." Taking up the rear were Ernest Roeber, Dan Hickey and Jack Stelzner in matching red sweaters, carrying water bottles, a bucket of sponges, towels, a pair of large fans and miscellaneous gear.

"Here I am, dear!"

It was Rose, seated behind Fitz's corner waving a little Stars-and-Stripes flag. Fitz, beaming, stopped and bent down to kiss her. Former Kansas senator Ingalls, sharing the box with Rose, discreetly averted his gaze.

"Good luck to you, Bob," she said.

Fitz told her again not to worry. He entered the ring and began slowly circulating around, exchanging pleasantries with people in the front rows.

"How are you, Fitz?" called out timekeeper William Muldoon from his seat in front of the bell. The spring-loaded device had previously been used to clang out a warning signal in one of the Comstock lode mines.

"Oh, bloody fine," Fitz responded.

He nodded to Bat Masterson, overseeing security on Fitz's side of the arena. He ignored Wyatt Earp, employed by Dan Stuart to provide the same service on Corbett's side.

Even louder cheering now for Jim Corbett. His supporters clearly outnumbered those backing Fitz. Jim came down the west aisle of the arena wearing a grayish brown bathrobe, hair parted in the middle and slicked down, face creased with a big smile, his seconds following in turtleneck sweaters. He paused to greet his father and brothers seated at ringside, then skipped up the steps and ducked through the ropes.

The Camera One operator started turning the crank the moment Fitz stepped into the ring. He may have also started humming a tune, something simple and with a strong beat. *Here's a how-de-do, If I marry you, When your time has come to perish. . . .* It was a trick that would come to be widely used by camera operators in the silent era to maintain a steady cranking speed, particularly novices who hadn't yet acquired the "feel" of exactly two turns per second. For Rector and his assistants, any trick to maintain rhythm would have been especially important, for they did not have much experience of hand cranking and were now embarking on a marathon session of it—eight minutes of turning the handle, a four-minute break, another eight minutes at the handle, another break, on and on for as long as the fight lasted. It was going to require concentration, and stamina too. To head off exhaustion from endless cranking—it was almost certainly more than one man could do—Rector had likely drilled his three-man teams to work in shifts, each man taking a turn operating the crank, then turning the reels.

In the foreground of the shot were the backs of several men seated at ringside, in front of the sign "Copyrighted by the Veriscope Company 1897" painted across the side of the platform. The three most prominent heads belonged to official timekeeper Muldoon at the bell in the center, Fitz's designated timekeeper Lou Houseman in a white hat to his right and Corbett's man James Colville to his left. Visible on the far side of the ring was the cluster of journalists in the press box. Beyond them, rising on tiers of benches in the background, were spectators. In the ring itself stood Corbett in his corner on the near right, Fitz in his on the far left, their seconds and referee George Siler milling about.

After acquainting themselves with the feel of the rosined canvas, Corbett dancing about on his toes, the two fighters stepped to the ropes nearest the Veriscope and stood facing the lens as Rector had requested. Fitz stood somewhat awkwardly, hands behind his back, shoulders slightly stooped, not particularly pugilistic. Corbett, hands on hips, appeared more confident, more aggressive. They remained still for a moment, squinting in the bright sunlight, then moved to their corners.

Rector, manning Camera Two, waited for the film in Camera One to be halfway used up, then started cranking his machine. *Oh my darling, Oh my darling, Oh my darling Clementine....*

Two cameras were now in operation. The Veriscope was making its duplicate record.

Master of Ceremonies Billy Madden took the center of the ring. This contest, he announced, was for the heavyweight championship of the world. It would be a fight to the finish. That meant that it would continue until one man was knocked out, gave up or was otherwise unable to continue. "As it is taking place," Madden instructed the audience, "you will please keep order, because if you make any noise or cause any excitement it will only interfere with the men— and besides, there are ladies present. I hope you gentlemen will not forget that fact." He then proceeded to introduce the officials, the fighters' seconds, and finally the fighters themselves, Corbett receiving again the loudest applause.

The gloves were passed up through the ropes. They had been locked in the safe in Dan Stuart's office after being checked and approved by the opposing side the previous day. Corbett's were a tan color, manufactured by A. L. Reach of Philadelphia. Fitz's were pea green. Their seconds laced them on over bare hands. Protective hand wraps had not been allowed. As he hovered about Fitz, Julian kept a suspicious eye on the opposite corner for any signs of small bottles, the sort that might be used to dose Corbett's gloves.

The two combatants slipped off their bathrobes. Corbett appeared to be in good shape, muscles hard, skin taut, somewhat leaner than when he had defeated Sullivan five years before. He was wearing a skimpy pair of red trunks to ensure maximum freedom of movement, cut so high in the back that they exposed most of his buttocks. Intertwined American and Irish flags decorated the belt around his middle. His wife had sewn it for him. Fitz's muscled upper body was equally impressive; his legs much less so. He had long since ceased being bothered by catcalls about his skinny pins. He wore more conservatively cut navy blue trunks edged with red and a belt of American flags. Both fighters had black leather boxing boots on their feet, the thin leather soles freshly rasped for traction. Their socks, white for Corbett, black for Fitz, were rolled down to the boot tops.

Referee George Siler approached each fighter. "I don't suppose it is necessary for me to instruct you?" he asked. "You both know the rules as well as I do."

Fitz nodded. Corbett responded with an impatient, "Yes, yes."

Rules taken care of, Siler said, "Shake hands, gents."

Corbett stepped forward and extended his hand. Martin Julian stepped in front of Fitz to block it. "No, no," he said, "we won't shake hands; we refuse you." It was payback for Corbett's refusal to shake Fitz's hand on the penitentiary road. Corbett shrugged and turned away.

The refused handshake elicited an approving laugh from Rose Fitzsimmons. From Corbett supporters across the arena came hissing and boos and cries of, "Smash him, Jim!" Fitz's backers responded with, "Soak him, Fitz!"

The seconds gathered up the robes and towels and vacated the ring. Referee Siler moved to the center, checked that the two fighters were ready, then pointed to timekeeper Muldoon at ringside.

Muldoon sounded the bell and started the stopwatch.

Round One.

CHAPTER 21

FIRST BLOOD

THE TWO FIGHTERS MET at ring center. Corbett held his hands low, down near his hips as was his usual practice, confident in his speed and ability to evade blows. Fitzsimmons adopted a more traditional stance, hands at chest level, head drawn back.

A feint from Corbett, prompting Fitz to step back. Feinting was a specialty of Jim's, getting his opponent to go one way, then stepping in to tag him. It worked against Fitz. He ate a jab, the first of many. He kept grinning.

A clinch. Both men were skillful at fighting in clinches, locking up their opponent with one arm and pummeling with the other as had been agreed to allow in the rules. They wrestled for a moment, then pushed apart, both swinging, Fitz connecting. "It was your own suggestion," he said. It was Corbett who had wanted hitting to be allowed on the break.

Fitz swung and missed. And again. Corbett was remarkably quick, dancing back and slipping punches. Peter Jackson was right: it was like trying to fight a ghost. Fitz was convinced, however, that the bigger man, for all his prowess at jabbing, lacked knockout power, something he himself possessed in both hands. He would just have to wade in and soak up the hurt and wait for an opportunity to land something big.

Two and a half minutes into the round, Fitz leaning back, waiting, stalking, Corbett weaving, jabbing, dodging. And then an opening. Fitz stepped in with his right. The blow snapped Corbett's head back and sent him pedaling backward, on the defensive, ready to ward off a rush.

It didn't come. Fitz hung back, his face flushing red to his hairline. The two fighters circled each other through the final moments of the round.

The sound of the bell and a scramble at the corners, the seconds piling through the ropes to get a chair placed for their man to sit down. Corbett was sponged off as Billy Woods vigorously fanned him with a towel. Be careful with this man, Billy Delaney kept saying. Don't take any chances. Keep him at arm's length and pick him apart.

On the far side of the ring Fitz had the sun in his eyes. He had lost the coin toss for corners. Hickey was standing over him shading him with a large fan. Roeber cooled him with a second fan while Stelzner and Julian bent in close with their sponges. Fitz, at the center of the huddle, showed no visible sign of the pain he was in. But he was hurting—"like the deuce," he would say after. The throbbing started in his right hand and radiated up to his elbow.

It had happened when he landed that punch, aiming for Corbett's jaw but connecting with his hard head.

I think I broke my thumb, he said.

Thirty seconds!

Inside the Veriscope, the man with the stopwatch called out the time: thirty seconds until the start of Round Two.

Enoch Rector was still humming and cranking, the reel of film passing through Camera Two nearly used up. He had not operated the machine before for this length of time—not in earnest with real film passing through it. Not even eight minutes of it and his right arm felt like it was about to fall off, the muscles in his shoulder on fire from the unremitting effort of cranking at precisely two turns per second, twelve photographs being taken with each turn.

Behind Rector, the two men assigned to his machine continued to manually rotate the reels, one unwinding the feed reel, keeping the film slack as it went into the camera, the other winding the exposed film onto the take-up reel as it stuttered out.

Four feet to his right, the Camera Three operator was humming and mouthing a tune of his own, the feed reel running through his machine halfway used up. He had begun cranking at the opening bell, overlapping Rector's machine by four minutes. For the rest of the fight two cameras would be kept in constant operation like this, the next machine in line starting up every four minutes.

Time! Round Two!

Outside, a muffled clang as William Muldoon sounded the bell. The Camera One operator started cranking and humming, embarking on the machine's second reel just as the film in Camera Two ran out.

Rector released the handle with a profound sense of relief. Less than four minutes until the machine had to start filming again. He flexed his arm and neck and shoulders, stretching his muscles, then he pulled off his jacket. The interior of the Veriscope was getting warm.

Behind him, the film on his camera was being changed. This was where the Veriscope proved its true worth, for being itself a darkroom meant that the cameras and film did not need to be housed inside light-tight cabinets. Everything was left entirely exposed in the red light, free from encumbrance, accessible in an instant. It therefore took only seconds for the exposed film to be removed from the take-up arm sticking up from the floor. It was returned to its can, the can was passed to the man in charge of the film stock and a fresh can received in return. The roll of film inside was loaded onto the camera and the second man on Rector's team took over at the crank.

The man with the stopwatch: *One minute!*

Corbett was looking good. He was dancing, dodging, blocking, jabbing. This was the "science" for which he was justifiably famous, the ring craft of the Marquis of Queensberry era. His confidence was rising now with each blow he drove home, with each big swing that Fitz loaded up with and missed.

The spectators were feeling it too. To most it looked like Corbett was dominating Fitz with superior speed and reflexes, blunting his attacks and picking him apart from a distance. It was those little left jabs, John L. Sullivan commented to a friend at ringside, remembering how they had worn him down in his loss to Corbett five years before. "Those punches made me so mad," he said, "that I could have eaten a pound of ten-penny nails."

It was Fitz, however, who was the aggressor. He kept moving forward, taking Corbett's shots with a fixed grin. He had trained for this. He had come expecting to absorb punishment so that he could get close and deliver a knockout.

He moved in again, took another jolt to the face and replied with a straight right, testing his hand. The pain was tremendous, racing up his arm and exploding inside his brain. It meant he no longer had knockout power in his right. With his injured thumb it was good for little more than blocking and jabbing. He would have to win with his left.

He rushed in again, a missed swing and they clinched, Corbett smiling over Fitz's shoulder at his father and brothers at ringside. The break, Fitz taking a punch in the mouth in the process. The blow drove his lower lip into his teeth, tearing the skin. He was not wearing a protective mouth guard. It had not yet been invented.

He grinned.

In the press box, Bill Naughton was calling out the punches to a stenographer who was passing them in turn to a telegraph operator standing by. Other newsmen were doing the same. These blow-by-blow descriptions of the fight were soon being received in cities across the country.

In San Francisco, thousands packed the street outside the offices of the major newspapers, the *Chronicle*, *Examiner* and *Call*, eagerly awaiting each new bulletin as it was painted in big letters on rolling canvas banners. I hope it's over soon, workmen on their lunch break were saying. They could stay out only until one o'clock. Posters had already appeared all across town announcing the "Triumphal Reception" that would be held for Jim Corbett at Mechanics' Pavilion the following evening. To the largely pro-Corbett crowds, Brady's gamble did not seem to be tempting fate...much.

In New York City, twenty-five thousand people jammed City Hall Park and Newspaper Row and spilled back more than five hundred feet to Broadway, a bigger crowd than had massed here at President McKinley's recent election. The *New York World* was posting bulletins on the outside of the Pulitzer Building and using two mannequins to give the crowd an idea of the key blows. Many were too far back to see either the words or the figures and had to rely on those in front to shout the news back. *Corbett delivered a right to the jaw!* would be called out, and *Fitz hit Corbett with a left to the wind!* Smaller throngs were imbibing the news in athletic clubs, pool halls, bars and hotels. At Proctor's Pleasure Palace on East 58th Street a paying audience was listening to bulletins read from the stage and watching two boxing instructors demonstrate the action. In the Gilsey House Café, a particularly animated group mouthed the messages as they were read off the stock ticker and illustrated the punches on themselves for the benefit of their deaf friend. "Ah," the friend would murmur approvingly every time Corbett got in a good lick.

Across the Hudson and Hackensack Rivers, a crowd of ten thousand was following the fight in Market Square in Newark. Most were rooting for Fitz, considering him Newark's own, as he had lived for several years in that city. One man who wasn't was "Captain" Charles Glori. Fitz's former manager, back on the Newark police force at the reduced rank of sergeant, was thirsting to see Fitz suffer the humiliation of a knockout, just retribution for being an "ingrate" and leading Glori to ruin. To cash in on such a sweet prospect, Glori had placed a number of bets on Corbett totaling two thousand dollars. He had even agreed, if Fitz won, to close the café he ran on the side and drape the front of the place all in black.

Corbett rushed across the ring at the sound of the bell and caught Fitz with two shots to the body and one to the ear. Fitz, a red mark starting to show on his stomach, swung back and missed and moved in for the clinch. Referee Siler again made no attempt to part them. So long as clinching did not become excessive, he would leave the fighters alone.

They were three rounds into it now. Fitz, thrown off by his injured thumb, was breathing harder than he should have been so early in the battle. Not having much luck reaching Corbett's elusive head, he tried for the stomach and landed a hard left. "It shook me up considerably," Corbett later admitted.

And then, from a front-row seat behind Fitz's corner, a shrill female voice:

"Punch him!"

It was Rose Fitzsimmons. She had sat quietly up to this point but the pent-up excitement had become too much.

"Punch him, Bob!" she roared, sending Senator Ingalls seated beside her in his pince-nez glasses cringing away. "Hit him! Punch that hound!"

Every set of eyes in the nearby press box swiveled over. It was unusual enough for a woman to be present at a prizefight, let alone to be shouting like this. Pencils began scratching on pads.

The bell ended the round. The two fighters returned to their corners. Fitz, breathing hard, took a big drink from the water bottle. Corbett in the opposite corner waved a bottle away.

Rose wasn't the only female prominently seated at ringside. In one of the other boxes was the "illusion dancer" Ida Fuller, appearing that week at the Carson Opera House. Fuller had been determined to see a pugilistic contest ever since hearing the argument in Spain that bullfighting, a sport she had recoiled from in horror, was not as cruel as prizefighting. She was having her curiosity satisfied now. What she was witnessing was in her opinion not the least bit brutal. It was manly, athletic, scientific. "If this was a fair sample of prize fighting," she would write a few days later in the *Carson City Morning Appeal*, "any lady can attend with more propriety than she can witness a bull fight. Indeed there is no comparison." The Spanish, in short, had it all wrong.

Further back in the arena, in his bleacher seat behind Fitz's corner, young Hugh Castle at last worked up enough nerve to ease his Kodak camera out from under his jacket. Holding it low, he advanced the film, then looked about for the guards with their big sticks.

All eyes were on the ring. No one was looking his way. He brought up the camera, clicked, and slipped it back under his jacket.

The image would soon be on sale in Carson City and appear in the *San Francisco Chronicle* the following week. It and a second photo Castle shot at the end would be the only still images taken of the fight.

-------- ✺ --------

Time! Round Four!

The reel of film stuttering through Camera Two was half used up. Enoch Rector, positioned behind the machine, unwound the feed reel as the man on the handle continued to crank. Edison would have considered this manual feeding-out of the film embarrassingly backward. But it worked. It also sidestepped the problem of tension on the film caused by the intermittent mechanism pulling on the great weight of the twelve-hundred-foot reel. With manual unwinding there was no tension, the man assigned to turn the reel making sure the film was kept constantly slack.

The Camera Two operator appeared to have settled into a rhythm. The best technique was to keep the forearm perpendicular to the machine and to crank with just wrist and forearm, maintaining a light grip on the handle and allowing the weight of the lower arm to do some of the work. It was still tiring to crank like this for eight minutes, exactly twelve frames per turn, exactly two turns per second. But it could be done.

Camera Three had just started up again, its three-man team rotating positions before embarking on a fresh reel. At the opposite end of the Veriscope, Camera One had just fallen silent, its second reel complete. Its operator was flexing his arm as the others changed the film. Now they were shifting positions.

One minute!

The pent-up anxiety that had preceded the fight was almost all burnt away now that they were well into the thing. Rector felt comfortable enough to take a more leisurely look out the red-tinted window as he worked. There was Fitz stalking, Corbett evading. No clear indication who was leading. There was Rose Fitzsimmons, conspicuous in her flowery hat behind her husband's corner. John L. Sullivan was over there. And Bat Masterson, in a flat cap rather than his usual derby. Rumor had it he had bet heavily on Pompadour Jim.

Rector's eyes returned to the interior. The two operating cameras were buzzing loudly, working smoothly. He glanced over his shoulder at the man at the back of the Veriscope superintending the film. He was sealing up the can containing the last reel to come off Camera One. Now he was labeling the lid. That made four reels of

film that had been shot. Four thousand eight hundred feet.
Two minutes!

More left jabs tagging Fitz in the face, sometimes two-hand combinations. The blows were greeted by cries from the stands of "Good boy, Jim!" and "Punch his head off!" and the entreaty to "Take your time, Fitz!"

Fitz's nose was thoroughly mashed now, his gums were torn, his lower lip split open. And his blood was flowing—the "claret" as it was sometimes called in sporting circles. It trickled out of his nostrils and from the side of his mouth and started to drip off his chin. The sight of it excited the crowd and prompted more cheering.

First blood went to Corbett.

It was Round Five.

Corbett kept up the pressure, jabbing Fitz in the face, smearing blood all over. His confidence was even higher now, his opponent visibly winded and damaged and showing signs of being rattled, clinching to stop the onslaught, forcing Siler to step in and order them apart for the first time. As for Fitz's blows that had gotten through his defenses, Corbett was finding them not as fearsome as everyone said, the right hand not at all. Fitz admittedly had hurt him a few times but nothing had come close to knocking him down or inflicting damage. The realization that he could take the blacksmith's dreaded hammer blows filled Corbett with pride.

"Pound him, Bob!"

It was Rose Fitzsimmons, on her feet again at ringside. Corbett glanced at her and laughed. Perhaps it was the thought of Corbett's own wife Vera or one of his prim sisters yelling at ringside that struck him as funny. They would never condescend even to set foot inside a boxing arena. They were following the fight in private at the Corbett family home back in Frisco via a special wire run over from Harry Corbett's saloon.

Rose, seeing Jim chuckle, snapped, "You can't whip him!"

"Calm yourself, madam," beseeched Senator Ingalls beside her. "Please calm yourself down."

Fitz heard his wife's exclamations through the general din. They gave him a feeling of grim determination, the thought flashing through his mind: "It shall never be the lot of that woman to be the wife of a defeated husband."

Corbett gave him another knock in the mouth, aggravating the cut on his lip. The claret was flowing even more freely.

Round Six would be worse.

Fitz was sponged clean when he answered the bell. He rushed at Corbett with left and right swings, both hands missing, then grabbed him and wrestled him back on the ropes to the accompaniment of disapproving cries of "Oh! Oh!" from the crowd.

It was rough handling, too much forearm to the face. Referee Siler issued a caution.

The exertion and Corbett's counterstrikes had started the blood flowing again. It was soon impeding Fitz's breathing, too much to swallow. Ingesting a lot of blood could make a fighter sick to his stomach. Fitz spat a red mouthful onto the white canvas and snorted more of it out his nose.

By mid-round the blood covered Fitz's face from his chin to his hairline. It was spattered on Corbett's chest and shoulders, it was sprayed in droplets across the ring canvas—it was even streaked on Corbett's thighs where the Californian had brushed his soaked gloves. There was open jubilance among the younger men in his corner, one of his seconds turning to someone at ringside and saying with a knowing nod, "Six rounds." In the opposite corner, Martin Julian's brow was furrowed with concern.

Corbett was fighting hard now, sensing that Fitz was ripe for the finish. Some of his blows were wild and missed altogether. But then a shot landed solidly under Fitz's right ear. It lacked knock-out power but it stunned him just the same. He dropped to one knee, head bowed. Corbett, almost wild to end it, hung over him, ready to smash him down the moment he tried to rise.

"Well, it's all over," John L. was heard to say around his cigar.

"Stand back," Siler instructed, unable to begin his count until Corbett had stepped away from his downed opponent as required by the rules.

Julian was up on the ring apron, roaring. "Stand back there and obey the rules! Why don't you stand back?"

Most of the spectators in the arena were on their feet now, shouting and cheering. Rose Fitzsimmons had left her seat and was standing beside her husband's seconds, crying out for Bob to be careful. Patrick Corbett remained where he was, silently stroking his beard, his eyes locked on his son as they had been the whole fight.

"Stand back, Jim," Siler repeated.

Corbett grudgingly backed up. Siler started to count, following timekeeper Muldoon who was calling out the seconds with downward strokes of his arm. Fitz had recovered but wisely stayed down, resting on one knee to take full advantage of the count. When he finally rose at the call of "eight," he was fully ready to defend himself.

Corbett came at him, looking for the knockout, pouring everything he had into the assault. Fitz took several good shots but was far from beaten, clinching to blunt the assault and getting in a few shots of his own, a couple to the ribs, a stinging short-arm punch to the nose. At the bell he was still on his feet.

His seconds dove through the ropes with the chair and got him seated. That left scarcely fifty seconds to work on their fighter. With Hickey holding up the sun shade and flapping the fan for all he was worth, Julian gave Fitz the water bottle for a rinse and spit while Roeber kneaded witch hazel, arnica and alcohol into their man's battered forearms to take down the swelling. A quick sponge-off of the blood, a sip of beef tea for fortification and Julian daubed the witch hazel on Fitz's split lip and shoved it up his nose to coat the septum. The astringent extract, stinging on contact, constricted the tissues and blood vessels to stop the bleeding.

Julian had just lost one of his bets: Fitz to win in six. But he wasn't thinking about that. He was examining his brother-in-law's face as he worked, assessing the damage. Only the battered nose and lip were oozing—nothing too alarming for an experienced fighter like Bob. It was good red blood too, not the dark stuff that indicated the nose had been broken. More importantly, the skin across Fitz's brow and around his eyes was undamaged—bruised but not torn. Even a small nick here could be disastrous, dripping blood into his eyes and obscuring his vision.

Rose was still on her feet behind Fitz's corner. She had often watched her husband spar in training but had never seen him in actual, bloody combat. In her excitement and concern she called his corner men "Idiots" and accused them of not handling him right.

"Never mind the blood," Fitz told her. "I've got him licked."

In the opposite corner, Corbett was still breathing hard, a coat held up to keep the sun off the back of his head. He had expended a lot of energy in Round Six trying to end it. Woods was flapping the towel to cool him. Delaney and White had sponged off his body, all of the blood Fitz's. Corbett remained uncut and appeared undamaged. But he was tired. As the one-minute rest period ticked down he continued puffing. He was having a hard time catching his breath.

Time! Round Seven!

Inside the Veriscope, six reels of exposed film were sealed in cans stacked against the back wall. At Camera Two, Rector was into his next shift on the crank, two turns per second, precisely two turns per second, on and on, the machine halfway through its third reel.

You are lost and gone forever, Dreadful sorry, Clementine . . .

Camera Three was starting its third reel, while Camera One had just finished its third and fallen silent, beginning its film-changing cycle. The exposed reel was stowed in its can and the can passed to the assistant stationed by the back wall. He labeled it, sealed it and added it to the stack. That made seven reels of film that had been shot. Eight thousand four hundred feet.

Rector now had the preliminaries and the first six rounds recorded. It was a total of thirty-four minutes of action, double the length of the longest film previously made, the bullfight filmed by Gray Latham and Eugene Lauste in Mexico City the previous year.

And he wasn't done yet.

CHAPTER 22

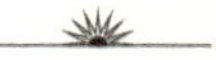

THE AWFUL BLOW

"Now do him up, Jim!"

"Knock his hair off!"

The calls rang out from the forty-dollar seats all the way back to the bleachers, Corbett's many fans expecting him to finish Fitz in this round, the seventh. Corbett began strong but soon grew tired as his opponent continued to stalk him, unfazed. It was like Charlie White had repeatedly told him in the corner: *Fitz can recover like no other man. He's as tough as a nickel steak. Be very careful.*

There Fitz was again, his face re-bloodied, holding his own as Corbett jabbed and danced and struggled to regain his breath after the great expenditure of energy in Round Six. Fitz got the worst of it but returned to his corner at the bell looking remarkably fresh. The injury to his thumb at the start of the fight, coupled perhaps with Carson City's nearly five thousand-foot elevation, had thrown him off, leaving him winded in Rounds Four through Six. But he had regained his composure now and settled into a rhythm, one that he felt sure he could maintain for many more rounds. The realization gave Fitz's confidence a boost, for he knew now that he could outlast Corbett. With his right hand hurting like a red-hot iron had been driven right through it, he came out for more in Round Eight, then Round Nine, then Round Ten, on the offensive, growing stronger, hitting harder, as if the earlier knockdown had done him good.

The reporter from the *San Francisco Chronicle* saw it, looking up from the press box at Fitz silhouetted against the blue sky. "There were blood drops trickling down every part of his body," he wrote, "and it was only by great efforts that he seemed able to keep the flow down his throat from choking him, but there he stood, aggressive and smiling, his fighting face more pronounced than I ever saw it, and his eyes twinkling in the sunlight as he watched for Corbett to come on."

The tide of the battle was turning. Fitz could feel it. It was in the waning power of Corbett's arms in the clinches and in the lack of snap in his punches—particularly one that landed full on Fitz's nose. It hurt, but not as much as it should have. "It was then I discovered that his blows were losing force," Fitz recalled after. "He struck less frequently than before and seemed to be playing for wind."

Corbett's vaunted offense was slipping. There was less to fear now from getting in close. He was also slowing, his dodging and evasions no longer so sharp. It meant that Fitz was able to reach him more often and with greater power—starting with a hard left to the belly. The punch made Corbett wince and affected his breathing, his face, previously hard-set and ruddy, becoming drawn and pinched.

Rose Fitzsimmons, bounding out of her seat, picked up on the effect. "Hit him in the slats, Bob!" she cried, an exhortation that would soon become world famous. "It's the only way to whip the hound!"

Corbett wasn't smiling now. Fitz's grin was slipping too. They both looked grim, locked inside the cocoon of their combat, the noise of the arena receding into the background. The nemesis facing was as far as consciousness extended. Apart from him there was the awareness of their own bodies: the pain of an injured thumb; the throbbing of a split lip and battered nose; the working of lungs straining to get in enough air; aching forearms from innumerable blocked blows; mounting fatigue in legs that were starting to feel like they were weighed down with lead.

The punches that landed still hurt after ten rounds. They had lost the shock that the first blows in a fight usually imparted but they hurt just the same. What had changed was the way the pummeling was perceived. It was natural now, as natural as moving and breathing.

Getting punched in the face and the body had become part of survival in the ring.

It was no longer merely warm inside the Veriscope. It was hot. Enoch Rector, jacket off, had sweated through his shirt and was craving fresh air, a break from the stifling atmosphere generated by so many bodies occupying such a small space. His apparatus was not designed for comfort. That was painfully clear.

End of Round Ten!

The man with the stopwatch called out the warning. Rector was manning the take-up reel now. Another glance out the window, then at the precious stack of exposed film against the back wall. There were ten cans of it now, twelve thousand feet. Was it good? Would it turn out? Rector's mind flitted again to the terrors of the developing process, the myriad mishaps that could spoil his exposed film, his accumulation of treasure. A miscalculation with the chemical baths, the emulsion lifting off the celluloid base—

Thirty seconds!

They had already suffered one film breakage. Even with all tension removed from the film, it could still catch and tear or jump off the sprockets. The strip had been rethreaded in a flustered hurry and the machine put into motion again, thirty seconds lost. It was an unwelcome hitch but not unexpected. Rector was filming the fight in duplicate as insurance against this very thing. Now, if both operating machines suffered breaks at the same time...that would be a major problem.

Time! Round Eleven!

Camera One, freshly loaded with film, buzzed back to life. Another few seconds and the film in Camera Two ran out. The operator released the handle and Rector and the third member of the team stopped turning the reels.

There was no time to rest. Rector set to work cleaning the machine's delicate mechanism, brushing and blowing away any debris, applying drops of oil to the gears. He was going to crank the camera himself for the next reel; the man whose turn it was had become overtired and erratic on his last shift. Behind him, the other two set to work removing the exposed reel—the fourth to be passed through the machine—and returning it to its can.

One minute!

One minute into Round Eleven; three minutes to go and Rector would have to start cranking again. They had been filming for... Rector did a quick calculation in his head, the preliminary action plus ten rounds plus this additional minute.

They had been filming for fifty minutes.

"Hey, Jim," Fitz breathed into Corbett's ear as they clinched, "this is the unlucky thirteenth for you. I'm going to knock you out."

Corbett didn't reply. He had remained largely silent throughout the fight, letting Fitz do the talking.

They broke. Fitz, stalking, wasn't going as much for the head. While Corbett's offense was weakening, he remained effective defensively with his dodging and slipping—so much so that Fitz had concluded he was expending too much effort trying to land a knockout blow on the jaw. He was directing more attention now to the body.

An opening upstairs. Fitz took it, landing a left on Corbett's mouth, then stepping in for some vicious in-fighting, less wary of Jim's punches now that they had lost some of their steam.

Another clinch, one arm locked up, the other swinging, then a break. Fitz came away with his nose and mouth bleeding again, red seeping also from a gash on the side of his face. It wasn't a fresh cut. Corbett's jabs had opened up a cut Fitz had received several days before, wrestling with Roeber.

Corbett's mouth was working, his tongue moving around. He spit something out.

It was one of his teeth, an artificial one pegged into his jaw.

Fitz's designated timekeeper Lou Houseman raised his white hat. It was the signal he had been using to warn Fitz that the round was almost over. The bell sounded five seconds later. The fighters returned to their corners.

On Corbett's side, Billy Delaney got his man seated and started rubbing strong liniment into his forearms, then gave him a drink. Delaney had been calm and confident through the first ten rounds but was anxious now about the stamina of his fighter. For Jim was dangerously tired. Delaney could see it in the way his movements were subtly slowing, in how his gloves were slightly dropping, in how Fitz was able to back him up in the clinches. And he could hear it now as Jim sat in his corner, taking in great gasps of air.

Fitz was not about to go down with another few onslaughts. He was too tough. And wily. Those wild swings he was taking that looked so amateurish—they were likely a trick to lull Jim into being careless, just the sort of thing Jack Dempsey used to do. The best course of action would be for Jim to back off for a round or two to recover, then embark on a long campaign, carefully pacing himself, to break his opponent. It would take real grit, digging down deep in ways Jim hadn't done in years. Did he still have the endurance Delaney had witnessed in him back in 1889, in that epic twenty-seven-round battle on the barge against Joe Choynski? Because it looked like he was going to need it.

The bell sounded. Jim rose from his chair. Delaney urged him one last time to pace himself and fight Fitz from a distance, to not be drawn in, to not mix it up.

Still puffing, Jim headed back into the fray intending to end it.

Time! Round Fourteen!

Enoch Rector glanced again out the window, anything to take his mind off the agony of cranking. The fighters were clinching again, then a break, Fitz pushing Corbett away, a powerful shove.

Ruby lips above the water, Blowing bubbles soft and fine, But alas, I was no swimmer, So I lost my—

The reel ended. Rector released the handle and let his arm drop. Camera One had now taken over in making the duplicate record, joining Camera Three which was halfway through its own reel.

A spark drew Rector's eye to Camera Three. It was the static electricity problem. The passage of film past the lens at the rapid rate of two and a half feet per second was generating enough static to cause occasional discharges. The resulting sparks would show up on the developed footage as streaks of light. Aggravating, but there was nothing he could do about it now. Fortunately it was not happening too often, the interior of the Veriscope being so humid, a benefit of all the close-packed bodies. Had the air been dry, the static discharge problem would have been worse.

A fresh reel of film was loaded onto Camera Two. Rector

threaded the celluloid strip through the machine and cranked through several feet of leader to be wound onto the take-up reel.

The handle seized up in Rector's hand. The film had jumped off the sprockets and caught in the mechanism. He yanked a screwdriver out of his pocket and went to work on the blockage. When it was cleared he rethreaded the film and, eyes on the gears, cautiously started cranking again. The film fed through the mechanism correctly this time.

He relinquished the handle to the next man on the team and took over at the feed reel.

One minute!

Dah-dit-dah-dit dah-dah-dah dit-dah-dit...

The bulletin raced out from the arena and across the country in a series of telegraphic dots and dashes. Translation: *Corbett left to jaw.*

Dan Stuart had relented at the last moment and allowed a special wire to be run into the arena all the way to the press box—the use of which cost extra, of course. For the newspapers and wire services unwilling to pay the premium price, bulletins were being physically carried over to the Western Union telegraph office, a sprint and forty-five-second gallop on horseback that was resulting in a five-minute delay.

Dit-dit-dah-dit dit-dit dah dah-dah-dit-dit...

Fitz left to mouth.

In downtown Manhattan, the crowd in front of the Pulitzer Building pushed and surged as it read the headlines and watched the mannequins being manipulated on the platform set up on the third floor. Here was another streetcar, wading through the crush of flesh at a crawl, police out in front to open a passage. *Insoles! Insoles! Brother, don't catch cold through your feet!* An intrepid vendor worked his way through the throng. No one paid him any attention.

Over on Wall Street turnover had slowed to a trickle in the final hour of trading as traders followed the fight on the ticker.

Fighters clinch... Fitz bloody... Corbett misses with the right... Good N—

A sudden panic at the abbreviated "Good night" that the ticker service used to sign off at the end of each trading day. A rush for the telephones, a flurry of calls to the ticker office. *Keep the wire open! Keep the wire open!*

Uptown in Harlem at East 125th Street, five thousand people were following the fight in front of the offices of the *New York Journal*. The reports were being written on a huge blackboard by a rapid-fire vaudeville artist billed as Verno, the Lightning Raphael.

Another bulletin was coming in at the telegraph station inside. *Dah-dit-dah-dit dah-dah-dah dit-dah-dit...*

The telegraph operator jotted the message on a slip of paper. It was rushed over to the window and thrust out to Verno to be chalked up on the board.

The two-foot-high letters read: *Corbett is down.*

It happened at the midway point of Round Fourteen, when Fitz threw his bad right hand at Corbett's chin after they broke from a clinch. Instead of parrying the blow or leaning forward and to the side to slip it, Corbett jerked his head back and momentarily exposed his midsection. The vulnerability lasted for only a split second but for canny ring veteran Fitz it was enough. He instantly drove his left into the pit of Corbett's stomach—a solid left, a sledgehammer left, a finishing left with his full bodyweight behind it.

The punch dropped Corbett to one knee. He felt paralyzed. He couldn't breathe. He heaved with his chest to get air into his lungs, a look of agony mixed with confusion etched on his face. "It was an awful blow," he would say after. "I thought it had killed me."

Referee Siler waved Fitz back. Then, following timekeeper Muldoon's prompt, he brought his hand down to start the count.

"One!"

Corbett kept heaving with his chest, trying to draw in a breath. His mind was clear. He was fully conscious, aware of what was going on around him. But he couldn't move.

"Two!"

Most of the spectators were on their feet now, excited. For William Brady the reaction was almost physical sickness at seeing Jim, so powerful, so vibrant, "with all the marrow gone out of his bones."

"Three!"

Jim struggled to rise. He couldn't. He had no strength. Another chopping hand from Siler accompanied by the loud count of: "Four!"

Still unable to breath, Jim started crawling toward the ropes, dragging his left leg as if it were dead. If he could just hang onto something he might be able to pull himself back to his feet.

"Five!"

Inside the Veriscope, Enoch Rector watched through the red-tinted window with growing alarm as Corbett crawled toward the near left corner on the ring, the one spot where he shouldn't go. At the most dramatic moment in the fight, he was dragging himself out of the shot.

"Six!"

Rose Fitzsimmons was wild with excitement, hopping up and down and crying, "Oh Bob, Bob!" Patrick Corbett remained silent, stroking his chin, eyes locked on his son.

"Seven!"

Another hand chop from Siler. Jim was at the ropes now. He reached out to grab one, missed, and almost fell on his face. He tried again and got hold.

"Eight!"

Hanging on with his right hand, Jim tried to pull himself to his feet. He couldn't. He desperately tried to signal Siler that he wasn't knocked out, that he just couldn't catch his breath, that this continued counting was somehow unjust.

"Nine!"

No, this wasn't right...

"Ten!"

Siler threw up his hands. The fight was over. Across the arena a cheer went up mixed with cries of "Foul!" from Corbett supporters. Hats were thrown into the air. Corbett's corner men, already up on the apron and moving toward Jim, swarmed through the ropes to aid their stricken fighter.

The spasms that had seized Corbett's solar plexus were easing. He was at last able to wheeze in some air. With the help of Delaney and McVey, he rose unsteadily to his feet and allowed himself to be led back to his corner as spectators flooded down the aisles and dove through the ropes. "Talk about Bedlam," Siler said after. "The vast house just lifted itself into the ring."

Within seconds the twenty-four-by-twenty-two-foot space was packed with men jostling to congratulate Fitz and commiserate with Corbett, some happy, some angry, some just overcome with excitement, some in a rage, calling "Foul!"

"No foul," announced Siler. "Fitzsimmons knocked him out fairly with a stomach punch. Fitzsimmons wins."

His declaration went largely unheard. The ring was getting alarmingly crowded now with all sorts of emotions. Siler ducked through the ropes and jumped down off the ring platform, fearing there might be trouble and that he as referee would be a target. He had been warned before the fight that Corbett's Frisco friends might get violent if he lost.

The Pinkerton men stationed around the arena were making their way to ringside to keep things under control. Wyatt Earp remained planted behind Corbett's corner, hand on his pistol, ready to head off any trouble. Bat Masterson left his post further back on the opposite side and began moving down the aisle.

By this time Corbett had regained the use of his limbs. Released from the strange paralysis, his boiling frustration suddenly burst forth. He broke free from the ministrations of his seconds and stormed across the ring at Fitz, thrusting spectators aside to get at his foe to continue the battle. He hadn't been beaten. He hadn't been fairly knocked out. It was just a lucky punch. The fight had to continue. He would *make* it continue.

Masterson broke into a run, roaring, "Get in there and keep those men apart! Part them! Part them!"

A melee broke out in the ring, Joe Corbett swinging in every direction. From Fitz's corner, brawny Ernest Roeber waded in to sort out some of the hotheads. Fitz himself did not know what was happening at first, only that he was being mobbed by delirious well-wishers and that hands were coming at him from all sides. One swung past his face. It had a glove on it. Another grazed his neck. By the time he realized that it was Corbett attacking, Corbett's seconds had seized their man and were pulling him back.

"Let me go!" Corbett cried in hysterical rage. "Let me at him! I'm not licked!"

William Brady, scarcely coming to Corbett's chin, wrapped his arms around him, trying to calm him. "Come on, Jim," he said. "You can fight him again. I'll back you twenty thousand tomorrow."

After a struggle with his corner men, Corbett allowed himself to be led through the crush back to his corner. Fitz, aglow with victory, let the attack go.

Martin Julian was less forgiving. "We knew it all the time," he crowed. "Now the people know who is the cur." And from an incensed Rose Fitzsimmons: "The coward!" She clambered up onto the ring and embraced her husband, unmindful of the blood smearing her face and the front of her green velvet dress.

After calming down, Corbett returned to Fitz and offered his hand. Fitz shook it but declined the inevitable request for a rematch, saying that he was retiring from the ring.

"You will have to fight me," said Corbett. "If you do not, there will be trouble. I will go at you in the street the first time we meet if you refuse."

"If you do," was Fitz's reply, "I will kill you."

That was the end of it. Corbett, his head bowed, his dressing gown thrown over his shoulders, was led from the ring and back to his dressing room under the bleachers.

"I can't believe it, boys," he said, the noise of the crowd thundering down through the ceiling. "I don't know how it happened. I had him almost whipped..."

He stopped. His face crumpled. He leaned against his brother Harry, who had just lost eleven thousand dollars in bets, and burst into tears.

The flood of emotion affected the others, all of them already deeply upset. "Pneumatic armor" Billy Woods sank into a corner with his cap over his face to cover his sobbing. Joe Corbett buried his face in his hands. White and McVey tried to soothe Jim but they were choking up too. Billy Delaney's eyes were also wet as he offered the only consolation he could by fanning the fallen champ with a towel.

"Brace up," Harry Corbett gruffly commanded. "Come on, boys, brace up now."

The interior of the Veriscope was silent. The last reel of film had been removed from the last camera and added to the pile stacked against the back wall. It brought the total to eighteen cans. That was twenty-one thousand six hundred feet of exposed film. Just over four miles.

Enoch Rector, sweaty and stifled in the warm air, his right arm heavy with fatigue, checked each of the cans to ensure they were properly sealed and labeled. Then he secured them in three light-tight boxes for extra protection, to be express shipped to New York, fully insured. It would be the height of foolishness now to take any chances with something so unprecedented, so valuable, so rare.

Less than three years before, he and the Lathams had been the first to reach the one-minute mark in capturing continuous action with the making of their first fight film, the Leonard-Cushing contest, a truncated affair made to fit the limitations of Edison's Kinetograph camera. Less than two years before, the Lathams extended the filming horizon to eight minutes with *Young Griffo vs. Battling Barnett*. Now, Rector had just filmed in duplicate an entire prize-fight, the heavyweight championship of the world as it actually happened, all fourteen rounds of action together with the pre-fight preliminaries and the confusion and excitement that followed the knockout. He had captured in its entirety the most sought-after sporting event in the world. He had not missed a moment. The whole thing had lasted an hour and a quarter.

He looked about at the ruby-tinged men who had helped him. He started nodding, a smile creasing his face beneath his full mustache. Relief, satisfaction, euphoria—it was all there.

All right, boys, he said. *Open the door.*

CHAPTER 23

DEVELOPING DREAD

BOB FITZSIMMONS, his battered face coated with liniment and with a stitch in his lip, returned to Cook's Ranch in raring high spirits, boyish exuberance bursting out. He seized Bob Jr. in his arms—*Hey, you old stiff!*—and danced him about as Sam the cook, wild with excitement, laid on a feast. For Bob had just won the heavyweight championship of the world and a fortune the papers were saying totaled fifty thousand dollars, his take from the purse and stakes and side bets, with the promise of more to follow from Rector's film that, according to Martin Julian, "will put us on Easy street the balance of our lives." With their financial wellbeing now seemingly assured, Bob granted Rose her wish that he leave the ring. "I am 36 years of age," he had announced after the fight, inflating the number just a little, "and have fought more championship battles than any two men in ancient or modern ring annals, and shall retire. I will never fight again."

That night, Bob had trouble sleeping, cramps seizing his limbs and lurching his awake. It was one of the aftereffects of a hard fight. He arose the next morning professing to feel fine but no doubt sore all over, his face tender, his right hand swollen, the left side of his torso one big bruise. When asked about his plans he continued to insist that he was through with fighting. "I'm out of the ring now, fellows," he airily said. Rose echoed her husband's decision. "It has been my prayer," she announced in a written statement, "that [Bob] would never enter the ring again, and he has answered it with his promise to retire."

As for Jim Corbett, he was feeling lower than low, scarcely able to comprehend that he had been beaten. He left the arena direct for the station and boarded the express train to Frisco, overwrought fans seeing him off with tears in their eyes. The solar plexus blow that had ended the fight continued to cause him discomfort throughout the journey and on into the next day, leading to rumors that he had died. There was of course no "triumphal reception" for him at Mechanics' Pavilion that evening. It had been hastily cancelled. Jim instead spent the time resting and having his broken tooth fixed by a dentist. Charlie White had recovered the original tooth from the ring and was carrying it in his pocket like a talisman, showing it around.

What would he do next? Jim said he didn't know. His friends assured him that his defeat would not affect his popularity as an actor; that he was a star in his own right, apart from the ring. But Jim must have found the prospect unnerving just the same of returning to the stage without the support of the heavyweight title. To ensure his continued theatrical success, he needed it back. And Fitz, with his talk of retiring, was not about to give him the chance.

In the coming weeks Corbett continued to press for a rematch, insisting that he was the better man; that he had been "fresh as a daisy" and leading up to the point when Fitz landed his "lucky punch." It was a view held by many Corbett supporters and one just as vigorously denied by those who backed Fitz. "There is no sense in saying that it was a chance blow," Fitz himself stated. "It was just the kind of a blow that I was waiting for a chance to deliver, and when my chance came I sent it home and won the fight. That was all the chance there was about it." To further fuel the controversy and build pressure for a rematch, William Brady proclaimed that Fitz had gotten a long count in the sixth and that he had fouled Corbett with a blow to the head after Jim was down in the fourteenth. What exactly had happened in Carson City thus remained a source of contention, accounts of the "Fight of the Century" differing depending on who was doing the telling. Just wait until the moving pictures come out, both sides were saying. They will show where the truth lies. They will prove we are right.

———— ✸ ————

Enoch Rector arrived back in New York confident that he had captured the whole of the Carson City battle. He was less sure about the next step, developing the four miles of exposed film. The necessary chemical treatments could ruin it if not done right. And what if the film itself was imperfect? What if the emulsion separated from the celluloid base in the chemical baths or frilled up at the edges as it dried? These problems were all too common. As Rector confided to Eastman Kodak sales manager Sam Mora, who paid him a visit toward the end of March, he had "great dread" of the developing work that lay ahead. It was arranged that he would telegraph Rochester if he ran into trouble and that Eastman Kodak would sent out an expert to assist.

The work commenced on March 30 at Veriscope headquarters at 244 West 23rd Street, the company occupying the building's entire sixth floor. To make the film easier to handle and to reduce the risk, the big reels of exposed negatives were cut into two hundred-foot lengths and developed in small batches. Working in red light under Rector's watchful eye, Veriscope employees wound the celluloid strips around drums and rotated them through a trough containing a developing agent. When the images had emerged to the proper degree, the drum was transferred to a second trough containing a neutralizing solution to halt the development process, then to a third trough containing a fixing agent to remove unexposed silver particles and make the film insensitive to light, then to a water bath to wash the chemicals away. After that the film was left to dry. And everyone prayed.

The first few batches turned out all right, the film emerging from the drying room with images sharp and the emulsion adhered. As a friend of Rector's revealed to the press on April 3, "the films are beauties. Every picture is as clear and distinct as could be wished." It would take another ten days to finish the work, but after that "the kinetoscope [sic.] exhibits of the fight are going to be the finest ever seen."

By this time something else had cropped up for Rector to worry about. The forces of morality, having already prompted the banning of prizefights in most parts of the country, were now taking aim at the exhibition of fight films, stirred to action by the publicity that the Veriscope venture was getting. State legislatures in Illinois, Minnesota and Massachusetts had already introduced bills to prohibit fight films, with Maine, Indiana and Wisconsin soon to follow. In Chicago, the Women's Temperance Union issued an appeal to the governors of other states to do the same, asserting that the nationwide exhibition of a Corbett-Fitzsimmons fight film would be "infinitely worse" than the staging of the fight itself, for it would expose a far greater number of people to the corrupting influence of the display. Up in Toronto an organization called the Moral Reform League would raise similar concerns to keep the film out of Canada. It was beginning to look like Rector's motion picture, regardless of how it turned out, might not be making a lucrative end-run around anti-fight legislation after all. News of its success and tremendous earning potential was attracting a whole new set of possible legal roadblocks all its own.

Rector responded by insisting that the drive to ban his film did not worry him in the slightest. For the truth was, he announced, that it had been a colossal failure and so there was nothing to ban. "Rector says the whole lot of snap shots look like the first efforts of a novice," reported the *Chicago Tribune*, one of the first to pick up the story. "When the plates [sic.] were developed every defect known to photography made its unwelcome appearance." And in the *Boston Globe*: "[O]f the many thousands of pictures taken at the ring side, none are good. Attempts have been made to develop the negative, and each successive trial to make something of them only served to emphasize the failure." And in the *Auburn Bulletin*: "Rector is staying at the Gramercy Park hotel. He is there to recover from the shock these underdone and overdone plates gave him, or he says."

At Eastman Kodak, the news was met with skepticism. If Rector had trouble developing the film, why had they received no cable from him? Why no frantic call for help? The whole thing, Eastman president Henry Strong concluded, was likely a "fake."

After a rest in San Francisco, Fitz worked his way East in easy stages, making public appearances along the way to cash in on his new title. Martin Julian, master of ceremonies for the show, introduced him as "the pugilistic marvel of the age; the champion middle-weight of the world; the champion heavy-weight of the world; the champion of champions, Mr. Robert Fitzsimmons!" Fitz would then bound out in red tights and give a punching display, making the bag dance with a rain of fists and elbows, then snapping the cord and sending it flying with a huge finishing blow. After that came an exhibition of wrestling, Fitz vs. Ernest Roeber, then a sparring session with Dan Hickey, Fitz demonstrating the now-famous "solar plexus punch" that had been Corbett's undoing.

If there was a fly in the ointment, it was Corbett himself. The former champion was proving ungenerous in defeat, following Fitz from city to city trying to stir up public pressure for a rematch. When Fitz appeared at the Grand Opera House in Salt Lake City, there was Corbett at the Salt Lake Theater, giving his own exhibition of bag punching, wrestling and sparring. "I am going to follow Fitzsimmons around," Jim stated, "until the sentiment of the public will force him to fight or stand as a rank quitter.... Every man who was at the ringside will admit that I had all the best of it until that fatal blow was delivered. I proved myself to be the more clever man, and now all I ask is another chance with Fitzsimmons." Fitz continued to insist that he was retired, adding that he would leave it "to the kinetoscope" to prove that he had been the better man. "If it does not show me leading in every round then I may be called a liar."

A grand reception awaited Fitz when he arrived in New York, throngs of people coming out to cheer him as his decorated carriage wended its way through the streets behind a brass band. A testimonial banquet would also be held at the Hotel Bartholdi, the entertainment to include such musical numbers as "Our Bob," "In One Punch" and "Listen to the Jingle of the Coin." By this time Fitz had dropped his retirement talk. Corbett's claim that his victory had been pure luck, a mere fluke, was too much. "I have not retired from the ring by any means," Fitz said, taking it all back. "I am still young and strong enough to defend my title.... [But] the talk about Corbett meeting me again is all bluff. He doesn't mean to fight me any more than my baby does, and that is true. He's a stiff, that's what he is. The only thing he has in his favor is his cleverness. He can't punch a little bit, and I wouldn't be afraid to let them tie my hands behind my back and allow Corbett to punch away until he got good and tired.... The truth is, I beat Corbett with one hand."

Fitz returned to the road with his show on April 19, one-week engagements booked for Philadelphia, Washington, Boston and Pittsburgh. Corbett remained behind in New York, preparing for a short run in *A Naval Cadet*, set to open that same evening. On display outside the theater was a large two-sheet poster showing Jim delivering a knockout, the "World Champion" titling underneath covered up with *Naval Cadet* advertisements. The lithograph, printed before Jim's Carson City loss, had cost good money and William Brady wasn't going to waste it.

Backstage, Jim must have felt some trepidation as he applied his makeup, wondering if his drawing power had diminished, if the applause would be tepid. Having lost his ring title, was he now about to be knocked out as an actor as well?

The answer came when he made his entrance in the first act. The entire house, packed to the rafters, let out a cheer and launched into a five-minute ovation, bringing the show to a halt and overwhelming Jim with emotion. He stood in the footlights, deeply moved, struggling to control himself as tears welled up in his eyes and trickled down his rouged cheeks. It happened again at the end of the second act and this time Jim was obliged to make a speech.

The evening was an unequivocal triumph, all the more so because the audience was composed not of fight fans but of regular theatergoers. And they still wanted to see him. As the *New York Press* observed the next day, after complimenting Jim on his skill as an actor, "Corbett has not had such a happy night in a year."

Over at Veriscope headquarters on 23rd Street, the bustle of activity belied Enoch Rector's insistence that his film had not turned out. The announcement had been a "fake" just as the president of Eastman Kodak surmised, an attempt to defuse efforts to get the film banned. The two sets of negatives were in fact in excellent shape, absolute "beauts," and were now being edited into a finished film. This was not "editing" in the way the term would come to be known, the splicing together of separately shot pieces of film to create a coherent sequence, It would be another few years before that was invented. For Rector, editing his raw footage consisted of simply examining the negatives with a powerful magnifying glass and choosing the best film for each round, that which had the sharpest image and the fewest imperfections such as white streaks caused by electric discharges. What he ended up with was a finished film that was 10,846 feet long—a static, uninterrupted view of the Carson City battle from the moment the two fighters stepped into the ring to the scrum of bodies that filled the frame after the knockout.

Using this precious negative, positive copies were next made for exhibition using what had now become 600,000 feet of film (one hundred thirteen miles!) purchased from Eastman, a slow and laborious process using crude printers, two teams of workmen laboring round the clock in twelve-hour shifts. Multiple projectors, as many as twenty-five, also had to be fabricated so that the film could be shown all across the country and overseas too, for it would be only through mass exhibition that it could realize its full financial potential. The plan was to sell regional concessions to the highest bidder, with each concessioner to receive a projector and at least two copies of the approximately seventy-five-minute film. The entire cost in production and advertising and everything else, Dan Stuart claimed, was expected to top one million dollars. It was a glorious, Texas-sized exaggeration—and perhaps not coincidentally the same amount Stuart said he expected to gross from the film.

By this time nearly a month had passed since the fight and all the feverish excitement that had gone with it. To Eastman Kodak president Henry Strong, this was too long. As he confided in a letter to George Eastman, Rector and the Veriscope Company "are making a great mistake in not getting their pictures on the market promptly as the interest is certainly waning." It was a valid concern, one that no doubt added to the pressure Rector was feeling as he put in long days overseeing all the work that had to be done.

And then came another threat: Imitators. On April 17 the following notice appeared in the *New York Clipper*: "Corbett and Fitz-simmons Films, in Counterpart of The Great Fight, in 14 Rounds, each film one round, will be ready for delivery this week." It had been placed by Philadelphia optician Siegmund Lubin, who had recently come out with a projecting machine of his own called the

Cineograph that he sold for ninety-nine dollars, together with a catalogue of blatantly pirated Edison and Lumière films. To cash in on public interest in the Carson City battle, Lubin hired a pair of laborers to represent Corbett and Fitz and recreated the fight in his backyard, directing the action by calling out blows from a newspaper account of the contest: *Corbett lands a right on the neck...Clinch... Break...Fitz takes a wild swing and misses....* The result was shoddy even by the low standards of the day, the ring being undersized with a sheet strung up behind as a backdrop; the rounds not even thirty seconds; "Fitzsimmons" outfitted in a ridiculous wig; the action clumsy to the point of burlesque. The deception, however, would not be apparent to most theatergoers until after they had purchased their tickets and taken their seats, for the significance of slippery words like "counterpart" and "facsimile" used in advertisements was not generally understood. Lubin was thus set to reap a handsome return from a minimal investment, selling his version of the fight for fifteen dollars per fifty-foot round.

The initial ad for Lubin's fake film brought Dan Stuart roaring out of his office to place notices headlined "WARNING!" in the *New York Clipper* and *Dramatic Mirror*. The Veriscope Company, he announced, was copyrighting its moving picture of the fight and intended to prosecute any infringement, which in the United States was "punishable by a heavy fine...and imprisonment." The great task was already underway at a cost of nearly thirty-five thousand dollars, so Stuart claimed, with copies being deposited in Washington, Ottawa, London, "and so on in all other Continental powers. A wicked war is to be waged against all fakirs, pirates, and persons manufacturing, selling or exhibiting imitations of this picture."

In copyrighting his film, Stuart was following the precedent set by William Dickson in 1893, when Dickson submitted paper prints of the frames of his "Edison Kinetoscope Records" film to the Library of Congress's copyright office. After a period of head scratching, library staff filed the film under "Photographs" and granted the copyright request. This application method was not too onerous with the earliest films, which were no more than fifty feet long and consisted of seven hundred-odd frames. The Corbett-Fitzsimmons fight film, however, was nearly eleven thousand feet long with a frame count exceeding one hundred thousand. Rather than printing this great mass of images on paper and applying for one copyright, Stuart took a shortcut. He printed one representative photograph for each round of the fight and had Veriscope Company vice president William Wheelock submit fourteen separate applications. The same procedure was used in England, fourteen separate copyrights taken out, Wheelock once again serving as front man. The applications were filed in Washington and London on the same day, May 15, 1897.

As it turned out, copyrighting the Corbett-Fitz fight film made no difference at all. For the fact was that Lubin had not illegally pirated the work. Its nonstandard width made it effectively impossible to copy, and in any event it had "Copyrighted the Veriscope Company" prominently displayed in each frame. As shoddy and dubious as it was, Lubin's "facsimile" was his own creation, a work that he legally owned and soon had copyrights for, as he trumpeted in subsequent ads. All Stuart could ultimately do, therefore, was to make empty threats to try to scare off exhibitors from buying Lubin's fakes. Martin Julian would later claim that Lubin siphoned $100,000 away from the profits for the real film.

The Lubin fake of the fight opened well before the real Veriscope film, projected by the Cineograph or Acmegraph, the Projectoscope or Magniscope or whatever other machine the exhibitor happened to own. In Victoria, British Columbia it was an Electrograph, the film being advertised as the only approximation of the Carson City battle the public would ever get to see, "[a]s the original pictures taken by the veriscope proved in the majority of rounds to be a failure." In New York the film opened at Huber's Museum, a stone's throw from the Academy of Music where Rector's real film was set to premiere, "10¢ to all, Kinematographe reproduction of facsimile of Corbett-Fitzsimmons Fight," with the inducement added later of "Free Pop Corn." By August it had spread across the country and to Europe and had reached as far as Singapore.

Many people paid to see the Lubin film thinking it was of the actual Corbett-Fitz fight. They went away disappointed, their vocabularies enriched by the words "facsimile" and "counterpart." In Little Rock, Arkansas the audience responded with cries of "Cheat!" and "Fake!" upon realizing the deception and nearly caused a riot until the manager agreed to refund their money. By and large, however, negative reaction was muted, no more than a handful of customers complaining after a show.

"We advertise a fac simile of the fight, and that's what we give," said a Chicago theater manager as he shooed disgruntled patrons away. "What do you expect for 10 cents, anyhow?"

Enoch Rector had now completed the final version of his Veriscope projector and was ready to begin making copies of the machine. It used an intermittent mechanism rather than the Eidoloscope's continuous movement, the momentary halt of each frame in front of the lens producing a brighter image. Like his Veriscope camera, Rector's projector was notable for its reliance on manual operation, the feed reel and the take-up reel both turned by hand, thereby avoiding the problem of excessive tension on the film. Electricity had not been entirely discarded, however. It was needed to run the intermittent mechanism and to light the powerful lamp that cast the image onto the screen. And that meant problems.

It started with the last-minute postponement of the film's debut, a private showing that had been scheduled for New York's Academy of Music on May 15, 1897. At issue was the theater's electrical supply. This would be an ongoing challenge at subsequent exhibitions, for electric power was far from standardized in the late 1890s, with the competing Edison and Westinghouse systems, direct current vs. alternating current, only the start. The power at New York's Knickerbocker Theater, for example, was 110 volts and 1,600 amps; at Carr's Third Avenue Theater it was 100 volts and 500 amps; at the Columbia Theater in Brooklyn it was 110-220 volts, 8,000 amps and a "three-wire" system; at Jacob's Theater in Newark it was 52 volts; at the Newark Opera House it was 110 volts and 30 amps; at the Columbia Theatre in Boston it was 110 volts and 2,000 amps. All this was complication enough for operating an electric light or fan, which could burn a bit brighter or dimmer, run a bit faster or slower, without being noticed. A projector, however, was more unforgiving. Rector's machine had to run at a constant and precise speed of twenty-four frames per second for the moving image to look right, which meant that the electrical supply had to be carefully adjusted. Wiring also frequently had to be extended up to the balcony where the projector was situated, for in many theaters the galleries where still illuminated solely with gaslight, which was softer and cheaper, electricity used only for lighting the stage.

Sorting out the problems with the Academy of Music's electric supply delayed the premiere of Rector's film by a week. The day before it was set to open, the *New York World* published a two-page spread featuring illustrations of actual frames of the film, which an intrepid reporter had managed to acquire in an unspecified but supposedly nefarious manner. "I don't know how it was done," Dan Stuart was quoted as saying, showing remarkable good humor over the theft, "but I do know that the pictures showed up splendidly and that it was a great piece of enterprise on the part of The World. How you people got access to the plates is a mystery to me and to every man around the shop, but you had them all right and they are mighty interesting."

The whole thing of course was a set-up, likely organized by William Brady, who had already viewed some of the film in private. For the Veriscope Company it was valuable publicity prior to the premiere, free advertising. And for Brady it was another opportunity to sow controversy over the fight, for as he now proclaimed, the picture of the knockout *showed* Fitz hitting Corbett after he was down. *A foul blow!*

"That picture means Fitzsimmons must fight me again," Corbett chimed in. "He has to; there is no getting away from that after that picture, which does not lie, will be seen by the people of this country.... I tell you that, although I have only seen seven rounds of the fight in the veriscope pictures, I am sure that they will open the eyes of some people. I don't think there will be any one who will claim it is not Fitzsimmons's place to fight me again, and that soon."

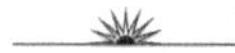

CHAPTER 24

THE FIRST FEATURE FILM

THE ACADEMY OF MUSIC on East 14th Street was one of New York's biggest theaters, with seating for twenty-one hundred patrons from the orchestra section to the cheapest perch in the back. It had once been the most genteel venue in the city, the home of grand opera, the social center for New York's elite. By 1897, however, those glory days were past. The Metropolitan Opera House had taken over that prestigious function and lower brow theatricals had become the Academy's usual fare, plays like *Humanity* ("A Rip Roaring Melodrama!"), *Two Little Vagrants* ("Two Hours of Solid Enjoyment!"), *The Sporting Duchess* ("A Beautiful Story, Containing Only the Grandest, Loftiest & Noblest of Ideas!") and *Under the Polar Star* ("Worth a dozen 'Sporting Duchesses'—N.Y. World"). It was also used for concerts, vaudeville shows, athletic exhibitions and political and religious rallies—and, on the evening of Saturday, May 22, 1897, for the premiere of the world's first feature film.

Enoch Rector's landmark movie did not have a specific title when it debuted. The first advertisements called it the "Corbett-Fitzsimmons Sparring Contest" to avoid antagonizing the moral forces arrayed against it. Thankfully, no laws had been passed yet banning the film, and all those involved with its exhibition wanted to keep it that way. In the coming weeks the word "sparring" would be dropped and "fight" almost never used, the film generally advertised as the "Corbett-Fitzsimmons Contest." It was only years later that the semantic pretense was discarded and the film came to be known by the title it generally bears today: *The Corbett-Fitzsimmons Fight*.

There were rumors on the eve of the premiere that it would not be allowed to take place. The threat, ironically, came not from the moral forces working to have the film banned but from Dan Stuart's former "fistic carnival" partner, Joe Vendig. The two had had a falling out earlier in the year, Vendig claiming that he had been cheated by Stuart, whose creative accounting never seemed to show any profits to share from the ventures he helmed, only expenses. The result was a lawsuit, then talk of an injunction blocking the screening of the Veriscope film until a settlement with Vendig was reached. Fortunately the injunction never materialized and the premiere went ahead.

The show was sold out, tickets going for twenty-five cents to a dollar, hundreds of patrons settling for standing room in the back to push the total turnout to nearly three thousand. It was by and large a theater audience, not a prizefight crowd, with tuxedoes much in evidence in the dollar seats and the boxes and a significant number of women scattered throughout. The one clue that this was a different kind of performance was the white canvas screen stretched across the stage. At thirty feet wide, it was somewhat smaller than an average-sized movie theater screen today. For a projected film in 1897, however, it was immense.

As the house filled to the accompaniment of popular tunes from the orchestra pit, Rector nervously waited in the projection booth that had been erected in a balcony in the back. It had taken considerable work to run wiring up here, where there was only gas lighting, and to adjust the current so that the projector ran at the correct speed. The problems caused by the Academy's eccentric electrical supply had been overcome, however, and the Veriscope was functioning properly at last, the first reel loaded and ready to go. A total of six reels would be shown this evening, the first and last roughly fourteen minutes, the others twelve minutes, in all some seventy-five minutes of actual screen time. Since three-to-five-minute breaks would be required to change the reels—there was only one projector—it would take a little more than an hour and a half to exhibit the whole thing. This, coupled with an introductory talk and intermission, would make the entire show just over two hours long, what would be billed as "a complete evening's entertainment."

The strains of *My Gal's a High-Born Lady* died away and the orchestra fell silent. A suave-looking gentleman in a fine evening suit emerged from the wings and positioned himself in front of the screen. He would serve as lecturer. He began by explaining that the audience was about to see an exact photographic representation of the championship bout that took place between James J. Corbett and Robert Fitzsimmons at Carson City, Nevada on March 17. The film would be presented in six parts by means of the celebrated Veriscope, with an intermission to follow the seventh round. They would now commence with the first part, showing the preliminaries and the first round.

The house lights dimmed. A buzzing started in the projection booth, loud enough to be heard throughout the theater. The canvas shone bright for a moment, then a torrent of flashes, then a black-and-white moving image emerged of a boxing ring, roughly life size. It had a flicker that was hard on the eyes, it occasionally bobbed up and down on the screen and a myriad of spots and flashes "streamed across the field of vision like gigantic motes." But when it was clear, the effect was amazing. Even the spectators on the bleachers far in the background could be made out. One of them was seen to take off his hat and swab his bald head, which made everyone laugh.

As the audience took in all these wondrous details, the lecturer, positioned to one side of the screen, pointed out referee George Siler, timekeeper William Muldoon, impresario extraordinaire Dan Stuart and others, then gave facts about Fitz and Corbett when they appeared to silent cheers from the spectators in the film and audible ones in the theater. More marvelous clarity—the fabric of the fighters' bathrobes, the fans and pails and other paraphernalia their seconds were carrying, Fitz squinting in the bright sunlight, the little American flags on Corbett's belt. It was all such a photographic triumph that one could almost forget the mounting eyestrain.

Up in the projection booth, the projector's intermittent mechanism continued buzzing away, electrically driven, as an assistant manually unwound the feed reel. The big roll of celluloid weighed at least fifteen pounds, far too much dead weight for a projector without a tension-eliminating loop to handle without breaking the film. As with his Veriscope photographing apparatus, Rector had sidestepped the problem by using manual operation to keep the film slack.

As for the risk of being roasted alive, he likely was too busy to give it any thought. The fact was, however, that the projection booth was a potential death trap. Rector's film, like virtually all motion picture film prior to 1952, had a nitrocellulose base that was as flammable as a gasoline-soaked rag—and it was racing past a nine thousand-candlepower lamp so hot that if it paused even for a moment it would burst into flames. In the wake of a projector blaze in a Cleveland theater just two weeks later, the city's fire warden would file a report condemning the machines, calling them "very dangerous in any building...even when handled with the utmost care by a skilled operator. The distance from the lens to the celluloid films is about eight inches, and if the film is not kept moving and the cap is off the lens, the film will ignite immediately." In the coming decades, as nitrate film continued to be used, fire prevention measures in movie theaters were mainly directed at confining the flames to the projection booth.

The first reel ended. As the orchestra played a short musical number, Rector and his two assistants loaded the next reel onto the projector, eighteen hundred feet of film, twelve minutes of screen time comprising Rounds Two, Three and Four. The lights then were dimmed and the show continued. The battle on the screen was heating up now and excited audience members, particularly in the back galleries, began calling out like spectators at a live fight. There were cries of "Oh, what a soaker!" and "Say, that was a peach!"; of "He's tiring now!" and "Fitz's got him!" and "Ah, go on, Jim's only playing with him!" The outcry was so great when Fitz was knocked down in Round Six that the lecturer gave up trying to speak over the noise. This audience volubility would be a regular feature at subsequent showings and would even be directed at the screen itself, viewers at times forgetting they were watching a movie. It sometimes resulted in outbursts of laughter—such as when someone called out to a ringside spectator in the film, who had stood up and was blocking the view, "Down in front!"

Another interesting feature of the response to the film was how viewers were captivated by what would seem utterly innocuous today. One example came in the eighth round, when a spectator borrows a match from Fitz's timekeeper Lou Houseman and lights a cigarette. The naturalness and reality of this simple action, the clarity of the smoke the man blew into the air—it amazed audiences in 1897. At a time when moving pictures were indistinct and typically recorded frenetic movements, it was a revelation to see a relaxed, unselfconscious moment so perfectly captured on film. As for Corbett's high-cut briefs and largely bare buttocks, in an age of supposedly Victorian sensibilities this merited no comment at all.

The intermission came after the third reel and the end of Round Seven, a welcome chance to stretch the legs and rest the eyes. The show then resumed with Rounds Eight to Ten on the fourth reel and Rounds Eleven to Thirteen on the fifth. A buzz of excitement greeted the start of the sixth and last reel, for as the lecturer reminded the audience, the finish was coming, the famous solar plexus punch that knocked Corbett out. When it came, however, few actually saw it. Fitz's back was turned and the blow delivered so quickly that Corbett was down before anyone knew what had happened. A collective "Oooh!" filled the theater, then cries of "Where's the foul? Where's the foul?" and a general tumult that once again forced the lecturer into silence. Then the ring was seen to fill with people, a crush of bodies pushing and shoving, Corbett charging at Fitz and being restrained. It was almost as interesting as the fight itself, a fascinating, surging tableau, some of the best footage in the whole film.

The screen went dark. The projector ceased its buzzing and the house lights came up. Calls for the last round to be shown again were ignored. Enoch Rector had done enough for one evening. Someone sang out "Three cheers for Corbett!" and three cheers were given. This was followed by "Three cheers for Fitzsimmons!" which met with a more tepid response. With that the audience rose from their seats and made for the exits, deeply impressed by what they had seen, both as an athletic exhibition and as a technological marvel. As Lady Colin Campbell would conclude her later review of the film: "[T]hough we leave the theatre with aching heads, we regret that so little that we determine to return as soon as we can, to witness again this combat of modern gladiators."

———— ☀ ————

Bob Fitzsimmons attended the matinee two days later, proclaiming that the film would prove he was nowhere near beaten in the sixth round and that the accusation that he had fouled Corbett at the end was a lie. As the film got underway, he leaned forward in his private box, elbows on the railing, and exclaimed to Martin Julian beside him, "There's me! And there's him too! What do you think of those bath robes? Ain't they peaches?"

Fitz kept up this running commentary all through the screening. In the first round it was: "Do you see how I am forcing him? See him backing away." When he was knocked down in the sixth round: "He threw me! Just got his arm under mine and twisted me over. It wasn't a knock-down." As he walked back to his corner after the bell: "What? Had me whipped in the sixth round? Not in a thousand years." In the seventh: "Here's where I nail him in the stomach … There goes my left." In the eleventh: "See him spitting out the tooth I knocked out?" And, with thick sarcasm as Corbett was seen to grow tired: "Why, what's the matter with this strong man Corbett? He's losing his speed and his steam."

During the final reel, as the fourteenth round unfolded, the theater filled with calls urging on both Corbett and Fitz. A shout of "Knock him out, Jim! Give it to him!" brought Fitz bounding to his feet to bellow a rejoinder.

"Don't get excited, Bob," Julian cautioned. "Keep your eyes on the fight."

More cries from the audience. "Just wait, boys. I'll do him," Fitz called out. And he did. Corbett went down, soundly defeated, and there was little indication of a foul. "There, see me step back?" Fitz exclaimed. "Why, I'm six feet away from him. But why doesn't he get up?" There was that sarcasm again. "He's strong enough to work along the floor like a caterpillar, but he doesn't get up. He's quit, sure enough." Then, when Corbett was seen bulling through the scrum filling the ring to take a swing at Fitz: "That's how he got his title of Gentleman Jim." That got a big laugh.

Fitz left the Academy of Music feeling fully vindicated. "Elegant," was his pronouncement on Rector's moving pictures. "They suit me. They show no foul, and I'm going to sue the World and Journal for damages."

The Corbett-Fitzsimmons Fight was on its way to be becoming a hit, receipts from its opening night totaling nearly three thousand dollars, the gross for the first week topping thirteen grand. It would continue at the Academy of Music until the end of June, two shows a day to mainly full houses, no shows on Sunday to be strictly decent. By this time it had debuted in other cities as well, starting with Boston on May 31 and Cincinnati on June 5, then Buffalo (June 7), Chicago (June 9), Detroit (June 21), Philadelphia (June 26) and Columbus (June 27). In July it spread further across the country: Atlantic City at the beginning of the month, then Grand Rapids (July 2), Pittsburgh (July 3), Cleveland (July 12), San Francisco (July 13), Milwaukee (July 18) and Portland, Oregon (July 27). It was a challenging time of year to make a go of a theatrical attraction, in the heat of the summer, before the age of air conditioning. The film nevertheless continued to do excellent business almost everywhere it played. In Chicago it had pulled in five thousand dollars in the first four hours of tickets going on sale. In Boston the take was nearly three thousand in just the first day. There were "large houses" in Buffalo, reported the *New York Dramatic Mirror*, "large patronage" in Philadelphia, "tremendous crowds" in New Haven and "S.R.O." (Standing Room Only) in Saint Paul. As William Brady observed, Dan Stuart had "struck a gold mine."

There was the odd town, however, where the film did not meet exhibitors' expectations—places like Aspen, Colorado and Lafayette, Indiana, where it attracted merely "fair audiences" in September, and Beloit, Wisconsin and Dallas, Texas, where business was "light" in November and December. This may have been due in part to a lingering lack of awareness of what a projected motion picture actually was. As the *Buffalo Courier-Record* noted, "there are still people who are ignorant of the marvelous invention of Edison, this veriscope, and they think that the battle as portrayed by it is something on the order of the scenes shown by a child's magic lantern." It is telling that when the film began a second run in Buffalo in August at the "popular price" of twenty-five cents, the exhibitors ran ads carefully explaining the nature of the show. "What will one see at the Veriscope Reproduction of the Corbett-Fitzsimmons Fight?"

it read. "First of all they will see a cozy auditorium with seats for 500 spectators and a great white screen. In due time the electric lights will go out. A few seconds you sit in total darkness, a whirr of the machine, a sizzling of the carbons warming up to work, a flash of light on the canvas and to all intent you have made a jump of 2000 miles from Buffalo to Nevada...."

The first international screening took place in Toronto on August 9, arranged by Clifton Turner, who had acquired the eastern Canadian rights. An attempt was made by Toronto's city council to pass a bylaw blocking the exhibition but it was narrowly defeated nine votes to eight. The film went on to enjoy great success in the city, the *Toronto World* hailing it as "a most wonderful reproduction of the greatest fistic contest of the century" and a "marvelous scientific achievement"—and noting that several people were heard to remark after the show: "'I can see nothing brutal or disgusting about that.'" To further highlight the decency of the exhibition, a special matinee was reserved "exclusively for ladies and children."

In Belleville, Ontario, meanwhile, "The great fac-simile ... reproduced by counterparts of Corbett and Fitzsimmons" had come and gone, screened by a projector called the "Feriscope." It was of course the Lubin film. It had been exhibited for "One Night Only!" before moving on to the next unsuspecting town. A disgusted *Belleville Intelligencer* reported on the flighty exhibition the next day under the headline "The Great Fake." The exhibitor was subsequently detained in Chatham, Ontario for false advertising and sent packing back to the States.

Enoch Rector had no time to rest on his laurels as his film made its triumphant march across the country. After the New York premiere he was sent to Chicago and Philadelphia and likely elsewhere to prepare theaters for openings and to run the projector—"a very delicate machine," the *Buffalo Evening News* reported after the problem-plagued initial screening in that city, with which "the slightest variation from proper adjustment of the film is greatly magnified on the screen." Rector also revamped the process for making prints of the film. Whatever this "new process of reproduction" entailed— better contact printing machines, better developing methods—a marked improvement was noted when fresh prints went into circulation. According to the *Chicago Tribune*, the new reels, screened for the first time on June 19, "are immeasurably clearer than the first batch, and the flickering which many complained of during the progress of the presentation of the pictures has been reduced so materially that...there was scarcely any shifting of the light, and the result was intensely gratifying."

While Rector was away in Chicago, Veriscope headquarters back in New York remained a beehive of activity, six days a week. Bookkeeper Charles Scribner was putting in especially long hours keeping track of the company's finances. He was back at his desk on Sunday, June 6, putting in a seven-day work week, operating the building's old-fashioned elevator himself because the usual man had the day off. "Scrib," as he was affectionately known, worked all through the afternoon and into the evening. Then he returned to the elevator, reached out to pull on the rope to bring it up from the first floor...and lost his footing. He fell down the shaft, six full floors, and was killed.

The death was viewed as an accident. Dan Stuart left New York the next day to be present at the film's Chicago premiere.

The remaining international rights to the Corbett-Fitz fight film were in the meantime being sold. William Brady acquired the concession for Great Britain and debuted the film at the Imperial Theatre in London on September 27, tickets going for as much as a pound, the equivalent of five American dollars. Bob Fitzsimmons and Martin Julian expressed interest in exhibiting the film in Australia but lost out in the bidding to a syndicate headed by Brady, which swept up the rights to the Sandwich Islands (Hawaii), Australia and South Africa and organized a world tour. It would be under the management of Brady associates Ed Cooke, who had assisted Enoch Rector in filming the fight, and George Welty. Rector himself, no doubt attracted by the prospect of overseas adventure, agreed to join them to run the projector. He decided to make a grand tour of it and take his wife Jesse along.

The trio of Cooke, Welty and Rector sailed from San Francisco on August 13 aboard the steamship *Australia*, the Veriscope and screen and related equipment totaling more than a ton and a half in the hold. The first stop was Honolulu. The initial version of Rector's projector had not drawn big crowds here when it was exhibited in February earlier that year. It now did much better, packing the Hawaiian Opera House for two sold-out shows, August 23 and 24, before the gear was packed up for the onward journey.

"There seems to be an impression that it is not an entertainment suited to the taste of ladies," Rector told a local reporter during the brief stop, addressing the moral concerns the film had stirred up. "This is a mistake, natural, perhaps, but when we think how many of the female colleges are adding athletics to their curriculum, it is really a surprise that such a rumor should exist. Why, in New York and Philadelphia we began the entertainment at a quarter before 9 o'clock, so as to accommodate society people who indulged in late dinners, and I have never once heard a lady find fault with the pictures or remark that they are demoralizing in any sense. I am not a sporting man by any means, but if I had sons, or even daughters, I would much prefer that they be taught to defend themselves with nature's weapons than to resort to fire arms. The exhibition by the veriscope is an object lesson, which should elevate, rather than lower the morals of the community."

From Honolulu the little party embarked for Sydney, where the film had its Australian debut on September 18, billed as "The Fitzsimmons-Corbett International Boxing Contest." It played to good houses, Ed Cooke serving as lecturer, Rector and two assistants operating the projector. The audience was enthusiastic and vocal in the usual way, even shouting at the black-and-white image of referee George Siler when he blocked the view of the fighters to "Get out of the way!" The *Sydney Arrow*, interviewing Rector, Cooke and Welty, found them to be "a thoroughly genial trio" and Rector in particular "well primed on all branches of sport, and though capital company at any time, he goes one better when the floodgates of reminiscence are opened." In plain English, Rector was fond of telling stories. These included tales of his adventures on the railroad in the interior of South America; of Texas Rangers, Judge Roy Bean and Mexican Federales on the Rio Grande; of the colorful Lathams and flamboyant William Dickson and of working in Thomas Edison's lab. Rector's Edison connection in particular would be subject to exaggeration during the Veriscope's Australian tour, Rector being touted as having been "for many years associated with Mr. Edison's laboratory" and even at one time his "partner." This was standard practice at the time for marketing any electrical product. The farther away one was from Edison, the safer it became to claim close ties to the great man. It was just good business.

The Veriscope film remained in Australia for four months. From Sydney it moved to Brisbane and Melbourne, then to Adelaide and along the south coast, then to West Australia and a tour by narrow-gauge railway through the booming gold rush towns of the outback, Rector billed as "one of the greatest electrical experts in the world." The tour ended in Fremantle on January 8, 1898, whereupon Rector and his companions boarded the steamer *Nineveh* bound for Durban in the British colony of Natal. "The Fitzsimmons Corbett Great International Boxing Contest" had its South African debut here at the beginning of February. It then moved on to Johannesburg for a two-week engagement, which included a "Grand Curio Souvenir Night" at which the audience received a piece of the actual film to take home—likely a snippet from a worn-out reel. "This is the First Time any of these Films have been given away or sold to anyone," announced an advertisement in the *Standard and Diggers' News*. "This is an opportunity of securing a Souvenir of this Celebrated Contest never offered to the public before in any country where these pictures have been exhibited."

The South African tour ended in Cape Town. From here Rector and his wife Jesse and their companions embarked on the long journey home via Europe to complete their trip round the world.

In the year that Rector was away, the Corbett-Fitz fight film continued to be shown in theaters across the country, from Albuquerque, Memphis, Paducah, Wichita and Topeka to St. Johnsbury, Vermont, Little Falls, Minnesota, Lincoln, Nebraska, Philipsburg, MO and Richmond, VA, with second and even third runs in major cities like Chicago and New York. The moral outcry that had preceded the premiere had in fact done little to stop it, with the numerous bills introduced in state legislatures now largely stalled and forgotten. In Montreal, the city council failed in its attempt to pass a bylaw to keep the film out. In Los Angeles, the opening was delayed by protests but eventually went ahead after the city council passed an ordnance to allow it. In Kingston, Ontario, the mayor could only plead with the opera house manager not to show it. He was ignored.

By any standard the film was a runaway hit. Enoch Rector therefore had good reason to expect a financial windfall when he arrived back in New York, for Dan Stuart had promised him a handsome share of the profits. A delighted Bob Fitzsimmons had already received two payments totaling $20,000 by December 1897 from his fifteen percent stake, with more to follow. Rector, assured twenty-five percent of net profits after Corbett and Fitz got their cuts, anticipated receiving a comparable sum—enough to make him wealthy in an era when a fine house cost only a few thousand dollars and a meal could be had at a decent eatery for twenty-five cents.

He would be disappointed. The months slipped by and no payment was forthcoming. Rector finally confronted Stuart only to be told that he had no interest in the Veriscope Company beyond being a paid employee. When Rector reminded him of his verbal promise of a quarter-share of net profits, which Stuart himself had earlier admitted exceeded $120,000, Stuart countered that that figure was for *gross* profits, not net. After Corbett and Fitzsimmons had been paid and all expenses subtracted, including under-the-table envelopes to state legislators to forestall anti-fight film legislation, there were no net profits. None whatsoever. The film had barely broken even. Or so Stuart said.

Rector had just been burned by what is today known as "Hollywood accounting," the use of creative bookkeeping and inflated expenses to show even the most successful film as having not made any profit. "Net points" on a movie? To industry veterans this is a joke. Back in the late 1890s, however, slight-of-hand accounting as applied to a film was not so well understood. It might even be said that Dan Stuart was the first movie producer to employ "Hollywood accounting," years before Hollywood ever existed—and that Enoch Rector was its first unfortunate victim.

In July 1899 Rector sued Stuart for fifteen percent of net profits from the film. The threat of legal action had worked for Corbett and Fitzsimmons two years before when Stuart was slow to pay out their shares. But they had written contracts, and Rector did not. All he had was a verbal assurance of a net share in a venture where the net profit was supposedly zero.

Rector's case was ultimately unsuccessful. And so the man who made the world's first feature-length film, the first "complete evening's entertainment" in cinema history, ended up with almost nothing.

EPILOGUE

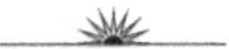

THE CORBETT-FITZSIMMONS FIGHT continued to be shown in theaters on into the first decade of the twentieth century, earning far more than *Corbett and Courtney Before the Kinetograph*, the most successful film to precede it. The total gross, according to William Brady, was between six and seven hundred thousand dollars, making it a huge theatrical hit and prompting others to try to repeat the success. Filming an actual prizefight, however, remained a difficult proposition. That it would be two and a half years before the next major fight film was released only served to highlight the immensity of Enoch Rector's achievement.

The fight game by this time had found a temporary haven in New York thanks to corrupt political boss "Big Tim" Sullivan, who pushed the Horton Law through the state legislature permitting limited-round bouts within the confines of athletic clubs. This was a boon for fight promoters, for there was no better place than New York, the biggest urban center in the country, for selling tickets. For making fight films, however, the shift to the Big Apple posed a major technical challenge, for it generally meant filming indoors, and at night, when the greatest number of fans could attend. There thus would be no bright sunshine to illuminate the ring as Rector had enjoyed in Carson City. The work had to be done under electric lights.

The first attempt was made on June 9, 1899, when Bob Fitzsimmons defended his heavyweight title for the first time—not against Jim Corbett, who would never get a rematch, but against Jim Jeffries, Corbett's former sparring partner and now a leading contender. It seemed a lopsided matchup, for Jeffries was built like a tank, two hundred ten pounds of rock-hard muscle to Fitz's one-sixty-eight of gristle and bone. It was in the lead-up to the battle that Fitz, like his wife Rose before him ("Hit him in the slats!"), uttered a quip that remains a popular idiom today. When asked about his tremendous weight disadvantage, Fitz retorted, "The bigger they are, the heavier they fall."

The fight, scheduled for twenty-five rounds, took place at the New Coney Island Sporting Club under the glare of intensely bright lights that seemed to bother Fitz when he stepped into the ring. Women were not allowed into the arena, so Rose was not at ringside to cheer him. She would watch from a passageway under the seats in the back. Fitz had assured her that he would win, and he believed it, assuming that Jeffries' size would make him too slow. But he was mistaken. Jeffries knocked him out in the eleventh round, an experience so unfamiliar to Fitz that he would later claim he had been drugged. As for the attempt by the Vitagraph Company to film the contest, it ended in failure. The ringside cameras worked but the indoor illumination did not, an electrical mishap knocking out more than half the lights before the opening bell. Only indistinct shadows could be seen on the film.

The next major attempt was made by an outfit called the American Sportagraph Company three months later, at the bantamweight title fight between Thomas "Pedlar" Palmer and Terry McGovern. This time light was not a problem, the fight being held in daytime in an open-air arena similar to the one Dan Stuart had erected for the Corbett-Fitz battle two years before. The apparatus used to film the fight, built by Edwin Porter, also appears to have been similar to Rector's Veriscope in Carson City, the *National Police Gazette* describing it as a "picture machine, sheathed in funeral-black tar paper, with two little glass windows that blinked in the sun like a pair of eyes." The big "machine" worked well. Unfortunately for the doomed American Sportagraph Company, the fight was a bust, McGovern knocking Palmer out in less than three minutes. The film was deemed to have no exhibition value and never released.

It was not until November 3, 1899 that the success of the *Corbett-Fitzsimmons Fight* was repeated with the filming of Jim Jeffries' first title defense against Tom Sharkey. The venue was the New Coney Island Sporting Club where Jeffries had won the crown from

Fitz. The American Mutoscope and Biograph Company that William Dickson helped found would do the filming, using two free-standing Biograph cameras set up on a platform forty-five feet from the ring. The big reels of extra-wide film, each good for four minutes, were sealed in light-tight canisters that could be attached to and removed from the cameras without the need of a darkroom. For illumination, four hundred lights of a combined total of 480,000 candle power were suspended over the ring. "The great search-light exhibited at the Chicago Exhibition was far less powerful," the *New York World* noted. The blinding array generated so much heat that the presiding electrician claimed he could endure to stand under them for no more than two minutes.

Jeffries and Sharkey stood it for nearly an hour and three-quarters, the entire duration of the twenty-five-round fight. And the Biograph cameras recorded it all—up to the final minute of the last round, when the filming camera suffered a breakdown. An attempt was made a few days later to record a reenactment of the missing last minute but the footage was so obviously staged that it wasn't used. The blemish this caused was generally overlooked when the nearly two-hour movie went on exhibition, for the images were stunning, the sharpest and steadiest ever seen thanks to the quality of the Biograph machinery and the two-and-three-quarter-inch-wide film.

Another lull followed in the filming of prizefights, in large part because promoters were coming to better appreciate what a gamble it was. A major investment in acquiring film rights and equipment and setting up an arena could be lost if a camera broke down, if there was a problem with the lighting, if the fight ended too soon or was not much of a show. To guard against this last possibility, the producers of the next attempt to record a fight, Bob Fitzsimmons vs. Gus Ruhlin at Madison Square Garden on August 10, 1900, shot cushioning footage beforehand of the two men in training. The project ended in failure regardless when one of the cameras malfunctioned on fight night and a large part of the action was lost. Whatever film that was shot was never released.

Following the repeal of the Horton Law on August 31, 1900, New York State once again shut down for fights and promoters were forced to look elsewhere for venues. The next fight where cameras were set up, Terry McGovern vs. Joe Gans on December 13 of that year, took place in Chicago, the city council there persuaded to relax its fight ban in the hopes of capturing the lucrative pugilistic market that New York had spurned. The filming, undertaken by the Selig Polyscope Company, was technically successful. The fight itself, however, was disappointing, Gans going down in the second in what was widely viewed as a fix. The resulting controversy prompted the city council to reinstitute its ban, barring fights from the city for another twenty-five years. The film that was subsequently exhibited of the fight was scarcely ten minutes long.

The filming of Jim Jeffries's heavyweight title defense against Gus Ruhlin in San Francisco's Mechanics' Pavilion on November 15, 1901 had a similar outcome. The work was undertaken by the Edison Manufacturing Company using a large apparatus similar to Rector's Veriscope, the *San Francisco Chronicle* describing it as "a temporary booth with glaring red peep holes." The big machine worked as expected. So did the powerful lights. But once again the fight was a bust, Ruhlin putting in a lackluster showing and quitting after only five rounds. The *Chicago Tribune* called it "the poorest [title fight] in the history of Queensberry fighting in America, and...a sad blow for the game." After the fight several boys dove through the ropes and began dancing around in the ring, hoping to be captured for posterity on film. One of the spectators in front of the photographing apparatus jokingly held his cap up in front of the lens to foil them. It was soon yanked away by the Edison crew and the man given a beating. But it was all for naught. The eleven-hundred-foot film that was subsequently released was never more than a minor attraction. Of the footage that still survives, there is no sign of the dancing boys.

After the release of the *Jeffries and Ruhlin Sparring Contest*, few real fight films were made until 1906, when improvements in motion picture technology lessened the chance of mechanical mishap and fueled a resurgence. The fake fight film business, meanwhile, continued to flourish, with Siegmund Lubin leading the way. Lubin built a new studio on a Philadelphia rooftop and began making marginally better productions using a bigger ring, painted backdrops and a few dozen spectators. For the most part he continued to employ actors to flail through clumsy reenactments of recent bouts. Occasionally, however, he hired the actual fighters themselves.

Such was the case following the Fitzsimmons-Ruhlin fight of August 10, 1900, where the attempted filming had failed. For an undisclosed sum, Fitz and Ruhlin went down to Philadelphia three days later and reenacted the lopsided bout for Lubin's camera, struggling to keep straight faces as they faked big swings and traded light taps and generally tried not to hurt each other. The film broke in the last round but that was no problem. The camera was reloaded and they simply started again. "Right, let go the right," instructed the referee when the time came for the knockout. Fitz lobbed a glove at Rublin's still-tender jaw and Ruhlin went down, adjusting his sprawl to coaching off-camera. Jim Corbett and "Kid" McCoy went through a similar performance for Lubin the following month, reenacting their recent fight at Madison Square Garden in which McCoy took what many believed to be a dive in the fifth.

Lubin made more than two dozen fake fight films between 1897 and 1908. His productions, although shoddy and obviously staged, were cheap and easy to make and proved reliable box office fodder, providing audiences with at least a pale imitation of fights that they could not otherwise see. He would go on to become a major player in the emerging motion picture business in the early 1910s, churning out hundreds of one- and two-reel comedies, dramas and westerns and giving a start to such stars as Alan Hale and Oliver Hardy. It was not such a big creative leap, after all, from talking two actors through a staged prizefight to directing a leading man to stride across a set, punch the villain in the nose and take the girl in his arms.

In December 1899, six months after losing the heavyweight title to Jeffries, Bob Fitzsimmons had a violent breakup with his manager Martin Julian. The incident left Julian with a black eye and reportedly included both men threatening each other with unloaded pistols. Julian went on to exhibit the Jeffries-Sharkey fight film and managed a Bulgarian wrestler known as the Terrible Turk. Fitz would largely go without a manager after that.

Fitz coasted comfortably for a time without Julian handling his affairs. He moved his family into a new house in the upper-class Bensonhurst section of Brooklyn, displaying his stuffed pet lion Nero in the parlor and the gloves he used to beat Corbett on the mantel. "I christen thee Rose Villa," he pronounced at the house-warming, breaking a bottle of beer over the porch railing. When Fitz heard of an old acquaintance back in New Zealand who had fallen on hard times, he generously invited him to come to America and join his growing household, which now included three children and his sister-in-law Theo. "I'm on easy street now, old boy," Fitz wrote in his letter. "Come and live with me and take a rest in your old age."

Fitz would get one more crack at the heavyweight title, in a re-match against Jim Jeffries in San Francisco in 1902. He dominated for the first seven rounds, pummeling Jeffries and leaving him bloodied, then let his guard slip in the eighth and was decked. That was the end of Fitz's quest to recapture the heavyweight crown. He won the newly created light heavyweight title the following year, the first fighter ever to hold titles in three weight divisions. It did not have nearly the same cachet with the public, however, and he soon returned to fighting at the ultimate weight. A notable fight from this later stage of his career was against rising contender Jack Johnson. It took place in 1907, when Fitz was in his mid forties. He was knocked out in two. Although now well past his prime, Fitz refused to give up boxing. It was all he knew and he needed the money. He continued to appear in the ring until 1914, when the New York Athletic Commission prohibited him from fighting and effectively forced him to retire.

Back at Rose Villa, Fitz's contentment had been shattered by Rose's death back in 1903, taken away by pneumonia at the age of just thirty-seven. He remarried and moved to a farm in New Jersey but he never found the happiness he had enjoyed with Rose and eventually turned to drink. His third wife left him and a fourth fol-lowed, a woman named Temo Ziller, an actress like wife number three. By the time of their marriage in 1915, "easy street" for Fitz was long past. He was almost broke and creditors were closing in on his farm. In the face of impending ruin, he turned his life around and gave up the bottle, becoming a born-again Christian and announcing his intention "to surrender my life to the Lord and enlist under the banner of temperance and clean living." He had only just embarked on a temperance lecture tour, appearing on stage in Chicago, when he caught a cold that turned into pneumonia. He died on October 22, 1917, at the age of fifty-four. Martin Julian, his fortunes diminished by a fire in a theater where he was heavily invested, followed two years later, in 1919.

Jim Corbett was training for a fight against Charles "Kid" McCoy, on the road back to title contention, when he received the worst blow of his life. It came via telegram on August 16, 1898 informing him that his father Patrick, who had been showing signs of increasing mental instability, had shot and killed Jim's mother and then taken his own life. The news left Jim prostrated with grief. The McCoy fight was postponed.

Recovering from the shock of violently losing both his parents, Corbett went on to get two shots at Jim Jeffries's title, in 1900 and again in 1903. He lost both by knockout. Neither was filmed. The experience of being punched unconscious was as unfamiliar to Corbett in 1900 as it had been to Fitz. "What is it?" he mumbled when he woke up back in his corner. "Jim," replied his second, "you were knocked out."

"And from that day to this," Corbett would write years later, "I don't remember ever being hit. I don't remember being on the ground at all."

Corbett retired from the ring after his second loss to Jeffries but remained in the public eye as a celebrity and an actor. In the 1910s, nearly two decades after his pioneering appearance in *Corbett and Courtney Before the Kinetograph*, he returned to working in front of the camera, making a string of low-budget serials, features and shorts with titles like *The Man from the Golden West* (1913), *The Burglar and the Lady* (1914), *The Midnight Man* (1919) and *The Prince of Avenue A* (1920). Most of these films are now lost. A heavy financial setback followed for Corbett when the stock market crashed of 1929. He survived it, but not the cancer that came after. He died at his home in Queens on February 18, 1933, age sixty-six, in the arms of Vera, his wife of thirty-seven years.

John L. Sullivan gave up drinking in 1905 and vowed thereafter to live a clean life. He remarried and retired to a farm outside Boston and, like Fitz, became a temperance speaker, delivering a lecture entitled "From Glory, to Gutter, to God." Holding court on his porch, vowing to live to a hundred, John L. maintained for some years the appearance of being comfortably off. But he wasn't. The fortune he had earned in the ring and on stage was all gone by this time and his farm was a failure. He died broke in 1918, age fifty-nine.

Peter Maher ended up a night watchman on the Hoboken docks—the same docks featured in the 1954 Marlon Brando film *On the Waterfront*. ("I could've been a contender. I could've been somebody!") He struggled with ill health through the 1920s and finally moved to Baltimore to live with his son. Having himself lost so much to booze, it is ironic that the last money he earned was from an advertisement for whiskey, "A champeen whiskey…extra fine for straight drinkin' or in fancy highballs…Silver Dollar. It's Got a Smooth Punch." Peter Maher died in 1940, age seventy-one.

Enoch Rector didn't make another film following the success of *The Corbett-Fitzsimmons Fight*. After being denied his promised share of the profits, he drifted out of the movie-making business and his idea of making longer films by using a giant camera manually operated from the inside soon became obsolete. He devoted the rest of his life to being an inventor. His first major invention was an amateur movie camera and projector system, the Ikonograph, that used 17.5mm film—standard 35mm film cut in half. Rector offered the system to George Eastman in 1902 but was unable to spark the tycoon's interest. Years later Eastman Kodak would come out with something similar, the Cine-Kodak, ushering in the era of 16mm home movies. By then Rector's Ikonograph had long since been forgotten.

The tepid response to his Ikonograph prompted Rector to give up on motion pictures altogether and direct his inventive energies elsewhere, first to a low-cost phonograph called the Rectorphone, then to the automobile. In 1929 he came out with the Rector Gasi-fier, a device that could be fitted onto any gasoline-powered engine to allow it to run on cheap fuel oil. Investors were rounded up and the Rector Gasifier Corporation was formed, but the invention ultimately failed to break the grip that gasoline had on the market. The Rector Gasifier, like the Veriscope, the Ikonograph and the Rectorphone, faded from the scene.

Rector lived out his later years in the Tudor City apartment complex on the east side of Manhattan. He continued working on inventions long past the age of retirement, still hoping to hit it big—"prospecting for gold" as his granddaughter Sara Chermayeff remembered—and became something of a health nut, a vegetarian who made allowances for bacon and roast pork. He was working on a simplified fuel injection system for car engines when Jesse, his wife of sixty-one years, passed away in 1956. Enoch didn't last a year after that. He died on January 27, 1957 at the age of ninety-four.

Dan Stuart tried for two years to arrange a rematch between Corbett and Fitzsimmons and make another lucrative film. He also flirted with the idea of holding a new "fistic carnival" in the Carson City arena before it was torn down. Nothing came of his efforts and he eventually gave up on the fight game to devote himself to horse tracks and racing. He also gave up on Texas and moved to New York, where he married at the age of fifty-four and had two children. He died in 1909, his health having never fully recovered from the near-fatal bout of pneumonia he had suffered in Nevada prior to the Corbett-Fitz fight. He left an estate estimated to be worth around one million dollars.

Otway and Gray Latham left the motion picture business after the collapse of their Eidoloscope venture and became New York real estate agents. Otway married artist and society girl Natalie Lockwood, then remarried when the union failed and Natalie moved to Europe. He died in 1906, carried away by a sudden illness at age thirty-seven. Natalie, who reportedly had never gotten over the breakup of their marriage, committed suicide in her Paris studio the following spring. Gray's marriage to celebrated magazine illustrator Rose O'Neill, inventor of the Kewpie doll, was similarly short-lived. It was Rose who insisted on the split as a matter of self-preservation, after Gray began calling at publishers' offices to commandeer her paychecks. In 1907, seven months after Otway's passing, Gray followed, falling off a Broadway streetcar and striking his head on the pavement. The death was called an accident but relatives claimed it was murder. Gray must have been pushed off the streetcar, they said—likely by pickpockets, for a large sum of money he had been carrying, the down payment on a real estate deal, was gone.

It was thus Woodville Latham's fate to outlive the two sons he had followed into the film business. His patent containing the crucial loop that Eugene Lauste had developed was ultimately acquired by the Motion Picture Patents Company, a trust for controlling the patents for making movies that included such firms as Edison, Vitagraph, Biograph and Lubin, and would become ubiquitous in movie cameras and projectors. Woodville faded into obscurity after that. He spent his final days living in a small room in Harlem, a broken-down Southern gentleman reduced to selling books door to door. A final bit of notice was taken of him in 1911, when the MPPC tracked him down to give testimony in their patent infringement lawsuit against the Independent Moving Picture Company, one of the legal battles fought over the thorny question of who invented the movies. Woodville died later that year. His death went unreported. The MPPC went on to lose the lawsuit and fall by the wayside and the motion picture patent wars became a thing of the past.

William Kennedy Laurie Dickson prospered after leaving Thomas Edison's employment. He was a founding member of American Mutoscope and Biograph, later known as the Biograph Company, which made the peephole Mutoscope to rival the Kinetoscope and then a large-format projector, the Biograph, that was superior to Edison's Vitagraph. The Biograph Company went on to play a leading role in the silent film era, giving directors like D.W. Griffith and Mack Sennett their start and introducing actors like Lionel Barrymore, Mary Pickford and Lillian Gish to the screen. Dickson was no longer involved in the company by then. He had retired to England, first to London and then to the island of Jersey, where he spent his final years in a hillside cottage overlooking the sea. He died in 1935, championing Edison's and in turn his own role in the development of movies to the end. Edison never forgave him for his perceived betrayal, however, and never regarded him again as a friend. For Dickson, it was the greatest regret of his life.

Eugene Lauste joined his old friend Dickson at the Biograph Company after parting ways with the Lathams, working as a camera operator and projectionist and later overseeing the company's plant outside Paris. He subsequently was employed at Dickson's research lab in London, where he continued working on a problem that had long interested him: adding sound to movies. Lauste believed that Edison had taken the wrong path with his Kineto-phonograph concept, for it was immensely difficult to achieve true synchronization when images and sound were recorded and reproduced by two separate machines. To lock image and sound together, Lauste turned sound waves into a pulsing blob of light recorded directly onto film alongside the corresponding pictures. He was granted a British patent in 1907 but never received any financial benefit from it, for when the seismic shift to sound films finally came in the late 1920s the patent had expired and the invention was in the public domain. Lauste spent his final years running a boarding house in Bloomfield, New Jersey, not far from the Edison lab where he had once worked. He died there in 1935, three months before Dickson, his worthless shares in the Eidoloscope Company displayed in a frame on the wall.

Thanks to improvements in motion picture technology, the fight film business experienced a resurgence between 1906 and 1912 and Lubin-style fakes disappeared. Then the rise of heavyweight champion Jack Johnson prompted a backlash. Many people, particularly in the South, were offended that a black man held the title and found it intolerable that films of him whipping a series of "Great White Hopes" were being shown across the country.

The result was the Sims Act, pushed through Congress in July 1912 by an alliance of congressmen and senators wanting to suppress films of Johnson and those more generally opposed to fight films on moral grounds. The act, which made it illegal to transport fight films across state lines, killed the business as effectively as an outright ban on their exhibition, for fight films were expensive to make and thus required nationwide distribution to make a profit. By confining their exhibition to the state where they were filmed, the Sims Act so undermined their earning potential that they were no longer worthwhile to make. It was the first step by the United States government, albeit a roundabout one, toward censoring films.

Fight films thus disappeared from the scene early in the second decade of the twentieth century, just as a new form of cinematic entertainment, the narrative film, was coming into its own. Pioneers like George Méliès in France and former Edison employee Edwin Porter in the United States had led the way, experimenting with editing and cross-cutting to tell ten-to-fifteen-minute celluloid stories like *A Trip to the Moon* (Méliès, 1902) and *Life of an American Fireman* and *The Great Train Robbery* (Porter, both 1903). What was arguably the first feature-length narrative film, *The Story of the Kelly Gang*, was made in Australia in 1906, running time seventy minutes. The Italians made the first screen epic, *Quo Vadis*, in 1912, two hours long, followed by the even more spectacular *Cabiria* in 1914, clocking in at two hundred minutes. Then the impetus shifted back to the United States with the 1915 release of D.W. Griffith's *The Birth of a Nation*, which took the art of filmmaking to a whole new level. The cinema as we know it today had arrived.

As movies continued to evolve in the decades that followed, *The Corbett-Fitzsimmons Fight* film was largely forgotten. A complete copy of it no longer exists. A reel was discovered in Portland, Oregon in the 1960s by handball champion and fight film collector Jim Jacobs, who would go on to co-manage Mike Tyson. Another portion was donated to New York's Museum of Modern Art in 1982 by Bob Fitzsimmons' granddaughter, Joy Blake Fitzsimmons, bringing total surviving footage to around twenty-nine minutes or just under forty percent of the original movie. This fragile nitrate film was preserved and transferred onto 35mm stock by the British Film Institute and was screened at London's National Film Theatre on the film's centenary in 1997. Most of this footage can be viewed on the internet today, but only in low resolution and with the edges cut off—a dim, truncated shadow of the images that so impressed audiences back in 1897, when Enoch Rector's production became the world's first feature-length movie and the cinema's first blockbuster hit.

NOTES

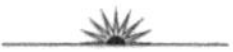

MC Papers: Merritt Crawford Papers, microfilm edition
GELC: George Eastman Legacy Collection, Eastman Museum, Rochester, New York
TAED: Thomas A. Edison Digital Collection, edison.rutgers.edu
TENHP: Thomas Edison National Historical Park, Orange, New Jersey

PROLOGUE

On restoration of *The Corbett-Fitzsimmons Fight* and centenary screening: *The Independent*, June 1 and 7, 1997; "Square Ring (A Bout Last Night)," *Sight and Sound*, June 1997, 73; Grant Lobban, "In the Splendor of 70mm," *The 70mm Newsletter*, Mar. 2002, www.in70mm. com/newsletter/2002/67/splendour_of_70mm. Brady, *Fighting Man*, 147, put the film's gross at $600K-$700K. On Jim Jacobs: *Binghamton Press*, April 8, 1962; Robert Boyle, "Really the Greatest," *Sports Illustrated*, Mar. 7, 1966, 64-72; *Yonkers Herald-Statesman*, Dec. 28, 1968; *Medina Journal-Register*, April 22, 1981; *Los Angeles Times*, Mar. 24, 1988. Also: author correspondence with Ashley Swinnerton, Museum of Modern Art, Mar.-April 2016.

1) THE PERSISTENCE OF VISION

On the Overland Mail: Ormsby, *Butterfield Overland Mail* (firsthand account); Harlow, *Old Waybills*, 207 ("I now know what hell is like"). The injuries Muybridge sustained in the crash were reported in his murder trial fourteen years later. Muybridge trial: *Daily Alta California*, Oct. 19, 1874 and Feb. 4, 6 and 7, 1875; *Sacramento Daily Union*, Oct. 20, 1874 and Feb. 4 and 8, 1875; *San Francisco Chronicle*, Dec. 21, 1874 (interview with Muybridge in cell); Haas, *Muybridge*, 63-78 and 81-82; MacDonnell, *Eadweard Muybridge*, 147-50; Ramsaye, *Million and One Nights*, chapter 2.

The story of Muybridge's sequential photography work begins with his five books published during his lifetime: *The Attitudes of Animals in Motion*, 1882; *Animal Locomotion*, 1887; *Descriptive Zoopraxography*, 1893; *Animals in Motion*, 1899 ("In those days" quote p. 1); and *The Human Figure in Motion*, 1901 ("There, governor" quote p. 7). Accounts of Muybridge capturing motion of horses: *Daily Alta California*, Aug. 3, 1877; *Sacramento Daily Union*, June 18, 1878; *Pacific Rural Press*, June 22, 1878; "A Horse's Motion Scientifically Determined," *Scientific American*, Oct. 19, 1878, 241. Also: *New York Sun*, Jan. 29, 1883 ("I conversed with him"); Stillman, *Horse in Motion*, 123-27; Haas, *Muybridge*, 94 and 109-11; MacDonnell, *Eadweard Muybridge*, 22-24 and 84-91; Clark, *Stanford*, 367-68; Leslie, "The Man Who Stopped Time." Muybridge's 1882 appearance at the Royal Institution: "Mr. Muybridge at the Royal Institution," *Photographic News*, Mar. 17, 1882, 137; *Spirit of the Times*, April 29 and Nov. 25, 1882.

2) A PUNCH IN THE FACE

On Fitz's early life in New Zealand: *Timaru Herald*, June 10, 14 and 15 and Sept. 11, 14 and 15, 1882 (Jem Mace tournaments); *San Francisco Morning Call*, Mar. 3, 1892 (Fitz interview); Pardy, "Famous Fighting Codes," *Ring*, Mar. 1942, 22ff (Fitz on London vs. Queensberry rules and his first bare-knuckle fight). Fitz's claim that he won the amateur championship of New Zealand in the Jem Mace tournament appears untrue. It was a local affair, Mace holding similar tournaments in Otago, Auckland, Dunedin, Lyttelton and elsewhere. (See *Auckland Star*, April 10, 1882; *Otago Daily Times*, June 26, 1882; *New Zealand Observer*, April 22, 1882; *Tuapeka Times*, Aug. 16 1882; *Bruce Herald*, Oct. 3, 1882; *Lyttelton Star*, Oct. 16, 1882.)

Bob's marriage: *New York Herald*, Oct. 7, 1893. For his ring career in Australia I waded through a large body of material in the *Sydney Evening News*, *Sydney Morning Herald*, *Sydney Referee*, *Sydney Globe* and *Australian Town and Country Journal* for the years 1886-90. Of particular note: *Globe*, April 6, 1886 (earliest published mention I found of Fitz in Sydney), April 19, 1886 (earliest published account I found of a Fitz fight) and June 4, 1886 (Fitz outclassed but fast improving); *Referee*, Mar. 8, 1888 (Slavin fight, Fitz greatly improved) and Jan. 23, 1889 (first Hall fight); *Evening News* and *Referee*, Feb. 12, 1890 (second Hall fight); *New York Herald*, Oct. 7, 1893 (Louisa Fitzsimmons stating that Bob told her he threw Hall fight); *Referee*, Feb. 26, 1890 (Fitz clowning in fight, called a "fool") and April 16, 1890 (departure for Frisco); *Morning Herald*, April 17, 1890 (description of *Zealandia* leaving port). The odorous fighter Bob faced was Edward "Starlight" Rollins. For Tom James' role in recruiting Fitz: *San Francisco Morning Call*, Jan. 16, 1891. According to *New York Press*, Mar. 5, 1893, Bob was so poor when he came to America "that he had to work his passage from Australia to San Francisco."

Additional Fitz sources: *Sands Sydney and Suburban Directory*, 1887-90; Odd, *Fighting Blacksmith*, chapters 1-3; Webb, *Prize Fighter*, 24-26 (childhood punch in the face); Rocap, *Remembering Bob Fitzsimmons*, 2-5 (early life) and 19-20 (Fitz throwing Hall fight); Fitzsimmons, *Physical Culture*, 61-114; Petersen, *Peter Jackson*, 38-39 (Fitz training under Jackson). Jackson was one of four men arrested in 1884 for aiding and abetting the fight that resulted in the mentioned ring death. *Sydney Evening News*, April 19, 1884 called them "a shady-looking lot."

On Corbett: Corbett, *Roar of the Crowd*, 3-7 (childhood fight with Carney) and 74-89 (Choynski fight); Fields, *James J. Corbett*, 5-31; Myler, *Gentleman Jim Corbett*, 7-31; *New York World*, Sept. 4 and 9 ("allow[ing] the boys"), 1892; Fox, *Life and Battles of James J. Corbett*, 7-8 (Carney fight); Irvine, *"Our Jim,"* 14-38; *Langley's San Francisco City Directory*, 1886-89; *Daily Alta California*, Aug. 29, 1885 (earliest report I found of Corbett fighting at Olympic Club: "Corbett's reach and strength were tremendous, but not equal to [his opponent Mike] Cleary's science and quickness.") and Feb. 13, 1886. On Corbett's initial foray into prizefighting as "Jim Dillon": *Salt Lake Tribune*, June 29 and July 1, 15 and 23, 1886; *Salt Lake Herald*, June 29 and July 9, 1886; *Daily Alta California*, July 19, 1886; *National Police Gazette*, July 31, 1886; *San Francisco Morning Call*, Jan. 2, 1891 (Patrick Corbett interview); *Reading Eagle*, Sept. 4, 1892 (Ollie Corbett interview). Also: *Daily Alta California*, Aug. 23, 1886 (Jim's return from Salt Lake City and marriage to Ollie), Mar. 7, 1887 ("squeamish about fighting for a prize!"), May 30, 1887 (hired as instructor at Golden Gate Club), Feb. 13, 1888 (hired at Olympic) and May 12, 1889 (training for Choynski fight); *Daily Alta California* and *Sacramento Daily Union*, May 31, 1889 (Corbett-Choynski fight in barn) and June 6, 1889 (Corbett-Choynski fight on barge). It could be disputed that Corbett invented the left hook. The significance of it appears to have escaped Corbett himself at the time, for he only began to speak of it years later.

3) ROOM 5

On Edison's philosophy of invention and vision for a lab complex: *New York Journal*, July 2, 1891 ("I like to begin"); draft letter, Thomas Edison to James Hood Wright, Aug. 1887, TAED NA011005 ("I will have the best equipped"); *New York World*, Nov. 17, 1889 ("Anything that won't sell"); Tate, *Edison's Open Door*, 126 ("I measure everything"). Description of Edison's West Orange lab: Horace Townsend, "Edison: His Work and His Work-Shop," *Cosmopolitan*, April 1889, 598-607; Dyer and Martin, *Edison*, vol. 2, 639-51; Baldwin, *Edison*, 193-94.

For Muybridge's work at UPenn, see *Animal Locomotion* (1887), available on-line at www.muybridge.org. Muybridge describes his photographic equipment and technique in *Descriptive Zoopraxography* (1893), 10-26. Also: Talcott Williams, "Animal Locomotion in the Muybridge Photographs," *The Century Magazine*, July 1887, 356-68; *New York Evening Post*, July 14, 1887; William Dennis Marks, "The Mechanism of Instantaneous Photography," in *Animal Locomotion: The Muybridge Work at the University of Pennsylvania*; *Orange Chronicle*, Mar. 3, 1888 (Muybridge lecture in Orange); *Orange Journal*, Mar. 3, 1888, quoted in Spehr, *Man*

Who Made Movies, 75 (A.N. Tinude letter); *New York World*, June 3, 1888 (Muybridge-Edison meeting); *Brooklyn Daily Eagle*, June 14, 1888 (Levison camera).

On the cylinder Kinetograph: Edison Caveat No. 110, Oct. 15, 1888, TAED PT031AAA; Edison Caveat No. 114, Mar. 22, 1889, TAED W100ABX; Edison Caveat No. 116, July 29, 1889, TAED W100AB7. (The date of May 20, 1889 on Edison's handwritten original for No. 116 was likely when he started compiling the long list of ideas that comprised the document.) Another useful source on motion picture work at Edison's lab in 1888-89 are the depositions recorded in the 1900 lawsuit Thomas A. Edison vs. American Mutoscope Company and Benjamin F. Keith, Equity No. 6928, United States Circuit Court, Southern District of New York, TAED QM001, in particular the testimony by Edison (pp. 91-124), Fred Ott (128-40) and Charles Brown (140-58; "monkey shines" quote on p. 158). Other sources: William Dickson to Merritt Crawford, Dec. 1, 1930, MC Papers, reel 1; Merritt Crawford, "William Kennedy Laurie Dickson: Movie Pioneer," unpublished manuscript, undated (circa 1930), MC Papers, reel 1; *New York Herald*, May 28, 1891 ("a pet hobby"); Dickson and Dickson, "Edison's Invention of the Kineto-Phonograph," 206-14; Remsen Crawford, "Patents, Profits and Pirates," 3-5 and 135-38.

Among secondary sources, I made most use of Paul Spehr's superb *Man Who Made Movies*, chapters 1-10 and Hendricks, *Edison Motion Picture Myth*, passim (rich in detail but with a strong anti-Edison slant). Also: Ramsaye, *Million and One Nights*, chapters 3-4; Ramsaye, "The Romantic History of the Motion Picture," *Photoplay*, April 1922, 20-23 and 110-14; Musser, *Emergence of Cinema*, 55-66; Israel, *Edison*, 292-94.

4) CHAMPION AND CONTENDER

For Fitz: *Daily Alta California*, May 11, 1890 (*Zealandia* arrival in Frisco); "A Remarkable Athletic Organization," *Harper's Weekly*, April 5, 1890, 262-64 (CAC description); *Daily Alta California* and *San Francisco Call*, May 15, 1890 (Bob tested as CAC); *Daily Alta*, May 26, 1890 ("ungainly in appearance"); *Daily Alta, Los Angeles Herald* and *Sacramento Daily Record-Union*, May 30, 1890 and *Maitland Mercury*, July 5, 1890 (McCarthy fight); *National Police Gazette*, Aug. 16, 1890 (Fitz-Upham fight); *Daily Alta*, Oct. 28 and 31, 1890 (Fitz's family arrives). Secondary sources: Odd, *Fighting Blacksmith*, 52-63; Rocap and Rocap, *Remembering Bob Fitzsimmons*, 24-33; Webb, *Prize Fighter*, 47-57.

Fitz-Dempsey fight: *Sacramento Daily Union*, Sept. 10, 1890; *Los Angeles Herald*, Sept. 24, 1890; *Daily Alta California*, Sept. 21, Oct. 31 and Dec. 15, 1890 and Jan. 16, 1891 ("Corbett is too clever"); *San Francisco Morning Call*, Dec. 31, 1890 and Jan. 8, 15 and 16, 1891; *National Police Gazette*, Oct. 4, 1890 and Jan. 24, 1891; *New Orleans Daily Picayune*, Jan. 11-16, 1891; *New York Herald* and *World*, Jan. 15, 1891; *Buffalo Express*,

Jan. 15, 1891; *Johnstown* (NY) *Daily Republic*, Jan. 16, 1891; *New York Dramatic Mirror*, Feb. 21, 1891 ("Never mind, mother"); *New York Press*, Jan. 16, 1891 (Sullivan's reaction). On audience interference at fights in the old days, which necessitated a barbed-wire fence around the ring: *Chicago Daily Tribune*, Sept. 8, 1892.

For Corbett: *Daily Alta California*, Nov. 3, 1889 (launch of *Illustrated World*); *Langley's San Francisco City Directory*, 1889-91; Corbett, *Roar of the Crowd*, 90-145; Fields, *James J. Corbett*, 36-48; Myler, *Gentleman Jim Corbett*, 34-45. It was in front of the Florence Hotel were Jim lived, incidentally, that Sam Spade's partner Floyd Thursby was gunned down a half century later in the Humphrey Bogart film *The Maltese Falcon*.

Corbett-Kilrain fight: Corbett, *Roar of the Crowd*, 93 ("I was dumbfounded"); *Daily Alta California, New York World, Herald* and *Sun*, Feb. 18, 1890; *Sacramento Daily Record-Union*, Feb. 23, 1890 (Jim's telegram to Ollie); *San Francisco Morning Call*, April 18, 1890 (Kilrain "squealing"); *New York Clipper*, April 25, 1890 (Corbett a "craze"). On Patrick Corbett's outburst: *Morning Call*, Jan. 1, 2 and 3, 1891.

Corbett-Jackson fight: *New York Sun*, April 15, 1890 ("the general impression"); *Los Angeles Herald*, Mar. 9, 1891 (Kilrain's prediction Jim would be "punched full of holes"; Kilrain's trainer William Muldoon additionally called Jim a "blatherskite"); *San Francisco Morning Call*, Mar. 14, 1891 ("slowest man in creation"); *Daily Alta California, Brooklyn Daily Eagle, New York World* and *New York Herald*, May 22, 1891. For Jackson in the role of Uncle Tom: *San Francisco Morning Call*, Feb. 13 and Mar. 20, 1893; Petersen, *Peter Jackson*, 167-69; Susan Clark, "Up Against the Ropes: Peter Jackson as 'Uncle Tom' in America," *The Drama Review* 44 (Spring 2000): 157-82.

Sullivan in Frisco: *San Francisco Morning Call*, May 26, 1891 ("potpourri of rubbish"); *Reading* (PA) *Eagle*, Sept. 4, 1892 (Ollie Corbett's comment); *Morning Call*, June 16, 21 and 25, 1891 and *Sacramento Daily Union*, June 25, 1891 (Corbett benefit); *Pittsburgh Post-Gazette*, Feb. 10, 1933; Corbett, *Roar of the Crowd*, 149 ("I can whip this fellow!").

The *Buffalo Evening News*, Dec. 11, 1894, observed that "Sullivan undoubtedly developed and perfected the knockout blow and was the first glove fighter to put it into practical usage. Before Sullivan's time the heroes of the ring fought their great battles with bare knuckles and usually won them by wearing out the strength of a foe...." Much of Sullivan's reputation as a knockout artist was earned while he was on tour challenging all comers, which generally meant unskilled local toughs whom he could readily put to sleep.

5) SWITCH TO CELLULOID

Edison's departure for Europe: *New York Herald, Press, Times* and *Tribune*, Aug. 4, 1889. Edison's first version of a Kinetograph using a celluloid strip was outlined in Caveat No. 117, Dec. 9, 1889, TAED PT031AAH. For Dickson's account of the projected image with sound demonstration upon Edison's return, see Dickson and Dickson, *History of the Kineto-graph*, 19 ("Good morning, Mr. Edison"); Dickson to Merritt Crawford, Dec. 1, 1930, MC Papers, reel 1; Eugene Lauste to Will Day, May 30, 1933, MC Papers, reel 1 ("[T]he pictures was blur"). Lauste was hiding behind the screen during the failed demonstration. He hid there at Dickson's instruction when Edison showed up because he was not authorized to be in the room. While Dickson's claim of projecting a moving image with synchronized sound in Oct. 1889 has been disputed, it is clear that this was subsequently attempted. In a list of questions concerning the Kinetograph sent to Edison by George Hopkins of *Scientific American* on April 25, 1893, for example, the following is asked: "Have you successfully shown it on the screen in connection with the phonograph?" Edison's scribbled response: "Yes." (TAED D9335AAP) See also Dickson and Dickson, "Edison's Invention of the Kineto-Phonograph," 206-14.

Among secondary sources, I made greatest use of Spehr, *Movies*, chapters 10-20 and Hendricks, *Myth*, chapters 9-19 and *Kinetoscope*, chapters 1-4. Also: Ramsaye, *Nights*, 50-73; Israel, *Edison*, 294-96; Musser, *Emergence of Cinema*, 67-74; Robinson, *From Peep Show to Palace*, chapter 2; Rossell, *Living Pictures*, chapter 4; Tate, *Edison's Open Door*, 253 and 302 (on Edison's focus on "useful inventions"); Baldwin, *Edison*, 213-19 (Edison's ore milling obsession).

Numerous writers in the past several decades have followed Gordon Hendricks' lead in claiming that Edison was primarily influenced to switch to film strips by seeing Étienne-Jules Marey's apparatus in Paris in September 1889. It should be noted that Marey was using paper-backed rather than celluloid strips at this time. The evidence seems clear, moreover, that Dickson had begun working with celluloid strips *before* Edison left for Paris. As Spehr states in *Movies*, 146, "he [Edison] did not experience the revelation of new and unfamiliar technology that Hendricks and others have postulated. The image of Edison slapping his forehead and saying 'why couldn't I have thought of that' is absurd. Edison was very familiar with machines that manipulated strips. His earliest inventions, the stock ticker and improved telegraph machines, used strips of paper—in fact, he had built his early career on manipulating such strips. The notion that Edison learned about the potential of celluloid from Marey is also misleading.... Edison experimented with it for the phonograph, Dickson was using it before Edison left and Newark, Edison's home base, and the home of the Celluloid Manufacturing Co., was a leading manufacturing center of raw celluloid. Edison, the avid amateur chemist, probably knew more about it than Marey did."

On the Kinetoscope's public debut: *New York Herald* ("The machine was started") and *New York Sun* ("My intention"), May 28, 1891. *New*

York Press, May 29, 1891, commented that now that Edison had succeeded in replicating sound with the Phonograph and sight with the Kinetograph, "he will doubtless apply the same principle to the senses of smelling and tasting." See also *Brooklyn Daily Standard-Union*, May 28, 1891 ("The worst of it"); *New York Herald*, June 14, 1891 ("How can we expect"); Lathrop, "Edison's Kinetoscope," 446-47; "The Edison Photophonokinetograph," *The Electrical Engineer*, May 20, 1891, 584.

Letters to Edison re. Kinetoscope: Eugene Elliott to Edison, June 5, 1891, TAED D9141AAA; G. Don Portez to Edison, June 11, 1891, TAED D9141AAC; John Lyons to Edison, Sept. 5, 1891, TAED D9141AAH; P. W. Singleton to Edison, Nov. 25, 1891, TAED D9141AAN. Reply: Tate to G. Don Porter [sic. Portez], June 16, 1891, TAED LB050017. Dickson's correspondence with Gundlach Optical Co. and Bausch & Lomb appears in Edison laboratory letterbooks for 1889-91, TAED LM102 and 1891-95, TAED LM103, in particular Dickson to Gundlach, Aug. 31, 1891, TAED LM102403 ("The lense [sic.] is entirely unfitted"); Sept. 16, 1891, TAED LM102413 ("I order a lens"); and Dec. 7, 1891, TAED LM103004 ("For what use").

On Dickson's quest for durable film: Dickson to Eastman Dry Plate and Film Co., Oct. 22, 1891, TAED LM102437 ("somewhat stunned"); Nov. 2, 1891, TAED LM102447 (initial film order); Dec. 7, 1891, TAED LM103006 ("chew up film"); and Feb. 8, 1892, TAED LM103046 ("skin very tough"). Dickson ordered film from Eastman 1½ inches wide. Dickson's perforating machine, in addition to punching holes on either side, also trimmed it to size. For the Eastman side of the story: Ackerman, *George Eastman*, chapter 2 and Brayer, *George Eastman*, 94 ("Praying Department"). An interesting letter from Eastman to his head chemist, Henry Reichenbach, July 23, 1891: "Enclosed is a small fragment of film furnished Edison.... He perforates it on both edges and delivers it by means of cog wheels.... The trouble with the film we have sent him is that the cogs tear the film slightly, as you will see by the enclosed, and gives blurred images." (Ackerman, *Eastman*, 67.)

6) THE HEAVYWEIGHT TITLE

Fitzsimmons as middleweight champ: *Pittsburgh Dispatch*, April 19, 1891 ("What I want to point out"). Fitz tours with *Fashions*: *Buffalo Express*, Mar. 31, 1891; *Chicago Tribune*, April 6, 1891; *Pittsburgh Dispatch*, April 14, 1891. Fitz-Hall fight in St. Paul prevented: *St. Paul Daily Globe*, July 3, 21 (Archbishop Ireland comment), 22 and 25, 1891. Fitz-Maher fight: *New Orleans Daily Picayune*, Feb. 28-Mar. 4, 1892; *New York Herald*, Mar. 3, 1892; *New York World*, Mar. 3, 1892; *Indianapolis Journal*, Mar. 3, 1892; *San Francisco Call*, Mar. 3, 1892; *New York Clipper*, Mar. 12, 1892; *Buffalo Courier*, Mar. 20, 1892 (different perspective on fight by "a literary man"). Maher tries to kill himself: *New York Press*, Mar. 6 and 7, 1892;

Reynold's News, Mar. 13, 1892. Fitz secondary sources: Odd, *Fighting Blacksmith*, 64-90; Rocap and Rocap, *Remembering Bob Fitzsimmons*, 34-38; Webb, *Prize Fighter*, 62-68.

Sullivan issues challenge: *Indianapolis Journal* and *Brooklyn Daily Eagle*, Mar. 6, 1892 (*Eagle* headline: "Let the Bluffers Quail!"); *New York World*, Mar. 8, 1892 ("Poor little 210-pound baby!"); *St. Paul Daily Globe*, Mar. 8, 1892 (Sullivan an "old woman"); *New York World* and *Herald*, Mar. 16, 1892 (Corbett-Sullivan agreement). Mitchell picks fight with Corbett: *New York Herald* and *San Francisco Call*, Mar. 22, 1892; *New York World*, Mar. 23, 1892.

Corbett hooks up with Brady and joins *After Dark* cast: Corbett, *Roar of the Crowd*, 151-53; Brady, *Showman*, 78-81; *San Francisco Call*, July 23, 1891; *Buffalo Courier*, Nov. 28, 1891 ("I haven't got a line to speak"). Descriptions of play: *St. Paul Sunday Globe*, Jan. 17, 1892; *Indianapolis Journal*, Mar. 1, 1892; *Los Angeles Herald*, Oct. 17, 1892. Brady background: *Pittsburgh Dispatch*, Sept. 21, 1890; Brady, *Showman*, chapters 1 and 2. According to the *Call*, July 31, 1891: "A letter from Jim Corbett to his brother says that the professor [Corbett] is seriously thinking of settling down permanently in the East. Having several theatrical engagements in view he thinks life on the road is a far better paying venture than life in the ring."

Sullivan in training: Sullivan, *Life and Reminiscences*, 254-67 (ideas on training) and 283-94 (doctor's report); *San Francisco Call*, May 26, 1891 ("shampoo and a shave"); *New York Sun*, July 10, 1892; *Salt Lake Herald*, Sept. 2, 1892; *Reading Eagle*, Sept. 4, 1892 ("fleshy" buttocks); *National Police Gazette*, Oct. 29, 1892 ("Corbett is so scared of me"). Corbett in training: *New York World*, Aug. 8 and Sept. 4, 1892; "Training a Fighter," *The Illustrated American*, July 23, 1892, 463-64. Corbett told Hugh Coyle that he attended the 1884 Sullivan-Robinson fight and was the first person through the gates. "Corbett says he got his first lesson in practical and professional pugilism that evening." (Letter from Hugh Coyle, Feb. 17, 1892, quoted in Sullivan, *Life and Reminiscences*, 278). The Sullivan-Robinson fight was reported in the *Daily Alta California*, Mar. 7, 1884.

Corbett-Sullivan fight: *New York World*, July 24, Aug. 30 and Sept. 2, 1892 (Sullivan's boots); *Los Angeles Herald*, Sept. 6, 1892 and *New York Sun*, Sept. 7, 1892 (belly wraps); *New York Evening World*, Sept. 7, 1892 (verbatim fight cables); *New York World*, *New York Herald*, *New York Sun*, *Chicago Daily Tribune*, *San Francisco Call*, *Los Angeles Herald*, *Indianapolis Journal* and *Pittsburgh Dispatch*, Sept. 8, 1892; *National Police Gazette*, Sept. 17 and 24, 1892; Corbett, *Roar of the Crowd*, 194-201.

Corbett in *Gentleman Jack*: *Buffalo Courier*, Oct. 1, 1892 (Jim Daly quits); *New York World*, *Herald* and *Press*, Oct. 4, 1892; *National Police Gazette*, Oct. 22, 1892; *New York Sun*, Nov. 8, 1892; *New York Dramatic Mirror*, Nov. 12, 1892. Sullivan in *Man from Boston*: *New York World*,

Oct. 4, 1894; *National Police Gazette*, Oct. 22, 1892. Bob Fitzsimmons's Athletic and Specialty Company: *New York Clipper*, April 9, 1892.

7) PREPARING FOR MARKET

On Dickson's Florida sojourn: *Orange Chronicle*, Feb. 11, 1893 ("gone to Florida"); Dickson to Al Tate, Feb. 6, 1893, TAED D9335AAG ("I feel very sure"); James Symington to Thomas Edison, April 24, 1893, TAED D9308AAJ ("It cost 11 dollars"); Tate to Dickson, Mar. 6, 1893, TAED D9310ACE ("attention is so much absorbed"). On the Columbian Exposition: Hubert Howe Bancroft, *The Book of the Fair* (Chicago: Bancroft Co., 1893). The Phonograph and Tachyscope exhibits were located in the Electricity Building; Muybridge's exhibit, Zoopraxographical Hall, was located on the Midway Plaisance (see pp. 420 and 863). Erastus Benson to Al Tate, May 5, 1893, TAED D9335AAR ("pay $1000 a day").

On the Kinetoscope's Brooklyn Institute debut: *Brooklyn Daily Eagle* and *Brooklyn Daily Standard Union*, May 10, 1893 (latter quoted in Hendricks, *Kinetoscope*, 37-38); "First Public Exhibition of Edison's Kinetograph," *Scientific American*, May 20, 1893, 310; Al Tate to George Hopkins, May 1, 1893, TAED D9310ADC (Edison's answers to questions Hopkins submitted to prepare for his lecture). According to Hendricks, *Kinetoscope*, 40-45, this single Kinetoscope may have been placed on display at the Columbian Exposition in late July.

On the stock market crash and subsequent depression: *New York World* and *Buffalo Courier*, May 4, 1893; *New York Herald*, May 6, 1893 ("cruel, cruel"); *Syracuse Courier*, May 6, 1893 ("The worst is probably over"); *New York Evening Telegram*, July 26, 1893 (NYSE closure plan). See also Douglas Steeples and David O. Whitten, *Democracy in Desperation: The Depression of 1893* (Westport, CT: Greenwood Press, 1998), chapters 3, 4 and 6. On the impact of the downturn on Edison: Spehr, *Movies*, 300; Al Tate to Francis Jehl, Sept. 11, 1893, TAED LB058091 ("the Electric business"); Edison lab staff list in Account: Distribution of Labor, 1893-96, TAED NL025A1. Another example of Edison's financial strain: John Randolph (Edison's bookkeeper) to Mrs. Ellen Edison (widow of Edison's brother Pitt), Sept. 7, 1893, TAED LB053593: "Mr. Edison desires me to state that he is very short of money just at present and that he will have to reduce the allowance to $40.00 per month."

On Eastman's production troubles and withdrawal from the film market: Ackerman, *George Eastman*, 89-90; Brayer, *George Eastman*, 89-91, 95 and 99; Spehr, *Movies*, 245-46; *Chicago Tribune*, Nov. 6, 1892; *Denver Republican*, Dec. 11, 1892. On the Blair Camera Co.: Dickson to Blair Camera Co., May 21, 1893, TAED LM103186 ("leathery consistency"). Prior to settling on Blair, Dickson reached out to Reichenbach's renegade outfit, the Photo Materials Company. It was apparently unable to meet his needs. See Dickson memorandum, no date [Feb. 1893], TAED D9335AAY.

On the Black Maria: *New York Sun*, Mar. 11, 1894; Hendricks, *Kineto-scope*, chapter 3; Spehr, *Movies*, 265-67; Phillips, *Edison's Kinetoscope*, chapter 14-15. Other sources for this period of Kineto development: Tate, *Edison's Open Door*, 282-87; Robinson, *Peep Show*, chapter 3; Musser, *Emergence of Cinema*, 75-81; Musser, *Before the Nickelodeon*, chapter 3. The original Black Maria was demolished in 1903. The replica at the Edison National Historical Park today was built in 1954. The lab employee initially contracted to build the first twenty-five Kinetoscopes was James Egan.

On Sandow and his visit to Edison's lab: *New York Herald*, Mar. 7, 1894; *Orange Chronicle*, Mar. 10, 1894 (quoted in Hendricks, *Kinetoscope*, 53-54); *New York Dramatic Mirror*, Mar. 17, 1894; *New York World*, Mar. 18, 1894; David Chapman, *Sandow the Magnificent: Eugen Sandow and the Beginnings of Bodybuilding* (Urbana: University of Illinois Press, 1994), 76-77; Charles Musser, " 'A Personality So Marked': Eugen Sandow and Visual Culture," in *Moving Pictures: American Art and Early Film, 1880-1910*, ed. Nancy Mowll Mathews (New York: Hudson Hills Press, 2005), 104-10.

8) OPEN FOR BUSINESS

For the Holland Brothers Kinetoscope Parlor and general New York back-ground: *New York World*, April 15, 1894 (advertisement); *New York Her-ald*, May 20, 1894 (theater listings); Phillips, *Edison's Kinetoscope*, 74 (1155 Broadway handbill); "The Kinetoscope," *The Critic*, May 12, 1894, 330; *New York Sun*, May 25, 1894; Spehr, *Movies*, 307-09; Hendricks, *Kinetoscope*, 56-61; Ramsaye, *Nights*, 87-88; Burrows and Wallace, *Gotham*, 951-1208.

For Enoch Rector's background: US census, 1870 and 1880 (1890 census records were lost in a fire); author interview with Rector's granddaughter Sara Chermayeff, Sept. 22, 2011 and Nov. 19, 2015; Charles Rector, "Morgan 'Goes A-Raiding'," 310-11 and 322 (on North-South split in Rector family); Callahan, *Genealogical and Personal History*, vol. 1, 837-38 (on step-mother Jane and step-brother William); *Catalogue of West Virginia University*, 1883-85; Enoch Rector passport application, Buenos Aires, April 2, 1890 (ancestry.com); Mulhall, *From Europe to Paraguay*, chapters 8-11; *Omaha Daily Bee*, Nov. 15, 1890 and *The Railroad Gazette*, Feb. 19, 1892, 143 (Mogyana Railroad); *New York Sun*, April 15, 1892 ("Matto Grosso in Revolt"); *Parkersburg Daily State Journal*, May 2, 1895 (Rector's marriage announcement gives some background info.); *New York Times*, Jan. 27, 1957 (Rector obituary); Ramsaye, *Nights*, 106-08; *American Machinist*, Dec. 31, 1891, 10 (Lang Motor Co.); U.S. Patent Office, "Spring-Motor," patent no. 481,714, Aug. 20, 1892 (application filed Dec. 14, 1891); *Official Gazette of the United States Patent Office* 60 (1892), 1248.

On the Lathams: US census, 1870 and 1880; *Richmond Dispatch*, July 18, 1861 (Woodville's Civil War enlistment); *New York Evening Express*,

Jan. 15, 1863 (Eliza arrested); *Catalogue of West Virginia University*, 1880-85; *Wheeling Intelligencer*, Sept. 22, 1883 (Gray in fight) and Aug. 2 and 6, 1884 (Woodville controversy at WVU); *Catalogue of the Officers and Students of the University of Mississippi*, 1886-89; Sansing, *University of Mississippi*, 152 (Woodville's dismissal; three other professors were dismissed at this time, one of whom committed suicide); *Daily Tobacco Leaf-Chronicle*, Nov. 3, 1891 (Gray as traveling salesman); *Western Druggist*, Dec. 1893, 499 (write-up on Otway); Formanek-Brunell, ed., *Rose O'Neill*, 53 and 73-76 (on Gray, O'Neill's first husband); Ramsaye, *Nights*, 104-08; Hendricks, *Kinetoscope*, 147-50.

Additional sources on the Lathams, Rector and the start of their Kinetoscope venture: Spehr, *Movies*, 313-15 and 320; Hendricks, *Kinetoscope*, 88-90; Streible, *Fight Pictures*, 29; correspondence between Otway Latham and William Gilmore, General Manager, Edison Manufacturing Co., May 16, 19, 21 and 25, 1894, TAED D9427.

9) UPS AND DOWNS

For Corbett in *Gentleman Jack*: *Sunday Morning Courier*, Lincoln, NE, June 18, 1893 ("From the rise of the curtain"); *New York Dramatic Mirror*, July 15, 1893 (Brady interview); *New York Sun*, Feb. 21, 1894 (play review); *Brooklyn Daily Eagle*, Mar. 13, 1894 (play attracts "better" class, including "doctors and lawyers" and "a surprising number of women"); *Philadelphia Inquirer*, Dec. 16, 1894 ("I do not think I flatter myself"). Also: Woods, "James J. Corbett: Theatrical Star," 162-75.

The attempt to hold the Corbett-Mitchell fight at the Coney Island AC and the legal brouhaha that ensued may be followed in the *Brooklyn Daily Eagle* starting on April 2, 1893, when the initial fight agreement was announced. See also *New York World*, April 3, 1893. Amended articles stipulating that the fight would be "a scientific glove contest of twenty rounds or more" were signed in September. (*Eagle*, Sept. 24, 1893; *Syracuse Daily Journal*, Oct. 2, 1893.) "Boss" McKane's downfall is chronicled in the *Eagle* starting on Nov. 7, 1893, with reports of his thugs beating up poll watchers.

Fitz's breakup with Carroll was reported in the *Rome* (NY) *Daily Sentinel*, July 12, 1892 ("I am done with Carroll forever"). On *Heroic Blacksmith*: *New York Clipper*, June 25 and July 9, 1892 (ads seeking "new comedy acts and startling novelties" for the show); *New York World*, Sept. 14, 1892 (Brooklyn opening); *New York Dramatic Mirror*, Oct. 22, 1892 ("poor business" in Selma, AL; "empty chairs" in New Orleans); *New York Clipper*, Nov. 12, 1892 (show closes). The Julians hailed from Oakland, CA, not from Australia as some sources state. See "The Julians of Oakland," *San Francisco Call*, Nov. 25, 1895.

Rose Julian (real name Rosalie Samwells) was remarkably hefty for a contortionist, one hundred forty-five pounds on a five-foot-three frame in 1892. Other female contortionists often used padding to simulate the curves that appealed to male audiences of that era but with Rose the bulges straining the seams of her outfit were real. (*Philadelphia Inquirer*, Nov. 19, 1893.) This, coupled with her pretty face, helped fuel the success of her stage act, for as the *Buffalo Morning Express* concluded on May 28, 1889, "she is not a great contortionist."

On the Fitz-Hall fight: *New York Herald*, Sept. 9, 1892 ("The price of a member"); *New York Press*, *New York World* and *Indianapolis Journal*, Mar. 9, 1893; *Buffalo Courier*, Mar. 10 (includes background on Martin Julian) and 11 (comment by Hall supporters), 1893; *Chicago Tribune*, Mar. 11, 1893 (Crescent City AC unable to pay purse); *New York World*, Nov. 2, 1893 (Bob's fight expenses); *Johnson City-Endicott Record*, Nov. 24, 1917 (Martin Julian's reminiscences). Bob's marital woes were reported in the *New York Herald*, Sept. 20 and 21 and Oct. 7, 1893; *New York Sun*, Sept. 21 and Oct. 7, 1893 and April 27, 1894; *Buffalo Express*, Sept. 23, 1893; *New York Tribune*, April 27, 1894. On Captain Glori: *National Police Gazette*, Sept. 1, 1894; *Buffalo Courier*, Feb. 26, 1895; *New York Morning Telegram*, Sept. 21, 1900; Newark Board of Trade, *Newark, N.J., Illustrated: A Souvenir of the City and its Numerous Industries* (Newark: William A. Baker, 1893), 39.

On the Corbett-Mitchell fight: *Syracuse Daily Standard*, Jan. 3, 1894 (fight might be held in woods); *National Police Gazette*, Jan. 20 and Feb. 17, 1894; *New York Press*, Jan. 21, 1894 ("greatest ring battle"); *New York World*, Jan. 7 (Electric Cloud Projector) and 23-26, 1894; *New York Herald*, Jan. 21, 25 ("This town never saw") and 26, 1894; *Philadelphia Inquirer*, Jan. 26 and 27 ("Brandy was not old enough"), 1894; *Reading* (PA) *Eagle*, Jan. 26, 1894; *Aurora* (IL) *Daily Express*, Jan. 26, 1894; Corbett, *Roar of the Crowd*, 209-20. Jim insisted that the purse be in cash so that it would not go unpaid if the authorities intervened. By prior agreement, the money would go to the man referee Kelly deemed to have had the best of the fight up to that point; in the event of a draw, it would be equally divided. (*New York World*, Jan. 23, 1894.) The earliest reference I found to Corbett using a "left hook," incidentally, was in this fight against Mitchell. (*Philadelphia Inquirer*, Jan. 26, 1894.)

Corbett in *Gentleman Jack* after Mitchell fight: *Salt Lake Herald*, April 30, 1893 (play dialog); *Buffalo Express*, Mar. 30, 1894 (*Modern Society*); *Buffalo Courier*, May 15, 1894 (reprint of *London Daily Telegraph* review); Brady, *Showman*, 139.

10) THE MOVIES REACH A MINUTE

The initial steps in the Latham-Rector Kinetoscope venture can be traced in the correspondence between Otway Latham and William Gilmore and Thomas Edison in May 1894, in particular Latham to Gilmore, May 16, 1894, TAED D9427AAD (Otway's order of ten machines); Gilmore to Latham, May 19, 1894, TAED D9427AAE (order accepted); Latham to

Edison, May 25, 1894, TAED D9427AAF ("strips of 100 to 150 feet"; Dickson's comment re. "bonanza").

On Jack McAuliffe: *Buffalo Courier*, Jan. 18, 1894; *Brooklyn Daily Eagle*, Aug. 23, 1894. Mike Leonard background: *New York World*, May 10, 1893 ("What d'ye think of the coat?") and *Brooklyn Daily Eagle*, April 16, 1934. On the proposed Young Griffo-Lavinge matchup and the Leonard-Cushing fight: *New York Sun*, June 16 and Aug. 4, 1894; *New York World*, June 16, 1894; *New York Journal*, June 16, 1894, clipping at TAED SC94009C; *Elmira* (NY) *Daily Gazette and Free Press*, June 27, 1894 ("draw blood if possible"); Hendricks, *Kinetoscope*, 88-97; Streible, *Fight Pictures*, 29-34; Spehr, *Movies*, 338; Musser, *Emergence of Cinema*, 82-83; Dickson and Dickson, "Kineto-Phonograph," 210 (Dickson tries artificial lighting). A small portion of the Leonard-Cushing fight film survives, an unidentified round. It can be viewed on the Library of Congress website www.loc.gov.

Jack Cushing may have been a more romantic figure than previously thought. In Ham's Fork, Wyoming in January 1889, a recently arrived "pugilist from Pittsburg" named Jack Cushing ran off with Alice Bloodgood, the wife of a mine foreman. The woman's husband, Calvin Bloodgood, accompanied by a posse of miners, chased down the couple before they reached the railroad. Calvin begged Alice to return and for a moment she wavered, asking, "Will you let Jack go?" When Calvin refused, Alice drew a pistol and killed him. She and Jack fled on horseback into the night and were believed to have boarded a train heading east. (*New York Herald* and *Sacramento Daily Union*, Jan. 21, 1889; *Utica Weekly Herald*, Jan. 22, 1889.)

On Rector's "Special Kinetoscope": Rector to Edison Manufacturing Co., July 30, 1894, TAED D9427AAH; "The Edison Kinetoscope," *The Electrical Engineer*, Nov. 7, 1894, 377 (diagrams of interior of standard Kinetoscope); Hendricks, *Kinetoscope*, 15-16, 88-91 and Illustration 55; Phillips, *Edison's Kinetoscope*, 27-35; Ramsaye, *Nights*, 108. Ramsaye states that Rector did the work "at the Edison plant," not in the Edison lab. This would have come from Rector himself, he being Ramsaye's primary informant on the Latham-Rector prizefight film venture.

After the flurry of coverage of his divorce in Oct. 1893, Bob Fitzsimmons' name largely disappeared from newspapers for several months. His renewed challenge to Corbett was reported in the *San Francisco Call*, Feb. 14, 1894 ("I'll go into a room"). Corbett's response: *Syracuse Daily Standard*, Feb. 15, 1894 ("Really, I wish people"); *Philadelphia Inquirer*, Feb. 18, 1894 ("I will never fight Fitzsimmons"). On the Fitz-Choynski fight: *New York Sun, Boston Daily Globe, Buffalo Evening News, Sacramento Daily Union* and *Seattle Post-Intelligencer* (Martin Julian mentioned as being in Fitz's corner), June 19, 1894 and *Boston Post*, June 20, 1894 (gate was $4,000). Fitz marries Rose: *New York Evening World*, June 25,

1894 and *National Police Gazette*, July 14, 1894. Fitz forms new theatrical company: *New York Clipper*, Aug. 11, 1894. Glori becomes Fitz's partner: *New York Morning Telegraph*, Sept. 21, 1900. Glori resigns from police force: *New York Herald*, Sept. 27, 1894.

In the final months prior to her retirement from the stage, Rose did her contortionist act with her brother Martin. It is interesting to note, as a sidelight on body image in this very different era, that she weighed 175 lbs at this point and Martin was himself quite chubby. (Article on Rose in *Philadelphia Inquirer*, Nov. 19, 1893.) John L. Sullivan was an ardent suitor of Rose's before Bob came along. "She was a peach," Sullivan recalled in 1901. "I had it all fixed with the old lady, her mother, who used to travel with her, for me to pay my addresses to Rose, but once when loaded I tried to talk sweet to the girl and it was all off." (*St. Louis Republic*, Feb. 21, 1901.)

On 83 Nassau St. parlor: Streible, *Fight Pictures*, 31 (handbill); *New York Press*, Aug. 4, 1894 (notice of opening); *New York Sun*, Aug. 4, 1894 (firsthand account of visit) and Aug. 14, 1894 (review); Hendricks, *Kinetoscope*, 97-100; Ramsaye, *Nights*, 109-10.

11) CORBETT-COURTNEY

On Corbett's return from England: *New York Sun* and *Herald*, Aug. 2, 1894. Also: Brady, *Showman*, 139 ("The English public"); *New York Press*, Aug. 8, 1894 ("Corbett made a mistake"); *New York Dramatic Mirror*, Sept. 1, 1894 (*Gentleman Jack* opens in Trenton); Woods, "James J. Corbett: Theatrical Star," 171-73.

It was reported in the press that Otway Latham contacted John L. Sullivan first to appear before the Kinetograph but dropped the idea when the ex-champ demanded $25,000. (*Chicago Tribune*, Sept. 10, 1894.) On Otway's communication with Corbett: *New York Sun*, Aug. 10, 1894; *New York Journal*, Aug. 10, 1894, clipping at TAED SC94027A (Otway's letter to Brady and Brady's reply); *New York World*, Sept. 8, 1894. Kinetoscope Exhibiting Co. incorporation notice: *New York Times*, Aug. 17, 1894. The fact that Corbett received royalties from the film came to light when the weekly payments—totaling $13,347 by Aug. 1895—stopped and Corbett took the KEC to court. (*New York Herald*, April 17, 1896 and April 5, 1898; *San Francisco Call*, April 18, 1896.) See also Musser, *Emergence of Cinema*, 84. On Courtney's earlier bout with Fitz: *New York Sun*, Oct. 3, 1894 ("clinching and sprinting"). Courtney on how he was chosen to fight Corbett: *New York Herald*, Oct. 14, 1894.

On the Corbett-Courtney fight: *New York Sun* and *World*, Sept. 8, 1894 (most detailed accounts); *New York Herald*, *New York Evening Telegram*, *Brooklyn Daily Eagle* and *Syracuse Daily Journal*, same date, and *Syracuse Standard*, Sept. 9, 1894. That much of the fight reportage was a publicity stunt was revealed by New Jersey journalist G. Wilfred Pearce in a letter to the *Boston Advertiser*, Sept. 18, 1894. "Corbett did not receive $1 for his services," Pearce stated. "He tendered his services and presented $25 to the Trenton man [Courtney] who was not knocked out until later in the day, when John Barleycorn, champion of the world, knocked him out in a Newark café." Other sources: Spehr, *Movies*, 347-50; Hendricks, *Kinetoscope*, 100-09; Musser, *Emergence of Cinema*, 83-84. Corbett makes no mention of the fight in *Roar of the Crowd*. Brady in *Showman*, 160-61, admits that it was a "phony fight" but gives a fanciful account.

Peter Courtney went on to enjoy a brief period of modest fame following his bout against Corbett, partnering with Peter Maher for exhibition fights in Hoboken and Philadelphia. In their Phillie appearance on Oct. 27, 1894 he "showed the white feather by falling down without being hit," fueling what the *Inquirer* called "a lingering suspicion that Peter Courtney 'laid down' to Jim Corbett.... [T]he fact that [Courtney] was afraid to stand up before Peter Maher makes it look as if Corbett and Courtney had an understanding." (*Philadelphia Inquirer*, Oct. 29, 1894.) The pair's performance two days later was called a "laughable setto. Maher landed when and where he pleased and he could have put Courtney out in a punch. Courtney has no science and there are a carload of middleweights in this city who can beat him." (*Ibid.*, Oct. 30, 1894.) Courtney did not long live after that. He died of consumption on May 11, 1896 at the age of twenty-eight. (*Brooklyn Daily Eagle* and *Auburn* [NY] *Daily Bulletin*, May 15, 1896.)

On the legal fallout: *New York Times*, Sept. 9 and 12, 1894; *New York World* ("I shouldn't be surprised") and *Brooklyn Daily Eagle*, Sept. 12, 1894; *Newark Evening News*, Sept. 12, 1894, quoted in Hendricks, *Kinetoscope*, 109 ("I was not there"); *New York Commercial Advertiser*, Sept. 14, 1894, TAED SC94028A (Edison subpoenaed).

That the Corbett-Courtney film debuted in late September (Sat., Sept. 22, 1894 is a likely date) is evident from a telegram from Otway Latham to William Gilmore, Sept. 26, 1894, TAED D9427AAS: "Please have another set of Corbett films as soon as possible. [signed] Latham." The later date of Nov. 17, 1894 erroneously given in many sources as the film's release date was when copyright was granted. According to *The Pharmaceutical Era*, Nov. 15, 1894, 452, "Otway Latham...is understood to be largely interested financially in the kinetoscope. A drug trade man tells the writer that at one of the kinetoscope places downtown [presumably the Broadway parlor] $180 a day has been taken in regularly." This figure seems impossibly high assuming a nickel per machine, the price charged for Leonard-Cushing, but would have been attainable if the price was a dime.

On Kinetoscope Exhibiting Co. developments: Otway Latham to William Gilmore, Sept. 24, 1894, TAED D9427AAR (films breaking); *The Pharmaceutical Era*, Aug. 15, 1894, 163 ("business is picking up") and Oct. 1, 1894, 308 (Tilden Co. John St. office closed); *New York Herald*, Dec. 13, 1894 (ad seeking cashier for restaurant at 83 Nassau, suggesting Kinetoscope parlor was closed); "Extract from Minutes of Kinetoscope

Exhibiting Company," attached to J. H. Cox to William Gilmore, Oct. 30, 1894, TAED D9427AAW; certified contract signed by Otway Latham assigning rights to KEC, dated Aug. 24, 1894, TAED D9427ABD; Tilden to Gilmore, Oct. 15, 1894, TAED D9427AAU; Gilmore to Cox, Nov. 7, 1894, TAED D9427AAZ; Cox to Gilmore, Nov. 11, 1894, TAED D9427ABA.

12) CHALLENGE ACCEPTED

Fitz's comments on Corbett-Courtney fight film: *San Francisco Call*, Jan. 17, 1895; *National Police Gazette*, Jan. 26, 1895. Fitz-Creedon fight: *New York Herald*, Aug. 14 (articles signed; "I've Fitz where I want him") and Sept. 27 ("he just cannot beat me"), 1894; *San Francisco Call*, Sept. 20, 1894 ("I invented that blow"); *New York Sun*, *New York World*, *Indianapolis Journal* and *San Francisco Call*, Sept. 27, 1894 (fight coverage); *Los Angeles Herald*, Sept. 29, 1894 (wrist blow); *National Police Gazette*, Oct. 13, 1894. Scholl cable to Corbett with Fitz's challenge: *San Francisco Morning Call*, Sept. 27, 1894.

The public exchange between Fitz and Corbett was chronicled in the *New York Sun*, Sept. 28, 1894 (Fitz's first letter to Corbett, dated New Orleans, Sept. 27); *Los Angeles Herald*, Sept. 29, 1894 ("If Mr. Corbett will say"; Corbett's first letter, dated Sept. 28, in which he calls Choynski and Creedon "second-class"; Sullivan's comment and Corbett's response) and *Buffalo Evening News*, Oct. 2, 1894 (Fitz's second letter to Corbett, Corbett's response and Scholl's ultimatum). Other sources: *New York Evening Telegram*, Sept. 29, 1894 ("lie"; Corbett "childish" with "streak of yellow"); *New York Herald*, Sept. 29 (editorial denouncing Corbett) and Oct. 4, 1894 (Corbett accepts challenge; Fitz's delight). A preliminary meeting took place between Fitz/Capt. Glori and William Brady on Oct. 1 but was little more than a shouting match, the word "cur" being thrown about. (*San Francisco Morning Call*, Oct. 2, 1894; *National Police Gazette*, Oct. 20, 1894.) Verbatim records of Oct. 11 Corbett-Fitz meeting are in *New York Evening Telegram*, Oct. 11, 1894 and *New York Herald* and *World*, Oct. 12, 1894. Reaction in Jacksonville: *New York Evening Telegram*, Oct. 12, 1894 (including *Florida Citizen* editorial).

Gray Latham's offer for Corbett-Fitz fight: *New York World*, Oct. 26, 1894; *New York Press*, Oct. 27, 1894; *New York Clipper*, Nov. 3, 1894. Fitz's response: *Syracuse Daily Standard*, Dec. 19, 1894 ("Why, that just suits me") and *National Police Gazette*, Jan. 5, 1895 ("Just think of $50,000"). Brady rejects offer: *New York Herald*, Dec. 28, 1894 ("Fitzsimmons has never had any experience"). According to *New York Press*, Oct. 28, 1894, "No larger bona fide offer has ever been made for a fight and none ever carried such strong inducements.... [The KEC offer to hold the fight in Mexico] is a most flattering and alluring proposition viewed from any standpoint." Gray also approached John L. Sullivan about filming a bout between him and Peter Maher. Although Sullivan had now warmed to the idea of having his image preserved "so that future generations may see him in the ring as well as Corbett," he demanded too much money and no deal was reached. (*Oswego Daily Times*, Nov. 8, 1894.)

Corbett's and Fitz's touring dates with their shows through the fall and winter of 1894-95 were tracked in *New York Dramatic Mirror* ("Corbett has improved" quote Sept. 8, 1894). Fitz "doing a very light business": *Oswego* (NY) *Daily Times*, Nov. 8, 1894. Fitz's hiring of Riordan noted in *New York Clipper*, Nov. 3, 1894. On death of Riordan: *Syracuse Evening Herald* ("Poor Conny!"), *Syracuse Daily Journal* ("Dunfee! Dunfee!"), *Syracuse Daily Standard* and *Brooklyn Daily Eagle*, Nov. 17, 1894; *Syracuse Sunday Herald* ("Go easy a bit"; "never put on a glove again"), *New York Press*, *New York Sun* ("disgusted"), *New York Herald*, *Chicago Tribune*, Nov. 18, 1894; *Syracuse Daily Journal* and *New York Press*, Nov. 23, 1894; *New York Herald*, Nov. 24, 1894 (coroner's inquest); *Chicago Tribune*, Dec. 24, 1894 (Fitz's account of incident); *Syracuse Courier*, Jan. 21, 1895 (indictment); *Syracuse Evening Herald*, July 3, 1895 ("monkey punch"). Totman's questionable reexamination of Riordan's brain was revealed in Bob's subsequent trial.

13) EUGENE LAUSTE'S LOOP

On the Lathams' projection venture: Woodville Latham testimony in Equity 5/167, Motion Picture Patents Co. v. Independent Moving Picture Co., April 25, 1911, Edison archives, TENHP; Emil Kleinert testimony in *ibid.*, June 15, 1911; Woodville Latham testimony in Woodville Latham v. Thomas Armat, Dec. 4, 1897, quoted in Musser, *Emergence of Cinema*, 92 ("I said to my son"); *Richmond Dispatch*, Dec. 29, 1894 (Lambda Co. incorporation); Thomas Armat to Earl Theisen, June 24, 1932, TAED X319AC (Edison's views on projection). Dickson's involvement with the Lathams: Dickson to Eugene Lauste, July 4, 1932, MC Papers, reel 1 ("If they had only known"); Dickson to Dyer & Seely (Edison's law firm), June 21, 1894, TAED LB061115 (Dickson transfers copyrights to Edison); Edison to Norman Raff, Feb. 5, 1895, TAED LB061413 (Edison objects to Dickson as "co-inventor"); Woodville Latham testimony in Patent Interference 18,641, Latham v. Casler v. Armat, 1897, in Spehr, *Movies*, 368 ("exhibited a morbid dread"). First private demonstration of Pantoptikon: *New York Sun* and *World*, April 22, 1895. Woodville's response to Edison: *New York Sun*, April 23, 1895.

Secondary sources for this chapter: Musser, *Emergence of Cinema*, 91-100; Ramsaye, *Nights*, 118-25 and 128-33; Ramsaye, "The Romantic History of the Motion Picture," *Photoplay*, May 1922, 32-35 and 95-98; Robinson, *Peep Show*, 53-55; Spehr, *Movies*, 356-75.

My main source on Eugene Lauste was the mass of unpublished material in the MC Papers, reel 2, which includes Lauste's typewritten memoirs and answers to questions sent him by Merritt Crawford and an unpublished biography of Lauste by Crawford, all circa 1930. Additional sources: *New York Sun*, April 15, 1890 (Lauste's wife runs off with boarder); John Randolph to Lauste, Mar. 16, 1892, TAED LB053170 (Lauste fired by Edison); Lauste testimony in Equity 5/167, Motion Picture Patents Co. v. Independent Moving Picture Co., April 6 and 7, 1911, Edison archives, TENHP; Spehr, "Eugene Augustin Lauste," 18–38.

On Rector's break with the Lathams and subsequent KEC reorganization: Ramsaye, *Nights*, 121; Samuel Tilden to William Gilmore, Sept. 2, 1895, TAED D9515AAB (redesigned KEC letterhead listing company officers). On Lathams' lawsuit: *New York Evening Telegram*, Feb. 18, 1895; *New York Tribune*, Feb. 24, 1895; Supreme Court, County of New York, General Term, First Dept., decision for Latham et. al. v. Tilden et. al., June 14, 1895, *The New York Supplement, Containing the Decisions of the Supreme, Superior, and Lower Courts of Record of New York State*, vol. 34, p. 1142; *New York Sun*, June 19, 1930 (letter to the editor from KEC lawyer Charles Brodek giving particulars of case).

Dickson would credit Lauste for the invention of the "Latham Loop." In a letter to Lauste in 1932, he wrote: "On those Lathams claiming your clever independent work & your famous adjunct of a 'Loop'—no, <u>you indeed knew that neither by word or action did I disclose any of our Edison lab. work</u>. I expect you often wondered why I hung around, never helping you or them." (Dickson to Lauste, July 4, 1932, MC Papers, reel 1, underlining in original.) It is telling that Dickson's first concern here was not to highlight Lauste's achievement but to assert that he himself had not been disloyal to Edison.

On Dickson's break with Edison: Dickson to Merritt Crawford, Aug. 10, 1932, MC Papers, reel 1; Dickson to Eugene Lauste, July 4, 1932, MC Papers, reel 1 ("The Lathams did work hard"); Dickson testimony in Equity 5/167, Motion Picture Patents Co. v. Independent Moving Picture Co., April 11, 1911, Edison archives, TENHP ("I soon became disgusted"); Spehr, *Movies*, 370-72 and 390-91.

14) GRIFFO-BARNETT PROJECTED

On Young Griffo: *Riverine Grazier*, July 4, 1893 ("perfect garden of ruffianism"); *Sydney Truth*, May 14, 1899 ("anything but aromatic"); *Adelaide Chronicle*, Sept. 7, 1933 ("as elusive"); *Sydney Referee*, May 17, 1893 (departs for America) and Jan. 18, 1928; *Sydney Truth*, quoted in *Warwick Examiner and Times*, May 27, 1893 ("one of the liveliest crowds"); *Illustrated Sydney News*, May 20, 1893 ("[O]ur joy"); *Maitland Weekly Mercury*, Dec. 17, 1927. Other Griffo sources: "Ring History of the Near-Champions. Chapter LXXXIII: Young Griffo," *National Police Gazette*, Mar. 4, 1922; Fleischer, *Young Griffo* (contains no mention of the Latham film); Richard Broome, "Griffiths, Albert (1871–1927)," *Australian Dictionary of Biography*, vol. 9, online at http://adb.anu.edu.au/biography/griffiths-albert-6487.

Griffo fight at Manhattan AC: *New York Press* and *World* and *Brooklyn Eagle*, Mar. 27, 1895. The *Eagle* reported the Griffo film deal on Mar. 29, 1895 ("More Honors for Griffo: He Will Shortly Appear Before Edison's Kinetoscope"). Griffo-Corbett altercation: *Chicago Tribune*, April 1, 1895.

On Charley Barnett: US Federal Census records for 1880 and 1900; *Trow's New York City Directory*, 1888-95; *New York Sun*, Mar. 13, 1895 (Leonard fight); various small items in New York newspapers starting in 1893 noting Barnett's fights. Nowhere in these 1890s sources, incidentally, is Charley referred to as "Battling" Barnett, the nickname first ascribed to him by Ramsaye in *A Million and One Nights* and now attached to the film, *Young Griffo vs. Battling Barnett*. There was a boxer active in the 1920s, when Ramsaye was writing, named Morris "Battling" Barnett.

On the Griffo-Barnett fight: *New York Evening World*, May 4, 1895; *New York World*, May 5, 1895; *Brooklyn Daily Eagle*, May 5 and 8, 1895; *New York Herald*, *New York Sun* and *Rome* (NY) *Citizen*, May 7, 1895. Debut of Griffo-Barnett film: *New York World*, May 26, 1895. The fight took place atop the second iteration of Madison Square Garden, completed in 1890 and demolished in 1924.

It has been stated in a number of sources that: 1) the Griffo-Barnett fight was a restaging of an earlier bout the two fought in MSG; 2) that it was six rounds, not four; and 3) that it ended in a knockout. This is all incorrect. I have found no evidence that Griffo and Barnett ever met outside their filmed encounter. The misconception that it was six rounds started with the mistaken headline in the *New York Herald*, "Young Griffo and Barnett Fight Six Rounds Before the Panopticon," but the article itself, together with every other newspaper report, gives the actual duration as four rounds. As for the KO claim, the *New York World*, May 5, 1895 specifically stated that "the four rounds were decidedly lively and Griffo did his best to get in a knock-out, but failed."

Only the *New York World*, May 26, 1895 noted the debut of the Griffo-Barnett film. The *World* gives the opening date as "Monday last" (May 20), although Saturday (i.e. May 18, as written on the ticket) was a more usual day for theatrical openings. The story of the first movie ticket was told in Grant Dixon's column "Lights of New York," *Ossining* (NY) *Citizen-Sentinel*, July 18, 1930: "C. B. Braunstein, formerly of Cincinnati, writes me from California that he has what is supposed to be the first paid admission ticket to the first picture show in New York. The ticket reads: 'IDOLOSCOPE, Exhibition No. 1, The Lamda Co., Admit One.' On the back of the ticket is written: 'Otway Latham, May 18, 156 Broadway, 1st paid admission.' But unfortunately no year is given. Perhaps somebody can supply it." This suggests that Braunstein (1852-1934) did not attend the screening himself but rather came to possess the ticket later. The misspellings "Idoloscope" and "Lamda" may be due to Dixon misreading Braunstein's presumably handwritten letter.

On the Eidoloscope: *Arizona Silver Belt*, Aug. 3, 1895 (description of early exhibition); *New York Herald*, July 22, 1895 (on Coney Island); *New York Sun*, July 19, 1895 (wrestling matches filmed); *Richmond Dispatch*, Oct. 28, 1895 (LeRoy Latham takes Eidoloscope to Virginia). Also: Ramsaye, *Nights*, 133-36, 180-91 and 290-91; Musser, *Emergence of Cinema*, 99-100; Streible, *Fight Pictures*, 45-46; Robinson, *From Peep Show to Palace*, 54-55; George Pratt, "Firsting the Firsts," *Image* 14 (Dec. 1971): 26-29. Lauste recounts his "twin camera" and the Woodville Latham projection incident in "Questioning and Answering of Mr. Eugene Lauste, Regarding the 'Invention' of Mr. Woodville Latham, the Eidoloscope," MC Papers, reel 2.

Griffo-Barnett film frame illustrations: *Brooklyn Daily Eagle*, May 8, 1895 and *New York World*, May 26, 1895. Barnett's later life: US Federal Census, 1900 and 1910. Griffo's later life: *Brooklyn Daily Eagle*, May 13, 15, 21 and 25 and Aug. 26, 1895 (arrested and jailed) and Aug. 13, 1896 (sentenced); *Sydney Truth*, May 14, 1899 (insane asylum); *Albany Evening Journal*, June 18, 1906 ("common loafer"); *Buffalo Courier Express*, May 2, 1927; *Saratogian*, Saratoga Springs, NY, Dec. 21, 1927 ("I don't know"); *New York Sun*, Dec. 7 and 8, 1927 and *Brooklyn Daily Eagle*, Dec. 8, 1927 (death).

15) ENTER DAN STUART

Jacksonville repealed its fight ordinance on Dec. 4, 1894; Florida's anti-fight bill was passed by the senate on May 6, 1895 and by the legislature on May 21. (*San Francisco Call*, Dec. 5, 1894; *New York Herald*, May 7, 1895; *Brooklyn Daily Standard Union*, May 22, 1895.) In New Orleans the Supreme Court on May 6, 1895 decided against the Olympic Club in its legal battle to host fights. "The result is a death blow to prize fights in this city," reported the *New York Herald*, May 7, 1895. Corbett-Fitz fight to be relocated: *New York Herald*, April 29, 1895 ("cast iron cinch"); *Canisteo* (NY) *Times*, June 6, 1895 (Quebec offer); *Galveston Daily News*, June 4, 1895 ("It will certainly"); *Topeka State Journal*, May 22, 1895 ("Will be in New York").

On Dan Stuart: *Galveston Daily News*, Nov. 30, 1890 ("a man whose word") and Mar. 24, 1895 (opens Dallas's first stock exchange); *Dallas Daily Times Herald*, Nov. 15, 1909 (obituary); *Memorial and Biographical History of Dallas County, Texas* (Chicago: Lewis Publishing Co., 1892), 547; *National Police Gazette*, June 22, 1895 ("nothing short of a revolution"); *Rome* (NY) *Citizen*, June 13, 1895 ("a mammoth structure"); Miletich, *Fistic Carnival*, 18-19.

The Lathams seek film rights to Corbett-Fitz fight: *New York World*, Oct. 26, 1894; *New York Press*, Oct. 28, 1894 (Gray, as KEC vice president, offers $50,000); *Clinton* (NY) *Courier*, Sept. 25, 1895 ("[A] gentleman named Latham"). Fitz demands compensation for being filmed: *Clinton* (NY) *Courier*, Sept. 25, 1895 ("Some people may think"); *Galves-*

ton Daily News, Oct. 13, 1895 ("I will insist"); *Rome* (NY) *Semi-Weekly Citizen*, Sept. 13, 1895; *St. Paul Daily Globe*, Sept. 16, 1895 ("not interested in that invention").

Rector's plans to film the fight, including specs for Kinetographs and film to be used, are detailed in William Gilmore to the Kinetoscope Exhibiting Co., Sept. 10, 1895, TAED D9516AAD. Rector's meeting with Gilmore to iron out details likely occurred on Sept. 4, according to Samuel Tilden to Gilmore, Sept. 2, 1895, TAED D9516AAC. Rector's claim to have invented the "Latham Loop": Ramsaye, *Nights*, 125. According to *El Paso Daily Times*, Feb. 27, 1896, "These [Kinetoscope] machines [for showing rounds of the Fitz-Maher fight] were to be so constructed that five people could witness the contest at one time, at a tariff of 10¢ per spectator." Also: Edison Manufacturing Co., Financial Records: General Ledger, 1893-1897, TAED CK502, p. 140 (entry for "Four Prize Fight Machines") and p. 160 (entry for "Multiscope").

Fitz's financial woes and break with Glori: *Philadelphia Inquirer*, Mar. 4 and 5 ("robbed right and left"; "financially crippled"), 1895; *New York Clipper*, Mar. 9 and 30 ("Capt. Chas. Glori"), 1895; *Buffalo Courier*, Feb. 26 (Glori rant against Fitz) and 27 ("That stationhouse story"), 1895; *Auburn* (NY) *Bulletin*, Jan. 29 and Feb. 9, 1895; *New York Evening Telegram*, Feb. 26, 1895 (Fitz and Glori nearly come to blows); *New York Herald*, Mar. 12, 1895; *New York Dramatic Mirror*, Mar. 16, 1895. Fitz trial: *Syracuse Journal, Courier* and *Evening Herald*, June 24-July 4, 1895, in particular *Herald*, July 4 (review of evidence). Also: *New York Herald*, June 25, 1895; *Buffalo Courier*, June 30, 1895; *New York Sun*, July 2, 1895; *New York Evening Telegram*, July 4, 1895.

Corbett's marital woes: *New York Herald*, July 16, 18 and 28, 1895; *New York Evening Telegram*, July 26 (divorce) and Aug. 15, 1895; *New York Herald* and *Sun*, Aug. 16, 1895; *New York Press*, Aug. 21, 1895 (marries Vera). See also Fields, *James J. Corbett*, 88-92. Nose-pulling incident: *New York Herald* and *Press*, Aug. 12, 1895 (eyewitness accounts); *Galveston Daily News*, Oct. 5 ("beastly drunk"), Oct. 6 ("this foreigner"), Oct. 7 ("Jim simply lies") and Oct. 12 ("Corbett doesn't know how"), 1895.

Corbett-Fitz fight in Dallas: *Galveston Daily News*, Oct. 13, 1895 ("electric treatment"); *Auburn* (NY) *Weekly Bulletin*, Aug. 1, 1895 (Dallas arena second largest in history); *New York Herald*, Oct. 3 ("I have been arranging") and Oct. 22 ("Will you kindly" and "[N]ow that he is compelled"), 1895; Miletich, *Fistic Carnival*, 75 ("It is all over"); *New York World*, Oct. 23, 1895 ("cur" etc.). Fight moves to Hot Springs: *Galveston Daily News*, Oct. 12 and 31, 1895; *New York Sun*, Oct. 29, 1895; *New York Herald*, Oct. 31, 1895. Fitz and Corbett arrested: *New York Telegram*, Nov. 1, 1895; *San Francisco Call*, Nov. 1 ("I want you men"), 2 and 3, 1895; *New York Clipper*, Nov. 9, 1895.

Corbett relinquishes title: *El Paso International Daily Times*, Nov. 13, 1895 ("Corbett surrenders"); Corbett, *Roar of the Crowd*, 247 ("I was so disgusted"). Fitz-Maher fight arranged: *San Francisco Call*, Nov. 4, 1895 ("eidoloscope people"); *El Paso International Daily Times*, Nov. 16, 1895; *New York Herald*, Dec. 5, 1895; *New York Sun*, Dec. 13, 1895 ("I am sure"); *New York Clipper*, Dec. 14, 1895 (fight articles signed).

16) STANDOFF IN EL PASO

On the ongoing saga of bringing off the Fitz-Maher fight: *El Paso Daily Times* and *Galveston Daily Times*, Jan. 1-Feb. 21, 1896; *New York Herald*, Jan. 12 ("It will be all over" and "Things are different"), Jan. 30 ("That man had better") and Feb. 15, 16 and 18, 1896; *National Police Gazette*, Feb. 22 and 29, 1896; *Brownsville Daily Herald*, Feb. 15, 1896; *Utica Daily Union*, Feb. 8, 1896 (Capt. Glori arrives in El Paso); *Houston Daily Post*, Feb. 2, 1896 ("good and thoroughly whipped"). Ahumada intervenes: *San Francisco Call*, Feb. 13, 1896 ("[I]f its promoters"). Fitz and Maher prepare: *National Police Gazette*, Feb. 8, 1896; *New York Herald*, Jan. 12, 16 and 30 and Feb. 14, 1896; *St. Paul Daily Globe*, Feb. 13, 1896; *San Francisco Call*, Feb. 15, 1896. Catron bill: *Washington Morning Times*, Feb. 7 ("Be it enacted") and 8, 1896; *Los Angeles Herald*, Feb. 11, 1896; *El Paso Daily Times*, Feb. 8, 1896 ("puffed toad"). The bill passed the House on Feb. 6 and Senate on Feb. 7. El Paso city council resolution against bill: *New York Herald*, Feb. 15, 1896 ("We regard"). Juarez bullfight: *New York Herald, Los Angeles Herald* ("Ask him"), *San Francisco Call* and *Galveston Daily News*, Feb. 17, 1896; *El Paso Daily Times*, Feb. 18, 1896.

Rector marries: *Parkersburg Daily State Journal*, May 2, 1895. Rector prepares to film fight: Samuel Tilden to William Gilmore, Sept. 2, 1895, TAED D9516AAC and Feb. 1, 1896, TAED D9617AAA; *Galveston Daily News*, Jan. 14, 1896 ("a malicious falsehood"); *Utica Globe*, Feb. 1, 1896 (official fight program); *El Paso Daily Times*, Feb. 1, 1896 (Eidoloscope Co. cable); Gilmore to Kinetoscope Exhibiting Co., Sept. 10, 1895, TAED D9516AAD ("have entire charge"); Gilmore to Edison, July 15, 1895, TAED D9517AAQ ("Young Heise sails for Europe this week with the Kinetograph..."); Continental Commerce Co. to Gilmore, Aug. 28, 1895, TAED D9517AAW ("unable to get any satisfaction"); Edison's handwritten note on W. Louis Sonntag Jr. to Edison, Feb. 21, 1896, TAED D9604AAQ, referring to "my regular man [in charge of lab photography] being in Mexico with Kinetoscope."

That William Heise was the Edison technician who accompanied Rector to Texas is revealed in *Catalogue of Title Entries of Books and Other Articles Entered in the Office of the Librarian of Congress*, No. 290 (Jan. 18-23, 1897), 20, where copyright is granted to Heise for photos entitled "Bull Fight," "Mexican Bull Fighters," "The Hand-Shake of Bob Fitzsimmons and Peter Maher Prize Fight" and "The Knock-Out of Bob Fitzsimmons and Peter Maher." (There is no record of these photos surviving at the LOC. According to reference librarian Julie Stoner [email to author, Mar. 16, 2016], "Many photographs that were submitted for copyright were not kept by the Library.") That Theodore Heise went along as assistant was deduced from "Theo. R. Heise European Expense a/c," July-Sept. 1895, Edison Manufacturing Co., Financial Records: General Ledger, 1893-1897, TAED CK502, p. 134, where a later entry has been appended dated Feb. 1896, the month of the Fitz-Maher fight.

The arrival of Rector and his companions in El Paso was noted in *Galveston Daily News*, Feb. 8, 1896. Weather details from *El Paso Daily Times*. Other sources on KEC involvement in fight: *Auburn* (NY) *Bulletin*, Dec. 25, 1895; *Washington Morning Times*, Feb. 7, 1896; *Brooklyn Daily Eagle*, Feb. 12, 1896. Filming materials loaded onto railcar: *Galveston Daily News*, Feb. 11, 1896. Julian confronts Rector: *Buffalo Evening News*, Feb. 12, 1896 ("I understand"). Rangers watching Rector: *New York Sun*, Feb. 13, 1896. Rector slips out of town: *Saint Paul Daily Globe*, Feb. 13, 1896; *Brownsville Daily Herald*, Feb. 14, 1896. Rector's frustration: *Galveston Daily News*, Feb. 18, 1896 ("You may say"); *New York Herald*, Feb. 20, 1896 ("Both Maher and 'Fitz'"). Attempt to film Sullivan: *El Paso Daily Times*, Feb. 16, 1896 (ad for the final performance of *Wicklow Postman*, noting that "An attempt will be made to photograph the Sullivan-[Paddy] Ryan sparring match for the Kinetoscope") and Feb. 18, 1896 ("loaded to the gunnels"). Other Rector sources: *Houston Daily Post, Los Angeles Herald* and *Oswego Daily Times*, Feb. 11, 1896; *Chatham* (NY) *Courier*, Feb. 26, 1896; *El Paso Daily Times*, Feb. 27, 1896; *Galveston Daily News*, Feb. 28, 1896 (Rector interviewed).

El Paso Daily Times, Feb. 23, 1896, noted that "Gray Latham, of New York, who has been in the city for some time, left yesterday for the City of Mexico." See also Lauste interview, MC Papers, reel 2 (re. Mexico trip).

Train departs for fight: *El Paso Daily Times* ("Those desirous"), *Galveston Daily News* ("Checks don't go"), *San Francisco Call* ("I understand that Fitzsimmons"; "dead cinch"), *New York Herald* and *Sacramento Record-Union*, Feb. 21, 1896; *New York World* ("They won't throw us") and *Brownsville Daily Herald*, Feb. 22, 1896; *New York Clipper* and *National Police Gazette*, Feb. 29, 1896.

The most comprehensive secondary source on Fitz-Maher fight is Miletich, *Fistic Carnival*, chapters 4-7. See also Streible, *Fight Pictures*, 54-57; Musser, *Emergence*, 194-95; Robinson, *Fist Fighting*, 4-21; King, "The Fight"; and Ramsaye, *Nights*, 281-84. Ramsaye's account, evidently based on an interview with Rector, is clearly embellished.

17) THE MAN INSIDE THE CAMERA

On the Fitz-Maher fight: *New York Sun*, Feb. 10 (Maher's scarred legs) and 22, 1896; *New York World* and *San Francisco Call*, Feb. 22, 1896; *New*

York Herald, El Paso Daily Times and *Galveston Daily Times*, Feb. 22 and 23, 1896; *Brownsville Daily Herald*, Feb. 22 and 24, 1896; *New York Times*, Feb. 22 and 29, 1896; *Houston Daily Post*, Feb. 22 and Mar. 15, 1896; *New York Clipper* and *National Police Gazette*, Feb. 29, 1896. Secondary sources: Miletich, *Fistic Carnival*, chapter 8; Robinson, *Fist Fighting*, 22-26; Odd, *Fighting Blacksmith*, 113-17.

Rector's story: *New York Herald*, Feb. 23, 1896 (Rector's pre-fight conference with Stuart re. weather and batteries); *New York World*, Feb. 22, 1896 ("Kinetoscope Scheme Failed"); *Chatham* (NY) *Courier*, Feb. 26, 1896; *El Paso Daily Times*, Feb. 27, 1896 (Stuart-KEC deal); William Gilmore to Kinetoscope Exhibiting Co., Sept. 10, 1895, TAED D9516AAD (Kinetograph and film specs); Ramsaye, *Nights*, 282-84; *El Paso Daily Times*, Feb. 23 (Gray Latham leaves for Mexico) and Feb. 26, 1896 (Rector films bullfight); *Galveston Daily News*, Feb. 28, 1896 ("the most bloody"); Eugene Lauste interview, MC Papers, reel 2 ("not very respectable"). Of the 25,000 feet of film Rector took to Texas, 20,000 was returned for a refund. (Kinetoscope Exhibiting Co., Memoranda, TAED D9516AAG.)

El Paso Daily Times, Feb. 27, 1896 included a report detailing how the KEC had been "primarily responsible" for the Fitz-Maher fight, putting up the purse and paying the forfeit money for the cancelled undercard bouts in addition to promising Stuart "a very liberal sum" and twenty percent of the profits if the filming succeeded. The promised "liberal sum" and profit-sharing was true; the fronting of the purse and forfeit money was not. As Rector stated during a stop in Dallas on his way home, "We have never given a single cent, either directly or indirectly toward the purses of the fights. Our contract was Mr. Stuart was entirely on a percentage basis, for the right to photograph the fight. Of course we had to take chances of getting sunshine, and the great cost of our machines, about $17,000, was risk enough for us to assume. This amount would have been a clear loss to us had we failed to catch the bull fight. This we got. Mr. Stuart did not allow us any say so at all in regard to the arrangements, and had we paid him anything for his privilege we would at least have requested a postponement until a bright day." (*Galveston Daily News*, Feb. 28, 1896.)

Background on Langtry and on Roy Bean's involvement in the fight: Skiles, *Judge Roy Bean Country*, 28-37; Sonnichsen, *Roy Bean*, 174-89; McDaniel, *Vinegarroon*, 126-33; White, "Judge Roy Bean"; King, "Fight". On Texas Ranger involvement and "Wild West" side of the Fitz-Maher story: Webb, *Texas Rangers*, 444-46; Weiss, *Yours to Command*, 101-18; Paine, *Captain Bill McDonald*, 194-98; DeArment, *Bat Masterson*, 348-50.

18) NEW FIGHT, NEW MACHINES

Fitz on Corbett: *Galveston Daily Times*, Feb. 23, 1896 ("I shall completely ignore"). Fitz's vaudeville show: *New York Herald*, Feb. 29, 1896; *Buffalo Courier*, Mar. 15, 1896 (ad); *New York Dramatic Mirror*, April 25, 1896.

Nero's death: *San Francisco Call* and *Brooklyn Daily Eagle*, April 17, 1896; *The Ring*, Sydney, June 25, 1896 (quoting Cleveland newspaper).

Corbett winds up *Naval Cadet* tour and heads to Frisco: *Los Angeles Herald*, May 4, 1896; *Salt Lake Herald*, May 28, 1896 ("It's this way"); *San Francisco Call*, May 31 and June 2, 1896. Sharkey's challenge: *San Francisco Call*, June 7, 1896 ("[C]an't a person"). Corbett-Sharkey fight: *Sacramento Daily Union* and *New York Sun*, June 25, 1896; *San Francisco Call*, June 25 and 26 ("the foulest fighter"), 1896; *Los Angeles Herald*, June 27, 1896 ("simply butcher Sharkey"). Numerous women tried to buy tickets to the fight but were refused, a National Athletic Club spokesman commenting that "It isn't their place." (*San Francisco Call*, June 19, 1896.)

On the demise of the KEC: *New York Herald*, April 5 and 17, 1896; *San Francisco Call*, April 18, 1896 (Corbett lawsuit); *Paterson* (NJ) *Morning Call*, June 7, 1898 (notice of KEC unpaid taxes going back to 1895). Distribution of Leonard-Cushing and Corbett-Courtney fight films went to Raff and Gammon. See Rector to Edison Manufacturing Co., April 6, 1896, TAED D9617AAD and Raff and Gammon to William Gilmore, April 10, 1896, TAED D9619AAA. The incorporation of Kineto-Multiscope Co. was noted in *Indexes to Corporate Filings* in the New Jersey State Archives.

On Rector and the Veriscope: *Boston Daily Globe*, April 10, 1897 (Gilmore recalls refusing Rector's request to alter Edison camera); Ramsaye, *Nights*, 284-86; *The Phonoscope*, Dec. 1896, 13; *The Great Sound Money Parade in New York* (New York: Republic Press, 1897); Ackerman, *George Eastman*, 126-27 (Eastman Kodak's new negative and positive Ciné film). Ramsaye doesn't mention Stuart in relation to arranging the Corbett-Fitz fight, instead crediting Rector (his information source), with playing a key role. For some of the other projectors that had entered the market by late 1896, see *The Phonoscope*, Nov. 1896, 12 and Musser, *Emergence of Cinema*, 109-18 and 133-45.

The Eidoloscope: *New York Tribune* and *World*, May 8, 1896 (bullfight film ads); *New York Dramatic Mirror*, July 25, 1896 (bullfight film in *Carmen*); *Indianapolis Journal*, Jan. 3, 1897 (review); *New York Herald*, Aug. 2, 1896 (Eidoloscope Co. office and equipment seized); *Brooklyn Daily Eagle*, Aug. 2, 1896 (company fails); *New York Times*, Oct. 7, 1896; Ramsaye, *Nights*, 290-95. The bullfight film was initially advertised as being twenty minutes long; the *New York Sun* write-up, May 8, 1896, specified seventeen minutes; reports of screenings during *Carmen* stated fifteen minutes. According to Woodville Latham, half the bullfight film was ruined when one of the "dark boxes" into which the undeveloped reels were packed was opening during shipment back to New York. (Woodville Latham testimony in Equity 5/167, April 29, 1911.) The Latham patent containing the crucial "Latham Loop" was acquired by the Anthony Co. in 1896, following the Eidoloscope Co.'s demise, and later by the American Mutoscope and Biograph Co. in 1908. (Spehr, *Movies*, 626, n. 944.)

Fitz challenges Corbett: *New York Evening Telegram*, Sept. 11, 1896. Corbett and Fitz meet: *New York Evening Telegram*, Sept. 12, 1896; *New York Herald*, Sept. 12 and 13 ("I read of your challenge"), 1896. Indictments and arrest: *New York Evening Post*, Sept. 19, 1896; *New York Evening Telegram*, Sept. 21, 1896; *New York Press*, Sept. 22, 1896.

Fitz-Sharkey fight: *San Francisco Call* and *Examiner*, Dec. 3 and 4, 1896; *New York World* ("I have given in"), *New York Sun* and *Brooklyn Daily Standard*, Dec. 3, 1896. Women were allowed at the fight. On the legal battle that followed: *San Francisco Call*, Dec. 10 (Sharkey trainers testify) and Dec. 18 (judge's decision), 1896; *Brooklyn Daily Standard*, Dec. 9, 1896; *New York World*, Dec. 11, 1896. It was alleged that Sharkey's groin injury from Fitz's alleged low blow was in fact administered in his hotel room after the fight. A mysterious "Dr. Lee" examined him in private and Sharkey was heard to groan in pain through the locked door. Then a team of doctors was sent for to examine the swelling. (*Brooklyn Daily Eagle*, Dec. 4, 1896.)

Veriscope in California: *Sacramento Daily Record-Union*, Dec. 7, 8 (voltage trouble), 9, 11 ("water bath"), 12, 15 (picture improved) and 17, 1896; *San Francisco Call*, Jan. 1, 1897 (Santa Cruz show). Veriscope in Hawaii: *Honolulu Evening Bulletin*, Feb. 4, 1897 ("Edison's Veriscope!"); *Hawaiian Star*, Feb. 4 and 6, 1897 (reviews); *Pacific Commercial Advertiser*, Feb. 12, 1897 (Veriscope proceeds to Hilo).

Corbett-Fitz fight articles signed: *New York Herald*, Dec. 18, 1896 (Corbett signs); *New York Herald* and *World*, Jan. 5, 1897 (Fitz signs). Passage of Nevada prizefighting bill and choice of Carson City: *Carson City News*, Jan. 14 ("not as brutal as football"), Jan. 23, Feb. 1 ("I do hate to see") and Feb. 5, 1897; *Carson City Morning Appeal*, Jan. 27 ("Let us have what benefits"), Jan. 30 (prizefight bill) and Jan. 31, 1897; *New York Herald*, Jan. 29, 1897 ("Nothing less than the death"); *San Francisco Call*, Feb. 2, 1897 ("make Stuart's head swim"); *San Francisco Chronicle*, Feb. 2-4 and 10, 11 and 12, 1897; *San Francisco Examiner*, Mar. 8, 1897 (chaplain's comment); *Saint Paul Globe*, Jan. 13 and Feb. 12, 1897; *Washington Evening Times*, Jan. 27 and 29 and Feb. 2, 1897. The Nevada prizefight bill passed the lower house by a vote of 20 to 9 and the senate by 9 to 6.

19) CARSON CITY

There was massive press coverage in the month prior to the fight, mid-February to March 16, 1897, of Corbett and Fitz in training—coverage that included the minutest details of what they were doing, saying, eating and feeling, along with all the goings-on in Carson City. These wonderfully detailed firsthand reports were my main source for this chapter, especially those in the *San Francisco Examiner*, *Chronicle* and *Call*; the *New York Herald*, *World*, *Sun* and *Clipper*; the *Brooklyn Daily Eagle*, *Carson City News* and *Carson City Morning Appeal*.

Of particular note on Corbett: *San Francisco Examiner*, Feb. 22 (pummeling Woods), Feb. 24 and Mar. 6 (letters received), Mar. 1 (Fitz "a wild man") and Mar. 16 (anxiety), 1897; *San Francisco Chronicle*, Feb. 16 (Fitz "a rat"), Feb. 18 (training camp description), Feb. 27 (Brady calls Julian "an ass"), Feb. 28 (snow knocked off roof), Mar. 1 (Jeffries sparring), Mar. 8 (meals), Mar. 12 and 16 (Brady and Julian meetings) and Mar. 14 ("sizing-up business"), 1897; *New York Sun*, Mar. 7, 1897 (Jeffries KO); *Carson City Morning Appeal*, Mar. 16, 1897 (Corbett's temper); Brady, *Fighting Man*, 139-44; Brady, *Showman*, 171-73; Corbett, *Roar of the Crowd*, 250-58; Miletich, *Fistic Carnival*, 194-95 (good-luck charms).

On Fitz: *Brooklyn Daily Eagle*, Feb. 20, 1897 (Julian to get up a "push"); *New York World*, Mar. 8 (dreams) and Mar. 12 ("I knocked it flat"), 1897; *New York Sun*, Mar. 6, 1897 (Fitz battered); *San Francisco Chronicle*, Feb. 21 (arrival in Carson), Feb. 24 (Julian fears poison) and Mar. 7 (Fitz in training; camp description), 1897; *San Francisco Examiner*, Mar. 3 and 4 (hate mail; Fitz playful), Mar. 6 (Fitz's battered face), Mar. 11 (Corbett encounter on road), Mar. 13 ("We give way as usual"), Mar. 14 (good luck charms; "I am a little boy") and Mar. 17 (Earp encounter), 1897; *New York Herald*, Mar. 4, 1897 (Fitz drinking spree); *New York Telegram*, Mar. 17, 1897 ("put him in furs"); Charley White, "Inside the Ring with the Great Fighters," *Syracuse Herald*, June 13, 1911 (Fitz's hot sauce and other dietary predilections).

On Stuart: *San Francisco Chronicle*, Mar. 4 (Masterson to police arena), Mar. 12 (arena construction), Mar. 13 (robbery rumor) and Mar. 14 (Law and Order League), 1897; *New York Sun*, Mar. 9, 1897 (arena construction); *San Francisco Call*, Mar. 17, 1897 (arena diagram); George Siler and Lou Houseman, *The Fight of the Century*, 45 and 57 (morphine withdrawal); Miletich, *Fistic Carnival*, 195.

Rector negotiated the huge purchase of film from Eastman Kodak on Dec. 30, 1896, as detailed in Henry Strong to George Eastman, Dec. 31, 1896, quoted in Ackerman, *George Eastman*, 124. Strong writes in his letter: "You may have taken some large orders for Ciné film, but I propose to knock you silly. I spent all of yesterday forenoon negotiating a contract for 300,000 feet of 2½ inch film to be taken within six months…. [A]*ll the concerns on the face of the earth, outside of ours, could not make this quantity of film and supply it promptly within the time specified. If we could capture Lumière and supply him with film, we would control the world.*" (Italics in original.) The film was delivered to Rector in New York in shipments of 30,000 feet.

The raw Eastman stock Rector used was 2½ inches (63mm) wide. Prints of the film were slightly smaller at 2⅜ inches (60mm) due to shrinkage during the developing process. Other print specs: frame width 2 inches (50mm); frame height 1¼ inch (32mm); frame aspect ratio 1:1.6. My thanks to Georgetown University Library archivist Lisette Matano for sending me photos of frame samples of the actual film lined up with a ruler. My measurements confirmed the dimensions reported in *The Phonoscope*, Jan.-Feb. 1897, 12.

Rector's cameras seized: *New York Herald*, Mar. 2, 9 and 11, 1897; *New York Evening Telegram*, Mar. 8, 1897. Rector arrives in Carson City: *New York World*, Mar. 12, 1897 ("bad weather"); *San Francisco Examiner*, Mar. 12, 1897. Veriscope construction and test: *San Francisco Chronicle*, Mar. 12, 14 (arena seating torn up) and 15, 1897; *San Francisco Call*, Mar. 14 and 15, 1897; *Washington Evening Times*, Mar. 12 ("purely experimental") and 15 ("I was a little fearful"), 1897; *New York World*, Mar. 15, 1897. *Chicago Daily Tribune*, Mar. 16, 1897 reported Rector as saying of filming prospects: "It is the greatest cinch on earth. Stuart does not care if one or two pay to see the big fight. We are satisfied that we will have a perfect picture of the contest, and this will see us to the good beyond any speculation."

Agreement on film rights: *New York World* ("Veriscope Matter Settled") and *New York Herald*, Mar. 17, 1897; *Rochester Democrat and Chronicle*, Sept. 30, 1899. The *Herald* stated that Rector was assured fifteen percent of the profits; the *Democrat and Chronicle*, reporting on Rector's subsequent lawsuit against Stuart, put the promised figure at "one-quarter of the net receipts after Fitzsimmons and Corbett had been taken care of." Other sources: Streible, *Fight Pictures*, 59-61; Musser, *Emergence of Cinema*, 195-96; Ramsaye, *Nights*, 285-86. There is no record of the Veriscope Co.'s existence in either the New York State Archives (Dept. of State, Division of Corporations, State Records & UCC) or in the New Jersey State Archives. Stuart never incorporated it as he did the Kineto-Multiscope Co., even though he led Rector to believe that he had.

20) PRELIMINARIES

On the final hours before the fight: *Carson City News, New York Evening Telegram, New York World, New York Herald, San Francisco Examiner* and *Brooklyn Daily Eagle*, Mar. 17 and 18, 1897; *Carson City Morning Appeal, San Francisco Call, San Francisco Chronicle, New York Daily Tribune, New York Sun* and *Los Angeles Herald*, Mar. 18, 1897; *New York World*, May 23, 1897 (Fitz's bathrobe). Hugh Castle sneaking camera into arena: *San Francisco Chronicle*, Mar. 24, 1897 and *Syracuse Daily Journal*, April 3, 1897. Some later reminiscences worth noting: Corbett, *Roar of the Crowd*, 260-61; Brady, *Showman*, 173-75; Martin Julian, "Corbett Insults Fitz…The World Title Fight," *Johnson City* (NY) *Record*, Dec. 22, 1917 (part of a syndicated series of reminiscences by Julian published Nov. 10-Dec. 22, 1917). Charlie White, a former Fitz trainer who was now working for Corbett, also wrote a syndicated series of reminiscences, "Inside the Ring With the Great Fighters," that included his memories of the Corbett-Fitz fight. The series was published in the *New York Evening World* starting on April 8, 1911 and continued through the summer.

On Rector assistant George Kellogg: *New York Times*, Dec. 20, 1944 (obituary); "George W. Kellogg, Pioneer Photographer," Rochester Museum of Arts and Sciences, circa early 1940s, on-line at www.fultonhistory.com, Montour Falls, NY scrapbooks 1-6; George Eastman Papers, Box 9, Folder 10, Reminiscences of George W. Kellogg, April 30, 1940 (University of Rochester, River Campus Libraries, Department of Rare Books & Special Collections). On Edward G. Cooke: *Sacramento Daily Union*, Feb. 12, 1897 (as Corbett's advance agent); *San Francisco Call*, Mar. 5, 1897 (as Corbett's press agent); *New York Sun*, Dec. 11, 1926 (recalling his role in Veriscope filming). On Edward (aka Edwin) Houghton: *Niagara Falls Gazette*, April 9, 1949 and May 19, 1956 (obituary); Mike Filey, *More Toronto Sketches: "The Way We Were"* (Toronto: Dundurn, 1993), 128; *New York Clipper*, Mar. 2, 1895 (*In Darkest Brazil*).

A description of how the Veriscope—misspelled "varioscope"—was to film the fight is found in *The Phonoscope*, Jan.-Feb. 1897, 12. The details in this report appear to be fundamentally correct with the exception of the statement that the cameras used 1,000-foot reels of film. Considering what is known of the filming (fight was recorded in duplicate with cameras starting at four-minute intervals; filming speed was 24 fps; each frame was 1¼ inch high; exhibited film was approx. 11,000 feet long and had a screening time of around 75 minutes), the reels must have been about 1,200 feet. The *Phonoscope* report includes an illustration evidently intended to represent Rector's camera but in fact of the electrically powered projector he built in late 1896. This same illustration appeared in the *San Francisco Chronicle*, Feb. 18, 1897, misleadingly labeled "Varioscope that will be used at the fight." Illustration of the Veriscope interior: *San Francisco Chronicle*, Mar. 16, 1897. Other Veriscope sources: *San Francisco Chronicle* and *Call*, Mar. 14, 1897; *Washington Evening News*, April 19, 1897; *Pacific Commercial Advertiser*, Honolulu, Aug. 23, 1897 (Rector interview in which he says "I began the series just as Fitzsimmons stepped into the ring."). The ring-size controversy was initially attributed to a construction error. That it was in fact made undersized to accommodate the Veriscope was revealed in the *San Francisco Call*, June 4, 1897.

That the Veriscope was a single machine has come to be largely forgotten, the external structure seen as little more than a shelter from the weather for Rector's three cameras. Its integrated nature was better recognized back in 1897. As one contemporary paper described it, it was "an immense camera, arranged on the principle of the little Kodak machine, which contained within itself miles and miles of prepared photographic film." (*Eau Claire* [WI] *Daily Leader*, Aug. 24, 1897.)

21) FIRST BLOOD

The description of the fight is based on the following newspaper sources, all Mar. 18, 1897: *San Francisco Examiner* (includes firsthand accounts by

Fitz, Corbett, Siler, Muldoon and Senator Ingalls), *San Francisco Chronicle* (includes illustrations of blows struck), *San Francisco Call, New York Daily Tribune, New York Evening Telegram, New York Herald, New York Journal, New York Press, New York Sun, New York World, Los Angeles Herald* (Rose at ringside) and *Carson City Morning Appeal*. Also: *Washington Evening Times*, May 22, 1897 (Sullivan at ringside); *Carson City Morning Appeal*, Mar. 21, 1897 (Ida Fuller account); *San Francisco Chronicle*, Mar. 24, 1897 (Castle's photo); *New York Sun*, April 16, 1897 (Rose interview). For happenings in Frisco: *San Francisco Call* ("triumphal reception") and *San Francisco Chronicle*, Mar. 18, 1897. In New York: *New York World*, Mar. 18, 1897. In Newark and on Capt. Glori: *New York Journal*, Mar. 18, 1897. Other sources: Corbett, *Roar of the Crowd*, 262-67; Fitzsimmons, *Physical Culture*, 163-71 ("It shall never be" on p. 166); George Siler and Lou Houseman, *The Fight of the Century*, 75-83.

Captain Glori would go on to fall even lower before disappearing from the historical record, being kicked off the Newark police force in 1903 for trying to arrange a reward for the return of stolen church vestments. (*New York Sun*, Feb. 22 and May 3, 1903.)

For insights into what was going on in the corners between rounds: *Utica Saturday Globe*, Mar. 20, 1897 (includes captioned illustrations of seconds ministering to their fighters with witch hazel and "A Little Stimulant" and kneading their bruises); "How to Second a Fighter in a Ring Encounter," *National Police Gazette*, May 18 and 25, 1901 (the May 18 article, credited to Fitz, is especially rich in detail).

In *Roar of the Crowd*, 263, Corbett claimed that Fitz received an unfair long count in Round Six, "fully fifteen seconds," referee Siler and timekeeper Muldoon neglecting to start the count right away. This has been repeated in subsequent secondary sources and is untrue. The count properly started the moment Corbett stepped back, as per the rules. As William Brady admitted in *The Fighting Man*, 145, "After the fight was over we claimed that he [Fitz] was down longer than ten seconds.... But we did that for effect. The truth of the matter is, Fitzsimmons was not badly hurt in this round and simply did what all experienced boxers do; took the benefit of the nine full seconds before getting up." If there had been an irregularity with the count, Corbett's designated timekeeper James Colville, seated beside Muldoon, would have raised a protest. He didn't.

It was variously reported in the press that Enoch Rector filmed the fight at 40 to 45 frames per second (see for example *Chicago Tribune*, June 9, 1897). This was an exaggeration. Judging from extant footage of the Corbett-Fitz fight film, Rector's actual filming speed was 24 fps (corroborated by *The Phonoscope*, Jan.-Feb. 1897, 12), somewhat slower than the 30 fps he intended to use at the Fitz-Maher fight (deducible from camera and film specs in William Gilmore to Kinetoscope Exhibiting Co., Sept. 10, 1895, TAED D9516AAD). Given a speed of 24 fps and a frame height of 1¼ inch, Rector's 1,200-foot film reels would have lasted eight minutes. Starting the cameras at four-minute intervals (according to *Phonoscope*) would have given a four-minute overlap, thereby allowing Rector to make a duplicate record of the fight with three cameras. With this information, one can map out a plausible approximation of the filming sequence and determine what each camera was doing at any given time. My description of filming inside the Veriscope in this and the following chapter is based on clues and deductions such as these, coupled with what is known about the challenges filmmakers faced at that time and of the practices of camera operators in the silent era. Antique movie camera expert Sam Dodge provided me with additional insights, including the telling comment, "I can't imagine cranking for 8 minutes. I don't think anyone could crank for 8 minutes. They had to have shifts at the camera." (Email correspondence with the author, Nov. 28 and 30, 2015.)

22) THE AWFUL BLOW

The continuing fight narrative is based on the same newspaper sources as in previous chapter. Of additional note: *San Francisco Chronicle* ("There were blood drops") and *Examiner* (Corbett's KO account; Siler fears trouble; "You will have to fight me"), *Buffalo Evening News* ("It was then I discovered"), *New York Press* ("It was an awful blow") and *Herald*, (Masterson: "Get in there"), *Saint Paul Globe* (Corbett dressing room scene), all Mar. 18, 1897; *San Francisco Call*, Mar. 19, 1897 (Fitz describes talking during fight; "Hey, Jim"). Other sources: Corbett, *Roar of the Crowd*, 264-66 ("Hit him in the slats!"; Corbett remembers KO); Brady, *Showman*, 176 ("with all the marrow"). New York happenings: *New York World* (Manhattan scenes; Wall Street) and *Journal* (Harlem; Verno), Mar. 18, 1897.

While several newspapers reported in their fight coverage that Rose Fitzsimmons exhorted Fitz to "punch him in the wind" (i.e. *San Francisco Chronicle*, Mar. 18, 1897), I was unable to find any reference to her uttering the exact words "Hit him in the slats." Possibly the earliest reference to Rose directing Bob to Corbett's "slats" (ribs) is a dialect-laden account intended as humor that was published in the *Kansas City Journal*, Mar. 22, 1897, which has Rose crying out, "Don't hit him on th' jaw.... Hit him on th' slats!" By the following year, "Hit him in the slats" had taken root as a "memorable slogan [that] will go down into history with 'England expects every man to do his duty' and 'Don't give up the ship.'" (*Buffalo Evening News*, Oct. 3, 1898). Rose herself would deny making any such outbursts, admitting only that "I couldn't control myself any longer" when Corbett went down. (*New York Sun*, April 16, 1897.)

Trainer Billy Delaney was critical of Corbett after the loss, saying that he ignored advice to ease up on training a few days before the contest; that he insisted on playing handball despite being told that it did him harm ("[I]f I hadn't been afraid of being caught I would have burned down the court."); and that "he wouldn't touch liquor in any shape…although I was telling him he needed some malt to supply the drain on his system by his hard work." (*San Francisco Chronicle*, Mar. 24, 1897.)

On the problem of static electric discharges while filming: "Static Electricity the Film Man's Belial," *The Billboard*, Nov. 29, 1913. One solution later used in the silent film era was to equip the camera with a condenser to absorb static buildup. After 400-odd feet of film had passed through the camera, the cameraman would lick his finger and touch the condenser, getting a slight shock and releasing the charge. See also Bitzer, *Billy Bitzer: His Story*, 21-22. On Rector's handling of the film after the fight: *San Francisco Call*, Mar. 18, 1897.

My estimate that Rector shot 21,600 feet of film (18 reels) making his duplicate record is based on the assumption that the three-camera filming sequence continued throughout the fight without major interruption. References to the length of the exhibited film vary in contemporary newspaper sources but are generally half this amount and thus confirm the estimate: *Washington* (DC) *Evening Times*, April 15, 1897 ("11,000 feet of films"); *New York Clipper*, May 1, 1897 ("The picture contains over ten thousand feet of film"); *Chicago Daily Tribune*, June 9, 1897 ("There are 10,800 feet of film on six reels").

23) DEVELOPING DREAD

Fitz after the fight: *Los Angeles Herald*, Mar. 18, 1897 ("I am 36"); *San Francisco Call* (bruised; "I'm out of the ring") and *Examiner* ("It has been my prayer"), Mar. 19, 1897; *Washington Evening Times*, April 12, 1897 ("will put us on Easy street"); *New York Press*, Mar. 19, 1897 ("There is no sense"); *Salt Lake Herald*, April 1, 1897 ("if it does not show"). Corbett after the fight: *San Francisco Examiner*, Mar. 19 (friends assure him he will still be popular; "fresh as a daisy") and 20 (White with broken tooth), 1897; *Buffalo Evening News*, Mar. 18, 1897 ("lucky punch").

Rector's "dread" at developing film: Eastman president Henry Strong to George Eastman (then in London, England), Mar. 29, 1897, George Eastman Legacy Collection (GELC), Eastman Museum, Rochester, NY. Initial reports of success: *Syracuse Daily Journal*, April 3, 1897 ("films are beauties"); *New York Clipper*, April 10, 1897. Making prints: "Big Fight on Canvas," *The Phonoscope*, May 1897, 5 ("Eastman…has one single contract with Mr. Stuart for 600,000 feet of the film, for which Mr. Stuart pays in cash $140,000." This price seems a Stuart exaggeration. According to Henry Strong to George Eastman, Dec. 31, 1896: "Our price [to Rector] is 5¢ per foot per inch wide [i.e. 12.5¢ per foot for Rector's 2½ inch wide film]. A 10% discount is to be given on the first 100,000 feet, if 200,000 feet are taken the discount is to be 15% and if 300,000 feet are taken within the time specified, 20%." [Ackerman, *Eastman*, 124.] This suggests a price, after discount, of $60,000 for 600,000 feet.)

Attempts to ban film: *Rome* (NY) *Semi-Weekly Citizen*, Mar. 21, 1897; *San Francisco Chronicle*, Mar. 23, 1897 ("infinitely worse"); *Chicago Tribune*, Mar. 26, 1897; *Syracuse Daily Journal*, Mar. 31, 1897; *Jamestown* (ND) *Weekly Alert*, April 22, 1897. Rector claims film didn't turn out: *Chicago Tribune*, April 4, 1897 ("Rector says the whole lot"); *San Francisco Call*, April 5, 1897; *Boston Globe*, April 10, 1897 ("[O]f the many thousands"); *Auburn* (NY) *Bulletin*, April 5, 1897 ("Rector is staying"); Strong to Eastman, April 8, 1897, GELC ("fake").

Fitz's show: *Salt Lake Herald*, April 1, 1897. Fitz and Corbett in Salt Lake City: *Salt Lake Herald*, Mar. 31 and April 1 ("I am going to follow"; Fitz's "kinetoscope" comment), 1897; *Deseret Evening News*, Mar. 29, 1897 (Corbett ad). Corbett's plans: *New York Dramatic Mirror*, April 17, 1897. Fitz arrives in New York: *New York Sun*, April 8 (reception) and 14 (arrival; "I have not retired"), 1897; "Grand Testimonial Banquet to Mr. Robert Fitzsimmons," New York Public Library, Rare Books Division, digitalcollections.nypl.org/items/510d47db-2d7b-a3d9-e040-e00a18064a99. Corbett returns to stage in *Naval Cadet*: *New York Press*, April 20, 1897.

Stuart said he expected to make "at least $1,000,000 within the next five years" from the film. (*Buffalo Evening News*, Mar, 22, 1897.) On his expected expenses and post-production details: *The Phonoscope*, May 1897, 1. This *Phonoscope* report gives the precise length of the finished film as 10,846 feet, a credible figure. The *Los Angeles Herald*, May 9, 1897 mentions Brady spending two hours examining the negatives "with a high-power glass," which suggests this may have been how Rector examined them as well doing his editing work. Also: Henry Strong to George Eastman, April 1, 1897, GELC ("are making a great mistake").

Lubin's fake film: Eckhardt, *King of the Movies*, 26-27; Musser, *Emergence of Cinema*, 200-02; Streible, *Fight Pictures*, 131-33. Lubin ads: *New York Clipper*, April 17 (Cineograph and fake fight film), May 15 and 29 (films are copyrighted) and June 19 (copyright certificate numbers given), 1897. Dan Stuart's "Warning!": *New York Clipper* and *New York Dramatic Mirror*, April 24, 1897. Also: *Dramatic Mirror*, May 1, 1897 and *Clipper*, May 1 (copyright application details; "A wicked war") and May 15 (Stuart threatens legal action against theater managers showing copyright-infringing films), 1897; *Johnson City* (NY) *Record*, Nov. 17, 1917 (Julian on Lubin fake); *Singapore Free Press and Mercantile Advertiser*, Aug. 23, 1897 and *Straits Times*, Aug. 19, 24 and 25, 1897 (fake film in Singapore).

Neither the real Corbett-Fitz fight film nor the Lubin fake are listed in the Library of Congress's *Catalogue of Title Entries of Books and Other Articles* or in H. L. Walls, *Motion Pictures 1894-1912 Identified from the Records of the United States Copyright Office*. The only record of their copyrights is to be found on handwritten cards from 1897 in the old card catalog at the US Copyright Office. The card for Rector's film is filed under "Wheelock, Wm. Kenyon, Dallas, Tex." It gives the name of the film as "Corbett-Fitzsimmons contest" with registration numbers starting at 26025 and is marked "rec'd May 15, 1897." A later notation is handwritten at the bottom: "Copies badly deteriorated destroyed Mar. 16, 1921." (My thanks to reference librarian Rosemary Hanes of the LOC Moving Image Section for this information.) Films in the US would continue to be copyrighted as photographs until 1912.

The British copyright documents for Rector's film are held at the National Archives in Kew under the title "Corbett v. Fitzsimmons Contest" and registrant name William Wheelock, reference numbers COPY 1/430/164 ("Photograph of first round") to COPY 1/430/177 ("Photograph of fourteenth round"), registration stamp dated May 15, 1897.

Lubin's film exhibited: *Victoria* (BC) *Daily Colonist*, May 22, 1897 ("[a]s the original pictures"); *New York Herald*, May 25 and June 7, 1897 (Huber ads); *The Phonoscope*, June 1897, 12 (Little Rock incident; "We advertise a fac simile") and Aug.-Sept. 1897, 8 ("It was surprising to see how many people there were who did not know the meaning of the compound word fac-simile. They know it, however, now.")

Rector's projector uses manual operation: *Chicago Tribune*, June 9, 1897 (film reels turned by hand). Film premiere delayed: *New York Herald*, May 15, 1897 (electrical problem at Academy of Music). Details on electrical supply in American theaters: *Julius Cahn's Official Theatrical Guide*, vol. 2 (1897). Advance pictures from film published: *New York World*, May 23, 1897 (Stuart: "I don't know"; Corbett: "I have seen").

24) THE FIRST FEATURE FILM

For details on the Academy of Music: *Julius Cahn's Official Theatrical Guide*, vol. 2 (1897), 7 and 37. Notices for plays at the Academy: *New York World*, 1896-97. Vendig sues Stuart: *Los Angeles Times*, Feb. 20, 1897. Vendig injunction might block premiere: *New York World*, May 23, 1897. Like most American theaters at this time, illumination at the Academy was a mixture of gas and electric. On the film's premiere: *New York Herald*, *World*, *Sun* and *Tribune*, May 23, 1897; *New York Press*, May 23 and 24, 1897; *New York Times*, May 26, 1897; *New York Clipper* and *Dramatic Mirror*, May 29, 1897; "Big Fight on Canvas," *The Phonoscope*, May 1897, 5; *Wellington* (New Zealand) *Evening Post*, Oct. 23, 1897, quoting article in *San Francisco Wave* ("streamed across the field of vision"). On fire risk: "Danger!" *The Phonoscope*, June 1897, 8; *Troy* (NY) *Daily Times*, July 7, 1897; Bitzer, *Billy Bitzer*, 14-15 and 18. Bitzer, running Dickson's Biograph projector at its debut in Oct. 1896, was *locked* inside the projection booth so no one could steal a glimpse of the machine. Also: *Wichita Daily Eagle*, May 29, 1897; *Chicago Tribune*, June 8 (intermissions between reels four to five minutes; whole show 2:10 long) and 9 (reels on projector turned by hand), 1897; *Owosso* (MI) *Evening Argus*, June 16,

1897 (three-minute intermissions); *Utica Daily Union*, June 29, 1897 (details on announcer, music); *Milwaukee Journal*, July 13, 1897 ("complete evenings' entertainment"); *New York World*, Oct. 20, 1897 ("[T]hough we leave the theatre"; Lady Campbell [pen name Véra Tsaritsyn] saw the film in London); Bitzer, *Billy Bitzer*, 13-18 (firsthand account of operating a Biograph projector in Oct. 1896).

Fitz sees the film: *New York World*, May 25, 1897; *Philadelphia Record*, May 26, 1897. Film opens in Boston: *Boston Herald* and *Journal*, June 1, 1897. In Cincinnati: *Cincinnati Post*, June 7, 1897; *New York Dramatic Mirror*, June 12, 1897. In Chicago: *Chicago Tribune*, June 6, 8 and 9, 1897. In Buffalo: *Buffalo Evening News*, June 8, 1897. The spread of the film across the country was tracked in *New York Dramatic Mirror*, June-Dec. 1897. Film grosses: *New York Press*, May 24 1897; *Chicago Tribune*, June 8, 1897; *Oswego* (NY) *Daily Palladium*, June 23, 1897 ("gold mine"). Second run in Buffalo: *Buffalo Evening News*, Aug. 21, 1897 ("What will one see").

The film in Toronto: *Toronto World*, Aug. 3 (Clifton Turner), 9 ("a most wonderful reproduction") and 10 (city council vote), 1897; *Toronto Evening Telegram*, Aug. 7, 1897; *Toronto Evening Star*, Aug. 9 and 12 ("exclusively for ladies"), 1897. The film went on play in thirty-five Canadian cities. The "Feriscope" in Belleville: *Belleville Daily Intelligencer*, June 2 and 3, 1897. On the Veriscope and "Feriscope" in Canada, see Paul Moore, "Mapping the Mass Circulation of Early Cinema: Film Debuts Coast-to-Coast in Canada in 1896 and 1897," *Canadian Journal of Film Studies* 21 (Spring 2012): 75-76.

Improved prints go into circulation: *Chicago Tribune*, June 20, 1897 ("new process"; "are immeasurably clearer"); *Buffalo Evening News*, June 8 ("very delicate machine") and June 15 (improved picture), 1897. *Chicago Tribune*, June 8, 1897 reported that Rector "arrived from New York last evening to manipulate the machines." Death of Charles Scribner: *New York Herald, Sun* and *Times*, June 7, 1897. Dan Stuart was not just president of Veriscope Co. but treasurer too, for which he paid himself an extra $75 a week. (*Rochester Democrat and Chronicle*, Sept. 30, 1899.)

Brady acquires UK film rights: *New York Evening Telegram*, May 29, 1897. The Australian debut was preceded by local notices from Stuart that the film "will be copyrighted in every country of the world" and that "we intend to prosecute all infringements." (*Sydney Morning Herald*, July 10, 1897.)

Rector's world tour: *San Francisco Call*, Aug. 14, 1897 (departs Frisco); *Honolulu Independent*, Aug. 20, 1897 (arrives in Honolulu); *Pacific Commercial Advertiser*, Aug. 21 (Veriscope write-up), 23 ("There seems to be"; film ad) and 24 (Honolulu screening), 1897; *Pacific Commercial Advertiser* and *Hawaiian Star*, Aug. 26, 1897 (departs Honolulu); *Sydney Referee*, Sept. 15, 1897 and *Newcastle Morning Herald and Miners' Advocate*, Sept. 16, 1897 (arrives in Sydney); *Sydney Morning Herald*,

Sept. 16, 1897 (film ad); *Sydney Arrow*, Sept. 18, 1897 ("thoroughly genial trio"); *Sydney Referee*, Sept. 22, 1897 (Sydney screening); *New York Dramatic Mirror*, Dec. 4, 1897 and Mar. 19, 1898; *West Australian*, Dec. 2, 1897 (tour through outback); *Kalgoorlie Miner* ("one of the greatest electrical experts"; Kalgoorlie was a gold rush town), Dec. 4, 1897; *West Australian*, Jan. 5 and 10, 1898 (final show in Fremantle); *Western Mail*, Jan. 14, 1898, *Sydney Sunday Times*, Jan. 30, 1898 and *New York Dramatic Mirror*, Mar. 19, 1898 (departs Australia); *Daily Commercial News and Shipping List*, Sydney, Feb. 1, 1898 (arrives in South Africa on Jan. 29); *Standard and Diggers' News*, Johannesburg, Feb. 12 and 14 (Jo'burg opening; it takes "three lantern men" to run projector), Feb. 9 and 15 (film ads), and Feb. 24 ("Grand Curio Souvenir Night"), 1898. Also: author interview with Sara Chermayeff, Nov. 19, 2015. The Chermayeff family has a photo of Jesse (Rector's wife) seated on a rickshaw, the inscription on the back reading "Durban, Natal, Feb. 1898."

The film's belated opening in LA: *Los Angeles Herald*, Dec. 4, 1897 and *Los Angeles Times*, Dec. 7, 1897 (city ordnance passed). In Montreal: *The Metropolitan*, Montreal, Aug. 14, 1897. In Kingston: *Toronto Daily Mail and Empire*, Dec. 3, 1897; *Kingston Daily Whig*, Dec. 7, 1897. Rector sues Stuart: *The Phonoscope*, July 1899, 18; *Rochester Democrat and Chronicle*, Sept. 30, 1899 and *Topeka State Journal*, Aug. 10, 1899; also *Buffalo Courier-Record*, Dec. 28, 1897 and *Brooklyn Daily Eagle*, Dec. 31, 1897 (Fitz gets film royalty checks). Rector vs. Stuart was heard in the New York Supreme Court. In August 1899 Judge Giegerich issued an order for Stuart to appear as a witness. Stuart's lawyers requested a postponement until October on account of their client's ill health. I was unable to find any evidence of the original records for this case at the New York County Archives, Division of Old Records, 31 Chambers St., New York. The documents have evidently been lost. The fact that there is no record of the case even in the old ledgers suggests that it did not proceed far.

EPILOGUE

The Corbett-Fitzsimmons Fight was still being screened—in Omaha, Nebraska—as late as 1904 (*Salt Lake Herald*, April 12, 1904). Brady's estimate of the film's gross: Brady, *Fighting Man*, 147. Fitz was quoted as saying "The bigger they are the heavier they fall" in the *Philadelphia Inquirer*, Mar. 10, 1899 and—three days before the fight—in the *Chicago Tribune*, June 4, 1899. The line as it is known today is of course "The bigger they come, the harder they fall." It has been asserted that Fitz used the line before facing a 300-pound behemoth named Ed Dunkhorst on April 30, 1900. He may have, but the Jeffries fight and the above newspaper sources preceded the Dunkhorst contest (second-round KO by Fitz) by almost a year.

Fitz-Jeffries fight (1899): *New York Morning Telegraph*, *New York Herald* and *Brooklyn Daily Eagle*, June 10, 1899 (lights and camera set-up);

New York Morning Telegraph, June 11, 1899 (filming details; first reports of failure); *Utica Daily Press,* June 15, 1899 (filming failed due to insufficient lighting); "The Films That Failed," *The Phonoscope,* May 1899, 14. Palmer-McGovern fight: *New York Times* ("The big camera of the vitascope loomed up at the top of the southern end of the inclosure") and *Morning Telegraph* ("the moving picture machine"), Sept. 13, 1899; *Indianapolis Journal,* Sept. 13, 1899 (venue similar to Carson City arena); *National Police Gazette,* Sept. 30, 1899 ("picture machine"); Streible, *Fight Pictures,* 103-04. Jeffries-Sharkey fight: *Brooklyn Daily Eagle,* Nov. 4, 1899; *New York World,* Nov. 5, 1899 ("The great search-light"). Fitz-Ruhlin fight: *Buffalo Express,* Aug. 5, 1900 (training footage shot); *New York Morning Telegraph* and *Chicago Tribune,* Aug. 11, 1900. Jeffries-Ruhlin fight: *San Francisco Chronicle* ("a temporary booth"), *Chicago Tribune* ("the poorest") and *San Francisco Call* (dancing boys), Nov. 16, 1901; *New York Clipper,* Dec. 28, 1901 (fight film ad). According to *San Francisco Call,* Nov. 15, 1901, the improved lighting array used to illuminate the ring generated much less heat. Lubin's fakes: Streible, *Fight Pictures,* 131-63; *Philadelphia Inquirer,* Aug. 14, 1900 and *Syracuse Evening Herald,* Aug. 15, 1900 (filming of Fitz-Ruhlin reenactment); *Philadelphia Inquirer,* Sept. 5, 1900 and *Buffalo Express,* Sept. 6, 1900 (Corbett-McCoy reenactment).

On Bob Fitzsimmons: *Daily Inter Mountain,* Butte, Montana, Dec. 16, 1899 (Fitz-Julian breakup); *New York Morning Telegraph,* July 25, 1901 ("I'm on easy street"); *Syracuse Herald,* Jan. 1, 1918 ("to surrender my life"); *New York Evening Telegram,* Oct. 22, 1917 and *Chicago Tribune,* Oct. 22 and 23, 1917 (illness and death); *Brooklyn Standard-Union,* Mar. 8, 1919 and *New York Sun,* Mar. 9, 1919 (Julian's death). On Jim Corbett: *San Francisco Call,* Aug. 17, 1898 (death of parents); Corbett, *Roar of the Crowd,* 294 ("What is it?"); *Brooklyn Daily Eagle,* Feb. 19, 1933 and *Brooklyn Daily Star,* Feb. 20, 1933 (death).

On John L. Sullivan: *New York Sun,* Feb. 3, 1918; *New York Tribune,* Feb. 10, 1918; *Washington Times,* Feb. 14, 1918. On Peter Maher: *New York Sun,* Oct. 31, 1924; *Buffalo Courier-Express,* April 16, 1927; *Milwaukee Journal,* April 1, 1937 (whiskey ad).

On Enoch Rector: Brayer, *George Eastman,* 209 (Ikonograph); *Milwaukee Sentinel,* Mar. 30, 1929 and June 29, 1932 and *Milwaukee Journal,* Nov. 9, 1929 (Gasifier); *New York Times,* Jan. 27, 1957 and *Chicago Tribune,* Jan. 28, 1957 (obituaries); author interview with Sara Chermayeff, Sept. 22, 2011 and Nov. 19, 2015.

On Dan Stuart: *Dallas Daily Times Herald, New York Herald* and *Chicago Tribune,* Nov. 15, 1909; *New York Sun* and *New York Herald,* Nov. 16, 1909 (obituaries). Stuart was sixty-two at the time of his death, not fifty-two as was widely reported. His wife was Harriet Brennan; his children Helen (born 1902) and Douglas (born 1904).

On Gray and Otway Latham: *New York Herald*, Aug. 13, 1906 (Otway's death); *New York Sun*, Mar. 26, 1907 and *New York Times* and *Herald*, Mar. 27, 1907 (Gray's death); *New York Herald* and *Baltimore Sun*, April 5, 1907 (Gray's death questioned as murder); Ramsaye, *Nights*, 294-98; Formanek-Brunell, ed., *Rose O'Neill*, 72-76. On Woodville Latham's end: Ramsaye, *Nights*, 553-58.

On William Dickson: Spehr, *Movies*, 618-46. On Eugene Lauste: *Bristol Evening News*, Aug. 26, 1897, clipping in MC Papers, reel 2 (Lauste states that Edison is on wrong track trying to incorporate phonograph with moving pictures to make sound films); Spehr, "Eugene Augustin Lauste," 26-36; Eyman, *Speed of Sound*, 30-32; Eugene Lauste, "Questionary [sic.] and Answering of Mr. Eugene Lauste," typed mss., MC Papers, reel 2 (Eidoloscope shares on wall).

Jim Jacobs discovers surviving film of fight: Robert Boyle, "Really the Greatest," *Sports Illustrated*, Mar. 7, 1966, 70. Film restoration and centenary screening: *The Independent*, June 1 and 7, 1997. The British Film Institute has 2,625 feet (roughly 29 minutes) of *The Corbett-Fitzsimmons Fight* on 35mm film. The original 60mm film, a total of some 4,200 feet (just under 29 minutes at 24 frames per second), is held at the Museum of Modern Art in New York. My thanks to Ros Cranston of the BFI's Non-Fiction Curatorial Team and Ashley Swinnerton of the MOMA Film Study Center for information on the length and provenance of extant footage.

BIBLIOGRAPHY

Ackerman, Carl A. *George Eastman*. Boston and New York: Houghton Mifflin, 1930.

Baldwin, Neil. *Edison: Inventing the Century*. New York: Hyperion, 1995.

Ball, Edward. *The Inventor and the Tycoon*. New York: Doubleday, 2013.

Bitzer, G.W. *Billy Bitzer: His Story*. New York: Farrar, Straus and Giroux, 1973.

Bonnet, Theodore, ed. *Annals of the Olympic Club*. San Francisco: F.H. Abbott, 1914.

Boyle, Robert. "Really the Greatest." *Sports Illustrated*, Mar. 7, 1966, 64-72.

Brady, William A. *The Fighting Man*. Indianapolis: The Bobb-Merrell Company, 1916.

————. "The Sporting Reminiscences of William A. Brady." *New York Telegram*, Feb. 12-Sept. 3, 1922 (30-chapter feature published on Sundays).

————. *Showman: My Life Story*. New York: E.P. Dutton, 1937.

Burrows, Edwin G. and Mike Wallace. *Gotham: A History of New York City to 1898*. New York: Oxford University Press, 1999.

Callahan, James Morton. *Genealogical and Personal History of the Upper Monongahela Valley, West Virginia*. Vol. 1. New York: Lewis Historical Publishing Co., 1912.

Clark, George. *Leland Stanford*. Paolo Alto, CA: Stanford University Press, 1931.

Collins, Theresa M. and Lisa Gitelman. *Thomas Edison and Modern America: A Brief History with Documents*. New York: Palgrave, 2002.

Corbett, James J. *The Roar of the Crowd: The True Tale of the Rise and Fall of a Champion*. Garden City, NY: Garden City Publishing Co., 1926.

Crawford, Remsen. "Patents, Profits and Pirates: An Interview with Thomas A. Edison." *Saturday Evening Post*, Sept. 27, 1930, 3-5ff.

Davis, Robert H. *Ruby Robert alias Bob Fitzsimmons*. New York: George H. Doran Co., 1926.

DeArment, Robert K. *Bat Masterson: The Man and the Legend*. Norman: University of Oklahoma Press, 1979.

Dickson, Antonia. "Wonders of the Kinetoscope." *Frank Leslie's Popular Monthly*, Feb. 1895, 245-51.

Dickson, Antonia and W.K.L. Dickson. "Edison's Invention of the Kineto-Phonograph." *The Century Magazine*, June 1894, 206-14.

Dickson, W.K.L. and Antonia Dickson. *History of the Kinetograph, Kinetoscope and Kineto-Phonograph*. New York: Albert Bunn, 1895.

Donnellon, Matt. *The Irish Champion Peter Maher: The Untold Story of Ireland's Only World Heavyweight Champion and the Records of the Men He Fought.* Bloomington, IN: Trafford Publishing, 2008.

Dyer, Frank Lewis and Thomas Commerford Martin. *Edison: His Life and Inventions.* 2 vols. New York: Harper and Brothers, 1910.

Eckhardt, Joseph P. *The King of the Movies: Film Pioneer Siegmund Lubin.* London: Associated University Presses, 1997.

Eyman, Scott. *The Speed of Sound: Hollywood and the Talkie Revolution, 1929-1930.* Simon and Schuster, 1997.

Fields, Armond. *James J. Corbett: A Biography of the Heavyweight Champion and Popular Theater Headliner.* Jefferson, NC: McFarland and Co., 2001.

Fitzsimmons, Robert. *Physical Culture and Self-Defense.* London: Drexel Biddle, 1901.

Fleischer, Nat. *Young Griffo: The Will o' the Wisp of the Roped Square.* New York: Printed by C.J. O'Brien, Inc., 1928.

Formanek-Brunell, Miriam ed. *The Story of Rose O'Neill: An Autobiography.* Columbia, MO: University of Missouri Press, 1997.

Fox, Richard K. *Life and Battles of James J. Corbett, the Champion Pugilist of the World.* New York: Richard K. Fox, 1892.

Haas, Robert Bartlett. *Muybridge: Man in Motion.* Berkeley: University of California Press, 1976.

Harlow, Alvin F. *Old Waybills: The Romance of the Express Companies.* New York: Arno Press, 1976 (originally published 1934).

Hendricks, Gordon. *The Edison Motion Picture Myth.* Berkeley: University of California Press, 1961.

––––––. *The Kinetoscope: America's First Commercially Successful Motion Picture Exhibitor.* New York: The Beginnings of the American Film, 1966.

––––––. *Origins of the American Film.* New York, Arno Press, 1972. (Compilation of *The Edison Motion Picture Myth*, *The Kinetoscope* and *Beginnings of the Biograph*.)

Irvine, L.H. *"Our Jim," The World's Champion.* New York and San Francisco: Crown Publishing Co., 1892.

Israel, Paul. *Edison: A Life of Invention.* New York: John Wiley and Sons, 1998.

Julius Cahn's Official Theatrical Guide. Vol. 2. New York: Publication Office, 1897.

"The Kinetograph: A New Industry Heralded." *The Phonogram*, Oct. 1892, 217-18.

"The Kineto-Phonograph," *The Electrical World*, June 16, 1894, 799-801.

King, Dick. "The Fight that Almost Kayoed Boxing." *Frontier Times.* Summer, 1959, 26-27ff.

Lathrop, George Parsons. "Edison's Kinetograph." *Harper's Weekly*, June 13, 1891, 446-47.

Leslie, Mitchell. "The Man Who Stopped Time." *Stanford Magazine*, May/June 2001, stanfordalumni.org/news/magazine/2001/mayjun/features/ muybridge.

MacDonnell, Kevin. *Eadweard Muybridge: The Man Who Invented the Moving Picture.* Boston: Little, Brown and Co., 1972.

Marks, William Dennis. "The Mechanism of Instantaneous Photography." In *Animal Locomotion: The Muybridge Work at the University of Pennsylvania*, 9-33. Philadelphia: J.B. Lippincott Co., 1888.

McDaniel, Ruel. *Vinegarroon: The Saga of Judge Roy Bean, Law West of the Pecos.* Kingsport, TN: Southern Publishers, 1936.

Miletich, Leo N. *Dan Stuart's Fistic Carnival*. College Station, TX: Texas A & M University Press, 1994.

Mulhall, M. G. *From Europe to Paraguay and Matto-Grosso*. London: E. Stanford, 1877.

Musser, Charles. *The Emergence of Cinema: The American Screen to 1907*. New York: Charles Scribner's Sons, 1990.

————. *Before the Nickelodeon: Edwin S. Porter and the Edison Manufacturing Company*. Berkeley: University of California Press, c1991.

Muybridge, Eadweard. *The Attitudes of Animals in Motion, Illustrated with the Zoopraxiscope*. London: William Clowes and Sons, 1882.

————. *Animal Locomotion: An Electro-Photographic Investigation of Consecutive Phases of Animal Movements*. Philadelphia: J.B. Lippincott Co., 1887.

————. *Descriptive Zoopraxography, or the Science of Animal Locomotion Made Popular*. Philadelphia: University of Pennsylvania, 1893.

————. *Animals in Motion: An Electro-Photographic Investigation of Consecutive Phases of Animal Progressive Movements*. London: Chapman & Hall, 1899.

Myler, Patrick. *Gentleman Jim Corbett*. London: Robson Books, 1998.

Newhall, Beaumont. "Light Sensitivity of Early Photographic Materials." *Image: Journal of Photography of the George Eastman House*, April 1955, 31.

Nicholson, Kelly Richard. *Hitters, Dancers and Ring Magicians: Seven Boxers of the Golden Age and Their Challengers*. Jefferson, SC: McFarland and Co., 2011.

Odd, Gilbert. *The Fighting Blacksmith: A Biography of Bob Fitzsimmons*. London: Pelham Books, 1976.

Ormsby, Waterman L. *The Butterfield Overland Mail: Only Through Passenger on the First Westbound Stage*. Lyle Wright and Josephine Bynum, eds. San Marino, CA: Huntington Library Press, 1942.

Paine, Albert Bigelow. *Captain Bill McDonald, Texas Ranger: A Story of Frontier Reform*. New York: J. J. Little & Ives Co., 1909.

Pardy, George. "Famous Fighting Codes." *The Ring*, Mar. 1942, 20ff.

Petersen, Bob. *Peter Jackson: A Biography of the Australian Heavyweight Champion, 1860-1901*. Jefferson, NC: McFarland & Co., 2011.

Phillips, Ray. *Edison's Kinetoscope and Its Films: A History to 1896*. Westport, CT: Greenwood Press, 1997.

Pollack, Adam J. *In the Ring with Bob Fitzsimmons*. Iowa City: Win By KO Publications, 2007.

————. *In the Ring with James J. Corbett*. Iowa City: Win By KO Publications, 2007.

Ramsaye, Terry. *A Million and One Nights: A History of the Motion Picture Through 1925*. New York: Touchstone, 1954 (originally published 1926).

————. "The Motion Picture." *The Annals of the American Academy of Political and Social Science* 128 (Nov. 1926): 1-19.

Rector, Charles. "Morgan 'Goes A-Raiding' and Views West Virginia: A Bit of Civil War History." *West Virginia Review* 6 (May 1929): 310-11ff.

Robinson, David. *From Peep Show to Palace: The Birth of American Film*. New York: Columbia University Press, 1996.

Robinson, K. R. *Fist Fighting Out West: Dan Stuart Versus General Mabry and the Texas Rangers*. West Kingsdown, Kent: English Westerners' Society, 2010.

Rocap, William H. and Pember W. Rocap. *Remembering Bob Fitzsimmons*. Wayne, ME: Archives Press, 2001.

Rossell, Deac. "'The New Thing with the Long Name and the Old Thing with the Name That Isn't Much Shorter': A Cinema Chronology, 1889-1896." *Film History* (special issue) 7 (Summer 1995): 115-236.

———. *Living Pictures: The Origins of the Movies*. Albany: State University of New York Press, 1998.

Sansing, David. *The University of Mississippi: A Sesquicentennial History*. Jackson, MS: University Press of Mississippi, 1999.

Sassaman, Richard. "Psst! Didja Know That Tom Edison Staged Illegal Fights for Flicks?" *Sports Illustrated*, July 12, 1982, 80-82.

Skiles, Jack. *Judge Roy Bean Country*. Lubbock, TX: Texas Tech University Press, 1996.

Sonnichsen, C.L. *Roy Bean: Law West of the Pecos*. New York: MacMillan, 1943.

Spehr, Paul C. "Eugene Augustin Lauste: A Biographical Chronology." *Film History* 11 (1999): 18–38.

———. *The Man Who Made Movies: W.K.L. Dickson*. London: John Libbey Publishing, 2008.

Stillman, J.D.R. *The Horse in Motion: As Shown by Instantaneous Photography*. Boston: James R. Osgood and Co., 1882.

Streible, Dan. "A History of the Boxing Film, 1894-1915: Social Control and Social Reform in the Progressive Era." *Film History* 3 (1989): 235-57.

———. "Female Spectators and the Corbett-Fitzsimmons Fight Film." In *Out of Bounds: Sports, Media, and the Politics of Identity*, edited by Aaron Baker and Todd Boyd, 16-47. Bloomington: Indiana University Press, 1997.

———. *Fight Pictures: A History of Boxing and Early Cinema*. Berkeley: University of California Press, 2008.

Sullivan, John L. *Life and Reminiscences of a 19th Century Gladiator*. Boston: Jas. A. Hearn, 1892.

Tefertiller, Casey. *Wyatt Earp: The Life Behind the Legend*. New York: John Wiley & Sons, 1997.

Townsend, Horace. "Edison, His Work and His Work-Shop." *Cosmopolitan*, April 1889, 598-607.

Webb, Dale. *Prize Fighter: The Life and Times of Bob Fitzsimmons*. Edinburgh: Mainstream Publishing, 2000.

Webb, Walter Prescott. *The Texas Rangers: A Century of Frontier Defense*. Austin: University of Texas Press, 1965.

Weiss, Harold J. *Yours to Command: The Life and Legend of Texas Ranger Captain Bill McDonald*. Denton, TX: University of North Texas Press, 2009.

White, Grace Miller. "When Judge Roy Bean Pulled a Prize Fight." *Frontier Times*, Aug. 1941, 477-80.

Woods, Alan. "James J. Corbett: Theatrical Star." *Journal of Sport History* 3 (Summer 1976): 162-75.

INDEX